the New Hampshire Legislature of 1883 as photographed by W. G. C. Kimball of Concord.

To
this day

our best to
alida millham,

Leon W Anderson
11/4/81

To
this day

*the 300 years
of the
New Hampshire Legislature*

by
Leon W. Anderson
with a Prologue by
J. Duane Squires

PHOENIX PUBLISHING
Canaan, New Hampshire

The New Hampshire Legislative Historical Committee, established pursuant to 1967, 379:20 and 1979, 380:11, provided funding for the preparation of the manuscript which serves as the basis of this publication. The Committee has not verified the accuracy of any statements made in this publication and shall not be responsible for any statements made or opinions or interpretations expressed in this publication.

Anderson, Leon W.
  To this day.

  Bibliography: p. 378
  Includes index.
  1. New Hampshire.   General Court—History.   1. Title.
JK2966.A53   328.742'09   80-28564
ISBN 0-914016-75-X

Printed in the United States of America
by Courier Printing Company
Binding by New Hampshire Bindery
Design by A. L. Morris

Publication of this volume
was in part made possible through the
generosity of James H. Hayes,
former member of the House of Representatives
and the Governor's Council,
and of the New Hampshire Charitable Fund,
New Hampshire Savings Bank,
and the Putnam Foundation.

This enterprise
is dedicated to
Harlan Logan for sponsorship,
Dr. J. Duane Squires for inspiration,
and my Mabel for caring.

CONTENTS

PREFACE

RODUCTION of this history of New Hampshire's 300-year-old Legislature was launched by the 1967 session, at the suggestion of Harlan Logan of Plainfield, retired New York publisher and educator, then serving a first term in the House of Representatives. The idea developed when he vainly sought information about the Legislature, and the nature of his responsibilities and obligations as a legislator.

The 1967 Legislature created a Legislative Historical Committee to handle the project, with Senate President Stewart Lamprey of Moultonborough as chairman. The other members were House Speaker Walter Peterson of Peterborough; the Republican majority floor leaders Senator Creeley S. Buchanan of Amherst and Representative Marshall W. Cobleigh of Nashua, and the Democratic minority floor leaders Senator Harry V. Spanos of Newport, and the late Representative Laurence M. Pickett of Keene.

The committee negotiated with the author, just-retired veteran political editor of the *Concord Daily Monitor*, to research and compile the history, and initial research disclosed that it was the first such project in the nation. The Library of Congress reported, upon inquiry, that to its knowledge, no other state had ever compiled a detailed history of its legislature, although some of them had publications presenting varied aspects of legislative life.

In 1978 the Legislative Historical Committee which continued to comprise the six top-ranking officials to the House and Senate, retained Dr. J. Duane Squires of New London, Granite State historian, to edit and authenticate the 440-page manuscript of the legislative history, after which it was approved and accepted. Then late in 1979 the committee voted not to publish the book and turned the manuscript over to the author.

Publication was given initial support by James H. Hayes of Concord, former legislator and all-time champion of the Governor's Executive Council, who arranged for copies to be distributed to schools, libraries, and historical societies in the state. Others who contributed materially to making its publication possible were the New Hampshire Charitable Fund, New Hampshire Savings Bank, and the Putnam Foundation. The author is deeply grateful to them all for making this volume a reality, as well as to Mrs. Constance T. Rinden who compiled the index.

Leon W. Anderson

Concord, New Hampshire
February 1, 1981

1680

The Comission constituting a Presidont & Councell f
Province of New-Hampshire in New=England.

Charles ý Second &c. To all to whom these psents shall come &
whereas our Colony of ý Massachusetts, al Massachusetts Bay in
New=England in _____ _____ _____ upon themselves to ex ___
Government & Jurisdiction over ý Inhabitants & Planters in
Townes of Portsmouth, Hampton, Dover & Exeter, & all other ý Townes
lands in ý Province of New=Hampshire, lying & extending from
___ miles northwards of Merrimack River, or any part there of
___ in Province of Maine, not having any legall right or a
___ to do; Submitt said Jurisdiction & all further exercise
___ of. We have thought fit by the advice of Our Privy Cou___
___ & restrain for the future; And do hereby inhibit an___
strain ý Same. And whereas ý Government of ý part of the
s'd Province of New=Hampshire, so limited & bounded as aforesaid
is not yet granted unto any person or persons whatsoever
ý same & still remains under Our imediate ca___
protection; To the end ý Our loving Subjects, ý Planters and
habitants within ý limits aforesaid, may be protected and
___ed in their respective rights, liberties & properties & ý
& impartiall justice may be duly administred in all cases
all & criminall, & ý all possible ___ may be taken f___
___ orderly Government of ý Same; NOW know ye, that W___
with ý advice of Our Privy Councell, have thought fit to order
establish & appoint a Presidont & Councell, to take care of ý said
___ of lands called The Province of New=Hampshire, & of the
___ters & Inhabitants thereof; & to Order, rule & Governe ý said
according to such methods & regulations, as are herein after
___ & declared. And for ý better execution of Our Royal
___ in this behalf, We do hereby nominate & appoint Our
___ & well beloved Subjects, John Cutt of Portsmouth Esq, to be

First page of the Petition of September 18, 1679,
used decoratively throughout this volume.
Collection: State Archives.

Prologue

The Foundations of New Hampshire, 1623 / 1681

O N APRIL 16, 1623, the first white settlement in what is now called New Hampshire began. Captained by David Thomson, twenty-one men landed at Odiorne's Point in the modern town of Rye. Their purpose was to trade with the Indians and to explore natural resources. Within a few years there were four recognized communities in New Hampshire: Strawbery Banke, renamed Portsmouth in 1653; Dover; Hampton; and Exeter. These four little republics were legally independent, and were not united officially until later in the century. In 1640 when the terrible Civil War broke out in England, the four New Hampshire republics asked for and were granted affiliation with the much larger colony of Massachusetts Bay. For nearly four decades this political relationship continued.

During these years with Massachusetts New Hampshire folk heard about the first ascent in 1642 of what today we term Mt. Washington; they learned of the exploration of the Merrimack River to Lake Winnipesaukee in 1652; they witnessed the original coinage of metallic silver money in British colonial America; they knew the impact of the first general education laws of Massachusetts in 1647; they noted the Massachusetts persecution of Quakers (but no executions occurred in New Hampshire); and they endured the costs of "King Philip's War" with the Indian tribes of Rhode Island.

But as the 1680s neared, a great change was at hand. After years of

3

hesitation King Charles II of England ordered that the union of New Hampshire with Massachusetts be terminated. The royal decree was dated September 18, 1679. Under its terms New Hampshire became a royal province and all legal authority of Massachusetts ceased. Thus the four seacoast towns of Portsmouth, Dover, Hampton, and Exeter achieved full autonomy as a British province, a fact fittingly commemorated three hundred years later in 1980.

By appointment of the King, "President" John Cutt and his council took office on January 22, 1680, and promptly began the task of organizing a representative assembly to balance the council, a familiar application of the bicameral principle in government. As soon as the certified lists of eligible voters in the four towns could be prepared, these names were made public. Portsmouth was found to have 71 men qualified for suffrage; Dover had 61; Hampton had 57; and Exeter had 20.

These 209 voters early in March elected eleven representatives, who became the first General Assembly of New Hampshire. This original legislature quickly voted itself the sole authority to enact all public laws and taxes. It voted extensive legal codes for the province; it instructed each town to choose selectmen to supervise all public life in that town.

So began three hundred years of what we would now call democratic institutions. The initial arrangements had to be modified as the province grew and new communities needed legal status, but basically they have endured.

Unfortunately "President" Cutt died on March 27, 1681, after a day of fasting had been ordered for his health. Oddly enough, the tradition of Fast Day thus began has continued for three centuries, and New Hampshire alone still observes "Fast Day" each spring.

Provincial New Hampshire, 1681 / 1775

The royal province of New Hampshire had seventeen governors appointed by the King of England. Some of these men in the 1680s and 1690s served very briefly in office. The reason was simple. England itself was going through revolutionary changes. The last two Stuart kings, Charles II (died 1685) and James II (expelled 1689), were replaced by King William and Queen Mary from Holland. The Queen was a member of the Stuart royal family, but King William was a different kind of ruler. Deeply immersed in European politics, his basic motivation as king was hostility to France. King William plunged England into bitter conflict with King Louis XIV of France. The result was to be four exhausting wars between 1689 and 1763.

The emergent world empires of Britain and France were now at death grips. Governors of New Hampshire appointed from London came and went, until finally in Benning Wentworth (1741-1767) a lasting magistrate was named by King George II. Provincial New Hampshire, as the closest of the thirteen original colonies to the power of imperial France in Canada, felt the impact of each new conflict. In "King William's War" (1689-1697) French raiding attacks from the St. Lawrence area occurred almost every year. Such towns as Dover, Salmon Falls, Exeter, and modern Durham were victims of these forays. Hundreds of New Hampshire people were killed or taken to Canada for ransom.

In 1697 in the present town of Boscawen an Indian war party returning to Canada was destroyed by an indefatigable woman named Hannah Duston; she and two other prisoners killed her ten captors while they slept. Then she safely fled back home to Massachusetts. A truce in 1697 ended this savage war until a new conflict ("Queen Anne's War") began in 1703. This war lasted ten years and was as cruel a time as New Hampshire has ever experienced. Hampton in 1703, Dover in 1704 and again in 1709, Durham in 1708, these were typical of the objectives of French and Indian raiding parties from Canada. Joseph Dudley, then the royal governor of New Hampshire, was energetic in hitting back at the French, especially in Nova Scotia. The peace treaty signed at Utrecht in Holland in 1713 on the whole favored Great Britain, and that gave New Hampshire much satisfaction.

After a sanguinary limited war against the Indians in Maine in the 1720s, there was an uneasy peace along the frontier until 1744. In that year a third major conflict—styled "King George's War"—between France and Britain erupted. This time the principal fighting by New Hampshire citizens was in the Connecticut River valley around Charlestown. There "Fort Number Four" was the key point of battle. Colonial troops, including a New Hampshire regiment, captured the mighty French fortress of Louisburg in 1745. But the peace treaty of 1748 was a *status quo ante bellum* agreement and all conquests had to be returned.

Finally, in 1755 the famous "French and Indian War" broke out. This was to be the decisive struggle between the two powers. It produced such notable New Hampshire leaders as John Stark and Robert Rogers, and ended with complete victory for the British army and the colonial forces. New Hampshire had played a vital part in the outcome.

During these decades of almost continuous warfare there were, of course, many other aspects of life in New Hampshire. Population increased from fewer than 5,000 in 1680 to 30,000 in 1763. New towns were chartered with speed. In 1689 there were just five incorporated towns in the province. King William and Queen Anne granted two more each. Then in the Hanoverian dynasty from 1715 to 1775 came charters for 138 new towns. Thus in 1775 there were 147 legally incorporated towns in New Hampshire with a total population of 82,000.

Homes, churches, and other buildings reflected the growth of population and wealth. The skills of cabinet making and furniture production; linen manufacture; the making of ordinary iron utensils for home and agriculture; maritime products beginning with masts; improved roads, stage lines and covered bridges; the start of modern medicine, including the introduction of the Fahrenheit thermometer; the founding of the ninth college in colonial America: Dartmouth College at Hanover, New Hampshire, in 1769; the initiation of an intercolonial postal system; new breeds of farm animals; the locating of taverns and inns along the principal roads—these were some of the new ideas in the social order previous to the Revolutionary War.

The provincial legislature began many innovations. In 1718 the members voted themselves immunity from arrest while going to or coming from a session. In 1740 they won a legal dispute with Massachusetts which resulted in the transfer of more than thirty towns from the jurisdiction of the Bay Colony to that of New Hampshire. In 1741 the legislature instituted daily opening prayers. In 1764 it reluctantly accepted a royal decree which established the western boundary of the province as the western bank of the Connecticut River.

The First Century as a State, 1775 / 1877

When the Seven Years War ended, New Hampshire had the finest force of militarily trained men in its history. So it is not surprising that the first overt action against the royal government occurred in our state. On December 14-15, 1774, hundreds of armed New Hampshire men seized Fort William and Mary near Portsmouth. Captured were its garrison and all its supplies. Early in 1775 the British army began retaliatory measures. The results of these were patriot victories in April at Lexington and Concord in Massachusetts, and the creation of an American army for forcible resistance. The leadership of the First New Hampshire Regiment was assigned to John Stark.

On June 17, 1775, came the renowned Battle of Bunker Hill near Boston. In this famous encounter Colonel Stark commanded more than half the troops, and his men inflicted severe casualties on picked British regiments from the Boston garrison. The First New Hampshire, a participant at Bunker Hill, was destined to become the longest-lived regiment in the Continental Army under General Washington, not being mustered out until December 1783.

New Hampshire troops went to Canada in the futile invasion attempt of 1775-1776; crossed the Delaware River under Washington in 1776; and were billeted at Valley Forge during the harsh winter of 1777-78. In the summer of 1777 a four-state army, commanded by General John Stark with New Hampshire troops in a majority, decisively defeated units of Burgoyne's invading force at the Battle of Bennington (August), and they helped compel his final surrender at Saratoga in October. In 1779 another American army under New Hampshire General John Sullivan ravaged the home lands of the Iroquois Indians in New York State. In 1781 New Hampshire men were active in the Virginia campaign which resulted in the surrender of the entire British army in that area. Two years later came the peace treaty.

Following this peace treaty of 1783 New Hampshire armed forces were disbanded. It is interesting to note that a New Hampshire man, Sgt. John Ordway of Bow, was a member of the Lewis and Clark expedition which explored the far west in 1804-1805. This state played a prominent part in the War with Mexico. Her native son, Franklin Pierce, who had been speaker of the New Hampshire House of Representatives at the age of twenty-six, rose to the rank of Brigadier General, U.S.A.

The greatest military effort of New Hampshire in the nineteenth century was its participation in the Civil War. Eighteen regiments of infantry were sent to the fighting front, and were active in all the battle areas. Some of the famous engagements—Gettysburg, the Shenandoah campaign of 1864, and the occupation of Richmond in 1865—had New Hampshire forces as key units. The state also contributed to the U.S. Navy. One of the most noted warships was the *Kearsarge*, named for a mountain in Merrimack County.

In purely state affairs the nineteenth century was a busy one. A great enthusiasm for sheep farming affected many communities. Factories sprang up along the rivers, and at least two thousand dams were constructed to provide power. In 1835 the first railroad entered New Hampshire, running from Boston to Nashua; by 1877 there were dozens of railroad companies operating over many miles. Manchester became the center of textile manufacturing, and in 1846 was incorporated as the original city in the state. By 1877 there were five more such New Hampshire municipalities.

Social and intellectual changes paralleled the economic ones. In 1784 a new constitution for New Hampshire went into effect, and most of it still is. In 1819 a previous decision to make Concord the state capital saw the opening of the capitol building. It was enlarged in 1864. Local academies, beginning at Exeter in 1781, were functioning in at least fifty communities by 1877.

The Shakers established great farms at Enfield and at Canterbury, and rose to popularity with many people. The Mormons took numerous converts from New Hampshire to Utah in the 1840s. Religious toleration was granted by law in 1819, and new denominations multiplied. Societies appeared for temperance reform.

Meanwhile maritime activity flourished for many years. From the shipyards around Portsmouth came some of the famed "clipper ships." The steam engine was soon applied to the problems of water transport, and before the Civil War there was steamboat traffic on the Connecticut River and on Lake Winnipesaukee. The "Lyceum" movements proliferated for the education of many. With ever more modern equipment lumbermen invaded hitherto inaccessible New Hampshire forests, and millions of board feet went down the rivers each spring. The White Mountains and the lake country became increasingly popular for summer tourists, and facilities quickly developed to care for them.

New methods of dairying were introduced and fine animals were brought over from Europe to upgrade the farm stock. The turnpike activity reached its height about 1830, and stage lines covered the state. The telegraph became practical a few years later; and in 1866 the first successful trans-Atlantic cable was laid from New Hampshire to Europe. A steam railroad up Mt. Washington began functioning in 1869. Workers in offices and factories started the process of organizing labor unions and of "striking" to achieve their objectives.

Complete Integration into the Nation 1877 / 1981

New Hampshire in the 1870s passed over the line between "the old days" and the modernity we know in the 1980s. Fittingly enough, its participation in the "Centennial Exposition" of 1876 at Philadelphia marked the division point. In 1879 the state government adopted the biennial system and the state senate was doubled in size to make twenty-four seats.

New Hampshire's interests in the affairs of the world increased after 1877. In the 1880s Secretary of the Navy, William Chandler of New Hampshire, began the historic change from a U.S. Navy built of wood to vessels of steel. In 1898 this new navy was first used in the Spanish War, and its renown spread throughout the world. Meanwhile, John Hay, Secretary of State under Presidents William McKinley and Theodore Roosevelt, acquired a large estate on Lake Sunapee in New Hampshire, and for a few weeks each summer guided American foreign affairs from that place. Thanks to Hay's successes, President Roosevelt became the mediator at the Portsmouth Peace Conference of 1905, when the Russo-Japanese War was terminated.

Because of the vast and complex "Progressive Movement" in American life, New Hampshire broke away from its traditional loyalty to the Republican Party, and in 1912 and 1916 voted for Woodrow Wilson to be President of the United States. Wilson's two terms embraced the years of World War I; a national draft law was enacted; and thousands of New Hampshire men were sent to Europe. After the German defeat in 1918, a powerful group called the American Legion was formed by many veterans, including several from New Hampshire, and it continued to influence public affairs for at least the two following generations.

In the post-war era of the 1920s, the University of New Hampshire took its modern name and form at Durham in 1923. During this same period labor unrest was continuous in the state and with greater or less success the elected officials strove to meet the needs of the workers. This effort culminated in the governorship of John G. Winant. While he was governor, the state began a charming monthly periodical entitled *The Troubadour*, devoted to attracting people to New Hampshire. To combat the "Great Depression," federal funds poured into the state in the "New Deal" programs of President Franklin D. Roosevelt. Somehow New Hampshire survived such a disaster as the closing of the giant Amoskeag Mills in Manchester in 1936, and came through the great flood of 1936 as well as the destructive hurricane of 1938.

As the 1940s began, it was clear that new crises loomed ahead. Hitler's successes in Europe and Japanese triumphs in Asia were ominous threats to world power. Finally, on December 7, 1941, the blow was struck, and the nation was at war again. Governor Robert O. Blood and his appointed defense council handled New Hampshire's war effort with skill and efficiency. Tens of thousands of its young men and women went into the conflict and into industry before victory was achieved in Europe and Asia.

The massive interstate highway system entered New Hampshire during Governor Dwinell's administration, and rapidly expanded in ensuing years. Shortly thereafter the "Iron Horse" bade farewell to passenger service in the state. Because of the absence of a state income or a state sales tax, however, people flocked to the Granite State. Population steadily increased until it passed 900,000 in the U.S. Census of 1980. It was an encouraging augury.

Such are some of the highlights in the more than 350 years of the history of New Hampshire. It is now my privilege to turn to the unifying thread which binds together the complex and fascinating story. This is the great accomplishment of Leon W. Anderson, whose luminous chapters comprise the body of this book. "Andy," with his unmatched knowledge of legislative records and his inimitable style, has provided that thread. He believes and I do, too, that the legislative process is the heartbeat of government. After reading his work, one can only marvel at the intricacy of our state's past, and the skill with which the author has re-created it.

J. Duane Squires
State Historian

Part 1

The Provincial Legislature

King Charles II, from a portrait by J. Smith after G. Kneller.
Courtesy Princeton University Library.

THE FORCED BIRTH

NEW HAMPSHIRE'S giant Legislature originated 300 years ago by force rather than choice. It was created by royal decree in the spring of 1680 and was imposed upon the people against their wishes.

This pioneer Assembly was dictated by King Charles II of England in a Royal Commission which forced upon New Hampshire its own provincial government, after nearly forty years of friendly affiliation with Massachusetts. The decree of 3,438 words spelled out that a prime purpose was to reactivate ownership of the New Hampshire territory for an heir of Capt. John Mason, who had been granted the area a half-century earlier by a royal charter. It declared that the new government was to be under the direct supervision of King Charles, listed grandson Robert Tufton Mason as proprietor of the entire territory, and emphasized that all property owners would be required to pay him annual rental fees or forfeit their holdings.

The royal edict was issued at London on September 18, 1679, and Mason's cousin, Edward Randolph, who played a prominent role in its development, was delegated to deliver and supervise its implementation. Randolph made the Royal Commission public in Portsmouth on January 1, 1680, and understandably was as unwelcome as his missive. Five years earlier he had generated the enmity of Massachusetts and New Hampshire officials when he toured the two areas, with royal sponsorship, in efforts to establish support for grandson Mason's proprietorship.

(The present Gregorian calendar is used in this narrative, rather than the old time measurement, (the Julian calendar) in use up to 1752, in which the year began on March 25.)

Legislative records show that the Mason Claim dated back to 1622. That was when the Council of New England in Plymouth first voted Captain Mason title to "Mariana," which eventually became New Hampshire. The following year, young David Thomson of Plymouth, England, was given a patent to settle what became Portsmouth and Dover, he being financed by Plymouth merchants. It was also in 1623 that Mason and Sir Ferdinand Gorges were jointly granted "Maine," with vaguely defined boundaries.

In 1629 Mason and Gorges were given more specific patents by the royal Council of New England. First they were jointly granted "Laconia," which was supposed to extend far inland toward the present Great Lakes region, to promote fur trade with the Indians. Soon thereafter yet another patent gave Captain Mason ownership of the territory which he then named New Hampshire, and the approximate present Maine area was given to Gorges.

Thomson's settlement prospered and then he died suddenly in 1628. The following year, 1629, Captain Mason took over Pascataway, as Portsmouth was first named under Thomson, and promptly invested substantial sums to enlarge the settlement. He financed several shiploads of English men and women, with cattle and workmen from Denmark. Then Mason died in 1635, after winning a final patent for "The Province of New Hampshire," as the Council of New England prepared to disband, without ever seeing his distant investment. Mason's widow was unsuccessful in continuing supervision of Pascataway and abandoned it to its settlers.

Hampton and Exeter were formed about 1638, and early in the 1640s the four towns which then constituted New Hampshire joined Massachusetts for protection against Indian raids from the north. Thenceforth, Massachusetts Bay Colony governed New Hampshire, certified property ownerships, and its population rose to about 3,000 by arrival of the Royal Commission of 1679.

Randolph, a minor British official, met with opposition in implementing the new government, but he persevered. He arrived with the title of Collector of Customs over all New England, with hopes of personal profits from the Boston and Portsmouth shipping centers, and firmly launched the new province.

The Royal Commission imposed a President and nine-member Council to head the government, and interestingly, in retrospect, it named the leading citizens of the four towns to fill these positions. The reason for these selections remains unknown, but whether or not Randolph had a part in it, it was obviously of clever design. Massachusetts Bay Colony was meanwhile chastised by King Charles II for its temerity in purchasing Maine from a Gorges heir without royal sanction. However, that territory remained part of Massachusetts until 1820, when it became a state. In this same period, the enterprising Bay Colony failed to purchase New Hampshire from Mason heirs.

Elderly John Cutt, a Portsmouth merchant, was appointed President. He and two brothers first settled on the Isles of Shoals some forty years earlier, and they eventually became rich and influential Portsmouth citizens. The Council appointees were equally prominent and respected, but some of them initially denounced the new government because of its Masonian threat to their properties. Randolph countered with an ultimatum. He warned them they would have to accept their royal assignments within twenty days or suffer possible fines or imprisonment. Cutt and his associates weighed the unhappy prospect of having less desirable appointees head the new government, so they accepted their positions on January 21, 1680, and assumed office the following day.

The 1680 Creation

DETAILS of the origin of this government and its Assembly have been preserved in the early volumes of the *State Papers*, as compiled by various legislative historians. Six men were named in the Royal Commission to the Council under President Cutt. They were Richard Martyn, William Vaughan, and Thomas Daniels of Portsmouth; Maj. Richard Waldron of Dover; John Gilman of Exeter; and Christopher Hussey of Hampton. They, in turn, were charged with naming three additional Councilors, and Elias Stileman of Portsmouth, Samuel Dalton of Hampton, and Job Clements of Dover were appointed to these positions.

The Council's first duty was to create the Assembly, so it ordered the four towns to submit lists of their property owners by February 16. From these data the Council posted special lists of "freemen" eligible to vote for "Deputies" to the pioneer Legislature. They totalled only 209 men: there were 71 for Portsmouth, 61 for Dover, 57 for Hampton, and only 20 for Exeter. The Council also decreed the three larger townships were entitled to each elect 3 men to the aborning Assembly; Exeter was limited to 2 members.

The Forced Birth

This manner of creating the Assembly was so arbitrary that, in issuing the details, the Council spelled out that it would not be repeated. It also promised that when the Assembly convened it would have the sole authority to determine how its members would be elected. In this connection, Governor Charles H. Bell, an eminent historian, observed in his 1888 *History of Exeter:*

There was no uniform rule determining the qualification of the voters, but they were selected arbitrarily; one consequence of which was that Exeter had a less number, in proportion to her population, than some of the other towns. Exeter had seventy taxpayers.

New Hampshire's first legislative election was set for March 1, at 9:00 A.M., and the certified freemen took oaths of allegiance before voting. The assemblymen reported for duty at Portsmouth on March 16, also at 9:00 A.M. The eleven first legislators were John Pickering, Robert Elliot, and Philip Lewis of Portsmouth; Peter Coffin, Anthony Nutter, and Richard Waldron, Jr., of Dover; Anthony Stanyan, Thomas Marston, and Edward Gove of Hampton; and Capt. Bartholomew Tippin and Lt. Ralph Hall of Exeter.

Attestation that the legislators met in taverns was recorded by a Governor and Council vote on October 13, 1682, as follows:

That Capt. Daniel & William Vaughan Esq. of the Counsel, take order for a convenient Meeting place for the Counsel & Deputies of the General Assembly in some private house in Portsmouth: It being his Majesty's Pleasure & Command not to have any in Taverns & such like places.

The solons elected young Waldron as first Speaker. The Reverend Joshua Moody of Portsmouth, staunch Puritan like most of the new officials, gave the opening sermon. An initial act of the tiny Assembly and its government was to vote regrets to Massachusetts for the forced separation, as follows:

The late turn of Providence made among us by the all-ordering Hand has given occasion for this present application, wherein we crave leave as we are duty bound:

1–Thankfully to acknowledge your great care for us and your kindness towards us while we dwelt under your shadow, owning ourselves deeply obliged that you were pleased, upon our earnest request and supplication to

*take us under your government and ruled us well whilst we so remained, so
that we cannot give the least countenance to those reflections that have
been cast upon you, as if you had dealt injuriously with us.*

*2–That no dissatisfaction with your government, but merely our submis-
sion to Divine Providence to his Majestie's Commands, to whom we owe
allegiance, without any seeking of our own, or desire of change, was the
only cause of our complying with that present separation from you that we
are now under, but should have heartily rejoiced if it had seemed good to the
Lord and his Majesty to have settled in the same capacity as formerly.*

The Royal Commission requirement that property owners pay an
annual rental fee of six pence to the pound to Robert Mason was firmly
rebuffed. The very first of a set of general laws voted by the Assembly
and concurred in by President Cutt and the Council declared:

TOWNSHIPS &C CONFIRMED–*To prevent contention & controversy, that may
arise amongst us by reason of the late change of Government; It Is Ordered
by this Assembly and the Authority thereof;* THAT *all Lands, Townships,
Town-grants, with all the other grants, lying within the limits of this
Province; and all other rights and properties:* SHAL *stand good, & are hereby
confirmed to the Towns and persons concerned, in the same state &
condition as they did before this late Alteration.*

This novice Legislature also declared itself the sole source of initiat-
ing governmental power and authority, on behalf of the people, in the
following statute:

*It is ordered and enacted by this General Assembly (including the Council)
and the authority thereof, that no act, imposition, law or ordinance be
made or imposed upon us, but shall be made by the same Assembly, and
approved by the President and Council, from time to time; that justice and
right be impartially administered unto all; not sold, denied or causelessly
deferred unto any.*

The freshmen lawmakers readily enacted an extensive array of basic
statutes, copied from the rigid Plymouth Puritans' restrictions on
personal conduct, and gave the towns freedom to elect their own
officials to "order the prudential affairs of a town." The first legislative property tax measured a penny per pound of valuation, and
because of a currency shortage, payments were permitted in wheat,

The Forced Birth

salt, Indian "corne," boards, or barrel staves. There was this initial definition of drunkenness:

It is to be understood as one that lisps or falters in his speech by reason of over much drink; or that staggers in his going; or that vomits by reason of excessive drinking; or that cannot by reason thereof follow his calling.

The death penalty was ordered for a long listing of personal misconduct, such as blasphemy, "Idollitry," treason, witchcraft, and even insubordination by children. Heading this array was:

It is enacted by this Assembly and the authority thereof: That if any person, having had the knowledge of the true God, openly and manifestly have, or worship, any other God but the Lord God; he shall be put to death.

None of these harsh penalties was ever invoked. It was not until 1739, some sixty years later, that New Hampshire's first legal death penalty was recorded. Portsmouth annals relate the public hangings of two women for an infant's death. The executions followed Sunday morning worship by the victims, in custody of the sheriff.

The first Legislature defined a voter, or freeman, as a male Protestant at least twenty-four years of age and possessed of property valued at least at £20. This action terminated the Council's original authority to define a freeman for the first election of the Assembly.

Interestingly, these pioneer legislators voted themselves free rides on Portsmouth's two toll ferries. They later extended this privilege to toll bridges and roads; as toll facilities disappeared, it did too. But the 1969 Legislature resurrected the free-ride policy for the present three toll highways.

The London government soon swung into action against the home-rule determinations of the doughty 1680 Legislature and President Cutt and his first Council. Customs Collector Randolph, who had settled at Boston, began submitting reports to his royal superiors at London, detailing their failure to comply with the Royal Commission commands, and especially Mason's proprietorship.

Randolph not only dispatched lengthy reports overseas but also crossed the Atlantic Ocean several times to deliver personal complaints. His biographers offer an interesting sidelight to this period in Randolph's life. At forty-eight he had been left a widower, with four daughters, just before delivering the 1679 Royal Commission; a second wife died in 1682; and a third wife died in 1684. It appears likely that his ocean travel related in part to his marital affairs.

Meanwhile, Randolph and his special agents in New Hampshire met with firm opposition from President Cutt and his Council. On several occasions they were ordered before the executive group, reprimanded for seizing vessels and impounding their cargoes, and told that authority for such acts could come only from official government channels.

Randolph's reports soon bore fruit. On September 30, 1680, the Lords of Trades and Plantations commissioned Richard Chamberlain, an employee, to become secretary and clerk of the Cutt government and to supervise its activities. Then on the following day, October 1, a royal "Mandamus" sent Mason to Portsmouth with authority to sit on the Council and personally to impose his rental fees and sell unoccupied lands at will.

While there are no available records to that effect, Chamberlain and Mason possibly came to Portsmouth together. Legislative records show they were both admitted to their new positions on December 30. Chamberlain was at first rebuffed in submitting his credentials, but Mason apparently had no trouble taking his Council seat.

Chamberlain told of his problems in a lengthy report on May 16, 1681, to his London superiors. He said he gave his commission to President Cutt on December 24; the Council did not give him audience until December 28; and then it debated Chamberlain's qualifications for three days, in his presence, before allowing him to assume his new duties.

Chamberlain reported continued harassment. He had difficulty obtaining the Council records from Councilor Elias Stileman, his predecessor, and was told they were not available because the province was "too poor" to compile them. By March 1681, he continued, he obtained partial records and was informed that other pertinent Council accountings had to be retained by Stileman, "as an Officer called Recorder, and is besides Clerk of Writs." Because of this arbitrary arrangement, Chamberlain wrote, the fees which had been expected from his position were collected by Stileman. So he asked that King Charles require the province to pay him an adequate salary.

Chamberlain reported that the Council repeatedly tried to impose a secrecy oath upon him, against dispatching details of its doings to London. He said this included dismissal threats and that the Council deliberated in private before voting final actions in his presence.

Chamberlain stressed that the Council firmly refused to support Mason, with his title of Lord Proprietor, in his efforts to collect rentals.

The Forced Birth

He even reported that some inhabitants tried to purchase undeveloped land from Mason, but the new officials denounced such transactions. As a result, Chamberlain wrote, Mason refused to participate in the Council meetings. Soon thereafter, Mason fled back to England to lay his frustrations before the royal government and to seek redress against the adamant New Hampshire settlers.

President Cutt became seriously ill early in 1681, and the Assembly's second session proclaimed March 17 a day of "public fasting and prayer" for his recovery. Dr. J. Duane Squires of New London listed this in his 1956 *Granite State History* as the beginning of New Hampshire's unique annual Fast Day holiday, which continues to be observed to this day.

President Cutt died on March 27, 1681. Chamberlain later wrote to London that he had been "an honest loyal Gentleman & stood for the Proprietor's rights." Then he added that Waldron, who succeeded Cutt as Deputy President, was of questionable loyalty, and his fault would be reported by Mason. Chamberlain said in addition that the tiny Assembly had rescinded some of its objectionable original statutes but refused to repeal its stand against the Masonion Claim (as it became known).

The Gove Rebellion

WALDRON, who became Acting President at sixty-five, was a veteran Indian fighter and had served twenty terms in the Massachusetts General Court, seven as Speaker. His brief administration enjoyed a spell of peace, owing to Mason's absence and to Randolph's being based in Boston.

Woes beset the province again late in 1682 when Mason returned to Portsmouth with a new executive to replace Waldron. He was Edward Cranfield, impoverished scion of a royal court family, with the title of Lieutenant Governor and Commander-in-Chief. He was armed with broadened authority and soon ruthlessly invoked it. Cranfield took office in October 1682, with special reason to enforce the Masonian Claim. Mason was alleged to have pledged one fifth of his rentals to King Charles II and to have mortgaged his claim to guarantee an annual payment to Cranfield for his support.

Governor Cranfield initially cloaked his guile with friendliness. He called the Assembly into session on November 14 and induced it to replace the original "Cutt Code" with new laws. Anxious to woo the new executive, the legislators voted Cranfield a flattering salary of £ 250.

Meanwhile, Cranfield's chicanery continued. The legislators approved his request that jurors be appointed by sheriffs rather than elected. Too late they realized that this gambit had placed the entire judicial system firmly in Cranfield's hands, for his new powers included authority to replace Council members at will (which he soon did), and Judges and sheriffs were appointed with Council concurrence.

The legislators did not at first know about Mason's briberies, but when they became known, the legislators refused to enact the additional statutes Governor Cranfield sought to help enforce the Masonian Claim. Thereupon he summarily dismissed the Assembly. Cranfield berated the assemblymen, and Edward Gove of Hampton in particular, as he ended their terms. Gove had vigorously challenged Cranfield's demands on the legislative floor.

As the lawmakers returned to their homes, they spread word of Cranfield's dictatorial manner. Public resentment festered, and Gove was reported to have met privately with his Hampton town leaders. Then Gove swung into action. Long a man of unbridled determination and quick to anger, with drawn sword, he took to horse in rebellion against the Cranfield regime. Admittedly fortified by strong drink (according to state records), he rode to Exeter and back on January 26, a Friday, over snow-covered roads, vainly exhorting the populace to join his armed revolt. He was accompanied by his son, John, and Mark Baker, a young employee.

Governor Bell's classic 1888 *History of Exeter* presents details of Gove's gumption. He recruited five Exeter laborers and a boy trumpeter in his one-day uprising. They were Joseph, John, and Robert Wadleigh, Jr.; John Sleeper; Thomas Rawlins; and youthful Nathaniel Ladd and his trumpet. By nightfall, as Gove and his tiny band returned to Hampton, it had also recruited William "Hely," a Hampton blacksmith, along with Ed Smith and John Young, not otherwise identified.

As Gove's impetuous revolt failed to muster support through his day-long entreaties, he meekly surrendered the following morning to his Hampton militia superiors; he was then a lieutenant of that unit.

Governor Cranfield had already taken action. He ordered a special detail to take Gove and his band into custody, and he is said to have personally interrogated the adamant rebel in Portsmouth on the fol-

The Forced Birth

lowing Sunday. Cranfield jailed Gove in chains on a charge of treason and ordered a speedy trial by his fellow citizens.

Councilor Richard Waldron, Jr., was appointed the Presiding Justice, and a twenty-one-member jury of leading citizens of the province was designated by Cranfield to serve on the case, with stiff fines or jail terms the penalty for refusing to do so. During the trial of Gove and his fellow rebels, witnesses testified to their rebellious activity. When members of his band admitted their participation in the revolt, Gove also confessed his guilt. Various minor penalties were imposed by the jury upon the other defendants, and only Gove was convicted of treason. Judge Waldron, long a friend of Gove, is recorded as having shed copious tears as he imposed the most severe sentence ever decreed in this country. It read:

You, Edward Gove, shall be drawn on a sledge to the place of execution, and there you shall be hanged by ye neck, and when yet living be cut down and cast upon the ground, and your bowels shall be taken out of your belly and burnt while you are yet alive, your head shall be cut off and your body divided into four parts, and your head and body shall be placed where our Sovereign Lord the King pleaseth to appoint. And the Lord have mercy upon your soul.

Governor Cranfield was required, under his commission of appointment, to send Gove to London for royal disposal of his sentence. The Governor profited from Gove's riddance. He confiscated the properties of this well-to-do real estate operator for his own use.

In England, Gove was confined to the Tower of London, where he remained for some three years. He was then freed by a new king and sent home. Upon his return to Hampton in 1686, Gove was again elected to various town offices and militia leadership. A new Assembly ordered restoration of his holdings, and records indicate this was done, at least in part, since Cranfield had by then left the province in royal disfavor.

As one historian has said, "History may question Rebel Gove's wisdom, but his spirit remains unsullied, for he pioneered American determination for freedoms." Gove's memory has otherwise been perpetuated in Granite State legislative lore. Through the past three centuries, at least twenty-two of his descendants have served in the same Legislature, according to family genealogy records. They have included 1835 Senate President Charles F. Gove of Goffstown, who was also an Attorney General, and 1874 Senate President William H.

Gove of Weare, following service as House Speaker.

Col. Jesse Augustus Gove of Weare, who became Deputy Secretary of State and was killed in the Civil War, was later honored as the Legislature sponsored his portrait in the State House, where it continues to grace a corridor adjacent to the Hall of Flags. Richard Gove of Laconia served in the 1881 House with much self-esteem. He wrote in the 1881 legislative *Brown Book* that he opened a jewelry business at eighteen, with "only my tools and seventeen cents ready money," in 1833, and "has built five large business blocks and fourteen dwelling houses, and now lives in a fine residence, costing $30,000." William Pinkham Gove, veteran Concord City official, served six terms in the House and Senate through 1969.

After his disposal of Gove, Governor Cranfield abolished the Assembly in 1684 when it refused his demands for fresh tax increases. He then imposed them by royal decree, but without much success, as householders greeted his tax-collecting constables with raised clubs and, in one recorded instance, an irate housewife's boiling water.

Years of Turmoil

THE OUSTED LEGISLATORS meanwhile pressed London charges against Cranfield's arrogance and finally met with success. The Privy Council ruled that only the Legislature had authority to impose taxes, even as the tiny Assembly declared when it first organized in 1680. When the new King James II government took over in February 1685, following the death of James's brother, and indicated that Cranfield would be called to account for misuse of his authority, the Governor fled on May 15, 1685. He went to the West Indies, where he won another appointment.

Deputy Governor Walter Barefoote succeeded Cranfield briefly and had a friendlier relationship with the settlers. A new type of government followed, to rule the Dominion of New England. Joseph Dudley, a wealthy Roxbury, Massachusetts merchant, became President of this overall administration on May 25, 1686. He served only six months, however, until the arrival at Boston of Sir Edmund Andros, on December 20, 1686, with the title of Governor over the New England area.

Andros imposed a tyranny considered without equal in American annals. He had been granted authority to rule New Hampshire without an Assembly, and he governed by decree. He denied freedom of speech; he forbade anyone from leaving the New England area without express permission (presumably to curb protests to London); and he prohibited town meetings, except for imposition of taxes.

Randolph and Mason served on Governor Andros's Council, and within two years his authority was broadened to include New York and the Jersey area. And soon thereafter, while accompanying Andros on a New York territory visit, the embattled Mason died, at the age of fifty-eight, and left his Masonian Claim to two sons, John and Robert. As the Revolution of 1688 led to the ousting of the King James regime in England, Massachusetts staged its own revolt, and Governor Andros and his hated officials were arrested and sent to London.

The mother country's upheaval left New England destitute of royal rule from 1689 into 1692. New Hampshire's settlers vainly considered a merger of the four towns for protection from raiding Indians. Portsmouth citizens then sponsored a petition for a second alliance with Massachusetts, which had set up an emergency Committee of Safety to join with its Boston Legislature as a temporary government. Nearly 400 signatures were obtained for the petition from the quartet of towns. The makeshift Massachusetts government then permitted New Hampshire to return to its former fold, with legislative representation.

Historians have noted that a significant feature of this petition was that ninety of the signatures were by "mark," for men unable even to write their own names. Remaining unnoticed in New Hampshire legislative records, but of interest in retrospect, the petition included one woman, Elisabeth Horne, otherwise identified by her mark.

Meanwhile, in England, London merchant Samuel Allen purchased the Masonian Claim and won appointment from the new King William III as Governor of New Hampshire, on March 1, 1692. He also arranged for his son-in-law, John Usher, wealthy Boston stationer, as Lieutenant Governor over the province.

Allen remained in London and Usher continued to reside at Boston. But Usher came to Portsmouth and launched a new Assembly in a friendly manner. He readily approved new legislation, allowed the lawmakers to set their own pay scale for a first time, and sent copies of all new laws to each town. The pay-scale statute read:

Whereas the sevirall Representatives of this Assembly can not officiate and discharge that honorable & greate truste reposed in them withoute being at greate Charges & Expense, be it therefore Ennacted by the Leftinant Governour & Counsill & Representatives convened in Generall Assembly

& it is hereby Ennacted by the authority of the same that the allowances to each Representative of the people shall be three shillings per diem to commence from there coming oute untill their returne home to bee paide oute of thee rates made in thee sevirall townes in the Province for defraying towne charges.

Governor Usher soon developed greed, however, to such degree that the Assembly retaliated by refusing to vote him any salary. The solons also blocked his efforts to collect Masonian rental fees from the citizenry for properties that they and their forbears had settled in good faith and developed into valuable holdings.

The Legislature became so exasperated with Usher at one point that it referred him to the Bible. As Usher repeatedly demanded funds for repairs at what became Fort William and Mary at Portsmouth, the legislators voted a historic answer. In early May 1694 their reply was: "See 14 Luke 28." This section of the Bible reads: "For which of you, intending to build a tower, sitteth not down first, and counteth the cost, whether he have sufficient to finish it." This drew the following sarcastic message from Lieutenant Governor Usher two weeks later, on May 24:

As you have the less to say to my speech, so you give me occasion at present to say less to you than intended: Butt you having spent days to give answer to my speech, hope you will not judge it hard if itt be 14 days before I compleat my answer fully to your text, 14 Lu. 28,—for which of you intend to build a tower and sitteth not down first to count yet cost—I, therefore acquaint you, by & with the advice of the Councill, judge it of absolute necessity to repair and secure their Maj'ties' Fourt, according to the power granted in the King's Commission; signifye to you, according to your answer to my speech, to make choice of 2 persons to join with 2 others of this House to set down and count the cost that they may lay before this Assembly a particular account of the same;—therefore expect your choice & returne of the names so chosen to the Board.

The legislators refused to abide by that message and continued to insist that the populace could not afford additional taxes, above the £ 700 levy already voted for that year, largely to support soldiery against Indian attacks. Usher's regime ended in 1698 when he was replaced at London, and Governor Allen rushed to New Hampshire in behalf of his Masonian Claim investment.

The Forced Birth

Bellomont's Benevolence

A RAY OF WELCOME royal sunshine beamed upon the Assembly in 1699. Richard Coote, Earl of Bellomont, arrived in New York in 1698 to become Governor of that area, and New Hampshire and Massachusetts as well. A year later, Lord Bellomont paid a memorable eighteen-day visit to this province.

Bellomont addressed the Assembly most graciously. He expressed appreciation of "the great sufferings you sustained all this last war by this Province being a frontier towards the Eastern Indians—a cruel and perfidious enemy in their own nature, but taught and encouraged to be more so by the Jesuits and other Popish missionaries from France. . . ." He also emphasized:

I recommend to you, gentlemen of the House of Representatives, the providing for the necessary support of the government, you being best able to judge what the charge will be, and its belonging to you of right to provide the means to defray such charge.

Gentlemen, you will do well to think of everything that may conduce to your own happiness and advantage, wherein you may depend on my concurrence with you, for I have all the disposition imaginable to do the King and this country the best service I am capable of.

This was undoubtedly the most friendly royal attitude the provincial Assembly ever enjoyed. Bellomont thus became the first to officially label the legislators a House of Representatives. He also was first to declare it should be the origin of taxation—which it remains to this day.

The assemblymen bloomed gratitude. They voted effusive thanks and spiked it with an appreciation gift of £500. This was an amazing demonstration, for it almost equalled the entire annual legislative tax of that period.

The "Journal of Council and Assembly," as the legislative Journal was then called, showed the legislators took Bellomont at his word, and he kept it. A three-level judiciary system was reorganized to furnish improved justice. It was headed by a remodeled Superior Court of Judicature, which then served for seventy years at Portsmouth, or until justice was spread through the expanding province in 1771 by creation of county courts.

Even more lasting was the fact that the 1699 House established its first rules of conduct, in written form, with executive sanction. They totalled only ten but comprised fundamental operating principles which continue to this day. They were, with exact spellings:

First. That every member of this Assembly that shall be absent att the time apointed for meeting, and att calling over, shall pay three pence to the Clark for every such defect.

Secondly. That whosoever, by any misbehavor in speech or action, justly offend any of the members of the House, he shall for the first be admonished; the second, fined, as the House think meet.

Thirdly. That none shall speak twise, untill every man have liberty to speak once.

Fourthly. That every member directs his speech to the Speaker, and not to another, and when they have a mind to speak to any case they ask leave of him to speak.

Fifthly. That none smoak tobacco in the House after calling over, on penalty of 3d [three pence] for the Clark.

Sixthly. That the speaker shall have a casting vote, when there shall be an equal vote.

Seventhly. That any member of the House shall have liberty to enter his Decent from any vote without giveing any reason thereof.

Eigthly. That if the Speaker be absent, the House may choose a speaker pro tempore, that the affairs of the House may be carried on notwithstanding such vacancy.

Ninthly. That if any member after being entered and qualified, shall absent himself a day without leave from the House, he shall pay a fine of five shillings; except he show to the House a sufitient reason for his soe absenting.

Tenthly. That if any member of this House shall be, by the major part of the House, thought unfitt and not qualified for said place, it shall be in their power to dismiss such person, giving notice to the town where he belonged, to choose another to fill up such vacancy.

The Forced Birth

Two years later, the Legislature added the following to its rules of conduct:

The publicque afairs of the House of Representatives being much obstructed by persons sitting and lying on the bed Voted that Whosoever hence forward either sitt or ly down shall forfeit three pence to the House for a fine for every such default after the House is called over.

Whereas the publicque afairs of this House be much obstructed by reason of several members thereof soe often withdraw themselves into the chimney to take tobacco and sitt talking and not attend the afairs of the House, Voted that whosoever shall soe doe for the future shall pay a fine of three pence to the clerk for every such offense except leave given, etc.

Then, in August 1722, the House rules were again added to as follows:

Voted that the third paragraph in the former orders of the House be mended, viz: That no member Speak twice, untill everyone have libberty to speak once to the matter or cause in question, whether it be vote, Resolve or Order Bill, etc.

Voted, That any member of this House that shall neglect to weare his sword or be found without it during the sessions of the Gen'll Assembly from this Day shall pay a fine of one shilling to the clerk of this House and the fine to be repeated as often as found without a sword.

New Castle had by this time been separated from Portsmouth and given legislative representation. So thirteen men sat in this historic session of 1699, with Samuel Penhallow of Portsmouth as Speaker and Theodore Atkinson of New Castle as clerk. The other members were Capt. John Pickering (later Speaker when Penhallow was promoted to the Council) and John Plaisted (also later appointed to the Council) of Portsmouth; Capt. Henry Dow, Lt. John Smith, and Lt. Joseph Swett of Hampton; Capt. Jonathan Tuttle, Capt. Jonathan Woodman, and Nathaniel Hill of Dover; James Randal of New Castle; and Theophilus Dudley and Moses Leavitt of Exeter.

Governor Bellomont died a few months later, at sixty-five, in New York. But his espousal of democratic self-determination nurtured New Hampshire's Legislature for years to follow. As it accumulated experience, it clung to the Bellomont-inspired freedoms with rugged persistence. Historian Jeremy Belknap, the Dover cleric, observed nearly a century later: "The government was now modelled in favour of the people, and they rejoiced in the change."

Portsmouth understandably dominated the Assembly's life through most of its ninety-five royal years. As a thriving seaport, it long was New Hampshire's major avenue of trade and contact with the rest of the world, and the province center of wealth and all-around leadership.

State records list nineteen legislative sessions in the initial twenty-year period up to 1700, and Portsmouth men served as Speaker and clerk in most of them. The first Speaker, Richard Waldron, Jr., of Dover, presided over the first seven sessions up to 1684, with John Pickering of Portsmouth as House clerk.

When the Assembly returned to power in 1692, Portsmouth men filled the Speakership in ten of the ensuing sessions; John Gilman of Exeter filled one term, and Henry Dow of Hampton one other. The Portsmouth Speakers in this period were: Pickering for five terms; George Jaffreys three terms; Richard Martyn; and John Plaisted.

Pickering filled the clerkship four times in the 1692-99 period when he was not Speaker, and Theodore Atkinson of New Castle was clerk in four sessions. The other clerks were Elias Stileman, Mark Hunking, and Richard Jose, all of Portsmouth. The records fail to list the clerk for 1697.

The Forced Birth

BATTLING FOR FREEDOMS

AS THE NEW CENTURY of the 1700s developed, so did New Hampshire's tiny band of legislators. Through the ensuing seventy-five years up to the Revolutionary War, they slowly but firmly built the foundations of the Granite State's giant House of Democracy. They were also successful in battling to safeguard the property rights of their constituents. Details of their trials and tribulations have been compiled in two massive legislative publications. They are contained in the *State Papers*, of forty volumes, which are well summarized in *Historical New Hampshire* in its 1976 fall issue, and in the priceless ten-volume *Laws of New Hampshire*, dating back to those enacted in 1680.

Historian William Fry of Columbia University observed in his 1908 *New Hampshire as a Royal Province:*

In the constitutional history of New Hampshire during the colonial period, the Legislature played a far more important role than the Executive, and its influence was much more extensive and far-reaching.

In this pioneering period, the Assembly, of never more than three dozen members, repeatedly repulsed attempts by royal Governors to usurp its powers. The legislators were forced to compromise at times, but they clung tenaciously to their newborn, home-hewn precepts of self-determination, and even strengthened them from time to time. They persevered as various royal Governors sought to impose changing patterns of supervision and domination over their affairs.

The legislators had more than Governors to contend with. There was also a royal Council, appointed by kings or the chief executives, and mostly beholden to them. The Council served with the Governor in ruling New Hampshire and also officiated as the upper half of the Legislature when it was in session, with authority to negate any House actions of which it did not approve.

Understandably, the Council, which at times numbered a dozen men, was mostly kept at arm's length by the House and was more tolerated than trusted. In the early years the two legislative bodies officiated in joint committees. Their concerns covered the raising of revenue, fortifications, receptions, and entertainments for new Governors, and citizen petitions for various redresses. The committees were initially equal in membership, but the Assembly soon insisted upon having a majority, and then successfully won the right to name its own appointees.

The provincial legislators were quick to establish their own qualifications. After the first election of 1680 had been supervised by President Cutt and his Council, the Assembly assumed that right, as allowed in Cutt's Royal Commission. It sponsored a law that a man had to be English, a Protestant, twenty-four years of age, possessed of £20 of taxable property, and "not vitious in life, but of honest and good conversation," for the right to vote or serve in that body. Then, when such a freeman was elected to the Assembly, he faced a fine of twenty shillings for each day of absence from a session, except when excused by the membership.

The 1680 Assembly launched annual sessions, to convene on the first Tuesday of March. But Governors eventually kept the legislators in office for longer periods, when to their advantage, or arbitrarily dissolved them when they failed to please a royal ruler. The Assembly cloaked itself in immunity on May 14, 1718. To protect its members from harassment while attending their duties with aides, as was the early custom, the House voted:

Every member of the Council, each Representative of any town or district, and each Judge of Assize within this Province, during their continuance in the said respective offices, employment, and trust, shall enjoy the privilege of having one son or servant, such as they shall choose dwelling in the House, exempted and freed from all impresses, detachments, and military exercises, except Watching in their turn, as the law provides; Any law, Usage or Custom to the contrary notwithstanding.

Battling for Freedoms

And further it is enacted by the authority aforesaid, that no members of the General Assembly, or his servant, during their time of the sessions, or going to or from thence, shall be arrested, sued, imprisoned, or any ways molested or troubled, or compelled to make answer to any suit, bill, plaint or declaration, or otherwise; cases of High Treason and Felony excepted.

When King George III took office in 1761, he sent instructions to Governor Benning Wentworth to curb this immunity, with this:

No Protection from Arrests allowed to a member of the Assembly further than in his person, and that only during the session of the Assembly.

In 1766 the same king asked Governor John Wentworth to require the Assembly to submit to the same restriction on immunity, but again it was of no avail. The 1718 legislative immunity provision remained in force until 1792, when it was repealed along with a mass of other old laws that had been superseded by the state's 1784 permanent Constitution and its updated general laws.

It was also in 1718 that the Assembly authorized five shillings per diem for the Councilors while attending legislative sessions. Nine years later the lawmakers raised their own pay to six shillings per day and the Councilors to eight shillings. Lieutenant Governor John Wentworth was granted twelve shillings per day while the Legislature was in session.

The provincial legislators early imposed rules upon their own conduct. Fresh from its beneficial relationship with Governor Bellomont, the Assembly took some members to task in February 1700 for being absent. It voted:

Whereas of late sundry members of this House have been wanting therein, ordered that the clerk send to them to appear on the Third to show reason if any they can for their conduct.

On the showdown day, Moses Leavitt of Exeter appeared and apologized. The following day Theophilus Dudley of Exeter showed up and paid a fine of twelve pence. The following May 12, House Clerk Theodore Atkinson of New Castle and John Plaisted of Portsmouth were each fined twelve pence for nonattendance. In 1701 the Assembly dismissed a member as unfit for the first time. He was Timothy Hilliard of Hampton, who was elected to fill a vacancy and then ousted for a "misdemeanor" not otherwise identified. In 1715 Jabez Dow of Hampton was disqualified from the House because he refused to give up his position as a royal constable.

As the pioneer Assembly membership of eleven slowly increased, its seatings took form. The sessions were held around a large table. The Representatives from the older towns sat closest to the Speaker; the others, in the order of their respective town's admission to legislative life.

An early Assembly rule required that a law had to be read three times over three days before final passage. Another rule declared that reconsideration of a measure was not permitted by a fewer number of members than were present when it was adopted.

Up to 1721, Assembly members served as their own clerk, with special fees in addition to their per diem pay. In that year, nonmembers became clerk at about £ 10 pay annually. This policy continued for thirty years, after which members again shared in the clerkship role to the end of the provincial period.

The Legislature began using opening prayers in 1741, when Governor Benning Wentworth became Chief Executive. Two Portsmouth clergymen, the Reverend Jabez Fitch and the Reverend William Shurtleff, rotated their services, and each was paid two pounds, ten shillings, for a year of such duty. The Council later adopted the same custom until its royal demise. As towns some distance from Portsmouth were granted legislative representation, members paid themselves modest travel allowances and per diem remuneration for days devoted to going from and returning to their homes.

The Assembly was chastised in May 1725 for lacking its own home. The royal Council proposed a bond issue to build a Capitol, saying:

Foreasmuch as the sitting of the General Assembly and holding ye Court of Justice at a common inn or tavern, as has been heretofore used within this Province, is not only a dishonour to the government, but attended with inconvenience too well known to need a mention.

The Council pointed out that the Legislature was paying £ 12 yearly in tavern rentals and said a proper Capitol could be financed by bonding payments of £ 30 annually. But the legislators brushed off the proposal, and it was only after lapse of another thirty years that they erected a provincial State House in Portsmouth.

Gov. Joseph Dudley. Collection: New Hampshire Historical Society.

Masonian and Pennycook Disputes

JOSEPH DUDLEY returned as Governor of New Hampshire and Massachusetts in 1702, when Queen Anne came to power, and served as Governor for fourteen years. During the following year Usher returned as Lieutenant Governor over New Hampshire, under Dudley. This time Usher was tied by a royal restraint, as it became known he had paid £ 1,500 to Allen, who had become impoverished, for a half interest in the Masonian Claim. Usher was specifically forbidden from pressing the claim.

Allen, who had remained in New Hampshire, struggled in vain to reap income from his Masonian Claim. So the aging Allen sought to recoup from his misfortune by offering to sell it, once and for all, to the New Hampshire citizenry. This development occurred early in 1705, and Governor Usher submitted the proposal to the Legislature in mid-April. On April 26 the legislators joined with the Council in ordering the five towns (New Castle had become incorporated) to elect two delegates each to meet at Portsmouth on May 1 to consider the offer.

On May 3 the special convention agreed to purchase terms for the Masonian Claim. Allen was to be paid £ 2,000 in two annual installments. He was also given ownership to unsettled lands of 500 acres in the Portsmouth-New Castle area, and 1,500 acres in each of the towns of Dover, Hampton, and Exeter. In addition, Allen was to become owner of all the unsettled New Hampshire territory outside the towns. The next day Allen died, at sixty-nine, and the agreement was never consummated.

The Assembly continued to battle Usher and his spending demands and consistently refused to vote him any salary, although he was occasionally granted expense allowances. Meanwhile, a juvenile problem surfaced, and the 1712 Assembly passed the following law:

Foreasmuch as ignorance, ill manners and irreligion are propagated by many parents and masters by neglecting to instruct youth under their care, etc.: It shall be lawfull for the Select men with a Justice of the Peace, to examine all youth of tenn years of age whether they have been taught to read, and all those who cannot read at said age to binde out to good masters who shall be obliged to learn them to read and write till they shall be of age, etc.

Governor Usher kept the legislators in session for record-breaking periods. His 1704 Assembly, with John Pickering as Speaker, ran into eighteen sessions through five years. The 1709 Assembly, with Mark Hunking as Speaker after five years as clerk, officiated through an all-time provincial record of sixty-one sessions, again through five years.

The royal government of the neighbor colonies was changed once again following Queen Anne's death in 1714. King George I first offered the joint Governorship to Col. Eleseus Burges, a noted army officer, but London friends of Massachusetts persuaded him to give up the commission for £ 1,000. This led to Samuel Shute's coming to Boston as the overall Governor in 1716, for a twelve-year period, and George Vaughan of Portsmouth became Lieutenant Governor of New Hampshire. But Shute dumped Vaughan, who failed to conform to the Governor's wishes, and John Wentworth of Portsmouth took his place in December 1717—the first of the three members of that wealthy family to preside over New Hampshire's provincial life.

Wentworth got along rather well with the Assembly. But he rolled up thirty-five sessions for the 1717 Legislature, through five years, and yet another thirty-one sessions for the 1722 Assembly, again over a five-year period. This policy became so unpopular that it resulted in the 1727 Triennial Act. This statute, in which Governor Wentworth and his Council concurred, restricted Assembly terms to not more than three years after 1727, and most of them ran to much less time from then on. It was successfully argued that this policy would make the legislators more responsive to their constituents than to the royal rulers.

This Wentworth administration became historic for two other reasons. The Legislature launched a 1726 battle with Massachusetts for having authorized settlement of Pennycook (which became Concord) by a band from the Haverhill, Massachusetts, area. And then it clashed with Governor Wentworth over appointment of the legislative Speaker.

Governor Wentworth informed the Assembly in April 1726 that the Bay colonists were to arrive at the Pennycook site the following month. He warned that the venture meant "invasion" of the "very bowels of this Province and will take in the most valuable of our lands." A joint committee was promptly appointed to trudge through the fifty miles of wilderness from Portsmouth to the threatened site. It comprised Richard Waldron, secretary to Wentworth; Assemblyman Theodore Atkinson; and Nathaniel Weare of Hampton, a prominent personage.

The Portsmouth committee reached Pennycook on May 14, shortly after the arrival of the band of some forty settlers and presented their official protest. History has recorded that they replied "in an amiable way," and that their presence was legal, by vote of the Massachusetts government. The Waldron group then "discreetly" left and reported back to Wentworth and the Assembly.

Governor Wentworth next filed futile protests with the Boston government, as his Assembly suggested the issue be laid before the king in England. But Massachusetts insisted that under an early grant its northern boundary included the Merrimack River and its valleys, along which Pennycook was laid out. The New Hampshire Assembly meanwhile paid the Waldron committee £ 31, seventeen shillings, and eleven pence for its time and travel expenses. In 1727 the legislators joined with Governor Wentworth in a most extraordinary solution to the Pennycook problem.

Governor Wentworth issued a controversial 1727 grant, called Bow. It covered not only the present township of that name but all of the Pennycook settlement and what is now Pembroke and Hooksett. The list of more than 120 Bow proprietors was the most impressive in New Hampshire history. It included all sixteen legislators, all the Councilors, Wentworth himself and his son, Benning (later Governor), and a host of their relatives and other citizens.

In this manner, the Legislature long refused to recognize Pennycook (later Rumford), because of its Massachusetts' sponsorship. The Bow owners never actually settled that town for a half-century. But as the Rumfordites prospered, the Bow proprietors vainly battled in the courts to collect rentals from them, despite royal rulings favoring Rumford over Bow.

The Legislature at Portsmouth denied Rumford's plea for townhood until 1765, and then it was granted only with most unusual details. It was declared to be a parish of Bow, without legislative representation, and its name was changed to Concord, which the Rumford settlers never asked for and long resented.

Another feature of this 1722-27 Assembly was a first fight with the Governor over its Speakership. Wentworth vetoed an Assembly's Speaker choice, and a stalement ensued as the legislators insisted they alone controlled that appointment and cited Parliament custom to prove their position. But as the Governor continued adamant, the House named a compromise Speaker, in a resolve which maintained its original claim. Wentworth approved this choice but also, in an accompanying statement, reiterated his executive prerogative.

A Massachusetts man who acquired royal polish during a long London residency became Governor of New Hampshire and his own colony in 1730. Eventually, he was trounced by the sturdy little Portsmouth Assembly in its final settlement of a protracted boundary dispute between the two governments. He was Jonathan Belcher, who bypassed New Hampshire's Lieutenant Governor, David Dunbar, and personally supervised the province from his Boston base.

Border Grabs and Snarls

THE ASSEMBLY had tried for some thirty years to win royal determination of New Hampshire's southern boundary. It claimed the line above the Merrimack River should continue westward from what is now the Lowell, Massachusetts, area, to the New York colony line. The Bay colonists in turn insisted the boundary extended three miles north of the Merrimack, to its northern source in Lake Winnipesaukee, some seventy-five miles above Lowell.

The Assembly became particularly alarmed as Massachusetts launched settlements deeper and deeper into the wilderness west of the upper reaches of the Merrimack. The obvious reason for this policy was to annex as much land as possible for bargaining purposes if and when the boundary battle came up for final determination. The Pennycook incident was a case at point. Historian Belknap wrote a half-century later:

Great inconveniences had arisen for want of a due settlement of the limits of the Province. The people who lived near the supposed line were sometimes taxed by both provinces, sometimes the officers themselves were at variance, and imprisoned each other. Several attempts had been made to remove the difficulty, and letters frequently passed between the two courts [Legislatures] on the subject, in consequence of petitions and complaints from the borderers.

Governor Belcher at first sided with New Hampshire, but he later connived against her. He wrote to the London government in 1733:

The poor borderers on the lines . . . live like toads under the harrow, being run into jails on the one side or the other as often as they please to quarrel. They will pull down one another's houses, often wound one another and I fear it will end in bloodshed, unless His Majestry . . . give some effectual order to have the bounds fixed.

Although, my Lords, I am a Massachusetts man, yet I think this Province alone is culpable on its head.

New Hampshire has all along been frank and ready to pay exact duty and obedience to the king's order and has manifested a great inclination to peace and good government, but, in return, the Massachusetts province have thrown unreasonable obstacles in the way of any settlement, and, offers to settle the boundaries with New York and Rhode Island in an open, easy and amicable way, yet, when they come to settle with New Hampshire, they will not come to terms, which seems to me a plain argument that the leading men of the Massachusetts Assembly are conscious to themselves of the continual encroachments they are making upon their neighbors of New Hampshire and so dare not come to a settlement.

In January 1736 the king created a commission to resolve the boundary battle. He designated five elder Councilors from each of the provinces of New York, New Jersey, Nova Scotia, and Rhode Island to make the decision, with any five of them constituting a quorum. Confirmed in October, the commission assumed office in April 1737, with a requirement that it convene at Hampton, New Hampshire, on August 1 to air arguments and then render a verdict.

New Hampshire and Massachusetts were supposed to appoint legislative committees to present their claims. But Governor Belcher had by this time shifted sentiments, and he kept the New Hampshire General Assembly prorogued so that it could not act. An earlier boundary committee was resurrected by the House, however, to appear before the boundary commission.

It was at this point that Belcher blossomed. He had become enamored of royal pomp and panoply while residing in London as agent for Massachusetts, so he ordered both Legislatures into session, virtually side by side, at the scene of the hearings. The New Hampshire lawmakers bowed to the Belcher mandate and met at Hampton. But they grimly refused his demands for special ceremonies in convening.

It was different, however, for their Boston counterparts. Governor Belcher ordered that they be escorted by a cavalcade to Salisbury, south of Hampton, and he rode with them, attended by a troop of horse. He recorded:

He was met at a Newbury ferry by another troop, who, joined by three more at the supposed divisional line, conducted him to the George tavern in

Hampton Falls; where he held Council and made a speech to the Assembly of New Hampshire.

40 Belcher's pomposity failed to impress the New Hampshire legislators and did not even pry a concession from them. But it produced a nugget for history lovers to savor. The novelty of Governor Belcher's kinglike display occasioned the following pasquinade (author unknown) in an assumed Hibernian style:

Dear Paddy, you ne'er did behold such a sight,
As yesterday morning was seen before night.
You in all your born days saw, nor I didn't neither,
So many fine horses and men ride together.
At the head, the lower House trotted two in a row,
Then all the higher House pranc'd after the low;
Then the Governor's coach gallop'd on like the wind,
And the last that came foremost were the troopers behind;
But I fear it means no good, to your neck or mine,
For they say 'tis to fix a right place for the line.

The Bay Colony's legislators remained in session at Salisbury, five miles distant from their New Hampshire opposites. Governor Belcher repeatedly sought concessions from the latter. But they remained so adamant that he could not even muster a quorum at times, and finally prorogued them in disgust late in October.

Only eight commissioners reported for the boundary hearings. Three were from Nova Scotia—William Skene, who presided; Erasmus James Phillips; and Otho Hamilton. The five others, all from Rhode Island, were Samuel Vernon, John Gardner, John Potter, Ezekiel Warner, and George Cornel. The commission issued a straddling report. It told the royal government at London that if the Massachusetts claim was correct, the boundary would be in its favor, and if the New Hampshire arguments were correct, the new line would please that province.

Both sides went into action, appealing to the London government for a final decision in their favor. Governor Belcher, meanwhile, was censured at London for his partiality toward Massachusetts and was later replaced.

New Hampshire's Assembly acted by itself to terminate the boundary woes. It bypassed the Council because it had sided with Governor Belcher in proposing a new merger with Massachusetts.

To This Day

The legislators turned to John Thomlinson, their longtime efficient London agent, and he prevailed.

Surprise Land Gains

IN THE KING'S ABSENCE on a European tour, the Privy Council took up the controversy at London, heeded Thomlinson's arguments, and on March 8, 1740, issued rulings which continue to this day. The Privy Council even set the New Hampshire boundary with Maine, then under Massachusetts jurisdiction. As for the southern boundary, the Privy Council ruled:

That the northern boundary of The Massachusetts shou'd be a Curve Line to Run three Miles north of the River Merrimack Parallel with it from the Sea as high as Pawtucket Falls [present Lowell area], *& thence a strait line should be drawn due west till it meets His Majesty's other Governments.*

The New Hampshire legislators became jubilant. They had won 3,500 square miles of territory long claimed and settled by Massachusetts. New Hampshire gained twenty-eight towns settled and governed by its opponent for more than a score of years. They included what are now Bedford, Goffstown, Suncook, Bow, Concord, Boscawen, Salisbury, Webster, and Contoocook, along the Merrimack River Valley; Amherst, Rindge, Peterborough, Lyndeboro, New Boston, Dunbarton, Weare, Hopkinton, Hillsborough, Washington, Warner, and Bradford, to the west of the Merrimack; and Hinsdale, Westmoreland, Walpole and Charlestown, in the Connecticut River region.

The Privy Council ordered the two colonies to jointly finance a survey of the new line, and Massachusetts refused, hoping it could be overturned by further London intrigue. The New Hampshire Assembly happily hired three men to run the new boundary, each with a crew covering one third of the distance. The New Hampshire Council refused to concur in payment to the surveyors, and it also blocked reimbursement to Thomlinson for his efforts. But these payments were authorized a year later under a new royal administration.

In the meantime, Thomlinson also settled the old Masonian Claim. A descendant, Boston seaman John Tufton Mason, who had just come of age, was talked into resurrecting the case by some Bay Colony legal sharps. The late Otis G. Hammond, former director of the New Hampshire Historical Society, compiled these details in 1916.

This Mason heir sold his alleged interests in that part of New Hampshire, long claimed and occupied by Massachusetts, for £500 and an expenses-paid trip to London to win royal approval of the transaction. The Massachusetts agent in London took Mason in tow, became bogged in royal bureaucratic red tape, and ordered the young seaman back home to save the costs of maintaining him. Mason resented this shabby treatment and turned to Thomlinson, with whom he had become acquainted. The upshot was that Mason signed an agreement to sell for £1,000 his entire claim against the New Hampshire settlers.

Under this arrangement, Councilor Benning Wentworth, son of the late Lieutenant Governor John Wentworth, and other wealthy Portsmouth officials were to pay the fee if the Assembly failed to do so. The ensuing negotiations were consummated after young Wentworth replaced Belcher in 1741.

FINAL PROVINCIAL YEARS

WHEN portly Benning Wentworth became Governor at forty-seven in 1741, he launched the most colorful of all of New Hampshire's provincial administrations. He governed for a quarter of a century (longer than any other man in American colonial history), and he both pleased and plagued the Legislature through it all. He had just lost a fortune in sea trade, sought to recoup wealth with the Governorship, and did so, almost beyond measure.

This Wentworth battled the Assembly over the years. Early in 1745 he staged a deadlock with the Assembly on two basic issues. He refused to concur on the Speakership and vainly tried to bestow legislative representation for towns of his choosing. The Legislature clung adamantly to its claim that such functions were its exclusive prerogative. Then Governor Wentworth gave up this confrontation for the time being, to turn his attention to settlement of Canadian war problems.

Four years later, in 1749, this two-pronged argument between Wentworth and the Assembly was revived and continued for almost three years. The forty-fifth Assembly of 1749 elected Richard Waldron of Hampton, whose father and grandfather of the same name had carved niches in New Hampshire history, as Speaker, and Wentworth vetoed the choice. This fifty-five-year-old Waldron had enjoyed lucrative royal appointments for twenty years and was ousted when Benning Wentworth became Governor. As a result, Waldron became his

Gov. Benning Wentworth, from a portrait by Joseph Blackburn of Portsmouth. Collection: New Hampshire Historical Society.

implacable enemy.

Governor Wentworth had also invited other towns to send Representatives to the Assembly, and the legislators once again firmly refused to allow them to be seated.

Governor Wentworth refused to budge, having announced he had obtained a royal ruling from London that he was correct on both issues. But the Assembly also stuck to its self-rule claim, and as a result of this deadlock the province became bereft of fiscal operations from January 5, 1749, to September 22, 1752. No taxes were levied; the courts were without funds; and even public records were not kept in this period, which ended only when the legislators' three-year term terminated. This stalemated Assembly held twenty sessions, passed no law, and approved only a single resolution. It permitted any person to print the session Journals, since the Assembly had no funds for that purpose.

In this period the legislators became acquainted with a new year. As indicated earlier, the British Parliament voted in 1751 to conform to the Gregorian calendar, which changed the start of a year from March 25 to January 1. This became effective in 1752, during which September 3 was adjusted to September 14, to eliminate eleven days in the new calendar.

Speaker Waldron continued in such high Hampton esteem that he was reelected to the 1753 House, from which he promptly resigned when Meshech Weare of Hampton Falls became the compromise Speaker. Waldron died soon thereafter.

The Masonian Owners

THE REVIVED MASONIAN CLAIM pestered this Wentworth administration for years. Its new owners vainly tried to turn it over to the Legislature, on behalf of New Hampshire's settlers, for the proposed selling price. But the legislators balked, time and again, because of a transfer qualification. It gave control of the Masonian land grants to the Governor and the Council, and the Assembly vainly insisted upon having that authority.

By 1746 the procrastinations had become so wearisome that another combination of rich Portsmouth area gentry engineered final purchase of the Masonian Claim for £ 1,500. This was negotiated with young Mason at Boston, during one of his infrequent returns from distant seafarings, who was also promised a share of the profits.

The new owners became known as the "Masonian Proprietors." As public resentments mounted when the surprise deal became known, they melted this antagonism with the announcement that they would quitclaim without charge all the improved properties in the settled townships. Records indicate that these proprietors sold some 135,000 acres in dozens of grants, out of an estimated area of 200,000 acres of claimed ownership. In 1790 New Hampshire's free government purchased from the surviving families the residue for a modest cash settlement and wilderness land.

Governor Wentworth had no knowledge of the 1746 sale until it was consummated. But the shareholders were all related to him, and he accepted the fact. In addition, the Governor had other profits to venture for. He soon began reaping, with grants in the western and northern sections of the province, beyond the Masonian "line," which extended inland from Portsmouth a distance of sixty miles. Then, when the French were driven from Canada, the wilderness of what is Vermont became attractive to adventurous land seekers, so Wentworth began to wholesale grants all the way to the New York colonial line, with substantial profits from fees and other such sources.

Governor Wentworth developed into an adroit operator. He promoted lasting friendships by including legislators and other prominent citizens in many of his grants, at little or no fees. For example, Dr. Josiah Bartlett of Kingston, who became a noted Revolutionary leader, did not join the Legislature at Portsmouth until 1765, but his activities as a town selectman drew Wentworth's attention, and he was given gratuitous shares in several new townships.

The influential New York government protested to the London government about Benning Wentworth's intrusions into the Vermont region. But Wentworth persisted, claiming that Massachusetts and Connecticut had been allowed to extend their western boundaries to the New York border, east of the Hudson River, and that New Hampshire, by precedent, was entitled to the same comparative distance inland.

Governor Wentworth granted nearly 140 towns in the Vermont area before the king issued a 1764 decree, setting New Hampshire's western boundary at the western bank of the Connecticut River —where it remains to this day. So from then on Governor Wentworth desisted. But by then he personally owned 70,000 acres in the Vermont grants, from his policy of keeping 500 choice acres in each grant for his own profit.

The Wentworths' Achievements

THE LEGISLATURE finally financed its own home in Portsmouth under Benning Wentworth some thirty years after the first Wentworth administration had proposed it. Part of this brick building, originally 80 by 30 feet in size, still stands as a historic shrine.

Benning Wentworth enlarged a residence at Little Harbor, in Portsmouth, into a massive mansion, facing the waterfront. It subsequently was reduced in size and was acquired by the Legislature a few years ago, as a tourist attraction. The site is where the state flower, the purple lilac, was first imported and planted in 1750.

This Governor Wentworth became housebound with the gout in his final three years of rule. He died in 1770, at seventy-four, three years following retirement. Three years later, his nephew, Governor John Wentworth, won a royal decree that Benning's approximately 200,000 acres of holdings in his grants, which he had willed to his childless widow, belonged to the province, with royal right to regrant these properties. But Benning Wentworth's memory continues in luster, for he named Bennington, Vermont, for himself, and it has long been site of the famous Battle of Bennington monument.

Governor John Wentworth's administration produced two major developments, both of which occurred in 1769, and that have continued to this day. One was creation of county governments; the other was the chartering of Dartmouth College. Wentworth personally helped sponsor both of these historic events, and the Dartmouth charter of December 13, 1769, was under his signature.

The Assembly long battled to spread provincial justice, centered for more than four score years in the Portsmouth seat of government. By the 1760s the populace had spread so far inland that the courts and public recordings had become virtually beyond their reach. While the seacoast population had grown to nearly 35,000, another 30,000 were planting roots and families in distant places, some even 100 miles westward along the Connecticut River, and northward into what is now Coos County.

The legislators argued that for many settlers, travel to Portsmouth for legal business was not only too far but too costly, because of the time involved in walking or riding over makeshift trails and make-do roads. They insisted that the province legal services, especially the registering of property ownership and recordings of deeds and other transactions, be made more accessible.

Gov. John Wentworth. Collection: State House.

The royal Council refused to concur on these legislative demands for several years. Then a showdown developed in 1769. Governor Wentworth stepped into the breach, as the Assembly refused to vote more taxes to enforce its demands. He used his influence to induce the Council to join in support of the spread of justice, so that a compromise measure to create New Hampshire's first five counties was passed on April 29, 1769. But it had a string attached; it was not to become effective until approved by the king. So it was not until March 19, 1771, to be exact, that county government received the royal blessing and became a reality. The statute contained a preamble which read.

Because of the great increase of the inhabitants of the Province, and the remote situation of many of them from Portsmouth, where the Courts of Judicature are now held, has rendered the administration of justice very expensive and difficult, and in some cases almost impractical. The people are not of sufficient ability to travel so far.

Governor Wentworth named the counties after Lords in distant England. First, encompassing Portsmouth, the seacoast, and inland to Concord, was Rockingham, named for Wentworth's royal benefactor. Then there was Strafford and Hillsborough. Cheshire and Grafton counties were not implemented until a couple of years later.

The state's five other present counties were created by the Legislature under its free government. Coos was formed out of Grafton on December 24, 1803; Merrimack from Rockingham and Hillsborough on July 1, 1823; Sullivan from Cheshire on July 25, 1827; and Belknap and Carroll from Strafford on December 23, 1840.

It was this final Governor Wentworth who developed a handsome estate on what became Lake Wentworth in Wolfeboro, which gave that town claim to being the first summer resort in the nation. In honor of his young bride, he also created Francestown, which has ever been a pretty New Hampshire town, in 1772.

Legislative statistics show that up to 1700, after twenty years of its own provincial government, New Hampshire had only 6 townships, Kingston and New Castle having been added to the original quartet. By 1730 the number had grown to 24. The following ten-year Belcher administration created 27 new townships. Then in the three dozen years of the two following Wentworth Governors' regimes, a total of some 150 new grants were laid out in New Hampshire, along with 128 in the disputed Vermont area.

Final Provincial Years

Social and Economic Gains

SOCIAL ECONOMICS claimed the attention of the provincial Assembly in its concluding years. In 1766 the legislators invoked price fixing on bread—to protect the seller rather than the consumer—the exact opposite of modern practice. This law read:

Whereas a just proportion between the price of flour and weight and price of bread is now a matter of importance as many people purchase the greatest part of their bread of bakers and without such regulation they are left to judge for themselves where their impartiality will be much questioned, and as it is reasonable they should be allowed a suitable profit in their business to encourage their industry and their fidelity in vending wholesome well made bread it is necessary a just medium should be established.

Then in 1769 the Legislature voted special protection for industry. Edward Emerson of Portsmouth was given the sole privilege of operating a potash works without competition within ten miles of the State House, "to encourage useful art," and to produce "a valuable commodity for exportation, for when several persons in different interests attempt the same thing, they often defeat the end at which they aim, and the business which under due regulation might have been of public service comes to nothing."

State records list only three divorces granted by the provincial Assembly, and two of them were subsequently denied, one by the royal Council, the other by the king in England.

On January 7, 1766, Samuel Smallcorn of Portsmouth was granted a divorce from Margaret Welsh because she had "admitted to her bed" one John Collier while her husband was away from home. The Governor and the Council concurred.

On April 5, 1771, Greenwood Carpenter of Swanzey was given a legislative divorce from the former Sarah Leathers of Charlestown, Massachusetts. They had been married for eleven years and had several children. Carpenter charged that his wife had left home and married another man, and said he wanted to marry again. The Governor and Council concurred, but more than two years later (September 1, 1773) this divorce was disallowed by the king.

The final provincial divorce granted by the Legislature was given to Eliphalet Pattee of Chester on January 22, 1773. He testified to having been married for nearly eight years when his wife, the former Abigail Elliott, went eighty miles from home and returned home pregnant sixteen months later. This divorce was disallowed by the Council four months later.

One other provincial divorce was recorded. In the first years of New Hampshire's provincial life, only the Governor and the Council had the power to grant divorces, and on February 11, 1703, according to legislative records, Thomas Holland of Portsmouth won his freedom from his wife, Elizabeth, for reasons unknown.

Legislative Leaders

THERE WERE FIFTY-FIVE elected assemblies during the ninety-five-year life of New Hampshire's provincial government from 1680 into 1775, and some of them had from eighteen to sixty-five sessions. There were twenty-two House Speakers and nineteen House clerks in this period.

Richard Waldron, Jr., of Portsmouth was Speaker of the first seven assemblies from 1680 to 1684, with John Pickering of Portsmouth as clerk.

Following the eight-year period when the province had no Legislature, Richard Martyn of Portsmouth became Speaker in 1692 and Pickering again was clerk. With just two exceptions, House members filled the clerkship, with special fees in addition to their per diem pay, throughout the years.

Andrew Wiggin of Stratham set a provincial record with service as Speaker for twelve terms, from 1728 to 1744, a period of sixteen years. James Jeffrey of Portsmouth, a nonmember, served as a salaried clerk for twenty-seven years, through fifteen terms, from 1717 to 1744.

After the Assembly was revived in 1692, Pickering was Speaker for seven scattered terms and clerk for an additional four terms.

The 1717 Assembly had a rash of leadership problems as it continued for thirty-five sessions through five years. Speaker Thomas Packer of Portsmouth was promoted to the royal Council and was succeeded by Joshua Peirce of Portsmouth from the clerkship. Other clerks in this Assembly were Joseph Smith of Hampton, Daniel Greenwood of New Castle, Ephraim Dennett and Henry Sherburne of Portsmouth, along with Jeffrey, the nonmember.

Richard Gerrish of Portsmouth had the distinction of being Speaker in the 1709 Legislature, which lasted through sixty-one sessions over a five-year period, with Samuel Keais of Portsmouth as clerk. Then Gerrish was Speaker in the three following assemblies, which lasted only two years in all.

Henry Sherburne, Jr., of Portsmouth and Andrew Clarkson of the same town teamed up as Speaker and clerk, respectively, for five terms, from 1755 to 1768.

Other provincial Speakers included John Gilman and Peter Gilman of Exeter; George Jaffrey, John Plaisted, Samuel Penhallow, and Nathaniel Rogers of Portsmouth; Peter Weare, Nathaniel Weare, and Meshech Weare of Hampton Falls; Daniel Tilton and Richard Waldron (vetoed in 1749 by the Governor but presided) of Hampton; and Ebenezer Stevens of Kingston.

Other provincial House clerks were Elias Stileman, Mark Hunking, Richard Jose, Richard Wibird, Matthew Livermore, William Parker, and Daniel Peirce (nonmember) of Portsmouth; Meshech Weare of Hampton Falls; Samuel Thing of Exeter; and Theodore Atkinson of New Castle.

The last of the fifty-five assemblies was a futile effort by Governor John Wentworth (third of that family as Chief Executive), convened on May 4, 1775, to restore peace with the rebellious legislators. Thirty-seven men from thirty-six towns reported for duty at Portsmouth, and the Assembly promptly refused to seat three of them.

Governor Wentworth had invited the loyalist centers of Plymouth, Orford, and Lyme to elect legislators. They respectively sent Col. John Fenton, Israel Morey, and Attorney Jacob Greene to Portsmouth. So the House revived its self-government determination and refused to seat them.

This final Assembly rebuffed all of the Governor's overtures, while reelecting another John Wentworth—of Somersworth and the Governor's cousin—as Speaker, and Meshech Weare as clerk. This third Governor Wentworth was still only thirty-eight, after a nine-year term, as he vainly strove to keep New Hampshire from breaking from the motherland. And only a few weeks earlier the Fort William and Mary cannon had boomed his joy upon birth of a first child, after six years of marriage, which he named Charles-Mary, after his long-time British benefactors, Lord and Lady Rockingham.

Wentworth prorogued the May 5 session after three days to June 12, 1775, and on July 15 he ordered another recess to September 28. By this time he had moved into Fort William and Mary with his family, and following a brief Boston visit, he took refuge on the Isles of Shoals, off Portsmouth, to avoid the mounting wrath of the Legislature and citizens in general.

Governor Wentworth feared cancelling the September 28 legislative date in person, so by message he set the next convening of the Assembly for April 24, 1776, which proved of less value than the paper it was written on. By that time, Wentworth had gone to Nova Scotia, to rule that area and later win a baronetcy from the king, and New Hampshiremen had begun their long struggle for freedoms never before known to mankind.

A seventy-five-year record total of thirty-four men from thirty-three towns qualified for that concluding provincial Assembly. There was then an estimated New Hampshire population of 82,200. So the per capita representation was 2,124, the greatest in the state's history, up to and including the 1971 apportionment statute. This also compared with a per capita legislative representation of 273, the all-time low, when the 1680 Assembly of eleven men represented an estimated population of but 3,000.

The thirty-two members of the last provincial Legislature besides Speaker Wentworth and Clerk Weare included John Langdon of Portsmouth, who did not serve, having become a delegate to the First Continental Congress at Philadelphia.

The thirty-one others in this historic conclave were Capt. Woodbury Langdon and Jacob Sheafe of Portsmouth; Capt. Caleb Hodgdon and Otis Baker of Dover; Josiah Moulton and Josiah Moulton, Jr., of Hampton; Col. Nathan Folsom and John Giddings of Exeter; Dr. Josiah Bartlett of Kingston; Maj. Richard Downing of Newington; Deacon Stephen Boardman of Stratham; Col. Stephen Holland of Londonderry; Ebenezer Thompson of Durham; Col. Clement March of Greenland; Col. Joseph Smith of Newmarket; Capt. Eliphat Merrill of South Hampton; John Webster of Chester; Col. John Hale of Hollis; Capt. John Chamberlin of Merrimack; Maj. Nathaniel Healey of Kensington; Deacon James Knowles of Rochester; Joshua Foss of Barrington; Col. Samuel Ashley of Winchester; Capt. Isaac Wyman of Keene; Elijah Grout of Charlestown; Paul Dudley Sargeant for Amherst and Bedford; Wyseman Claggett for Nottingham West (Hudson) and Litchfield; Jacob Butler, Jr., for Salem and Pelham; John Calef for Plaistow and Hampstead; and Henry Prescott and Samuel Jenness for New Castle and Rye.

As the provincial Assembly concluded ninety-five years of existence, it left a legacy of battling taxes without representation. It had vainly tried in 1764 to substantially broaden its membership. It voted on May 9, 1764, to allow a legislator for every 100 voters in each town, and the merging of tinier towns which could not muster that quota, for joint representation. The Governor and the Council approved this policy, but it was vetoed by King George III on June 26, 1767. But this apportionment principle was finally adopted when New Hampshire launched its own free government in 1776, and it continues to this day, in modified form.

While 33 towns were represented in the final provincial Assembly, a total of 146 towns was being taxed to support the royal government. Among the more heavily assessed towns denied legislative seats up to the end were Epping, Brentwood, Concord, Nottingham, New Ipswich, Lee, Madbury, Deerfield, and Hopkinton. Each paid more provincial taxes annually than did some of the towns with Assembly representation.

The provincial Legislature cultivated an unusual lawmaking policy, which its free successor continued for some years and then discarded. It restricted the life of statutes dealing with public conduct to from one to five or seven years' duration. This time limit latch was apparently based on the experience that if a new restraint or policy voted upon the people did not prove in the public interest, or became unworkable, it allowed for good riddance on the expiration date; if it proved worthwhile, the law could readily be reenacted.

Part 2

The First Century Of Statehood

Early engraving depicting Franklin Pierce leaving the Eagle Hotel in Concord after his election to the Presidency. Courtesy Mrs. Carl Gesen.

NEW HAMPSHIRE GOES FREE

NEW HAMPSHIREMEN rose to the challenge when their royal government foundered and dissolved their provincial Assembly in June 1774.

The legislators reconvened illegally in the State House at Portsmouth and then shifted their deliberations to a nearby tavern when Governor John Wentworth appeared with a sheriff and ordered them off. There they launched a "Provincial Congress" to replace their Legislature, and within eighteen months New Hampshire pioneered the first free Constitution in American history, on January 5, 1776, six months before the immortal Declaration of Independence was created.

This transition from royal rule to a free government was rife with fears and frustrations, for the colonists were forced to conduct a long and wearisome war to maintain it. But they dared and developed, by trial and error, to prove to the world that common people could manage their own public destiny.

Time has measured New Hampshire's new government of those formative years as both imperfect and inefficient. But her people had been schooled in self-reliance through more than a century of struggle to civilize the wilderness, so they persevered and prevailed.

As New Hampshire ventured into independence, her people were as different in makeup as they were distant from each other. Former House Speaker Richard F. Upton of Concord graphically reflected this in his 1936 book, *Revolutionary New Hampshire*, (which was reprinted

Richard F. Upton

in 1971) in explaining how the province had developed into three distinct sections, as follows:

The first section roughly coincided with the seacoastal plain, eighteen miles in length, and the Great Bay tidewater region. This area comprised almost half the population and paid nearly two-thirds of the total province taxes. . . . Because of their relative prosperity and close contact with royal officials, the people of this section seemed to have been somewhat conservative in viewpoint down to the actual outbreak of the Revolution.

The second section embraced roughly the area of the Merrimack Valley and contiguous territory. As many of the towns had been granted by Massachusetts Bay and settled by Massachusetts men, it was not unnatural that their inhabitants should look to Boston for political guidance. They seem to have been completely imbued with a Puritan disrespect for English institutions and the vested interests of the seacoast oligarchy.

The third section was the frontier, coinciding with the Connecticut River Valley, the scene of many a French and Indian raid in the past. This region was settled in great part by pioneering men from Connecticut who had pushed up the river for newer lands. . . . Ordinarily accustomed to an extremely democratic government, these political radicals resented the fact that they were given little or no part in the government of their adopted province.

Another reflection of New Hampshire life of two centuries ago was contained in a three-year law concerning Christmas, which expired as the provincial Assembly also came to an end. It was labeled "An Act To Prevent And Punish Disorders Usually Committed On The Twenty Fifth Day Of December Commonly Called Christmas-Day The Evening Preceeding & Following Said Day And To Prevent Other Irregularities Committed At Other Times," and read as follows:

Whereas it often happens that many disorders are Occasioned within the Town of Portsmouth by Loose Idle Persons going about the streets in Companies in a roisterous & Tumultuous manner hallooing huzzaing firing guns beating Drums to the great disturbance & Terror of many of the Inhabitants on the evening Preceeding & and evening following said Day and Whereas a barbarous inhuman custom of throwing Clubs at Tame Fowl on said Day & other Days hath long prevailed against all private Remonstrances which practice often Occasions Quarrels to the Disturbance of the peace and mischief often happens by boys & Fellows playing with balls in the public Streets for Preventing whereof—

Be it Enacted by the Governor Council & Assembly that no Person or Persons within the Town of Portsmouth shall on the Evening or Night next immediately preceeding the Christmas Day Assemble with others in a roisterous & Tumultuous manner aforesaid or Travel thro the Streets with beating of Drum or Drums & firing Guns or hallooing & huzzaing as aforesaid nor the evening after said Day on the Pains & Penalties herein after mentioned And that the practice of throwing Clubs at Fowls be & hereby is wholly forbid thro-out this Province and the shooting at fowles in any Public Place whereby any of his Majesty's Subjects shall be in danger is hereby also forbid And any boys playing with balls in any streets whereby there is danger of breaking the Windows of any building public or Private may be ordered to remove to any place where there will be no such danger.

And whereas on Public Days of any kind of rejoycing or Assembling of the People it has been Common for Negros & Servants to exercise & Practice Sundry sorts of games for money which may tempt them to pursue unlawful means to furnish themselves with money for that purpose therefore all such sorts of Gaming or playing in the streets highways or public places is hereby forbid—

New Hampshire Goes Free

And it is hereby further Enacted that all Persons are hereby Forbid to ride on a Gallop or other Swifter motion or Pace than after the Rate of five Miles an hour–thro' the Public Streets & Populous places of the Town and any Person Offending in any of the Particulars aforesaid shall be Subject to pay a fine not Exceeding five Shillings or Suffer Imprisonment not Exceeding forty Eight hours or Set in the Stocks not exceeding two hours and any justice of the Peace any Judge of the Inferior or Superior Court or the Majority of the Selectmen of the Town may and hereby are authorized respectively to take cognizance of the cases aforesaid & it is hereby ordered that boys under Twelve years of age be excepted from Suffering the Penalties aforesaid

And it is hereby further Enacted that the same restriction of Riding thro the Streets shall extend to all kinds of Carriages as well as to those on horseback.

This Act shall be in force for the Term of three Years & no longer. (Passed December 23 (Friday), 1771.)

Christmas was not observed in the colonies in those days, and the Legislature met on it when December 25 was a weekday. The German mercenaries, who fought for the British against the Americans, were among the first to plant Christmas observance, with joy and sharing, in the United States.

The Provincial Congress

NEW HAMPSHIRE'S Revolutionary government was created by methods that by necessity were makeshift and without precedent. The defunct 1774 Assembly had formed a novel Committee of Correspondence before it was outlawed, and it stepped into the breach. It called the ousted assemblymen into illegal session to pave a new government.

Judge John Wentworth of Somersworth, three-term Assembly Speaker, was chairman of this temporary group, whose main purpose was to promote alliance with the other colonies against the British oppressions. His committee associates, all former legislators, were John Sherburne, William Parker, Jacob Sheafe, and John Pickering of Portsmouth; Dr. John Giddings of Exeter; and Christopher Toppan of Hampton.

The July 6 tavern meeting issued a call for a convention, or Congress, of town delegates to deal with the province's rudderless public affairs. It was a surprisingly democratic appeal, for each of the 155 towns was invited to elect as many delegates as it pleased to the emergency Congress, at Exeter on July 21, 1774. The towns were informed the main purpose of this first Congress was to elect two delegates to the proposed Continental Congress at Philadelphia, and they were asked to send along modest allotments of money to defray their expenses, estimated at £ 200. Word also went out that the Exeter site was chosen to avoid possible royal recrimination, and the deliberations and membership were to be kept secret for the same reason. There was a postscript to the call. It read:

Considering the Distressing situation of our public affairs, Thursday the 14th is recommended to be kept as a day of Fasting, Humiliation and Prayer through this Province.

Subsequent compilations listed eighty-five men at that first Provincial Congress from at least sixty-four towns, making it more than twice the membership of any provincial Assembly. The seacoast area furnished most of the delegates, as the inland towns declined, for the most part, to participate. There were seven delegates from Portsmouth; five each from Dover and Exeter; four each from Hampton and Kensington; and three each from Kingston, Sandown, and South Hampton.

This first Provincial Congress elected Pickering and Dr. Josiah Bartlett of Kingston as delegates to the First Continental Congress at Philadelphia, but they both declined, the latter because his home was destroyed in a night fire. So Maj. John Sullivan, the prosperous Durham lawyer and militia leader, and Col. Nathaniel Folsom, wealthy Exeter merchant, became New Hampshire's first delegates to that historic meeting, which was in session during September and October 1774.

A second Provincial Congress convened on January 25, 1775, at Exeter, with an impressive 144 delegates. The Merrimack River towns were well represented; Hampton set the pace with 9 delegates, along with 7 from Portsmouth and 6 from Chester.

A third Provincial Congress met at Exeter on April 21, 1775, following the Battle of Lexington and Concord in Massachusetts, and, because it had been hastily called, this session mustered only 68 delegates from thirty-four towns. This session called upon the towns to share food and other supplies with Boston inhabitants, because of a rigid British blockade, and this drew substantial response.

Judge Wentworth was President of the first three Provincial Congresses. And it was in this period that New Hampshire patriotism was put to challenge.

The Committee of Correspondence first sponsored a lengthy "Covenant," which the towns were asked to circulate for signatures. It pledged refusal to use or deal in any British products, especially tea, and the names of men who failed to sign this document were to be posted as public enemies. One copy of this oath has been preserved in Concord history, and it lists "Mother Hannah Osgood," the famous Revolutionary tavernkeeper who catered to legislators with special concoctions, as probably the only woman in American history to sign such a document.

A second loyalty pledge was sponsored by the Continental Congress, and New Hampshire's Provincial Congress put it to wide use early in 1776, after it had legalized the first colonial Constitution of freedom against British oppression. This was a pledge to risk life and fortune "To oppose the hostile proceedings of the British fleets and armies against the United American colonies."

A fourth Provincial Congress convened on May 18, 1775, two weeks after royal Governor Wentworth had convened his final provincial Assembly, and quickly prorogued it, before fleeing the province. Dr. Matthew Thornton of Londonderry (later of Exeter and then Merrimack) became President of this session, and Dr. Ebenezer Thompson of Durham served as its secretary. It was this Congress which later in the year laid the groundwork for creation of New Hampshire's famous January 5, 1776, Constitution of freedom.

The First Constitution

THIS FOURTH PROVINCIAL CONGRESS launched the Committee of Safety, whose members inspired and piloted New Hampshire through the tedious war years. This Congress held several sessions in the summer and fall and laid the foundation for a new government. It sponsored troops for the Battle of Bunker Hill; launched a postal system; imposed a tax of £ 3,000 upon the towns; seized the royal records and moved them from Portsmouth to Exeter; and, finally, produced a pioneer election machinery for creation of a new government.

It was on November 13, 1775, two days before final adjournment, that this fourth Provincial Congress appointed a fourteen-man committee "to prepare a Plan for Representation of the People of this

Colony in the Future." It was headed by President Thornton and Secretary Thompson. The other members were Col. Samuel Hobart of Hollis, Col. William Whipple of Portsmouth, John Dudley of Raymond, Benjamin Giles of Newport, John Cragin, Jr., of Temple, Col. Timothy Walker, Jr., of Concord, Nathaniel S. Prentice of Alstead, Col. David Gilman of Pembroke, Col. Israel Morey of Orford, Deacon Samuel Knowles of Rye, and Ebenezer Smith of Meredith.

The committee reported an election formula the following day, with several significant features, for a new Provincial Congress, scheduled for December 21, 1775. The membership was apportioned on the basis of population, with taxpayers being the key measurement. All taxpayers were allowed to vote for the delegates, but the latter were required to possess at least £200 worth of real estate.

Another restriction in the election formula was:

That no person be allowed a seat in the Congress who shall by themselves, or by any person at their Desire Treat with Liquors etc. any Electors with an apparent view of gaining their votes, or by Treating after an Election on that Account.

The election plan also said:

In case there should be a recommendation from the Continental Congress for the Colony to assume Government in any way that will require a House of Representatives, That the said Congress for this Colony be empowered to Resolve themselves into such a House as may be recommended and remain such for the aforesaid term of one year.

The Exeter Congress had voted in October to ask the Second Continental Congress at Philadelphia for permission to establish a formal government, and an affirmative reply was voted on November 3, in the following resolution:

Resolved that it be recommended to the Provincial Convention of New-Hampshire to Call a Full and Free Representation of the People, and that the Representatives, if they think it Necessary, Establish Such a Form of Government, as in their Judgement will best Produce the Happiness of the People, & most Effectually Secure Peace and good order in the Province During the Continuance of the Present Dispute between Great Britain & the Colonies.

The apportionment formula was based upon a census voted by the

New Hampshire Goes Free

Congress in late August. It yielded a population of 82,200. Portsmouth showed the highest population, of 4,590 and was allowed three delegates. Granted two each were Londonderry, 2,590; Exeter, 1,741; Dover, 1,666; Chester, 1,599; and Amherst, 1,428. In contrast, given only one seat each were Barrington, 1,655; Epping, 1,569; and Rochester, 1,548. More than two thirds of the 155 towns were so sparsely settled that they were classed into districts of from two to eight each, for single seatings. All told, the membership was apportioned at 89. Each town, or classed group, was required to contribute the per diem for its delegate, but travel payments were to be allowed from the colonial Treasury.

The fourth Provincial Congress comprised a bustling body of record proportions. It contained 133 members from 101 towns. Many of them were common, so to speak, being little known beyond their neighbors, and this display of developing American democracy in action drew considerable public attention.

As selectmen issued fifteen-day "precepts" for election of the fifth Provincial Congress, specifically to create a new government, New Hampshire's two Continental Congress delegates wrote from Philadelphia urging restraints. Dr. Josiah Bartlett and John Langdon suggested that the legislative membership be held to a minimum, that a Council of fifteen named by the new House of Representatives should constitute its upper branch, and that there be no Governor to start with. Sullivan, newly named a Brigadier General by the Continental Congress, wrote from Boston, where he was a top aide to Gen. George Washington, at the memorable siege of the British army of occupation, and sent a letter to Exeter suggesting that if the position of Governor was created, his term should be curtailed, and the people, rather than the Legislature, should elect him. Sullivan also urged strong curbs against bribery at the voting polls.

Seventy-six delegates joined in the fifth Provincial Congress at Exeter on December 21, 1775, for its history-making session, with Dr. Thornton again as President. On December 27, a Wednesday, a five-man committee was appointed to "frame or draft a new government." It comprised Thornton and Thompson, again the Congress' secretary; wealthy Attorney Wyseman Claggett of Litchfield; Benjamin Giles of Newport; and Meshech Weare of Hampton Falls, soon to become chairman of the Committee of Safety.

Nine days later, New Hampshire's first-in-the-nation Constitution was ratified on January 5, 1776, by an almost 2 to 1 vote of the delegates. It contained only 911 words, of which 372 were in a preamble.

The entire document was composed in fifteen sentences (as shown in the appendices). It outlined a government which centered all authority in a Legislature, and there was no Governor. It also spelled itself as being of a temporary nature and expressed a conciliatory tone, with hope for early settlement of the taxation controversy and restoration of peaceful allegiance to Great Britain.

Official state records have, since the turn of the twentieth century, labeled the fifth Provincial Congress a Constitutional Convention, because its delegates were elected for the express purpose of forming a new government, as suggested by the Continental Congress. This declaration was a feature of the 1902 *Manual of the Constitution of New Hampshire,* by Professor James Fairbanks Colby of Dartmouth College. This volume of 318 pages represented the first history of New Hampshire's constitutional life, and was prepared for use by the Constitutional Convention of December 1902. The *1917 New Hampshire Manual for the General Court* listed Professor Colby's designation of the January 5, 1776, action as a constitutional convention. Then the 1948 Constitutional Convention called itself the thirteenth such New Hampshire session, and used the Colby history to note that when the fifth Provincial Congress convened at Exeter on December 21, 1775, it became the "First Constitutional Convention."

WARTIME PROBLEMS

NEW HAMPSHIRE'S pioneer constitutional government went into operation on January 6, 1776, as the fifth Provincial Congress voted itself into a House of Representatives, with sweeping powers. In their new role, the legislators elected their own membership to most of the dozen Council seats. One member, Meshech Weare, already chairman of the powerful Committee of Safety, became Council President, and soon thereafter he also became Chief Justice of the highest court. He held all three of these top positions throughout most of the eight-year war period.

President Wentworth and Secretary Thompson of the extinct Provincial Congress were promoted to the Council, and the latter became secretary of the colony. Phillips White of South Hampton became Speaker, and a few days later he was also given a lucrative Probate Court Judgeship, as the legislators parcelled scores of judicial and other civil appointments among themselves. Dozens of them became Justices of the Peace, a position then a coveted source of fees. This political nepotism, by the way, continued for years and festered popular resentments.

Controversy flared as details of the pioneer homemade Constitution became known by word of mouth, since the Legislature did not make a copy available to the "press" until six days following its enactment. Petitions poured upon the Legislature at Exeter from Portsmouth and other seacoast towns and were tabled for hearing. But when Editor Daniel Fowle of the tiny *Portsmouth Gazette & Historical Chronicle,* New Hampshire's first weekly (founded in 1756 by invitation of the provincial Assembly), denounced the document, the legislators voted sharp resentment.

Editor Fowle, jailed in Boston twenty years earlier for criticizing the Massachusetts General Court, from which he sought freedom of expression in Portsmouth, blasted the new Constitution as foolhardy and doomed to failure. His editorial ran almost twice the length of the Constitution, and Fowle justified it by concluding:

Was any man to see his neighbor's house in flames, would he fold his arms and silently sit at home; it would be madness! Such is my case; and tho' I burn my fingers in the attempt I will try to extinguish it, lest the whole city be in flames.

Fowle wrote that the colonies did not have sufficient resources or manpower to win independence. He rationalized that even if freedom was achieved, the young nation could not support it. He warned that the American rebels were "without arms, without ammunition and without trade," and had but 30,000 fighting men against an enemy force of 150,000, and not a single vessel of war to guard 1,000 miles of coastline against 500 British warships. Fowle also wrote that were the colonies to win independence, taxes would have to be increased tenfold for its defense, including fortifications along the Canadian border.

The Legislature voted an official censure of Editor Fowle, ordered him to appear for questioning, and labeled the editorial:

An Ignominious, Scurrilous & Scandalous Piece . . . so much Derogatory to the Honour of this Assembly, as well as of the Honorable Continental Congress and Injurious to the Cause of Liberty Now Contending for.

No record can be found of the outcome of Fowle's confrontation. But the Journal of the session, which contains the voluminous editorial, shows that he continued as a legislative printer, and his paper resumed publication following a brief shutdown.

Not only did Portsmouth spark the criticisms of the new government, but it circulated protest papers which were endorsed by residents of Dover, Newington, Rochester, Stratham, North Hampton, Rye, Newmarket, Kensington, Greenland, and "part of Brintwood."

The Council and the House granted the protestors a joint hearing on January 18, with John Pickering of Portsmouth as spokesman, and tabled the petitions. Nine days later, to help quiet the opposition, the Legislature voted to ask Chairman Weare of the Committee of Safety to contact the Continental Congress for its approval of the new government. This action had been demanded in a joint petition signed by a dozen legislative members—Samuel Sherburne and Peirce Long of Portsmouth, Stephen Evans and Otis Baker of Dover, Richard Downing of Newington, Nathan Goss of Rye, Ezekeil Worthen of Kensington, Benjamin Barker of Stratham, James Knowles of Rochester, Hercules Mooney of Lee, Daniel Beede of Sandwich, and Dr. Levi Dearborn of North Hampton. Legislative records indicate the requested endorsement never materialized at Philadelphia.

The New Legislature

A S THE FLEDGLING LEGISLATURE groped through its first year, it struggled with domestic as well as war problems. It opened a river and two brooks to fish traffic, as tiny dams to power sawmills and grain mills blocked them. The legislators ordered installation of sluiceways on Beaver Brook in the Londonderry-Windham and Pelham areas; "Great Cohass Brook," out of Lake Massebesic in Derryfield (now Manchester); and the Piscataquog River in the Goffstown sector. Three new laws emphasized that spring spawnings of alewives and salmon were vital food sources. Each town was authorized to establish a committee for enforcement of the sluiceways, and fines were to be shared with protesters.

This first Legislature argued its own pay. Both branches agreed it should be five shillings per diem, including Sundays. The House members wanted to collect their pay from the colony, but the Council successfully insisted it be defrayed by the respective towns. A new mileage formula, of two pence per mile, was enacted to cover frequent recesses of two weeks or more of the Exeter sessions. Solons living beyond fifteen miles of this wartime capital received mileage for each recess, and those within that limit could do the same, but the latter would then forfeit their Sabbath pay.

The 1776 legislators capped another freedom milestone on June 15. They approved a "Declaration For Independence," which was rushed to Philadelphia, to bolster the Continental Congress in deliberating what became the national Declaration of Independence three weeks later.

This historic New Hampshire declaration was bereft of the conciliation hopes of the January 5 Constitution and defiantly called for permanent freedom from Great Britain, in a single sentence of 345 words, as follows:

Whereas, it appears an undoubted fact, that notwithstanding all the dutiful petitions and decent remonstrances from the American colonies, and the utmost exertions of their best friends in England on their behalf, the British ministry, arbitrary and vindictive, are yet determined to reduce, by fire and sword, our bleeding country to their absolute obedience; and for this purpose, in addition to their own forces, have engaged great numbers of foreign mercenaries, who may now be on their passage here, accompanied by a formidable fleet, to ravage and plunder the seacoast; from all of which we may reasonably expect the most dismal scenes of distress the ensuing year, unless we exert ourselves by every means and precaution possible; and whereas, we, of this colony of New Hampshire have the example of several of the most respectable of our sister colonies before us for entering upon that most important step of a disunion from Great Britain, and declaring ourselves free and independent of the crown thereof, being impelled thereto by the most violent and injurious treatment; and it appearing absolutely necessary in this most critical juncture of our public affairs that the honorable the Continental Congress, who have this important object under their immediate consideration, should be also informed of our resolutions thereon without loss of time, we do hereby declare that it is the opinion of this Assembly that our delegates at the Continental Congress should be instructed, and they are hereby instructed, to join with the other colonies in declaring the thirteen United Colonies a free and independent state, solemnly pledging our faith and honor that we will, on our parts, support the measure with our lives and fortunes; and that in consequence thereof, they, the Continental Congress, on whose wisdom, fidelity, and integrity we rely, may enter into and form such alliances as they may judge most conducive to the present safety and future advantage of these American colonies; provided, the regulation of our internal police be under the direction of our own Assembly.

Meanwhile, John Langdon of Portsmouth, a noted Revolutionary leader, who had suffered a legislative business rebuff, lamented by letter to Dr. Bartlett:

The House have in a great measure lost the confidence of the people. . . . The most that is done is puning. Laughing, appointing officers one day, reconsidering the next; not a single act yet passed of any importance.

Wartime Problems

As the Legislature received an official copy of the Declaration of Independence, it voted to implement one of its provisions. It changed New Hampshire's title on September 10, 1776, to state. Officially it had been a province for some ninety-five years; then the fourth Provincial Congress of May 1775, began calling New Hampshire a colony, in its six months of deliberations, and the label of colony featured enactment of the first Constitution of January 5, 1776.

Two days later the Assembly elected Dr. Thornton, who had been ill, as a Continental Congress delegate. This gave him the distinction of becoming New Hampshire's third man to sign the Declaration of Independence, long after the state's two other delegates, Dr. Bartlett and Capt. William Whipple of Portsmouth, had done so. On October 19 the Legislature proclaimed New Hampshire's first constitutional Thanksgiving Day, as follows:

Voted and resolved that the third Thursday of November next be & hereby is appointed to be observed as a day of Public Thanksgiving throughout this state, and that the Committee of Safety of this state form a proclamation to be signed by the President and printed and dispersed throughout this state for that purpose.

As the self-appointed Legislature of 1776 adjourned in December, it voted precepts for its successor. The Councilors were for a first time to be elected by the male taxpayers, like the Representatives, and each man elected had to possess at least £ 200 worth of property. The apportionment formula approximated a House seat for each 100 families, and the Council members were chosen on a county basis.

As this first free Legislature reached adjournment on Friday, December 13, it voted a memorable action. It changed the name of the tiny hilltop town of Camden to Washington, to honor Gen. George Washington, the Commander-in-Chief of the intrepid American rebel forces.

The official Journal of that session had this final line:

GOD SAVE THE UNITED STATES OF AMERICA

Each following legislative session ended its official records in like manner throughout the war years.

This pioneer Legislature drew vigorous criticisms from the distant towns along the Connecticut River and isolated upper areas of the state. Officials of young Dartmouth College at Hanover (founded in

1769) sparked this dissent. They sponsored pamphlets claiming that sparsely populated areas had been unfairly denied individual legislative representation. They denounced the legislators for voting themselves most of the lucrative, judicial and civil appointments in the new government. The property requirement for election to the Legislature was also protested as undemocratic.

The 1777 Langdon Sessions

JOHN LANGDON, the shipbuilder who became wealthy by privateer raids on British merchantmen for valuable supplies for the rebels, became Speaker of the 1777 Legislature and piloted it through another events-packed year.

This Legislature quickly imposed wholesale price controls. They covered foodstuffs, clothing, rum, iron, and molasses, and even the wages of farm laborers and mechanics. By early summer the price controls had become so widely disregarded that the legislators ordered the local Committees of Safety to enforce them. But in November this wartime measure was repealed as the legislators admitted the controls' failure, "as having been very far from answering the salutory purposes for which they were intended."

When Vermont appealed for help to stop General Burgoyne's planned drive from Canada down Lake Champlain and the Hudson River, to sever New England from the other colonies, the Legislature convened in emergency session at Exeter on July 17, 1777. It authorized a volunteer army led by Gen. John Stark to defeat the British invaders at the Battle of Bennington a month later. It was in this session that Speaker Langdon is said to have sparked the legislators' patriotism by declaring from his rostrum:

I have a thousand dollars in hard money; I will pledge my plate for three thousand more. I have seventy hogshead of Tobago rum which will be sold for the most it will bring. They are at the service of the state. If we succeed in defending our firesides and our homes I may be remunerated. If we do not then the property will be of no value to me.

There is no official record that Langdon ever made this statement. It was first published by Editor Isaac Hill of Concord in his *New Hampshire Patriot* weekly as part of an Independence Day speech at Portsmouth on July 4, 1828. Hill reported he got the details of the statement from Judge Timothy Walker of Concord, who sat as a

John Langdon, from a painting by Tenney after Turnbull. Collection: State House.

Councilor with the Legislature at that 1777 session. Some historians later added to the statement:

Our friend, John Stark, who so nobly maintained the honor of our state at Bunker Hill, may safely be entrusted with the honor of the enterprise and we will check the progress of Burgoyne.

Throughout 1777 the Dartmouth-inspired criticisms of the temporary Constitution gained increasing support from neighboring towns and other parts of the colony, as the pamphleteering was continued. A major issue became protests that the people should be allowed to directly devise and approve their own government. This resentment became so widespread that when the third annual Legislature convened on December 17, 1777, with Langdon back as Speaker, it rose to the challenge. Within ten days it voted:

That it be recommended to the towns, parishes and places in this state, if they see fit, to instruct their Representatives, at the next session, to appoint and call a full & free representation of all the people of this state to meet in convention at such time and place as shall be appointed by the General Assembly, for the sole purpose of framing and laying a permanent plan or system for the future government of this state.

This remarkable action met with such general endorsement that when the Legislature reconvened in February, following a January recess, the two branches jointly voted on February 26, the following history-making resolution:

Whereas, the present situation of affairs in this state make it necessary that a full & free representation of the inhabitants thereof should meet in convention for the sole purpose of forming & laying a permanent plan or system of government, for the future happiness and well-being of the good people of this state, & this House having received instructions from a considerable part of their Constituents for that purpose; Therefore

Voted and resolved that the Honorable the President of the Council issue to every town, parish and district within this state a precept recommending to them to elect & choose one or more persons as they shall judge expedient to convene at Concord in said state on the 10th day of June next, for the purpose aforesaid, saving to the smaller towns liberty to join two or more

Wartime Problems

together, if they see fit to elect & send one person to represent them in said convention:

74 *And such system or form of government as may be agreed upon by such convention being printed & sent to each and every town, parish & district in this state for the approbation of the people, which system or form of government, being approved of by three-quarter parts of the inhabitants in this state in their respective town meetings legally called for that purpose, & a return of such approbation being made to said convention and confirmed by them, shall remain as a permanent system or form of government of the state, & not otherwise; & that the charge and expense of each member of said convention be defrayed by the respective electors.*

On March 10 the Legislature ordered the state's first constitutional Fast Day observance as follows:

A Proclamation for a General Fast throughout this state on Thursday the sixteenth day of April, next, being read and considered,

Voted, that the same be transcribed, printed and dispersed throughout this state.

Four days later, as the Legislature recessed its spring session, the final action was:

Voted, That it is offensive to this House that any member of this House should play at cards or any other unlawful game in Publick houses and that they be desired to desist therefrom.

New World Achievement

NEW HAMPSHIRE'S second Constitutional Convention convened in Concord on June 10, 1778, as the first of its kind in world history. Never before had a common people been allowed to elect themselves into convention for creation of their own government, with a key proviso that it had to be returned to them for final ratification or rejection.

Details of this convention were not completely preserved. But more than sixty years later they were researched by G. Parker Lyon of Concord, a historian, from town records, which indicated that only seventy-four delegates from ninety towns and parishes attended. The protesting western towns boycotted the session entirely, as their leaders warned that if they participated, they would be beholden to the outcome, even if it were not to their liking.

The convention continued for a year, mostly in recesses. Finally, on June 5, 1779, a new Constitution was approved. The incomparable Meshech Weare was listed as the opening President, even though he was not a delegate. But when copies were distributed to the towns and published in the few newspapers, they bore the name of John Langdon as President pro tem.

This new document continued to center the government in the Legislature, but with substantial restrictions against legislators serving in other public capacities. The property requirement for a legislator was raised to £ 300. Each town was allowed a House seat for every 100 male Protestant taxpayers, and smaller settlements could unite to meet the qualification. The Council was continued as the upper legislative branch, with a self-appointed President to serve in place of a Governor, with virtually no authority.

The delegates returned to Concord on the third Tuesday of September 1779 to tally the referendum returns. They reported rejection of the proposed Constitution and adjourned. So it was thus that New Hampshire became a first people ever to reject a government proposal in a peaceful and democratic process.

Development of this significant milestone principle of government of and by a people for their own welfare has never been given its proper due in history. The late Allan Nevins, noted American historian, gave it passing mention in his 1924 *The American States During and After the Revolution*. He wrote that the 1778 Constitutional Convention was the "first such body in the United States or the world." A *Manual for the 1918 New Hampshire Constitutional Convention* said of the 1778 session:

New Hampshire was the first state to draft a Constitution on this principle and the example was followed by Massachusetts in 1780, Vermont in 1786, and by the United States in the Federal Constitution (of 1788).

Two years elapsed before another attempt was made to create a permanent Constitution, as the wartime Legislature turned to even more pressing and vexing problems. Several of the Connecticut River towns were in open rebellion to such degree that they became a part of Vermont for a brief period, tried to create their own state of New Connecticut, and defied all efforts of the New Hampshire Legislature to woo them back into some semblance of unity. Soaring inflation and

Wartime Problems

increasing demands from the Continental Congress for more and more fighting men, and supplies for them, also beset the legislators.

The 1779 Legislature enacted a first draft law, after bounties of cash, land, and even clothing failed to muster sufficient volunteers for the Continental army. Pay scales ranged from $6.66 a month for privates to $166 for generals.

As this session ended, the Reverend Jeremy Belknap of Dover, who was to become New Hampshire's revered colonial historian, censured the legislators. He wrote to Ebenezer Hazard, a Philadelphia printer:

A member of our late House of Representatives in their last session at Exeter, returning from the Court to his Lodgings in the close of the day, passed by a house where a joiner had been shingling, just as he had thrown down his hammer and was descending the ladder.

The representative picked up the hammer, carried it to his lodgings (which were in a tavern) and pawned it for a jill of rum. The joiner, finding on inquiry which way the hammer went, followed it to the tavern, and demanded it, but was obliged to pay for the rum before he could have it.

Being a man of spirit, the joiner then publicly, in a crowded room, and in the presence of divers other representatives, warned the landlord against receiving stolen goods from the members of the General Court.

This is a speciman of the little villany of the cattle by whom we are . . . governed, for as that Assembly is dissolved, 'tis no blasphemy to tell the truth.

Early in 1780 the Legislature ordered the towns to produce 1,120,000 pounds of beef for the Continental army. A following law required them to raise 10,000 gallons of rum for the same purpose. The legislators then capped these requirements with a ban against shipment of cattle or beef, or rum or molasses, out of the state.

Rampant inflation harassed the wartime legislators, as they frequently voted increased issues of state paper money and supported the printing of paper currency by the Continental Congress to defray its war expenses.

The 1777 Legislature voted to make the state's paper money legal currency and said that if it were not accepted for payment of debts, the debts would become void automatically. Four years later, when people refused to accept the state's cheap paper money for old debts and swamped the courts with litigation, the 1781 Legislature enacted a strange fiscal formula. It set a ratio of 120 to 1 for paper money against gold or silver for 1781 debt payments, and lesser proportions for each of the five preceding years.

The waves of new paper money, including the issues of the Continental Congress, continued to depreciate in value so badly that "Not worth a Continental damn" became a slogan of disrespect—so much so in fact that the next Legislature voted that the towns could pay their annual tax assessments in rum, beef, leather shoes, cloth, wheat flour, felt hats, or blankets in lieu of money.

President, Chairman, and Chief Justice Weare wrote a friend in 1780:

I am in pain when I consider at what an enormous rate every thing has now got, 12 or 1,300 dollars for a cow, 40 dollars per bushel for corn, 80 for rye, 100 pounds per yard for common broadcloth, from 50 to 100 dollars per yard for linen, etc. etc. and still daily increasing.

Historian Upton compiled graphic details of the tribulations of the young wartime Legislature in his 1936 book. It turned from the unpopular price controls policy to granting bounties and tax exemptions to boost the ailing economy. It voted special payments for production of guns, powder, salt, sulfur, potash, and other goods, as British fleets blocked importation of such vital supplies.

The Legislature granted a loan of £200 to Richard Jordan of Exeter to start a papermaking mill and ordered town selectmen to sponsor collection of rags for it. Then it set up a special lottery to raise £2,000 for Robert Hewes of Boston to complete a glass factory at Temple after he had exhausted his own funds on the project.

The problems of counterfeiting claimed the continuing attention of the Legislature, and it passed repeated laws penalizing loyalists for remaining friendly to the royal motherland.

The Final Creation of 1784

IN THE SPRING OF 1781, as the Revolution sputtered and General Washington voiced pessimism about the outcome, the New Hampshire Legislature bowed once again to clamor for its improvement. On April 5 the House called for another Constitutional Convention, to convene on June 5 at Concord, with instructions to remain in session until a permanent new government was approved by the people. The

Council concurred the following day.

This convention precept candidly declared "the present situation of affairs in this state make it necessary" to replace the temporary 1776 document, "this House having received instructions from a considerable part of their constituents for that purpose." The prolonged propaganda from the Dartmouth College environment had borne fruit. In one major pamphlet approved by Professor Bezaleel Woodward, son-in-law of Dartmouth President Eleazer Wheelock, it was argued that every town, regardless of size, should have legislative representation, regardless of cost. It contended, in part:

It is objected by some, that a large and full representation will be more expensive, and a small number can do the business sufficiently. To which we answer—by the same parity of reasoning we may say that one man is sufficient to do the business, which will make a greater saving still, and so put out our eyes, and trust to others to lead us. . . .

We think it of the utmost importance that every inhabited town have the liberty, if they please, of electing one member, at least, to make up the legislative body—As it may be much questioned, if any one distinct corporate body be neglected, or deprived of actual representation, whether, in that case, they are in any ways bound, or included, by what the others may do.

This third Constitutional Convention failed to muster anticipated popular support. The June 5 opening disclosed a statewide boycott. Only an estimated 44 delegates from the state's 155 towns and parishes reported for duty.

Only a few convention records were preserved, and it was not until seventy years later that historian Lyon compiled the basic details from town statistics for the 1852 edition of the annual *New Hampshire Register*. They showed that the recalcitrant Connecticut River towns had again declined to participate. More surprising, many towns in the seacoast and Merrimack Valley areas had failed to elect delegates to the Concord session.

Thirteen towns which specifically voted not to sponsor delegates were Bow, Brentwood, Candia, Deerfield, Dunbarton, Epping, Greenland, Hampstead, Kensington, Northwood, South Hampton, Weare, and Wolfeboro, and they so informed the convention. Nineteen others did the same but did not see fit to report their negative actions.

This comparative handful of delegates labored more than two years, and were twice repudiated by the voters, before finally winning approval of a permanent Constitution, effective on the first Wednesday of June 1784.

Prior to the 1782 annual March town meetings, the convention issued an unusual appeal for more delegates. It stressed in a resolution printed in the tiny *New Hampshire Gazette* at Portsmouth that "There should be a full and free representation of the people to said convention, to advise, deliberate and determine on a matter of such moment to themselves and posterity." As a result, nine towns sponsored ten additional delegates.

Portsmouth assumed a leading role in this historic convention. It had furnished five delegates (more than twice that of any other town). One of them, George Atkinson, became President; another, Jonathan Mitchell Sewall, became the convention Secretary.

Following its June 5, 1781, organization, the convention named a committee of seven delegates to draft a new Constitution and then recessed to September 14. At that time the convention approved details of a new government, reduced the referendum ratification requirement from three quarters to two thirds of the votes cast, and requested that any town which might reject it inform the convention of the reasons for so doing. Then the delegates recessed to the fourth Wednesday of January 1782 to canvass the returns.

The 1781 draft for a new government proposed a more restricted Legislature. It would be limited to fifty House members, elected in county conventions by delegates elected by the voters, with a Senate replacing the Council, and property requirements at £ 400 for the Senators and £ 200 for Representatives. In addition, there was to be a strong Governor, with veto privileges; a worth of £ 1,000 was requisite to hold that office. Even more drastic, a man had to possess property of at least £ 100 value to vote for these officials.

The convention vainly strove to win approval of its initial plan of a new government. It distributed a lengthy letter, signed by President Atkinson and Secretary Sewall, extolling its supposed virtues. It said of curbing the legislative membership:

Experience must have convinced every one who has been in any degree, conversant with the transacting of business in public bodies, that a very large assembly is not the most convenient for the purpose. There is seldom so much order, and never such dispatch, as is found in a smaller body. There would be probably a greater proportion of suitable men than in a

Wartime Problems

The Legislature convened its first Concord session in the Old North Meetinghouse (top) in March of 1782. The lawmakers found it so cold they reconvened in the hall over Judge Walker's store (below) which still stands on North Main Street. Courtesy Concord Library and Mrs. Carl Gesen.

To This Day

larger body. The debates would, of course, be conducted with more wisdom and unanimity.

The circular appeal also emphasized:

A perfect system of government is not to be expected in the present imperfect state of humanity. But could a faultless one be framed, it would not be universally approved unless its judges were all equally perfect. Much less, then, may we presume to hope that the plan here offered to view will meet with universal approbation.

The letter took sharp issue with the temporary Legislature and with the manner in which the membership had been voting itself most of the lucrative appointments in the judicial and civil branches of the wartime government. It warned that the legislators were opposed to the proposed new Constitution because it would prohibit such political nepotism, and it stressed:

The love of power is so alluring, we had almost said infatuating, that few have ever been able to resist its bewitching influence. Wherever power is lodged there is a constant propensity to enlarge its boundaries. Much more then, will those with whom it is entrusted, agonize to retain all that is expressly delegated to them. . . . Can it seem strange then, that such persons, and indeed all who are vested with the aforementioned powers, should be backward in receiving and approving of a Constitution that so remarkably retrenches them?

The voters killed the 1781 proposal, and their repudiation reasons were reflected in a second draft. This provided for the twelve-man Senate, but the House membership formula became more acceptable as each town was permitted to elect a member for each 150 taxpayers (ratable polls); an additional member for each additional 300 taxpayers, and the tinier towns were allowed to group themselves for a single House seat. The strong Governor principle was continued; his property qualification and that of the legislators was cut in half; and the property rule to vote was eliminated.

The convention approved this second draft in August 1782 and returned to Concord on the last Tuesday in December, when it was learned the second draft of the proposed Constitution had also been defeated by the people. The towns reported great opposition to the strong Chief Executive concept. So the convention recessed once again to the first Tuesday in June 1783, when a third draft was

Wartime Problems

prepared and sent to the towns, and the delegates agreed to reconvene on October 31 to canvass the outcome.

Concord meanwhile enticed the Legislature to its bosom for a first time early in 1782. Representative Timothy Walker, Jr., took advantage of unhappiness among his fellow solons over inflationary lodging prices in prosperous Exeter, during a brief winter session, and suggested that Concord would offer more attractive accommodations. The legislators took Walker at his word, but when they convened in Concord on March 13 they were greeted with a cooler reception than was anticipated. The session was scheduled for the Old North Meetinghouse, but it was not heated. So young Walker promptly turned his store and home on upper North Main Street over to the Assembly and its Council upper house, for warmer deliberations. These buildings are still standing.

The 1783 June and October sessions of the Constitutional work were shifted to a small hall over John Stevens's store, on the northwest corner of present Main and Pleasant streets, because the Legislature occupied Concord's Old North Meetinghouse (where the Walker School now stands) on those dates. So it was in this modest two-story wooden structure that New Hampshire's permanent Constitution was created and proclaimed. This historic building was moved a few feet to the north in the 1850s to make way for a Masonic Temple brick block, and was destroyed in 1927 for site of the capital city's first supermarket.

The third draft of this third Constitutional Convention was successful. It was given a two-thirds referendum approval in the towns, even as the War of Independence came to a successful conclusion with the signing of a peace treaty at Paris early in September 1783. The new Constitution, proclaimed on October 31, was to become effective on the first Wednesday of June 1784, following implementation by a spring election of a new Legislature and a Chief Executive. This document was admittedly a compromise in desperation, because the temporary 1776 Constitution was for wartime duration only, and even with its emergency one-year extension voted by the old Legislature, it was on the verge of expiration.

The new Constitution eliminated the strong Governor concept entirely, along with the very title itself, because of pent-up resentments against the dictatorial and self-serving royal Governors. It was replaced by a President with limited authority. He was to preside over the Senate and was forced to share appointive powers with a five-man

Executive Council named by the Legislature from its own member-ship.

Rigid Qualifications

UNDER THE NEW CONSTITUTION, taxpayers aged twenty-one and over were allowed to vote, without religious qualification, as required in the 1780 Massachusetts Constitution. The President and the legislators were required to be Protestants. And there was a property qualification of £ 500 for the Chief Executive, along with £ 200 for Senators and £ 100 for Representatives.

The twelve-member Senate was initially apportioned by counties, and then by taxable wealth. The House was apportioned by a formula of one member for a first 150 taxpayers and an additional seat for twice that qualification yardstick; smaller towns were permitted to group themselves for a single seat. This plan purposely favored the smaller towns over the more populous ones, as there were more of the former than the latter.

This permanent Constitution contained a Bill of Rights, safeguard-ing individual freedoms and the privacy of homes, which was copied for the most part from that of Massachusetts. It also launched the concept of three divisions of government—the legislative, executive, and judicial, in that order—which was to become the hallmark of American democracy.

The Legislature was given the basic authority to develop, regulate, and finance the executive and judicial branches, and this prerogative continues to this day. On the other hand, the new document not only divested the Legislature of its long-criticized appointive powers but barred the members from holding most other remunerative state government positions, and this policy continues in force.

The 1784 Constitution favorably reflected the basic so-called Dart-mouth College criticisms. But it also contained a sharp rebuff, in apparent retaliation for the success of that better government crusade. The new Constitution barred the Dartmouth faculty from election to the Legislature. This prohibition, shocking in retrospect, was con-tained in one of the final articles of the new document, which read:

No person holding the office of judge of the Superior Court, secretary, treasurer of the state, judge of probate, attorney-general, commissary-general, judge of the maritime court, or judge of the Court of Admiralty,

Wartime Problems

military officers receiving pay from the Continent or this State, excepting officers of the militia occasionally called forth on an emergency, judge of the inferior court of common pleas, register of deeds, president, professor or instructor of any college, sheriff, or officer of the customs, including naval officers, shall at the same time have a seat in the Senate, or House of Representatives, or Council; but their being chosen or appointed to, and accepting the same, shall operate as a resignation of their seat in the Senate, or House of Representatives, or Council; and the place so vacated shall be filled up.

This restriction against Dartmouth College (long the state's only institution of higher learning) continued for eight years. It was abolished when wholesale improvements of the Constitution were ratified by the voters in 1792. Its most direct impact was against Professor Woodward, who was serving a first legislative term when the anticollegiate constitutional ban was imposed.

While President Atkinson presided over most of the third Constitutional Convention's deliberations, Nathaniel Folsom, the Exeter army leader, signed the new Constitution as President pro tem, and it was attested by Secretary Sewall.

Fifteen of the convention delegates also served in the 1783 Legislature, which held two sessions in Concord in June and October, the same months in which the new Constitution was finalized. They were Atkinson and Folsom, along with John Pickering of Portsmouth, Archibald McMurphy of Londonderry, Mark Wiggin of Stratham, Ephraim Pickering of Newington, John Dudley of Raymond, Nathaniel Peabody of Atkinson, John McClary of Epsom, Timothy Walker, Jr., of Concord, Ebenezer Smith of Meredith, Benjamin Giles of Newport, Francis Worcester of Plymouth, Davis Page of Conway, and Reuben Morse of Dublin-Marlboro.

The thirty-eight other delegates who joined in producing New Hampshire's Constitution, much of which lives to this day, were:

John Langdon and Ammi Ruhami Cutter of Portsmouth, Joshua Wingate and Otis Baker of Dover, Thomas Sparhawk and John Bellows of Walpole, Daniel Grout and William Markham of Unity-Acworth, Amos Emery of Dublin-Marlboro, John Taylor Gilman of Exeter, Samuel Emerson of Plymouth, Nathaniel H. Dodge of Hampton Falls, Joseph Cilley of Nottingham, Abraham Drake of North Hampton, Nathaniel Goss, probably of Rye, Robert Collins, probably of Sandown-Hawke (now Danville), Jeremiah Clough of Canterbury-Loudon, Simeon Cummings of Merrimack, Jacob Butler,

Jr., of Pelham, and Joshua Kimball of Pembroke.

Also, there were James Davis of Madbury, Joseph Badger of Gilmanton, James Brewer of Sandwich, Timothy Smith of Nottingham West (now Hudson), Jonathan Lovewell of Dunstable (now Nashua), Joshua Bailey of Hopkinton, Ebenezer Webster of Salisbury, Jonathan Martin of Wilton, Benjamin Mann of Mason, Timothy Farrar of New Ipswich, John Cragin, Jr., of Temple, William Smiley of Rindge-Jaffrey, James Underwood of Litchfield, Daniel Newcomb of Keene, Reverend Edward Goddard of Swanzey-Fitzwilliam, Moses Baker of Campton, John Wheatley of Lebanon, and John Sullivan of Durham.

Nine Legislatures served during the Revolutionary period, from January 6, 1776, to April 17, 1784, on an annual basis. They held forty-two sessions in that period, the majority in Exeter. Brief sessions were held in September 1777 and October 1780 at Portsmouth. Then from early in 1782, most of the remaining sessions were held in Concord.

Phillips White of South Hampton was Speaker of the first Legislature; John Langdon of Portsmouth presided over the next six; and John Dudley of Raymond served the final two terms as Speaker. Noah Emery of Portsmouth was House clerk for six terms, followed by John Smith of Durham for two terms and by John Calfe of Hampstead for the last year.

Meshech Weare became New Hampshire's memorable symbol of persevering patriotism by serving through all the eight wearisome years as President of the state, while presiding over the Council (the upper branch of the Legislature)—and simultaneously filling the busy positions of chairman of the State Committee of Safety and Chief Justice of the Superior Court of Judicature throughout most of the same period. Of this concentrated authority, the bulk was in the Committee of Safety chairmanship, for that handful of men, less than a dozen at a time, actually ruled New Hampshire when the Legislature was in recess or adjourned, which was most of the time, and it even functioned with a firm hand when the lawmakers were in session.

In 1853 the Legislature sponsored a modest marble monument to Weare's memory in Hampton Falls, which still reads, in part:

To perpetuate the memory of her illustrious son whose early efforts, sage counsel, and persevering labors contributed largely towards his country's independence, and shaping the future destiny of his native state.

Ebenezer Thompson of Durham was Secretary of State through the

Wartime Problems

war period. Col. Nicholas Gilman, the Exeter financier, served as State Treasurer for seven years and died in office. He was succeeded by a son, John Taylor Gilman, who subsequently became a fourteen-term Governor while also handling state finances through many years.

The wartime Legislature went out of existence on April 17, 1784, at Exeter, which was fitting, for that town was its haven of safety from the enemy throughout the Revolution.

Legislative records of the Revolutionary years cast many interesting reflections. Its membership of eighty-three in 1776—more than twice that of any provincial Assembly—continued sturdy and rose to ninety-five in the final year of 1783-84. The Legislature set its own pay in this period from five shillings per day, including weekends, up to sixteen shillings, and then it wound up at six shillings.

Public policy on holidays was reflected in a 1778 law creating a Naval Officer to regulate trade and navigation in Portsmouth Harbor. It specified that he would be:

Exempt from business on the Lord's Day (Sunday), all Fast and Thanksgiving Days appointed by Authority, and also on the anniversary of Independence.

When the legislators returned to Exeter in February 1780, following a recess, they voted themselves an extra pay allotment because a snowstorm had hampered their return home on New Year's Day. The following June they took a position on slavery, as follows:

According to the order of the day, the petition of Nero Brewster and other Negro slaves praying to be set free from slavery, being read, considered and argued by counsel on behalf of the Petitioners before this House, It appears to this House, That at this time, the House is not ripe for a determination in this matter: Therefore ordered that the further consideration and determination of the matter is postponed till a more convenient opportunity.

The final act of the wartime Legislature was apportionment of the annual state tax for support of the new and permanent government taking office in June 1784. The towns were required to file a comprehensive inventory of the official tax sources of that period, and by that time all money was taxed like any other property.

The inventory was officially listed as follows:

Polls from 18 to 75 years of age.
Male Negroes & Mulatto servants, 16 to 45.
Female Negroes & Mulatto servants, 16 to 45.
Acres of orchard land.
Acres of tillage land.
Acres of mowing land.
Acres of pasture land.
Horses and mares.
Oxen.
Cows.
Horses and cattle, 3 years old.
Horses and cattle, 2 years old.
Horses and cattle, 1 year old.
Yearly rent of mills, wharfs & ferries, repairs being deducted.
Sum total of the value of all buildings and real estate unimproved—owned by inhabitants.
Sum total of the value of all real estate, not owned by the inhabitants.
Sum total of money in hand or at interest, not in public funds.

Portsmouth, as usual, shouldered the heaviest state tax assessment, since it was the largest and wealthiest town. In contrast with present top population and wealth centers, the nine next-highest tax loads of 1784 were imposed, in order, upon Londonderry, Chester, Amherst, Epping, Rochester, Dover, Exeter, Barrington, and Gilmanton.

THIRTY CROWDED YEARS

GRIEVOUS POSTWAR economic woes beset New Hampshire's Legislature through the eight years existence of the compromise 1784 Constitution, up to its wholesale improvements in 1792.

First Years Under the Constitution of 1784

PAPER MONEY continued virtually worthless, and both the Legislature and private citizens were hard pressed to cope with their fiscal obligations. The New Hampshire *State Papers* offer this retrospective observation:

The long war had left the people impoverished, burdened with debt, and, everywhere, suffering grievously in consequence—There was a loud cry for more money. It was demanded that the Legislature provide for the emission of paper bills of credit, to be made a legal tender for all debts, private as well as public. The agitation was constant and exciting; the demands of creditors clamorous and pressing, and the calm judgment of men in many cases overcome by their own needs, and the dire necessity of many about them.

The distress became so severe that it led to an armed attack upon the Legislature, not to mention a giant hoax, and the state government was not even able to finance New Hampshire participation in the historic creation of the Federal Constitution in 1787 at Philadelphia.

The 1784 Legislature held three sessions. After convening in Concord on June 2 to launch the new permanent government, it learned that the venerable Meshech Weare, who had been elected President, remained confined to his Hampton Falls home by illness, so the following week the Senate elected one of its members, Woodbury Langdon of Portsmouth, as senior, and he then automatically became President pro tem.

This historic opening session continued for only two weeks. The Reverend Samuel McClintock of Greenland presented an hour-long invocation at the Old North Meeting House, for which the Legislature paid him £ 15, a substantial emolument for those days. The revitalized Legislature also streamlined its operating procedures.

Special exercises were arranged for this June birth of the permanent state government, and they were greeted with such public favor that the practice was continued, with embellishments, for nearly a half-century. On that opening day, the legislators marched to the sound of music along what is now Concord's North Main Street, to their meeting center, and they tapped the State Treasury to pay for a public dinner for themselves and invited guests.

On Saturday, June 12, the session was recessed to the following Tuesday, to convene at Exeter for a single day, to permit the ailing Meshech Weare to take the oath of office as first President of New Hampshire. It was administered by Langdon, the senior Senator who had been Acting President the first few days of the new government. Then the Legislature adjourned to an October meeting in Portsmouth, and a third and final session was held in Concord in February 1785.

Paper Money Incidents

A S THE 1786 LEGISLATURE prepared to convene at Concord, various towns mustered delegates to converge upon the lawmakers in a first giant lobbying effort for relief from debts.

Historian Belknap presented the following backdrop to this episode in his 1792 state history:

The clamor for paper currency increased, and, like a raging fever, approached toward a crisis. In every town there was a party in favor of it, and the public papers were continually filled with declamations on the subject.

It was said that an emission of bills of credit would give a spring to commerce and encourage agriculture; that the poor would be able to pay

William Plumer

their debts and taxes; that all the arguments against issuing paper were framed by speculators and were intended to serve the wealthy, who had monopolized the public securities, that they might raise their value and get all the bargains into their own hands; that other states in the Union had issued paper bills and were rejoicing in the happy effects of their currency, without any depreciation; that the people had a right to call upon their Representatives to stamp a value on paper, or leather, or any other substance capable of receiving an impression; and that to prevent depreciation a law should be enacted to punish with banishment and outlawry every person who should attempt by any means to lessen the value.

The Inferior Courts were represented as sinecures for judges and clerks; the defaulting, appealing, demurring, abatements, fees and bills of cost, without any decision, were complained of as burdens, and an abolition of these courts became part of the popular cry.

A young law student, William Plumer of Epping, swung into action against the easy-money forces. He had served in the previous Legislature but was denied reelection because he had moved to Londonderry to study law, and was then in Concord to earn some income in representing petitioners before the Legislature. From this role, Plumer—destined to become one of New Hampshire's most historic civilian leaders of all time—perpetrated the most unusual hoax ever visited upon the Legislature.

Historian Belknap compiled a voluminous account of the fakery, as did youthful Editor Jacob Bailey Moore in his 1824 *Annals of Concord*. And William Plumer, Jr., in his 1857 biography of his illustrious father, related how his parent boasted of his sponsorship of the affair.

As five protesting delegates awaited the arrival of others, young Plumer induced fellow lawyers and law students to join in a fake meeting with the unsuspecting quintet. What ensued is portrayed in the Plumer biography as follows:

Satisfied from the character of the men and the temper of the times that reasoning would be lost upon them, my father . . . conceived the idea of turning their proposed convention of delegates into ridicule, and thus rendering their pernicious purpose harmless. He was aided in the project by several active young men. . . . The plan was for these persons to join the convention, to take part in the proceedings, and ultimately to expose the folly and absurdity of its measures and pretensions.

Thirty Crowded Years

On entering the convention they were received without question, as delegates from their respective towns, and took at once the lead in its proceedings. After a debate of several hours, in which the pretended delegates, eleven in number, vied with the true ones in their zeal for reform, taking different sides, however, to avoid an appearance of concert, a series of resolutions was adopted by the meeting, and a committee, of which my father was chairman, was appointed to report a petition to the Legislature.

This petition, which was reported the next morning, embodied the substance of the resolutions, and was unanimously adopted by the convention. It requested the Legislature, among other things, to abolish the Court of Common Pleas, to establish town courts, to restrict the number of lawyers to two in a county, and to provide for the issue of state notes to the amount of three millions of dollars, the same to be a legal tender in payment of all debts.

These were the favorite measures, especially the last, of the discontented and debtor party, through the state; and they went not at all beyond the popular demand. The mock members, indeed, with all their disposition to render the convention ridiculous, could hardly keep pace with the real ones, in the extravagance of their suggestions.

Dr. Jonathan Gove of New Boston, who represented ten towns in Hillsborough County, said, "While we are money-making, 'tis best to emit as much as will discharge all our debts, public and private, and leave enough to buy a glass of grog and a quid of tobacco, without being dunned for them twenty times a day. For these purposes I move that the amount be twelve millions of dollars." It was on my father's motion that the sum was fixed at "only three millions!"

The convention went in a body to present their petition to the Legislature, which received them very gravely, and laid their memorial on the table. The Speaker (John Langdon) and some of the leading members, had been informed of the character of the convention, and received the visit with ceremonious attention, or, as one of the delegates said, "with superfluous respect."

. . . Gove left Concord without presenting the petition with which he was charged, and others disavowed their connection with the convention. The ridicule which this brought upon them checked their activity for a time, and

prevented their success with the Legislature, where they had many friends and had felt a great confidence of success. "The whole affair," writes the author of this clever stratagem to his brother, June 9th, 1786, "was so farcical that the very name of a convention is here a term of reproach."

While Plumer, Jr., obviously relished recounting his father's leadership in this hoax, he was quick to explain it was of but slight avail, and the demands for fiscal relief soon multiplied to such intensity that the Legislature was subjected to an armed insurrection less than three months later.

It was on September 20, a Wednesday, that an armed mob of 200 aroused men surrounded the Legislature in the First Church at Exeter, and held its members captive until nightfall. They had convened at nearby Kingston from several inland towns and marched into Exeter early in the afternoon with threats of holding the legislators prisoner until they voted a new issue of easy money.

Governor Charles H. Bell (1881-83) graphically records the details of this episode in his 1888 *History of Exeter*, his hometown. He wrote this background:

After the war was over, there came a time of peculiar stress. The Utopia that so many had looked forward to, as the natural result of independence, was not realized.

Times were hard and cash was scarce. Ignorant and unreflecting people fancied that the panacea for these ills was for the government to issue fresh bills of credit. But, fortunately, there were those in authority in the state with sufficient knowledge of political economy to prevent the Legislature from resorting to that deceptive remedy for financial troubles.

But they could not convince the "greenbackers" of those days; and at length matters came to such a pass that the infatuated clamorers for paper currency determined to make an attempt to dragoon the Legislature into sanctioning it.

The rebels entered Exeter in military array, as some of their leaders had served in the Revolutionary army. Bell explained that Joseph French of Hampstead, James Cockran of Pembroke, and John McKean of Londonderry were their principal officers. Half of the invaders were afoot, armed wih guns and swords; the others followed on horseback, bearing clubs and whips.

The Legislature was in the third week of its fall session, in the First Church, in the center of the village, while the Superior Court was sitting at the same time in the Town House, on the opposite side of the street. The insurgents at first surrounded the latter building by mistake and, Governor Bell wrote:

If their object had been to overawe the legal tribunal within it, they would have signally failed, for Judge Samuel Livermore was presiding, and so far was he from being daunted, that he ordered the business of the court to proceed, and sternly forbade every one from looking out of the windows.

Upon recognizing their error, the rebels arrayed a cordon of men around the church, where the legislators were huddled in suspense. Meanwhile, a large number of townspeople had converged upon the scene, and some of them declined to give way to the mob. The rebels prevailed, however, and stationed sentinels at the doors and windows. Then, as Bell relates, after ostentatiously loading their firearms, the leaders loudly declared their purpose to compel the Legislature to pass a law for the emission of abundant paper money, to ease debts and taxes, and their determination to hold the lawmakers captive until the demand was complied with. When one or two solons sought to escape, they were driven back inside with insults.

Governor Bell's description of what ensued excels embellishment. He wrote:

It fortunately happened the Chief Executive of the state was a man of courage and resolution, and not unacquainted with arms, John Sullivan, who had gained the rank of Major General in the Revolution. He appeared at the entrance to the meeting house and listened to the requirements of the assemblage. In a temperate and reasonable reply he gave them to understand that they need not expect to frighten him, for he had smelt powder before. "You ask for justice," he continued, "and justice you shall have." But he did not order them to disperse; he perhaps thought it was wiser to let them keep together, in order the more effectually to stamp out the tendency to insurrection against the constituted authorities.

The afternoon wore away; the General Court was still prisoner, and no progress had been made towards an adjustment. By this time many of the better class citizens of Exeter were filled with shame and indignation at the unchecked riotous demonstration, and one of them, Colonel Nathaniel Gilman, with the assistance of others, successfully practiced a "ruse de guerre," in order to raise the siege. He caused a drum to be beaten briskly at a little distance, while a body of citizens approached with a measured military step, and then cried out in his stentorian voice, "Hurrah for the government! Here comes Hackett's Artillery."

The cry was echoed by others, and the insurgents did not wait for more. Their valor was not up to the fighting point, and they rapidly retreated, standing not on the order of their going. They afterward made their rendezvous on the western side of the Little river, on the road to Kingston, and there a great part of the night was spent.

The imprisoned Legislators had meanwhile acted on their own behalf, under the leadership of Senate President John McClary of Epsom and Speaker John Langdon of Portsmouth. They huddled in joint session in the Senate chamber and voted "That His Excellency, the President, be desired to call forth a sufficient number Militia to protect the General Court in their present session."

President Sullivan quickly called out the militia to crush the revolt. Messengers were sent into the neighboring towns requesting officers to muster their commands and march at once to the scene. In Exeter, citizens enrolled themselves under the command of Capt. Nicholas Gilman, another war veteran. Governor Bell depicted the final details as follows:

The next morning saw possibly 2,000 men under arms in Exeter. President Sullivan assumed the direction of the column, which at once moved against the insurrectionary force, the volunteers of Exeter claiming the post of honor in the van. Arrived at within about an eighth of a mile from their antagonists, they were halted by order, when a small troop of horsemen under Colonel Joseph Cilley, a Revolutionary officer of distinction, galloped forward, forded the river, and made prisoners of the principal leaders of the insurgents; after which their followers surrendered at discretion.

Thus terminated the most formidable demonstration against the government which was ever made on the soil of New Hampshire. The happy result of it was in no small degree due to the loyal feeling and prudence and pluck of the people of Exeter. The attempt to dictate legislation by force having proved so ignominious a failure, it was not deemed necessary to inflict serious punishment upon the offenders.

Thirty Crowded Years

President Sullivan kept his word. The Legislature passed a bill authorizing the printing of more cheap money, but tied it to final ratification by the voters in a statewide referendum. A month later the electorate vetoed the measure by overwhelming majorities in the various towns, and so the will of the majority freshly demonstrated its faith in the Legislature.

Following dispersal of the rebels on Thursday morning, the Legislature voted £ 200 to pay the militiamen for their efforts, and passed the following resolution:

Voted that the President be requested to return the thanks of both Houses to the brave Officers and Soldiers of the Militia for the great zeal and Alacrity they have discovered in supporting the Constitutional Authority of the State, and for displaying a Spirit of Patriotism and public virtue, which while it affords the highest satisfaction to the Legislature merits the acknowldgements of every good citizen of the State.

Two days later, while the legislators prepared for final adjournment, the Senate proposed eight-day jail terms for the leaders of the revolt, but the House declined to concur, and then won approval of having them appear before the Legislature itself for judgment. This resulted in the leaders being voted their freedom, after which some of them lost their militia ranks.

The legislators also voted:

That the thanks of this House be presented to His Excellency, the President, for his firm, zealous and decisive exertions in suppressing the late audacious insurrection of a body of unprincipled men against the legislative authority of this state, and assure His Excellency that his conduct in the whole affair meets with their highest approbation and esteem.

This civilian uprising was not unique. Massachusetts had been torn by Shays's Rebellion in the western part of that state, and there were similar confrontations in other states, owing to the acute economic stresses and strains suffered by the people.

The Legislature became so destitute of cash in 1787—like its people—that it could not even finance delegates to the Philadelphia convention which created the Federal Constitutuion that summer. National leaders wrote entreating appeals to President Sullivan, then in his second term, stressing that New Hampshire's support was sorely needed to create the new document.

Henry Knox, the Massachusetts warrior, wrote to Sullivan on May 21:

As an old friend, a number of gentlemen have pressed me to write you soliciting that you urge the departure of the delegates from New Hampshire. . . . There are here a number of the most respected characters from several states, among whom is our illustrious friend, General Washington, who are extremely anxious on the subject of the New Hampshire delegates. If they come all the states except Rhode Island will be shortly represented.

On June 27 the Legislature elected four delegates. They were John Langdon and John Pickering of Portsmouth, Benjamin West of Charlestown, and youthful Nicholas Gilman of that noted Exeter family. But the legislators were unable to muster even travel cash for them, and history has recorded the incident as follows:

The representation of this state even at that late date was secured only by urgent appeals from abroad and extraordinary effort at home. The finances of the state were in a deplorable condition and it is impossible to realize at the present time what an undertaking it was to provide cash for any considerable public expense. It was reported in the newspapers of the day that the expenses of Mr. Gilman and himself were defrayed by Mr. Langdon from his private purse.

Neither Pickering nor West ever got to the convention. Thanks to Langdon's private purse, he and young Gilman, and the state of New Hampshire, became immortalized as among the twelve states and

John Sullivan

Thirty Crowded Years

thirty-nine men who sponsored and voted the Federal Constitution on September 17, 1787, for ratification by at least nine of the thirteen states.

Impeachment Snagged

THE 1790 LEGISLATURE featured the most unusual impeachment proceedings in New Hampshire history. Soon after it convened in Concord on June 2, the House of Representatives impeached Judge Woodbury Langdon (John Langdon's brother) of the Superior Court of Judicature for dereliction of office, and petitioned the Senate to concur in the ouster.

The charges against the Portsmouth man, who served as first President of the State Senate in 1784, were contained in a resolution passed by the House on June 17, by a close 35 to 29 roll call vote. It read:

Whereas Woodbury Langdon Esquire one of the Justices of the Superior Court of Judicature for said state has at divers times neglected his duty in said office in not attending at the times and places prescribed by Law for holding said Court (viz) at Amherst on the second Tuesday of May last and at Plymouth on the fourth Tuesday of said May—And likewise by means of his not attending upon his said duty the Court which by Law was to have been holden at Plymouth within and for the County of Grafton on the fourth Tuesday of May AD, 1789 was not holden at said time but adjourned until the Monday next preceeding the third Tuesday of October in the same year by means whereof no business could be done at said Court which Occasioned much inconveniency damages and uneasiness among the good citizens of this State—

And whereas it is Absolutely necessary that the Superior Court should be composed of Gentlemen who can and will attend to the important business that must unavoidedly be brought to said Court and the true genius of Republicanism dictating that it is Absolutely essential that no Office in Government should be held as a Sincecure—

Therefore Resolved that this House do impeach the said Woodbury Langdon Esquire of crimes and misdemeanors and that a Committee be chosen to exhibit the articles of impeachment to be laid before this House for their approbation and likewise to manage the prosecution in behalf of this House before the Honorable Senate.

The Senate launched its hearings on the impeachment two days later, on June 19, and a three-member House committee of "managers" filed a voluminous bill of particulars against Judge Langdon. The trio comprised Representative William Page of Charlestown and Representative Jeremiah Smith of Peterborough, both lawyers, and youthful Attorney Edward S. Livermore of Holderness, then practicing in Concord, as their aide. Smith was on the committee even though he voted against the impeachment two days earlier. They were bolstered by another five members of the House, to serve as witnesses. They were Elisha Payne of Lebanon, Daniel Warner of Amherst, Jeremiah Stiles of Keene, Joseph Kimball of Plainfield, and William Wallace of Henniker.

The gist of the indictment submitted to the Senate read:

The public are at all times entitled to the services of their officers receiving salaries—And whereas the said Woodbury Langdon Esquire hath wilfully and corruptly in various instances misbehaved in his said Office and hath neglected to attend the duties thereof by means whereof the said Courts have not been holden at the times and places by Law established and the administration of Justice delayed to the great injury of the good citizens of the state.

Senior Senator Nathaniel Peabody of Atkinson presided, as President Josiah Bartlett of Kingston disqualified himself as not being an elected member of the Senate. Then a sheriff's writ was issued for Judge Langdon's appearance at a continued hearing on July 28 at Exeter. Later the same day President Bartlett and his Council adjourned the Legislature to January 7, 1791, in Concord.

Judge Langdon showed up at the Exeter hearing, obviously tongue-in-cheek. It immediately developed the inquest was out of order because under the state Constitution, the Senate could not function while the Legislature was adjourned. So the Senate postponed the trial to January 7 and then, when the Legislature reconvened, issued another sheriff's writ for Langdon to face questioning on January 25.

Judge Langdon had meanwhile neatly taken care of himself. He won a well-paid federal appointment from President Washington to serve on a three-man commission to adjust Revolutionary claims by the states against the new national government, which the United States Senate confirmed on December 24, less than two weeks before the Legislature reconvened. Then he quietly submitted his judicial resignation to President Bartlett and left for his new post at Philadelphia.

When the Senate opened its scheduled impeachment session on January 25, it turned the case back to the House prosecutors for disposal. The following day the House voted to abandon the entire affair, after first voting to urge President Bartlett and his Council to appoint a replacement on the Court, and the Senate promptly concurred.

Judge Langdon had become noted for his tongue tartness and sarcasm against critics. During his four years of service on the high court he had repeatedly complained of the small pay and long hours, and in particular he denounced the Legislature for overturning decisions of the tribunal, as it could under the compromise Constitution of 1784.

Governor William Plumer of Epping, who compiled history and penned biographical sketches in his retirement after 1819, said of Langdon:

On the 17th of January, 1791, on the eve of his departure for Philadelphia, he addressed a letter to the President of the state resigning his office as judge, as being incompatible with that of commissioner.

In that letter he stated freely his opinion of the importance of the office of a judge of the highest court in the state, the inadequacy of the salary, and complained of the encroachments of the Legislature upon the judiciary, in passing bills to annul their judgments.

He observed "Many are impatiently waiting to fill my place, yet I hope the Executive will be directed to make a choice of such a gentleman as will be a credit to the appointment—not an ignoramus—no sluggard—no sycophant."

His letter was accompanied with a vindication of his official conduct as a judge, and his answer to the articles of impeachment.

The Legislature's request for a replacement for Woodbury was voted by the Governor and the Council on March 18. He was Timothy Farrar of New Ipswich, who served for a dozen years. Woodbury Langdon's haughtiness reaped public disfavor, and he later was twice defeated in Congressional bids. But his portrait continues to grace the Senate chamber, in solitary esteem, as the Senate's first presiding officer.

Transportation Trends

LEGISLATIVE AFFAIRS became different in the nine-year peacetime period following establishment of the 1784 permanent state government. They were still hampered by the unstable monetary system, but transportation and communications became major public concerns.

The Legislature granted numerous ferry franchises on the Merrimack and Connecticut rivers, and they became lucrative sources of profit, since bridges were too costly to build and maintain. Scores of special acts authorized towns to levy extra taxes on real estate, and especially on nonresident landowners, for construction and repairs of roads. Modest postal routes were established to mesh the growing towns into closer contact with each other.

Friendliness developed for Dartmouth College, despite the constitutional barrier against its faculty holding elective state office. Professor Woodward was named by the Governor and his Council as a Justice of the Grafton County Court of Common Pleas in 1785, and the following year he was elected to the positions of County Treasurer and County Register of Deeds, both coveted income sources. The Legislature also authorized the first of a series of lotteries to support the young Hanover institution.

The compromise Constitution required the towns to defray the wages of their House members, so many forfeited their representation, because of the fiscal crisis, as too costly. While the 1784 House had 91 members, the total slumped to 63 in 1787, and the nine-year average was 80. By comparison, in the eight-year period immediately following the 1792 revisions of the Constitution, when the state assumed all legislative costs, the House membership soared to an average of 137.

The 1784 Constitution formally imposed upon New Hampshire's Legislature the title of General Court, which continues to this day. It was borrowed from Massachusetts, the only other state to call its Legislature by that name. The term developed in the colonial period when Massachusetts had a chartered royal government and its Legislature was a final tribunal of appeal in all public and private disputes. In contrast, New Hampshire's royal government was by commissions creating Governors and their Councils, from time to time, and they were the court of final appeal.

The term "General Court" was most apt for the nine-year period that the compromises of the 1784 Constitution existed, for the Legislature then was the court of last resort, both public and private and including divorces. In this brief period the Legislature often overruled decisions of the court system.

When the permanent government became effective in 1784, the Legislature discarded the provincial policy of restricting the duration of laws, which was continued through the war years of the temporary Constitution of 1776.

The 1790 Legislature set a lawmaking record in its winter session of January 5 to February 18, 1791. It enacted 95 laws in 39 working days. It was not until 1828 that the Legislature exceeded that performance, by passing 130 new statutes in a one-month summer session. As usual in those formative years of free government, most of the 95 laws were local in character, concerning only individual towns and counties and, in many cases, individuals and their properties.

This record batch of legislation included curbs against wolves and profane language. One new law established a six-pound bounty on wolves and half that amount on their whelps. Stiff fines were invoked against "profane cursing and swearing," along with optional penalties which reflected the law-and-order values of those times. Fines ranged from eight shillings for a first offense, sixteen shillings for a second conviction, and twenty-four shillings for every subsequent penalty. For persons unable to pay such fines, the judge had the option of imposing a ten-day jail term, one hour in the town stockade, or a public whipping of not more than ten lashes. But there was an unusual restriction to this anticursing law. Prosecution for such an offense became void if not invoked within ten days of its occurrence.

The avalanche of new laws developed a new legislative policy as to their application. As the session approached final adjournment on February 18, 1791, the Legislature voted that all the forty-four new statutes of a general nature would not become effective until more than eight months later—to be exact, on November 1. The reason for this was summed in the following resolution:

It would be highly improper that the said acts should take effect or be in force until they be printed and distributed through the state for the information of the people at large.

This resolution also provided that all the laws which were repealed or superseded by the forty-four new acts were to continue in force until the November 1 effective date.

The 1790 Legislature also authorized a first collation and revision of

New Hampshire's laws, and this action compounded the problem of letting the people know about the new statutes before being forced to obey them. It assigned the streamlining of the laws to Attorneys Jeremiah Smith of Peterborough (later of Exeter) and Nathaniel Peabody of Atkinson, members of the House, and John Sullivan of Durham, then President of the state. The House had approved John Samuel Sherburne of Portsmouth, youthful Revolutionary veteran, to the commission, but the Senate insisted upon Sullivan in his stead.

When the 1791 Legislature convened in June, it learned the printing of the 1790 laws had been delayed, so it advanced the November 1 effective date to February 1, 1792, along with nine additional general laws voted in the 1791 summer session, to the new effective date. When the 1791 Legislature reconvened in January 1792, it learned that the printing of the record bundle of 1790 statutes had been delayed again, so it postponed the general effective date from February 1 to July 1, 1792, with a single exception, which read:

Provided nevertheless that an Act entitled An Act to prevent incestuous marriages and to regulate divorces shall not be suspended hereby.

This was not the end of the often postponed effective date of the 1790 session laws. When the 1792 Legislature convened in June, it was forced to delay the effective date again. By this time the law revision commission had completed its work with such effectiveness that the long-delayed 1790 statutes were drafted into the single new volume of updated law. And as more time was required to print the new volume, the frequently postponed effective date was once again advanced, this time to September 15, when they actually went into force.

The winter session of the 1790 Legislature closed on yet another historic note. On the final day the legislators voted flattering thanks to the town of Concord for providing them with a new meeting place. In August 1790 the town voted £ 100 to match $555 in labor and materials subscribed by fourteen leading citizens, "to build a house for the accommodations of the General Court." This was the first of several major efforts by Concord to reap the benefits of hosting the Legislature.

The town erected a one-story wooden structure on the elevated present site of the Merrimack County government building. It was 80 feet long, 40 feet wide, with a 15-foot posting, facing North Main Street. The House chamber was to the north, and the Senate met in a smaller hall on the south side. There was a narrow stairway leading to a small gallery overlooking both branches of the General Court.

Concord held its first special town meeting in the new building on December 13 and then turned it over to the Legislature, which grew in it until its own State House was opened in 1819.

The Legislative thanks went as follows:

Resolved, that the thanks of the General Court be returned to the town of Concord for the generous and very polite offer made by the Select men in behalf of said town of the use of the well designed and elegant public building lately erected for the accommodation of the General Court. This mark of attention and liberality in the town of Concord will be gratefully remembered by the Legislature whose deliberations will be facilitated by improving the fabric of the laudible purpose for which it was erected, and the rising prosperity of this town will at all times add to the happiness of the General Court.

As the Legislatures of 1791 and 1792 concluded state operations under the 1784 compromise Constitution, the New Hampshire Medical Society was chartered on February 16, 1791, and in the same year four postal routes were created, with postmasters appointed at Portsmouth, Exeter, Concord, Amherst, Dover, Keene, Charlestown, Hanover, and Plymouth. Their pay was two pence for handling a letter, and the postage was four pence for up to forty miles and six pence for delivery beyond that distance.

The Legislature chartered the state's first bank, the New Hampshire Bank, at Portsmouth on January 3, 1792, and voted to purchase $10,400 of its stock to help it function. This investment was used in 1840 to help establish what is now the State Hospital in Concord.

The nine Legislatures of the 1784-92 period held twenty-four sessions and passed 641 laws, for an average of 21 per meeting. Eleven of the sessions were in Concord, eight at Portsmouth, three at Exeter, and one each at Charlestown and Dover. The legislators convened at Charlestown September 12-29, 1787, and at Dover June 6-22, 1792. The 1791 session repealed 212 laws, some from the provincial era, but many of recent origin, as recommended by the 1790 commission, which updated the statutes into a single book.

Four men served as President of New Hampshire in this nine-year period. Weare retired from public life following one term, and died on January 14, 1786, just two days short of his seventy-third birthday anniversary. John Langdon served two terms (1785 and 1787); John Sullivan had three terms (1786, 1787, and 1789). Dr. Josiah Bartlett was

President during the final three years and then became Governor in 1793 under the revised Constitution of 1792.

Seven men served as House Speaker in the nine-year span. First was George Atkinson of Portsmouth, followed by John Sullivan and John Langdon, in that order. John Sparhawk of Portsmouth presided in 1787, died in September of that year, and was succeeded by Thomas Bartlett of Nottingham, who continued as Speaker the ensuing three years. Nathaniel Peabody of Atkinson was Speaker in 1791 and John Samuel Sherburne of Portsmouth in 1792.

The redoubtable John Calfe of Hampstead was House clerk throughout this period, except for 1790, when William Plumer, the brash young lawyer from Epping, briefly held the clerkship.

Historian Belknap was given a modest legislative appropriation to help publish his classic three-volume history of New Hampshire, the first volume of which was printed in 1784, and disseminated the following outline of what he considered the good life:

Were I to form a picture of happy society, it would be a town consisting of a due mixture of hills, valleys and streams of water.

The land well fenced and cultivated; the roads and bridges in good repair; a decent inn for the refreshment of travellers, and for public entertainments.

The inhabitants mostly husbandmen; their wives and daughters domestic manufacturers; a suitable proportion of handicraft workers, and two or three traders; a physician and lawyer, each of whom should have a farm for his support.

A clergyman, of any denomination which should be agreeable to the majority, a man of good understanding, of a candid disposition, and exemplary morals; not a metaphysical nor a polemical, but a serious and practical, preacher.

A schoolmaster, who should understand his business, and teach his pupils to govern themselves.

A social library, annually increasing, and under good regulation. A club of sensible men, seeking mutual improvement. A decent musical society.

No intriguing politician, horse-jockey, gambler or sot; but all such characters treated with contempt.

Such a situation may be considered as the most favorable to social happiness, or any which this world can afford.

The 1792 Improvements

NEW HAMPSHIRE'S GENERAL COURT donned an improved format in 1793, and the House membership blossomed. Under the 1784 Constitution, the people were automatically given another Constitutional Convention after seven years, to consider possible amendments, and this led to wholesale improvements in the Legislature and the entire state government in a 1791 convention.

The wages of the House members were shifted from the towns to the state, in the revised document, and the towns promptly began electing all the Representatives they were legally entitled to, rather than only those they could afford. New standards of conduct were imposed upon the Legislature, as both branches became required to operate with open public galleries, and members were forbidden to accept fees or other recompense for services relating to legislative affairs.

The revised Constitution required that the Journals of both the House and Senate be printed and published "immediately after adjournment," so that the general public would have access to such information as speedily as possible. The secondary name of the General Court was changed from "Assembly" to Legislature at the same time.

The voters killed a 1791 proposal to change the convening of the annual legislative sessions from the first Wednesday in June to the last Wednesday in October, to avoid conflict with summer farming pursuits.

Voting qualifications became more democratic in the revised Constitution. Males were allowed to vote at twenty-one, without the former requirement that they also pay taxes, with two exceptions. Men on public relief and those exempted from paying taxes, at their own request, were denied suffrage. On the other hand, property qualifications for the Governor continued at £ 500, along with £ 200 for Senators and £ 100 for Representatives. The Protestant requirement was also continued.

The compromise position of state President was abolished and the title of Governor was restored, but with sharp restrictions. An Executive Council elected by the people rather than by the Legislature was given negative authority over the Chief Executive, which continues to this day.

The 1791 adjustments to the Constitution were so numerous that seventy-two questions were required to present them on the referendum ballot for May 7, 1792. When the convention reconvened on May 30, the delegates learned that forty-six of the amendments had been approved and the other twenty-six were killed. The net result was that the Constitution became replete with confusion and disarray, so the delegates drafted an overall single amendment covering all the deficiencies, and on August 27, 1792, it was approved by a vote of 2,122 to 978, or only 56 more than the required two-thirds majority.

The revised Constitution established a permanent method for future amendments. It required the Legislature to submit the question of having a Constitutional Convention to the people every seven years. The massive 1791 overhaul proved so successful, however, that nearly sixty years elapsed before the voters approved a fifth Constitutional Convention for 1850.

Youthful William Plumer, then only thirty-three, dominated the entire 1791 convention deliberations, and was credited with sponsoring the legislative reforms. But he lost repeated efforts to reduce and restrict the House membership. The revised document became known as "The Plumer Constitution." It was also labeled as New Hampshire's "Second Constitution," and the Legislature used that title in its official documents for the following half-century. But then it became generally recognized that the 1792 changes were only amendments and that much of the 1784 document continued in existence without 1791 reenactment.

Plumer deplored lack of public interest in the 1792 amendments. He pointed out that the total vote of 3,100 registered for the final endorsement of the amendments was less than 50 percent of the gubernatorial vote earlier in the same year, and many towns failed entirely to turn in any balloting. The percentage actually was 37 percent, because in March of that year the total vote for Governor was 8,389, as Dr. Josiah Bartlett was reelected without opposition. Historically, this was the lowest percentage of participating voters ever to approve an amendment to the New Hampshire Constitution.

The 1791 amendment barring legislators from collecting fees for legislative activities apparently became questioned, as to scope, for the ensuing Legislature of 1793 spelled it out in greater detail. The article, still in force, reads:

No member of the General Court shall take fees, be of counsel, or act as advocate, in any cause before either branch of the Legislature; and upon due proof thereof, such member shall forfeit his seat in the Legislature.

The 1793 House appointed a committee to clarify this constitutional restriction, and it reported:

That no member of this House shall either directly or indirectly take any fee or reward for bringing forward or supporting any petition or motion before the Legislature or either branch of the same or committee thereof, and by receiving the same or accepting any promise or compensation thereof he shall forfeit his seat in the House.

This interpretation was endorsed by the House on June 11 and added to its general rules of conduct.

The 1793 Legislature created a Senate of twelve districts, for a first time, as the revised Constitution had abolished the former formula of electing the dozen Senate members from the five counties.

Political labels developed through the 1790s, and partisanship began to influence legislative affairs. John Taylor Gilman of Exeter, the autocratic State Treasurer (as was his father before him), became leader of the Federalists and won the Governorship for an all-time record fourteen terms, beginning in 1794. The opposition became known as Republicans, and their principal spokesman became John Langdon, who battled Gilman through two decades and managed to win election as Governor six times.

Thanks to creation of the permanent federal government in 1788 by New Hampshire's "key" ninth ratification vote, and its stabilizing influence on the monetary system, the state's economy became flourishing, its population boomed, and the Legislature labored to foster the public welfare.

The first of many toll turnpikes promoted by private companies, to augment town roads, was chartered by the 1796 Legislature, to link Portsmouth with Concord. This proved so profitable that within the following dozen years some 500 miles of toll roads, costing about $600,000, had fanned through the state, all with legislative sanctions. On the social front, the Legislature incorporated some fifty-nine public libraries in the seven-year period going into the 1800s.

In 1797 William Plumer became the first House Speaker to be allowed to appoint committees, as the traditional nominations by members were terminated. This custom continues to this day. This session also adjusted the poll tax to cover males from eighteen to seventy years of age, with exemptions for "militiamen aged 18 to 21, instructors and students of colleges, ordained ministers, preceptors of academies and paupers and idiots."

Governor Gilman was forceful and took issue with the Legislature on occasion. He won a 1797 pay raise in an unusual manner. He filed a demand for a $200 increase in his $1,000 salary through a House attaché to Speaker Plumer, and it was approved by the Legislature. But the following year he was refused another $300 raise.

Gilman invoked extraordinary executive authority against the Legislature in 1800. When the General Court asked him to adjourn the summer session on June 10, a Saturday, the Governor refused to do so. He explained he joined with his Executive Council in fearing the legislators might violate the law by traveling home on Sunday. So the adjournment was issued the following Monday, but no session of the Legislature was recorded for that day, and posterity can only ponder over how many of the Representatives bowed to the Gilman dictum.

The Legislature continued to hold brief annual June sessions to avoid conflict with haying and plantings, and it delayed most of its deliberating to early winter meetings, into 1800. Then the General Court of that year voted on December 10, the final day of its fall session:

Resolved that in the opinion of the Legislature, one session of the General Court for the ensuing year will be sufficient to transact the necessary business of the state and that the Secretary [of State] be directed to cause the same to be published in the several newspapers of the state.

Still a legislator, Plumer sponsored this policy for the avowed purpose of reducing legislative costs. It continued for a half-century, with but few exceptions, and a quadrennial proviso. Fall sessions every four years became custom for reapportionment of the annual state tax upon the towns, which more often than not ran into many days of arguments and debates over the merits of the local assessments and valuations.

The Legislature set a mobility record in the 1793-1800 period by holding sessions in six different towns. Of the two sessions yearly in this eight-year span, nine were held in Concord; three in Exeter; and one each in Portsmouth, Amherst, Hanover, and Hopkinton. Amherst hosted the Legislature in 1794 for the June 4-21 session, and

Thirty Crowded Years

it is recorded the town's liquor licenses multiplied from three to twenty-one for the occasion. The following year the legislators bestowed their presence upon Hanover for its June 3-18 summer session, and Dartmouth College staged a gala reception for the second-term inauguration of Governor Gilman. The Reverend John Smith of Hanover gave the traditional election sermon as the Legislature convened with more than customary pomp and panoply.

The Legislature held the first of its three sessions in Hopkinton, June 6-20, 1798. This town had seven regularly licensed taverns, so, town history records, only five extra liquor licenses were issued by the selectmen, and they were limited to the stay of the lawmakers.

The House membership grew slowly but steadily in the 1793-1800 years. It went from 119 to 150, to keep pace with the increasing population of the growing towns. Calfe continued as House clerk. The Speakers were Nathaniel Peabody of Atkinson, 1793; John Prentice of Londonderry, 1794 and 1798-1800; Russell Freeman of Hanover, 1795-96; and William Plumer, 1797.

National Horizons

GOOD TIMES greeted the Legislature as it headed into the 1800s, and its horizon assumed national scope. It often was in communication with the Legislatures of other states relative to slavery, as applied to creation of new states, and proposed amendments to the young Federal Constitution, then the vogue through the developing nation.

The Legislature handled a booming Hogg business. From June 1801 to December 1808 it voted name changes for sixty Hoggs. Entire families in several towns had their surnames changed to Prentice, Shepherd, Tennant, Huntley, and Moore, along with three Wilders and three Raymonds.

Military matters also claimed the attention of the Legislature, since the federal government had not yet assumed a substantial national defense posture. The General Court voted $8,000 in 1803 to purchase rifles and cannon for custody by the towns; it financed construction of gunhouses in 1805; and two years later it authorized the Governor to spend $19,000 for rifles and cannon for the towns.

Construction of New Hampshire's first state building, a granite prison, was authorized by the Legislature in 1810, and Concord became the site as the townspeople offered two acres of land for it and agreed to haul 3,000 tons of stone from nearby Rattlesnake Hill for its walls. It was opened in 1812 as a second war with England broke out. It was located off what is now the corner of North State and Beacon streets and remained in use until 1880 when the prison was moved to its present location.

Former House Speaker Russell Freeman of Hanover became victim of the most bizarre murder case in New Hampshire history while languishing in a debtor's jail at Haverhill in December 1805. Following two terms as Speaker in 1795-96 and five ensuing terms on the Executive Council, this prominent merchant suffered business reverses and was imprisoned by his creditors, as was customary in those years.

Freeman was confined in a single room with two other debtors, Capt. Joseph Starkweather, Jr., and Josiah Burnham, both of Haverhill. The latter, notorious town handyman, murdered the other two with a sheath knife in the evening of December 18. It was later said that Burnham resented chiding concerning a lady acquaintance.

Burnham went on trial the following spring before the Superior Court of Judicature at Plymouth, and youthful Daniel Webster, then a novice lawyer at Boscawen, was one of two men appointed by the court to defend him. The result was that Burnham was publicly hanged at Haverhill on August 12, 1806, his sixty-third birthday anniversary.

The Haverhill town history relates that upward of 10,000 people from throughout the sprawling north country converged upon the scene. Sheriff David Webster mustered a military escort for Burnham from the jail to the scaffold atop Powder House Hill. While he stood beneath the gibbet with a noose around his neck, there was a mournful singing program, after which the Reverend David Sutherland of Bath preached probably the most unusual sermon ever given at such an event in the state.

After exhorting Burnham that his death was deserved, the clergyman told the spectators:

Possibly there are some among you, who if your crimes were as well known as those of Josiah Burham, should like him be brought to an untimely end. Others of you are now living in the commission of sins, not cognizable indeed by human laws, but for which God will call you to account.

You esteem it a matter of alarming consequence to be arraigned at a human tribunal, tried, convicted and hanged; and you think right for so it is. But, alas, many of you think nothing of the probability of your being condemned

Thirty Crowded Years

at the bar of the eternal Judge. . . . In a few minutes you will shudder to see a fellow creature launched into eternity! but, oh remember that it shall be much more intolerable to fall into the hands of the living God, who is angry at the wicked every day.

All the temporal judgments that overtake unGodly men are only as a single drop in comparison with that overflowing cup, the very dregs of which they shall be forced to wring out in the eternal world. Consider this, therefore, yee that forget God, lest he tear you in pieces and there be none to deliver.

The Legislature was in session at Portsmouth when Freeman was murdered, but it recorded no attention to the deed, nor his memory.

John Calfe of Hampstead served the House of Representatives so long and well that following his death in October 1808, at the age of sixty-seven, the November session went into official mourning, with the following resolution:

Whereas it has pleased God, in his wise Providence, to remove by death the Honorable John Calfe, Esquire, who during our Revolutionary War, rendered important service to our common country, and for more than twenty-five years, successively, has faithfully served this state as clerk of the House of Representatives, therefore, voted, that in testimony of our respect to the memory of the Honorable John Calfe, the members of this House wear crape on the left arm during this session.

This Hampstead lawyer had served eight terms in the wartime Legislature, while also being assistant House clerk for three terms and then becoming clerk in 1783. He filled that clerkship for the remainder of his life, except for a brief 1790 interlude, and at the same time served as Judge of the Rockingham County Court of Common Pleas throughout this same period. Calfe's one possible fault was excessive compassion for others, and one biographer wrote that "he made many errors as judge for he had too much pity for the poor and unfortunate to the detriment of the rights of opponents."

Political Influence Sets In

POLITICS GREW in legislative influence through the first decade of the 1800s. Federalist Governor Gilman was finally ousted in 1804, after eleven terms, and Republican John Langdon succeeded him for four terms.

The Legislature became concerned with international affairs in 1807 as Great Britain and France, then at war, each ordered the United States not to trade with their opponent. Both nations began capturing American ships, to enforce their embargoes, and England went so far as to blockade Portsmouth's thriving seaport.

A major political development occurred in 1810 as William Plumer, the veteran Federalist champion, shifted to the Republican party. He had broken with Federalist international appeasement policies while serving a single term in the United States Senate up to 1808, and then retired to private life. But in 1810 the Republicans elected him to the State Senate, where he served two terms as President, after which Plumer served as Republican Governor through four history-laden terms.

Langdon won another two terms as Governor when the War of 1812, supported by Plumer, began. Then in 1813, Governor Gilman was reelected for an additional three terms, and he immediately engineered New Hampshire's first political ouster of the judiciary. He induced the Federalist Legislature to abolish the courts and replaced them under new names with Federalist appointees. In this maneuver, the Superior Court of Judicature was replaced by a Supreme Judicial Court and a Circuit Court of Common Pleas. But as it turned out, this was easier voted than accomplished. When the new Judges went into action in the fall of 1813, they received no attention. The Republican sheriffs continued to wait upon and serve the old Judges, who insisted their ousters without due cause was unconstitutional.

Governor Gilman took swift action to restore order in the courts. He became New Hampshire's first Chief Executive to call a special session of the Legislature since the 1792 reorganization of the state Constitution. It was convened on October 27, 1813. The colorful details are presented in Chapter XV.

It was in Gilman's administration that the 1814 Legislature voted to build a State House, as the House membership had grown to 184 and no longer fitted comfortably in Concord's 1790 Town House. In fact, the overcrowding had become so acute that the 1815 House voted:

Every member may wear his hat or not at his pleasure while in the House, unless when addressing the Speaker or during the presence of His Excellency, the Governor, and the Honorable Council.

Actual construction of the Capitol did not start until 1816, when Governor Plumer returned to the executive chair for another three terms, and then retired to private life as it was dedicated by the 1819 Legislature.

Meanwhile, when peace returned in 1815, and Gilman bowed out of politics, the Federalist party began to fade into oblivion, and the Republicans (later Democrats) began domination of state affairs, with but few brief intervals, until creation of the present New Hampshire Republican party in 1857. The Federalists developed into the Whig party, which never did very well in New Hampshire, and eventually became the Republican party. The early Republicans, meanwhile, became known as Republican-Democrats for a brief period; in the 1830s, they developed into the Democratic party, which continues to this day.

The Legislature suffered a historic setback by the United States Supreme Court during Governor Plumer's final administration. As he took office in 1816, the Dartmouth College trustees, of Federalist leaning, had discharged President John Wheelock, the aging son of the college founder, so Plumer asked the Legislature to reverse that dismissal.

The lawmakers approved a measure boosting the Dartmouth board of trustees from twelve to twenty-one, added a twenty-five-member board of overseers with veto power over the trustees for good measure, and gave the Governor and the Council authority to make all the appointments. Indicative of the political partisanship involved, when the House approved the measure by 96 to 86, not a single Federalist voted for it, and only 2 Republicans opposed it.

The trustees appealed the reorganization statute, and their counsel went before the resurrected Supreme Court of Judicature. Upon taking office, Plumer and his Republican Legislature had promptly repealed Gilman's 1813 revamping of the judiciary, so the high court once again became Republican in makeup. Interestingly, the Dartmouth and judiciary realignments bills became effective simultaneously on June 27, 1816.

Plumer restored Wheelock as president, the restored high court ruled in November 1817 that Dartmouth's reorganization was legal, and Wheelock died the following April.

The ousted trustees turned to the Supreme Court at Washington for redress, and New Hampshire's noted Daniel Webster, by then residing in Boston, entered the dispute, winning lasting fame as a result. He presented such devastating arguments against the Legislature before the United States Supreme Court that he won a February 2, 1819, decision which restored the original trustees to Dartmouth controls and freed the Hanover institution from legislative infringement for all time.

Ownership of what became New Hampshire's unique Indian Stream Republic of 1832-35 first faced the Legislature in 1820. After two land companies had disputed the area, which became the town of Pittsburg, for a score years, Representative Jeremiah Mason of Portsmouth demanded state sovereignty over the 160,000-acre territory, and this led to protracted legislative wranglings on the subject.

This problem was keyed to a single word in the 1783 Paris Peace Treaty which gave the United States its independence, relating to New Hampshire's northern boundary. It set the line at the "Northwesternmost" headwaters of the Connecticut River. The Canadian government claimed this meant the upper lakes of this stream, while New Hampshire insisted it was the source of Hall's Stream, a main artery of the Connecticut River, to the northwest of the so-called Connecticut lakes.

As officials of these opposing governments harassed them with edicts and intrusions, in 1832 the 400 Indian Stream settlers created their own government by a 56 to 3 vote of its adult males. As they vainly struggled for peace and tranquility, and Canada continued to try to impose its rule upon the Indian Stream area, the New Hampshire Legislature in 1835 sponsored a military takeover of the territory, and it came, by force, under its protectorship.

In 1840 the Legislature named the disputed area Pittsburg, and two years later ownership was settled. Daniel Webster, New Hampshire's noted statesman, representing the American government, won agreement from Lord Ashburton of Great Britain that the Hall's Stream borderline was correct.

On the Fourth of July in 1860 the Legislature gave full title to every Pittsburg settler and their heirs to all land in their possession on that date.

HIGHLIGHTS OF THE EARLY 1800s

THE STATE HOUSE was opened by the 1819 Legislature on June 2, with a unique display of brotherliness. It was in sharp contrast to the protracted battling over its site. (See Chapter XX.)

Attorney Matthew Harvey of Hopkinton became House Speaker, and his older brother, Jonathan, a Sutton farmer, became Senate President. They presided with such friendliness that Matthew was reelected Speaker, and Jonathan served three additional terms as President.

Churches Lose Tax Support

THE HARVEY BROTHERS' joint administration produced an even more important historic episode, as the 1819 General Court enacted the "Toleration Act," which terminated use of public funds to support churches, till then mostly of the Congregational denomination. This was the culmination of years of contention against the traditional policy of public financing of specified churches and their pastors. It was argued this constituted an infringement upon freedom of worship, as new denominations spread through the state, which could not share in such largesse because they were in the minority among voters.

The Reverend Dan Young of Lisbon, a Methodist clergyman, battled through four annual terms in the Senate to win enactment of the

1830 woodcut of the 1819 State House showing the original narrow dome and four corner chimneys.

Toleration Act. After he had induced the 1819 Senate once again to sponsor this highly controversial issue, it finally won passage by a close 96 to 88 House roll call vote.

Five House members debated the church bill with such vigor and in such detail that it required four editions of the weekly *New Hampshire Patriot* of Concord to print their arguments in full. Dr. Thomas Whipple, Jr., of Wentworth, House sponsor of the measure, was joined by John Pitman of Portsmouth in the showdown debate. Speaking in opposition were Ichabod Bartlett of Portsmouth, William Butters of Pittsfield, and Henry Hubbard of Charlestown.

Editors roundly denounced this purge of Puritanical religious domination. They wrung their type in horror against this separation of state from church. One called it "Repeal of Religion"; another headlined "Bible Abolished"; and a third observed, "When the wicked rule the righteous of the land mourn."

Governor Samuel Bell of Londonderry supported the bill and

Highlights of the Early 1800s

signed it into law on July 1, 1819, the day before final adjournment of the session, and he was reelected for three more annual terms.

The House membership totalled 193 for this 1819 session. The lawmakers sat at long desks facing west, with the Speaker's rostrum against the west wall. It was flanked by six raised seats on each side for the Senate members, when in joint session, so the upper branch actually looked down upon the House when together.

The 1819 inauguration was a gala affair. But it was delayed from the traditional second day of the session because Judge Bell, the incoming Chief Executive, insisted upon completing his chores on the Supreme Court of Judicature, at Haverhill, so he missed the Thursday exercises and did not take office until the following Monday.

Concord's *New Hampshire Patriot* reported on Tuesday, June 1, the day before the Legislature convened:

Citizens of Concord have made arrangements to escort the Governor-elect to the metropolis on his return at the close of the Court, to take upon himself the highest office in the gift of the people of New Hampshire.

The escort will start from in front of the State House on Friday at 2 o'clock P.M. and proceed to Johnson's (formerly Chandler's) tavern near the Contoocook river in Boscawen, where the Governor is expected to arrive at 4 o'clock.

Captain Abbott's company of cavalry will accompany the escort. The committee appointed on this occasion cordially invites the citizens of Concord and gentlemen from every quarter, without distinction of party, to join in the proposed escort.

Despite Governor Bell's absence, the Legislature convened as usual on June 2, the first Wednesday of June, when the members took their oaths, along with the Council. Retiring Governor Plumer substituted for Bell as the Legislature on Thursday led a colorful march to the Old North Meeting House for the traditional election sermon. As voted by the General Court, the line of the parade was as follows:

1–Military escort.
2–Committee of arrangements.
3–His Excellency the Governor and the Honorable Council.
4–Secretary and Treasurer and chaplain of the Legislature.
5–The preacher of the day and the reverend clergy.

6–President of the Senate, the Honorable Senate and clerks.
7–Senators and Representatives of the U.S. and military officers.
8–Speaker of the House of Representatives and the members, four deep,
  and their clerks.
9–Gentlemen of distinction; Samuel M. Richardson, Daniel Hoit, Peter
  Patterson, Samuel Harrington, Josiah Bellows, 3rd, and Israel W. Kel-
  ley, marshals of the day.

The 1819 session received an unusual report as it celebrated the opening of the Capitol. Secretary of State Samuel Sparhawk of Concord said that public improvements had claimed much legislative attention in roughly the first forty years of New Hampshire's freedom from the royal yoke. He reported that from 1776 through 1818 the Legislature had chartered 161 public libraries, 95 religious organizations, 22 academies, 27 musical societies, 10 banks, and 5 county agricultural associations. He also listed legislative authority for 53 bridges, 52 toll turnpikes, 18 canals, 38 cotton and "woollen" mills, 4 insurance companies, 8 fire engine companies, and 5 Masonic lodges.

The General Court flexed its image in its new home, and both branches launched standing committees for a first time in 1820. Until then, the House and Senate had for the most part held joint committee hearings with small committees appointed from time to time for each bill or petition.

The House created six committees, and the Senate had four. They were designed to handle the more important legislative business, and their titles and rank were illuminating on that score. The two major units in the House were a Committee on Elections and a Committee on Incorporations, each to consist of ten members. Comprised of only seven members each were a Committee on Agriculture and Manufactures, a Committee on Military, a Committee of Revisal and Unfinished Business, and a Committee of Accounts.

As New Hampshire's public life developed in those early years, voting returns from the towns were lax and inefficient and were often adjusted by the Legislature. This was also the period in which religious, educational, and literary groups, along with agricultural and manufacturing organizations, clamored for legislative incorporation and tax exemption benefits.

Four years later, the 1824 House substantially expanded its committees to cope with its broadening affairs. Then established were committees on Finance; the Judiciary; on Roads, Bridges and Canals; on Public Lands; Alteration of Names; and a Committee on Towns,

Parishes, and Schools.

Three joint House-Senate committees took form in 1825. They were on Engrossed Bills, State House and State House Yard, and on State Library. They continued until 1949, when the latter two were merged into other committees. The first continues to this day, but with a new title of Committee on Enrolled Bills.

Lafayette's 1825 Visit

THE 1825 LEGISLATURE made history by entertaining General Lafayette, the French hero of the American Revolution, and the event produced New Hampshire's celebrated nickname of the "Granite State." Mrs. Grace Amsden, who died at eighty-eight in 1960, compiled the details in her history of Concord's early life, which remains unpublished in a New Hampshire Historical Society's vault.

Lafayette was on a two-year national tour financed by the federal government to mark the golden anniversary of his joining the War for Independence. He reached Concord in grand style on June 22, 1825, a Wednesday, after an overnight stop at Pembroke, en route from Boston. He was driven to the State House in a barouche drawn by six dapple gray horses, escorted by Amos A. Parker, youthful publisher of the weekly *New Hampshire Statesman* of Concord.

The distinguished hero entered the town over the lower bridge, which was festooned with a giant arch of flowers, where an artillery unit greeted him with a national salute and eight companies of militia were lined at attention. Mrs. Amsden related that Lafayette rode up Main Street with the air perfumed by garlands on which girls had labored for days to prepare. The townspeople had also primped their premises to reflect their esteem.

As General Lafayette prepared to address the Legislature, he was escorted to the Capitol up the center walk of the yard and into the main foyer, then called Doric Hall, to greet 200 Revolutionary veterans under Gen. Benjamin Pierce. Following the legislative speech, a luncheon drew some 700, which was more than any establishment could serve, so it was held in the State House yard. Lafayette spent the remainder of the afternoon shaking hands and returned to the yard early in the evening for the same purpose, so great was his reception.

Lafayette was honored at a levee that evening, followed by an oratorio and grand reception, all of which used up most of the night. But the next morning the aged hero was off for Portsmouth at 6:30 A.M., en route to Maine. Lafayette's democracy was in sharp contrast to his

The Lafayette Elm

royal breeding—his name being Marie Joseph Paul Yves Roch Gilbert du Motier, Marquis de Lafayette. He joined the American Revolution at nineteen as a private soldier a few days after a royal wedding. He rose to become one of General Washington's trusted aides, with Major General rank. He time and again expended substantial personal sums to feed and clothe hungry and freezing soldiers under his command.

The General was accompanied to Concord by his son, George Washington Lafayette. He wore a wig by that time, and a Concord paper reported:

The Marquis de Lafayette was one of the finest looking men in the army, notwithstanding his deep red hair, which then, as now, was rather in disrepute. . . . His mien was noble–his manners frank and amiable, and his movements light and graceful. He wore his hair plain, and never complied so far with the fashion of the times as to powder.

Former Secretary of State Philip Carrigain, youthful Concord attorney who was a poet of local renown, composed a song for the Lafayette luncheon. He set it to the war song, "Scots Who Ha' Wi' Wallace Bled," and it comprised seven stanzas. Entitled "La Fayette's Return," the first stanza went:

Highlights of the Early 1800s

North and South, and East and West,
A Cordial welcome have addressed,
Loud and warm, the nation's guest,
Dear son of Liberty;
Whom tyrants cursed, when Heaven approved,
And millions long have mourned and loved,
He comes, by fond entreaties moved,
The Granite State to see.

It was in this manner that New Hampshire's symbol of strength and durability, as the Granite State, was launched.

The day following General Lafayette's departure from Concord, an elm tree was planted where he sat during the luncheon. The Legislature later sponsored two granite markers in his honor, at the entrance to the center walk of the State House yard.

The tree flourished and dominated the right front of the Capitol until it became diseased in 1956, and the state paid $300 to dump it into oblivion. Governor Lane Dwinell of Lebanon salvaged a few engraved gavels from the Lafayette elm, and some citizens used slabs from the huge trunk for coffee tables. Lafayette Lodge of Masons in Manchester received one of the gavels. The Lafayette posts were transferred to the main entrance of the State Hospital in 1892, to make way for the $20,000 granite arch which the Legislature allowed Concord to erect on the plaza to memorialize its veterans of all wars. The two markers were recently moved, for a second time, to flank the entrance to the new State Archives building on South Fruit Street in Concord.

On October 19, 1825, citizens of Franconia and surrounding towns dedicated an adjacent peak in the name of Lafayette, and it has been honored as such ever since on federal and state maps. The event was staged on the anniversary of the surrender of General Cornwallis and his British army at Yorktown, Pennsylvania, on October 19, 1781, to Generals Washington and Lafayette.

Carrigain had a checkered legislative career, which Mrs. Amsden's history suggests was due to his loose living as a bachelor of convivial habits. He became Secretary of State, by vote of the Legislature, for four terms beginning in 1805, while Republican Governor Langdon was in power; and it was in 1807 that the Legislature hired Carrigain to produce a first official map of the state and gave him a $5,000 advance payment for 500 copies. The 1814 Legislature threatened to sue him, as he insisted he would restrict the map to 250 copies and demanded another $5,000 for the full amount.

Several legislative committees negotiated over a period of three years, and Carrigain finally won an additional $3,750 payment for the 500 copies. They were handsomely colored, on heavy cloth paper, 50 by 56 inches in size. They were distributed to state officials and each town. Twenty remained in custody of the Secretary of State, some of which later went to educational centers. One remains to this day in the Secretary's vaults.

This Carrigain map includes most of New England, a strip of Canada, and Nova Scotia, for comparison purposes. It did not show what is now the town of Pittsburg, for that area was then being disputed by Canada. Copies of this pioneer map have been distributed by the State Department of Resources and Economic Development in recent years and have become a popular retail item.

Interestingly, Carrigain won his added $3,750 legislative payment when Federalist Governor Gilman was in office, and he dedicated it to Gilman, rather than Langdon, the original map sponsor.

There is no memorial, as such, to honor Carrigain for originating New Hampshire's prized nickname, the Granite State. But his map continues to be distributed by the state as a historic memento, and an impressive residence he built in 1799 on Concord's North Main Street has ever since been historically called "Carrigain's Folly." He borrowed to build it to impress his intended bride, the daughter of the Dartmouth College president, but she jilted him and he never married.

Born in Concord on February 20, 1772, and son of Dr. Philip Carrigain of New York City who began practice in Concord in 1763, Carrigain died on March 20, 1842, following an unsuccessful law practice in Chichester, in what one historian has described as "straightened circumstances."

Historian Mrs. Amsden told this delightful vignette of the 1819 Capitol's early years:

Sad to relate, in spite of its grandeur, irreverent youth played stunts with their proud edifice.

Boys of adventurous spirit found they could climb up the lightning rod from the ground to the dome and then crawl across the eagle and set astride his golden neck.

Highlights of the Early 1800s

Franklin Pierce

One boy, we are told, Abiel Carter by name, went up this perilous ascent the night before the Glorious Fourth and hung a flag on the eagle. When daylight came it revealed to his chagrin that the flag hung "Union down" so he climbed up again and righted it.

When the State House was first enlarged in 1864, the lightning rod was placed inside the walls, both to balk juvenile pranksters and for beautification purposes.

Franklin Pierce's Record

FRANKLIN PIERCE, New Hampshire's only United States President, began making political history in 1829, at the age of twenty-four, when he was elected to the first of four terms in the House of Representatives. He thus became the only person to serve in the Legislature, with a father as Governor, as Gen. Benjamin Pierce of Hillsborough filled that position in 1829 for a second term.

Young Pierce became chairman of the House Committee on Education and helped sponsor two unusual political developments. To celebrate Democrat Andrew Jackson's 1828 Presidential victory over John Quincy Adams, the General Court changed the name of the tiny town of Adams, in the White Mountains, to Jackson. Governor Pierce signed the resolution into law on the Fourth of July, 1829, and Jackson has existed since. Then Pierce and his legislative associates passed a law restricting the public printing of the session's laws to only news- papers of Democratic persuasion. This was done in the name of economy, according to records, as there were more Whig papers than of the prevailing party.

Two years later, Pierce became Speaker of the 1831 House, at twenty-six, the youngest ever to fill that position, and was reelected to that post the following year. The second youngest Speaker has been William E. Chandler of Concord, at twenty-seven, in 1863, who then went on to become a major Republican officeholder and party patriarch for half a century. Third youngest Speakers, each at twenty-eight, have been Ira Allen Eastman of Gilmanton, in 1837, and Harry Hibbard of Bath, in 1844.

Following election to the Congress in 1833, at twenty-eight, as the youngest New Hampshireman ever to sit in the national House, the Legislature of 1837 handed Franklin Pierce yet another historical distinction by electing him to the United States Senate at thirty-two, making him the state's youngest man ever to serve in that body.

Historic Spending Spree

IT IS RARE that a government suffers from too much money—but that is what bogged the General Court in 1836 into its second longest session in a century. On that memorable occasion, the legislators dawdled and debated at great length over what to do with an amazing $892,115.72 federal windfall. The national government had given New Hampshire substantial reimbursements for its support of the Revolutionary War and the War of 1812, but this surprise fortune from Washington almost staggered the imagination of the Granite State solons. All of this is understandable to this day, because the windfall was fourteen times the size of the Legislature's annual spendings at that time—and the equivalent of more than $7 billion by 1978 comparison.

After protracted haggling, the 1836 legislators voted to accept the huge cash offering—but with a rebuff, rather than thanks, for the Congressional generosity. They insisted—even as they grabbed it —that federal financial aid to state governments was degrading and an infringement upon their integrity. They unanimously resolved that:

Any distribution of the surplus revenues of the general government would be not only contrary to the true spirit of the Constitution, but if adopted will tend to the establishment of a consolidated government, degrading to the states and reducing them to servile dependence upon the general government.

126

New Hampshire's windfall developed from an overflow of funds into the national Treasury from sale of public lands as the western frontiers boomed with investors and pioneering settlers. This heaped a record surplus of $42.5 million in the federal till, after financing a $32 million annual budget.

Senator Henry Clay of Kentucky, destined to become a noted national statesman, had advocated distribution of the land sales revenue to the states, for fear it would become argument for reduction of high federal tariffs. President Andrew Jackson opposed the idea. He argued it was wrong because it doled out money not in the same proportion the people paid it into the government, and represented unfair redistribution of wealth.

Treasury Secretary Levi Woodbury, former New Hampshire Governor, also denounced the distribution proposal. He recommended the surplus be set aside and invested by the government for use in future fiscal emergencies. But when the proponents hit upon the scheme of dividing the surplus as a "deposite," rather than an outright gift to the states, President Jackson reluctantly yielded to the Congressional clamor.

Controversy flared as the 1836 Legislature convened in quadrennial November session for customary reapportionment of town property valuations, and quickly turned its attention to the whopping windfall. Governor Isaac Hill, Concord's caustic-tongued editor, denounced the federal largesse as dangerous to state sovereignty. He disputed Clay, saying the surplus should be devoted to reduction of tariffs.

Realizing, however, that the Legislature was determined to accept the free cash, Governor Hill recommended that the "deposite" be invested by the state, with interest earnings earmarked to reduce the yearly state tax upon the towns.

Hill cited precedents for his economy proposal. He pointed out that when Congress gave New Hampshire $300,000, starting in 1790, for support of the War for Independence, it was invested and provided earnings of an equal amount, which financed half of the state government's costs for thirty years, so tax assessments upon the towns were that much less. He also recalled that the state retained $40,000 received from the federal government for similar purpose after the War of 1812. Finally, Governor Hill stressed to the Legislature that Congress had tied a possible reimbursement string to the bonanza, so it should be kept intact to meet such a conceivable demand.

Governor Hill wasted his warnings. The contemplated glitter of what the giant largesse could do for the towns prevailed against all argument. The 244 legislators (12 in the Senate) hemmed and hawed deep into the winter, in their poorly heated State House. Finally, they threw caution aside and voted to divide the $892,115.72 among the 241 towns and grants.

The session opened November 23 and lasted till January 14, 1837, for fifty-three days. It became the second longest session in history up to 1879, when biennial sessions were launched. There had been a sixty-day session from December 25, 1793, to February 22, 1794, as the lawmakers implemented the mass of amendments then voted into the state Constitution.

The legislators first spent a month arguing the merits of the federal fiscal favor. The four-man Portsmouth delegation led a vain fight to refuse it entirely. This was climaxed on December 8 when the House killed the following resolution, sponsored by Thomas P. Treadwell of Portsmouth:

That a revenue drawn from the pockets of the people by any law of Congress of the United States for the purpose of distributing same to the states, is not only unconstitutional but highly dangerous to the liberties of the people, and that any act of that Congress tending either directly or indirectly to make the states dependent upon the general government for the means of enriching their treasuries is highly to be deprecated, leading as it would to consolidation and colonial dependence.

The House voted on December 15 to accept the windfall, by a 204 to 7 roll call. The swamped minority comprised Treadwell, Isaac Waldron, Augustus Jenkins, and Josiah G. Hadley, all of Portsmouth; James Pickering of nearby Newington; George P. Meserve of Jackson; and Robert Ingalls of Berlin.

After the Senate concurred in the acceptance, the legislators spent another three weeks battling over how it should be split among the

Highlights of the Early 1800s

towns. Some wanted it matched against voters; others argued for a property valuation yardstick. The upshot was compromise—the ever leavening denominator of democracy. The division formula became based half upon the voting populace and half upon property assessments.

The Legislature tied its own strings to the boodle. The towns were required to sign notes of reimbursement if the federal government should demand its return. It also voted the towns could spend only the interest earnings from their allotments and specified the inhabitants would be personally responsible for possible repayment if a town should default its pledge.

The legislators even went so far as to protect the scruples or timidity of a town which might fear to accept the strings tied to the windfall. They voted that if a town declined to assume the responsibility of its portion, the state would handle it and give the town the earnings derived therefrom.

Congress had arranged to have the surplus sent to the states in four quarterly installments, and the first allotment arrived early in February 1837, three weeks after the Legislature adjourned. On February 10, State Treasurer Zenas Clement of Concord prepared and published the amounts each town was to receive. He disclosed that Portsmouth was the greatest beneficiary, with $30,756.92; Nashua was posted for $21,359.40; and Concord placed third, with $19,308.

The Capital voted to spend its share before getting it. The Legislature gave Concord special permission, in the final hours of its marathon session, to raise a $30,000 loan to help finance the proposed Concord Railroad (which opened in 1842) and use the surplus to help pay it off. The town floated the loan, and Governor Hill promptly became "agent" for this investment of public funds in a private enterprise. This was ironical because the solons had earlier criticized Hill for suggesting exactly such use of the federal surplus at the state level.

Editorial criticism hit the Legislature. The weekly *Exeter News Letter* commented:

The true doctrine of most states is to scold bitterly, then scramble for the spoils. A man who is offered a bribe does all that is required of him by the fashionable system of ethics if he denounces bribery in good set terms while pocketing the bribe.

The surplus was supposed to promote the public welfare, but it soon plunged the young nation—and New Hampshire, to a degree —into economic chaos. Fiscal panic erupted in October; government revenue declined; and distribution of the fourth installment was cancelled. Some states had inflated their economy by launching massive public works projects or by distributing the cash among their citizens on a personal basis, thus giving false impetus to purchasing power.

Whatever the guise, time has shown there was but slight sincere intent that the states ever repay their largesse. Congress soon transferred the reimbursement authority from the Secretary of the Treasury to itself and has never invoked it. And by 1841 the Legislature had repealed restrictions on the allotments to the towns and allowed them to spend the principal without restraints.

Treasurer Clement ran the gamut of two legislative probes for handling the giant cash gift. He claimed that interest earned from the fund while it was briefly in his custody belong to him by right of custom. He argued before legislative committees that in 1812 Treasurer William A. Kent of Concord was permitted $180 for handling $36,000 for construction of the State Prison. He also cited that when the State House was built, former Secretary of State Albe Cady of Concord was granted 1 percent of the $64,000 in his charge for that project. Finally, Clement contended, Treasurer Samuel Morrill collected a $74.38 interest allowance in 1828 from a $55,000 literary fund allotment turned over to him for distribution to the towns.

Treasurer Clement won his point, but it also resulted in a fresh state fiscal policy. The Legislature agreed he was entitled to $678.72 of interest, along with $38.97 as interest from the interest, because reimbursements were delayed until the 1838 legislative session. Then the General Court ordered termination of the interest-retention custom and said earnings from state funds should henceforth accrue to the state; they have done so ever since.

What the towns did with their allotments remains scattered through their records. Dublin purchased a poor farm; Newington repaired a church; Francestown put its share into roads; and Portsmouth distributed most of its lion's share among taxpayers.

Half a century later, Treasurer Solon A. Carter of Concord told the Legislature it could forget the $669,086 it received from Washington. He disclosed in his 1894 report that all records of the transactions with the towns had disappeared, probably by intent. Carter said only $1,009.44 of the principal, along with $2,257.57 of interest, remained in the State Treasury and recommended it be dumped into the general

Highlights of the Early 1800s

fund and the account closed. The Legislature did so.

In 1966 Comptroller Arthur Levitt of New York resurrected the ghost of the Great Surplus of 1836. He suggested Congress should demand its return or vote never to do so, to wipe this dormant item off New York's slate. Levitt boasted that the Empire State had kept its allotment intact at the state level. A bill to abolish the "deposite" was filed in Congress for Levitt, but nothing came of it.

The Levitt ploy claimed the attention of New Hampshire's Congressional delegation. But so far as the General Court is concerned, it remains on record as opposed to any federal forgiveness. It resolved on January 13, 1837, even as it parcelled the surplus funds to the towns, to request the Granite State's members of Congress to firmly oppose "the alteration or change of the laws now existing regulating the deposite of public monies so as to distribute or relinquish the repayment of the same."

Time often alters legislative policy—as it does much of the modes of men and their minds. Over the past forty years, federal fiscal support of state Legislatures and their governments has become a major source of their dependence. National grants and matching funds have developed into a major portion of New Hampshire's General Court budgets, and the trend continues to increase. And the qualms of 1836 continue as well.

New Hampshire has joined other states in recent years in revolt against the insidiousness of such dependency upon the federal establishment because the fears of the 1836 episode have materialized. The national government has increasingly dictated and imposed rules and restrictions upon state affairs, to obtain this largesse. Because of this manipulated infringement upon the sovereignty of the Legislature, it has joined its sister counterparts in striving to shed the federal strings while yet continuing to enjoy the national fiscal favors.

Recently retired Senator Norris Cotton of Lebanon pioneered a Congressional proposal for distribution of federal cigarette taxes back to the states, without customary use restrictions. He argued, in vain, that Congress should not dictate state conduct, even in return for needed federal fiscal support. Former Governor Lane Dwinell, also of Lebanon, joined in support of this fresh concept of federal aid, in 1957, as chairman of a National Governors' Conference committee to study federal-state relations. This group recommended outright "block" distribution of federal funds to the states, free from all spending qualifications. This has come to pass recently, but still in modified form. The bulk of federal aid, especially for education, highways, and public welfare, remains firmly tied to rigid operating formulas which are both cumbersome and excessively costly to observe.

Colby Snags the Governorship

A POLITICAL UPHEAVAL featured the General Court's 1846 session, following a bitter split in New Hampshire's long dominant Democratic party over the slavery question.

As a result, Anthony Colby of New London became the Whigs' only Governor in the state's history, and John Parker Hale of Dover, expelled from the Democratic party for defying the Legislature, went to Washington as the nation's first antislavery United States Senator.

The Democrats thus lost control of the Legislature for the first time in a quarter of a century because of their summary treatment of Hale a year earlier, while he was serving a second term in Congress. The 1844 Legislature had voted to instruct Hale to vote for the annexation of Texas as a slave state, and in January 1845 he shocked the state with defiant repudiation of that edict. Congressman Hale issued a statement saying that it was morally wrong to extend slavery into any new state and that he would so vote.

Chairman Franklin Pierce of the Democratic State Committee immediately called a special convention for February 12, at which Hale was officially read out of the party and his third term nomination was withdrawn. Ten days later, on February 22, the Independent Democrats' party was organized by Attorneys Amos Tuck of Exeter and John L. Hayes of Portsmouth and rallied its new banner around Hale.

Hale was among a small bloc of Independent Democrats elected to the 1846 Legislature, along with a few others of the Free Soil label, and they joined with the minority Whig legislators in taking control of the session.

The 1846 gubernatorial election was thrown into the Legislature because none of the three major candidates, including Colby, mustered a majority of all votes cast, which was a constitutional requirement up to 1914, when the plurality rule went into effect. Democrat Jared W. Williams of Lancaster led the field with 26,740 votes, or 48 percent of the total. Colby received 17,707 votes for 32 percent, while Free Soiler Nathaniel S. Berry of Hebron polled 10,379 votes, and there were 568 scattered votes.

When the Legislature convened on June 3, the political trading was

Anthony Colby

launched, and Hale was elected House Speaker by 139 to 118 over Democrat Samuel Swasey of Haverhill. Then a joint session of the House and Senate elected Colby as Governor by a 146 to 124 vote over Williams.

Besides trading with each other, the coalition of House minority groups also had to deal with the Senate, still controlled by the Democrats, on the key issue of filling a vacancy in the United States Senate, caused when Levi Woodbury of Portsmouth resigned on November 20, 1845, to accept appointment to the United States Supreme Court. So the Senate was permitted to choose a Democrat to fill the remaining eight months of that term, upon agreement to support Hale for the ensuing six-year term starting on March 3, 1847. This pact was necessary on Hale's behalf, because each branch voted separately on election of United States Senators in those years. Both branches approved the Hale appointment to the Senate on June 9, and three days later Democrat Joseph Cilley, prominent Nottingham farmer, was given the short-term seat.

The fifty-six-year-old Governor Colby chalked up a vigorous administration, with the support of Speaker Hale and his influence with the Democratic State Senate. He was no novice, having become a longtime spokesman for the Whig party during seven terms in the

Legislature and three previous nominations for Governor.

Colby sponsored a law dividing the state into Congressional districts for the first time. New Hampshire was entitled to four seats in the Congress, and the Whigs had for years vainly argued for this division, so they might win a Congressional election in the seacoast area, where they were strongest. As a result of the 1846 law creating four Congressional districts, Amos Tuck promptly won three terms in the national House of Representatives.

Governor Colby also clipped the Democrats on another front. He told the Legislature that it should publish the annual session laws in all the newspapers and not just those of Democratic persuasion, as had been the custom for some years. He put the issue in this manner:

Each citizen is bound to obey the laws, and should have an opportunity to learn what they are, with the least possible trouble or expense to himself, after paying his proportion of the expense for making them.

No one should be compelled to take a newspaper in which he has no confidence, and any party in power which will refuse such equitable distribution, when they speak of their democracy and love of equal rights should speak softly.

Whig Governor Colby was outspoken on the brewing slavery question. He said in his legislative inaugural address:

Texas has been annexed by the United States for no higher object than to perpetuate an institution which degrades the human race and dishonors the God of Heaven. . . .

If Congress have not the constitutional right to abolish slavery in the District of Columbia, it would look better for them to remove the seat of government to some free state.

Colby, founder of what is now Colby-Sawyer College, at New London, helped pioneer state supervision over public education. The 1846 Legislature created the office of Commissioner of Common Schools, with the primary function of visiting each school district annually and reporting his findings to the General Court. This agency, first filled by Professor Charles B. Haddock of Dartmouth College, a nephew of Daniel Webster, developed by stages into the present State Board of Education.

Governor Colby lost a reelection bid in 1847, when the Democrats regained control of the Legislature, and Speaker Hale went to Washington to become such a noted antislavery Senator that nearly fifty years later his statue was erected in the State House yard. Through the ensuing years, Colby took delight in observing that he had accomplished so much in his lone year as Governor that the voters did not think he had to be reelected to equal his predecessors' achievements.

There was yet another distinction to Governor Colby's coalition administration of 1846. The House of Representatives contained sixteen Samuels; another was on the Executive Council; and then Samuel F. Wetmore of Concord was Deputy Secretary of State. The Councilor was Samuel Jones of Bedford, and the House Samuels included Swasey of Haverhill, defeated for Speaker. The other House Samuels were Noyes of Atkinson, Anderson of Auburn, Webster of Kingston, Hart of Newington, Cleaves of Portsmouth, Wentworth of Somersworth, Butterfield of Andover, Ayer of Hillsborough, Smith of Manchester, Nay of Sharon, Patridge of Chesterfield, Burnham of Goshen, Garfield of Langdon, Stevens of Bristol, and Peavey of Landaff.

A member of the 1849 House conducted an unusual survey, of historic value. When fear was expressed in a published statement that "professional gentlemen had an undue proportion of influence in the Legislature," the Reverend David Page of New Boston, a new legislator, compiled the following, as printed in the 1850 *New Hampshire Register:*

Executive Council—One tanner-currier and four farmers. Senate—Two lawyers, two merchants and eight farmers. House—One each of tanner-currier, school teacher, sea captain, lumber dealer, stable keeper, stage proprietor, bookbinder, ticket master, drover, brickmaster and Register of Probate; also three iron founders, two taverners, three printers, six deputy sheriffs, five physicians, twelve manufacturers, twenty-four merchants, twenty-five mechanics, nine clergymen, thirteen lawyers and one hundred and sixty-one farmers.

THE CRITICAL 1850s

Pierce Becomes President

THE DEMOCRATS continued to dominate the Legislature as New Hampshire swung into the second half of the 1800s. Their party chieftain, Franklin Pierce, fresh from service in the Mexican War, with rank of Brigadier General, won added prestige as President of the 1850 Constitutional Convention, and then became President of the United States in the 1852 national election. But the Democrats' reign was terminated soon thereafter in a realignment of political forces which gave birth to New Hampshire's Republican party in 1857.

Convention President Pierce was joined by former Governor Levi Woodbury of Portsmouth, then a member of the United States Supreme Court, in sparking an impressive array of amendment proposals. The convention recommended abolition of the Executive Council (the only time this proposal has ever faced a popular referendum) and of the religious and property qualifications for voting or holding state office. It also proposed reorganization of the General Court and popular election of certain state and county officials.

The voters resoundingly rebuffed these proposed constitutional amendments. The wholesale rejection was so shocking that Governor Samuel Dinsmoor, Jr., of Keene observed before the 1851 Legislature:

This popular reception of the amendments . . . is a remarkable incident in our history. Considering the character of that very respectable body (the convention), composed it was known to have been, of the most able and

135

*distinguished representatives of the various classes, occupations and in-
terests in the state, and enjoying, perhaps, in as high degree as any former
political assembly in New Hampshire, the confidence of their constituents,
it was not to have been anticipated that they would be so unfortunate in
apprehending the wishes of the people as to fail in securing their acceptance of even one of the numerous amendments submitted for their approval.*

But the Pierce and Woodbury leadership persevered. It successfully pressed for reconvening of the convention, out of which but
three amendments were resubmitted to the people. They called for
removal of both the ban on Catholics holding state office and of the
property qualification for holding state office, and they called for
giving the Legislature authority to propose constitutional amendments. Only the property qualification removal won approval, following which Judge Woodbury observed that it had not been enforced for
several years.

The Democrats became so happy when Franklin Pierce was suddenly nominated for President in June 1852, at a stalemated Democratic national convention at Baltimore, that they erected in the State
House yard what is believed to have been the tallest flagpole ever to
grace New Hampshire.

Admirers hauled two huge pine trees from the Dunbarton farm of
Democrat James Stone to Concord, to be spliced into a "Liberty Pole"
which rose 143 feet into the sky. This was slightly higher than the
Capitol's "Eagle" was then perched. First flown from it was a pennant
with the names of Pierce and United States Senator William Rufus
King of Alabama, his Vice Presidential running mate.

The main mast of the towering Pierce tribute was 93 feet long, and
the top pole measured 64 feet in length. There was a 5-foot splice, and
the bottom pole was sunk 9 feet into the ground, in a reinforced hole.
Ten yoke of oxen hauled each timber to the site for an August 12
dedication ceremony. A severe snowstorm on December 28, 1866,
shattered the upper half of the giant flagstaff, from which the American flag had been flown since 1853. Soon thereafter it was removed,
and the Legislature voted to fly the national emblem from the State
House roof, a custom that continues to this day.

The Know Nothing Party

A SECRET POLITICAL ORGANIZATION won control of the General Court in 1855, and it gave birth to New Hampshire's present Republican party two years later. It was a conglomerate of Whigs, Free Soilers, antislavery Democrats, and prohibitionists that engineered this coup under the banner of the short-lived American National party, better known as the "Know Nothings." This political phenomenon was based in the secret lodges of the oath-bound Order of the Star Spangled Banner, which spread through the nation in the early 1850s, in opposition to the influx of Catholic immigrants from Europe, to slavery, and to liquor. It flourished in varying degrees through the country. Members were instructed to say "I know nothing" when questioned about their affiliation or objectives.

The Know Nothings gained control of the Massachusetts government in 1854, and had mustered sufficient influence in the Granite State's Legislature to block the long-entrenched Democrats from filling two United States Senate seats in the June session of that year. By December 1854, it was recorded that the Know Nothings had 249 lodges through the state, based within local school districts; and early in 1855 leaders of the various anti-Democratic factions sponsored a Manchester convention, which produced a full slate of successful Know Nothing candidates for the March annual election. Attorney Ralph Metcalf of Newport, fifty-six-year-old former eight-term Democrat Secretary of State from Concord, was nominated for Governor. The coalition party's Congressional nominees in the state's then three districts were James Pike of Newfields, Mason W. Tappan of Bradford, and Aaron H. Cragin of Lebanon.

Metcalf and his fellow nominees campaigned primarily against the extension of slavery into new states and they were swept into office by substantial majorities. The new "American Party," as it was officially called, also captured control of both branches of the Legislature. Governor Metcalf reflected the Know Nothings' objectives in his inaugural address to the Legislature. He recommended a strong prohibition law and curbs on citizenship rights for foreigners. He emphasized in part:

The great influx of foreigners to this country has, of late, become a matter of deep interest and alarming anxiety to the people. . . . At this time, half a million aliens, most of them, we regret to say, ignorant and uneducated, are annually added to our numbers.

The religion which they have been taught from their birth, which has "grown with their growth and strengthened with their strength," is a religion acknowledging a foreign power for its supreme head, teaching and requiring its adherents to passively submit their consciences to the keeping of the priesthood, to seek no higher sources of spiritual instruction and consolation than that order; a religion that excludes the Bible from the common people, and allows its subjects to owe no allegiance, spiritual or temporal, to any power but what the sovereign Pontiff, may, at any time, and upon any emergency, annul and dissolve; a religion that pronounces all creeds heresy but their own, and boldly avows that it "nourishes most when watered by the blood of all heretics."

Metcalf also minced no words about liquor. He told the legislators:

For years past, the traffic in spirituous liquors has been felt by nearly all, and conceded by a great majority of the people of the state, to be an alarming evil.

No offense punishable by our laws, short of a capital crime, spreads so vast a desolation or inflicts such overwhelming misery upon a community, as the sale and use of intoxicating drinks.

Larceny, forgery, counterfeiting and their kindred crimes are limited in their operations, and trifling in their consequences, when compared with those resulting from the sale of spirituous liquors.

Governor Metcalf also recommended that the Legislature restore subsidies for agricultural societies to promote farming and to require the towns to furnish free books in the public schools, but these two suggestions were not approved.

The Know Nothing Legislature readily enacted a strong prohibition statute, which remained in force for nearly half a century, and plagued many following sessions because local communities failed to enforce it, owing to lack of popular support. Interestingly, this law did not include hard cider, nor did it prohibit the manufacture of intoxicating beverages, so Portsmouth's beer industry flourished into national dimensions.

The Legislature in 1855 approved two unusual resolutions. One called upon the Congress to deny citizenship for aliens until after at least ten, or up to twenty-one, years of residency. The other expressed disdain of secession threats by the slave states, as follows:

Resolved, that all threats of dissolution of the Union coming from the slave states, unless they are allowed to regulate the policy of the general government, on the subject of slavery, have lost their terrors with the people of New Hampshire.

The freewheeling Know Nothings reorganized the judiciary, to oust all the Democratic Judges, sheriffs, and other personnel of the courts. They also reshuffled the twelve state Senate districts, to reduce Democratic membership in that chamber. These political gambits were led by John J. Prentiss of Claremont as House Speaker and William Haile of Hinsdale as Senate President.

The two United States Senate seats which became stalemated in the 1854 session were filled by the Know Nothings. One went to former Senator Hale of Dover, who sparked the 1846 revolt against the Democrats. The other went to James Bell of Gilford, thrice unsuccessful Whig candidate for Governor.

Governor Metcalf stood for reelection in the 1856 March election and got more votes than Democrat John S. Wells of Exeter, but failed of a majority. Thus, the choice was dumped into the Legislature, where Metcalf nosed out Wells by a scant 25 votes for a second and final term.

The American Party meanwhile lost its national image because of sectional disputes and disappeared into history, even as the New Hampshire Know Nothings continued to run the Legislature for a second year. Youthful Concord druggist Edward H. Rollins, who had acquired behind-the-scenes repute as an organizer of the secret Know Nothing lodges, maneuvered himself into the 1856 House Speakership over Prentiss, who sought reelection, and then helped develop the newborn Republican party the following year.

Birth of Republicanism

BIRTH OF NEW HAMPSHIRE'S Republican party followed more than a year of incubation. Editor George G. Fogg of Concord's *Independent Democrat* weekly was liaison man in the inception. He became secretary of a national antislavery conference at Pittsburgh in February 1856, which sponsored the June 17 national convention at

Edward H. Rollins

Philadelphia, where the Republican party assumed national form and nominated Gen. John C. Fremont for President.

New Hampshire sent fifteen delegates to the Philadelphia session, chosen at a May 10 Concord rally. But Governor Metcalf and Speaker Rollins avoided this development, to safeguard their narrow legislative majority. Not a single Know Nothing legislator joined the delegation, headed by Editor Fogg and former Congressman Amos Tuck, the Exeter Free Soiler.

Speaker Rollins sparked support for Fremont, following his June 19 nomination, with a novel political maneuver designed to minimize possible disruption of the Know Nothings' control of the state government. He organized the Fremont Club No. 1 of Concord, with himself as president, and sponsored dozens of similar Fremont campaign committees through the state. By this device, Rollins and his coalition associates campaigned as "Fremonters," while carefully skirting identification with the new Republican label to avoid possible alienation of some of the Know Nothing factions.

This unusual campaign proved highly successful and established Speaker Rollins as a sagacious political chieftain for many years to follow. He conducted an unprecedented canvass and announced that

Fremont would carry the state by 6,000 votes and hand the Granite State Democrats their first Presidential campaign loss in 32 years. Fremont won by 5,700 out of a total vote of nearly 70,000 votes, and Rollins gained wide prominence from his forecast.

Historian James O. Lyford of Concord detailed the official founding of New Hampshire's Republican party in 1857 in his 1906 biography of Edward H. Rollins. This volume includes the first half-century of the party's life. It sprang from a Concord convention on January 8, 1857, at which a forty-five-man Republican State Committee was formed, with Speaker Rollins as chairman and Attorney Sylvester Dana of Concord as secretary. Nine of Rollins's 1856 House associates were on this pioneer committee. They were Thomas L. Tullock of Portsmouth, James M. Lovering of Exeter, M.C. Burleigh of Somersworth, Richard N. Ross of Dover, J.P. Morrison of Gilford, Charles H. Campbell of Amherst, Daniel McCaine of Francestown, George S. Towle of Lebanon, and former Speaker Prentiss of Claremont.

Two legislators vied for the initial 1857 Republican gubernatorial nomination. They were William Haile, the Hinsdale manufacturer and 1855 Senate President, and Ichabod Goodwin, Portsmouth import merchant. Haile topped Goodwin on the first ballot by 181 to 130, but seventeen others shared 136 convention votes, so it was not until a third roll call that Haile won majority approval. The delegates also nominated the three incumbent Know Nothing Congressmen, Pike, Tappan, and Cragin, for second terms.

The Republican slate swept to victory in the March 10 annual election, as Haile buried Democrat John S. Wells of Exeter by a vote of 34,474 to 31,235. When the Legislature convened on June 3, it showed an overwhelming change in membership. The twelve-member Senate comprised eight new members and was two-thirds Republican. The House became Republican, 194 to 126, with 189 new members, or 59 percent of the total.

Young Rollins was reelected Speaker without opposition, and Moody Currier, Manchester banker, became Senate President. In his inaugural address, Governor Haile reaffirmed the popular Know Nothing stands against slavery and liquor, and for more stringent citizenship qualifications for aliens.

This first Republican General Court launched a public economy policy and improved its toilet facilities. The House created a Committee on Retrenchment and Reform, and the forty-year-old outdoor water closet facilities were transferred into the State House basement.

The 1857 Legislature celebrated its Republican birth by voting $300 to implement the following law:

Chapter 2000—That the Governor and Council are hereby authorized to appoint some suitable person to remove and dispose of the building immediately south of the State House, now used as water closets, and belonging to the state, and to make and furnish, under the direction of the Governor and Council, in the basement of the State House, water closets suitable for the proper accommodation of the state, and to pay into the state treasury the proceeds from the sale of said building.

By the spring of 1881, steam-heating apparatus had been installed in the Capitol basement, and a Concord newspaper reported that bathtubs were among the new fixtures. Then the 1883 Legislature voted $3,000 as follows:

For the purpose of removing the water closets and urinals in the basement of the State House to a more convenient place in the basement; for increasing the number of water closets and urinals, and for proper draining, trapping and ventilating of the same.

New Hampshire's Legislature devoted considerable time through the Civil War years of 1861 to 1865 to its own affairs, even as it joined with Governors in providing funds and manpower to help win that conflict. As Governor Nathaniel S. Berry of Hebron sparked enlistments of 15,000 men, and personally signed 700 officers' commissions in the first two war years, the legislators authorized bounty payments to enlistees and voted bond issues of $994,000 to support their service.

State House facilities became center of wartime projects. Concord's weekly *New Hampshire Statesman* reported in August 1861:

Ladies of the Soldiers Aid Society have undertaken to sew for the Third Regiment 2,000 pairs of shirts and drawers. Every week day afternoon the members of the Society in this city assemble in the Senate Chamber to cut and prepare the garments. Portions are sent to other towns of the state for completion.

In September 1861, Concord printer Edward E. Sturtevant personally pitched a recruiting tent in the State House yard and lived in it while he signed up soldiers. Then he went to war with them, rose to the rank of Major, died in battle, and was buried in an unmarked grave. After the Concord Post of the Grand Army of the Republic was named in Sturtevant's honor, the 1883 Legislature voted to permit Concord citizens to hang his portrait in the State House, where it still remains.

The 1862 Legislature enacted the state's most unusual lottery of all time. It was devoted to assignment of seats in the House of Representatives as each session convened. (Details of the colorful origin and operation of this lottery through the ensuing ninety years are related in Chapter XVII.)

Retrenchment and Reform

THE HOUSE COMMITTEE on Retrenchment and Reform became a Republican party symbol for half a century, during which it conducted two successful studies of State House personnel costs. The 1864 House ordered the committee to make a first such study in New Hampshire history for the following purpose:

To ascertain and report to the House the number of clerks and other persons, not regular officers of the state, that have been employed in the various departments of the state government, the nature of the services rendered, and the compensation paid to each.

Following a three-week survey, the Retrenchment and Reform Committee reported that the Governor and the Council, and three agencies then operating in the State House, employed a total of four full-time and three part-time clerks, and that their compensation was merited. The Governor and the Council employed a combination doorkeeper-messenger for $300 a year, with a substitute paid $89.50 for the past year, while a military aide dealing with wartime bonus payments and similar things was paid $655 over the previous year, including travel expenses.

The Secretary of State employed one part-time clerk, at an annual cost of $112; the State Treasurer employed two clerks at $2 per day, and the Adjutant General had two full-time clerks, the pay of which had not yet been set by the Legislature.

Orren Perkins of Winchester was in charge of this pioneer survey, as chairman of the Retrenchment and Reform Committee. The nine other committee members were Eliphalet R. Sargent of Dunbarton, John U. Davis of New Ipswich, Asa Thurston of Lyme, Moulton Knowles of Manchester, Henry A. Yeaton of Portsmouth, David L.

Main Street, Concord in the 1860s. The John Stevens store at the right, in which constitutional conventions of the Revolutionary period were held in an upstairs hall, was moved in 1858 to make way for the Masonic block shown in the center.
Courtesy Mrs. Carl Gesen.

Warren of Moultonborough, Benjamin F. Taylor of Effingham, Joseph M. Chapin of Gilsum, and John P. Colby of Warner.

The Retrenchment and Reform Committee conducted a second survey of State House personnel in 1907. This study developed into the most dramatic episode of its kind in legislative history. (See Chapter XVIII.) But, by way of comparison, the three State House agencies of 1864 had grown to nine in 1907. They then included the State Library (in an adjacent building), a Board of Health, a Board of Agriculture, a Bureau of Labor, a Public Printing Commission, and the Attorney General's agency. Seventy years after its inception, the 1927 House abolished the Retrenchment and Reform Committee as outmoded and obsolete.

New Hampshire's Legislature is no more perfect than the people who constitute it. When the summer session of 1864 drew to a close, it jumped the chapter number of new statutes from 3,099 to 4,000, and no one detected the error until long after the legislators had adjourned and the new laws were printed. This hop over 900 numerals remains a part of legislative records to this day, which show Chapter 3099 listed ahead of 4000 even though the latter became effective four days prior to the former.

Chapter 3099 read as follows:

That the sum of one hundred twenty-nine dollars and fifty cents ($129.50), be allowed Stephen Smith & Co.; that one hundred twenty-five dollars ($125.00) be allowed Thomas Groom & Co.; that one hundred five dollars and fifty cents ($105.50) be allowed Cheney & Co.; and that twenty-five dollars ($25.00) be allowed Uriel L. Comings, and that the same be paid out of any money in the treasury not otherwise appropriated, and that the governor is hereby authorized to draw his warrant therefor.
Approved July 16, 1864.

Chapter 4000 read as follows:

That Parker Blood be allowed the sum of forty-four dollars and eighty-seven cents ($44.87) in full of expenses incurred by him in the Groton contested election case; that the same be paid out of any money in the treasury not otherwise appropriated, and the governor is hereby authorized to draw his warrant therefor.
Approved July 12, 1864.

The 1864 Legislature ran into a surprise special session on August 9, less than a month following a hectic annual summer session. The legislators were called back to Concord by Governor Joseph A. Gilmore, the rough-and-tough Concord Railroad superintendent, upon whom they had imposed restraints in the regular session. This second special session erupted into what have become considered the noisiest and nastiest legislative deliberations in New Hampshire history. (See Chapter XV.)

Governor Gilmore, a native of Weston, Vermont, died two years later at fifty-five, following a long illness. He came to Concord in 1842, when the railroad arrived, and became a wholesale grocer. He became a railroad official six years later.

The State House was doubled in size in 1865, by vote of the 1864 Legislature. There were prolonged and colorful arguments over the enlargement, as Manchester battled to move the Capital to that city. (See Chapter XX.)

The 1869 Legislature approved a State Police agency, subject to a rare referendum ratification. It was to comprise a $1,500 constable, with not more than twenty deputies at $3 per diem, and not more than five in any county. Prohibition forces urged approval of the measure to help curb illicit liquor sales, which flourished in many towns despite the 1855 prohibition law. But it was killed by a 13,812 to 6,031 vote in special November 8, 1869, balloting.

TWO DECADES OF TENSIONS

Blizzard of Roll Calls

A BLIZZARD OF ROLL CALLS engulfed the 1871 General Court as the state government became Democratic by the closest vote in history. The March election was so tight that it failed to produce a majority vote for Governor, so the choice automatically went into the Legislature, resulting in the most amazing political situation ever recorded in New Hampshire. When the session convened on June 7, the House of Representatives was listed with a Democratic majority of 1, or 165 to 164 over the Republicans. And the Senate stood deadlocked, 5 to 5, with two vacancies to be filled by the Legislature in joint voting.

James A. Weston, Manchester's popular Democratic mayor, had come within 112 votes of winning the March gubernatorial contest over James Pike of Dover, his Republican opponent. Weston's total vote was 34,799 to 33,892 for Pike. But 1,132 ballots were cast for other candidates, so Weston failed by 112 votes to win the required majority of 34,912.

All concerned agreed the outcome of the pending legislative balloting was virtually anyone's guess. While the Democrats admittedly had a one-vote edge in the House, their 165-vote majority included twelve members who had been elected on Labor Reform tickets, but jointly declared themselves for Weston for Governor. The Republican leadership held hope this coalition might be breached to swing two or more votes and win the showdown.

The welcome arch which greeted Onslow Stearns of Concord when he became Governor in June of 1869. The then new iron posts were installed at the entrance to all State House walks to bar peddlers and auctioneers with their carts and wares from the premises.

As Clerk Josiah H. Benton, Jr., of the previous House, called the June 7 opening to order, the Democrats nominated William H. Gove, Weare Quaker, for Speaker, against Republican James O. Adams of Manchester. This occurred shortly after it became known that two Republicans, Kendall C. Scott of Keene and Thomas F. Johnson of Pittsburg, were absent because of illness.

Gove became Speaker by a 164 to 162 roll call vote, and this was followed by a sensational series of thirty more roll calls through three hectic days and an all-night session. It was not until Saturday, the fourth day of the session, that the Legislature finally elected Weston as Governor by a 167 to 159 roll call. As a result, while Governors traditionally took office on the second day of a session, Weston's inauguration had to be postponed until the following Wednesday.

The thirty ensuing roll calls through Wednesday, Thursday, Friday, and into Saturday morning concerned House organization details only and are without equal in General Court annals.

With Attorney Harry Bingham of Littleton, the Democratic legislative patriarch, engineering his party's maneuvers, he proposed that James R. Jackson of Littleton and James H. Colbath of Barnstead be jointly elected clerk and assistant clerk, respectively. Republican Asa Fowler of Concord demanded an amendment to vote for clerk by secret ballot, won out on a 160 to 159 roll call, and then bowed in defeat as Speaker Gove voted to create a losing deadlock vote of 160 to 160.

149

The Republicans next proposed to substitute the name of Clerk Benton of Lancaster for reelection, and this was lost, 162 to 161. They next moved that the two clerical positions be voted upon separately; this was downed on a 164 to 161 roll call. A following motion to table the entire question was defeated by a 165 to 160 roll call.

The Republicans raised a point of order against Bingham's proposed combination election and when Speaker Gove ruled the question out of order, Fowler and Bainbridge Wadleigh of Milford demanded a vote of confidence. While Speaker Gove pondered that gambit, Fowler moved for adjournment and lost out on a 163 to 163 deadlock roll call.

The Fowler-Wadleigh challenge of Speaker Gove's ruling went to a roll call vote and carried by a surprising vote of 164 to 162. This rebuff proved so disconcerting to the Democrats that when Republican George A. Cummings of Concord moved for adjournment late in the afternoon, he prevailed by a 163 to 149 roll call. Drama continued through Thursday, as the deadlocked Senate, having agreed upon compromise temporary officers, waited patiently for the House to organize so it could join in election of a Governor and filling its two vacancies in joint session.

When the Thursday session opened, Bingham unloaded a bombshell. He disclosed that the previous afternoon's 164 to 162 repudiation of Speaker Gove's ruling had been a mistake. Republican Clerk Benton told the House that Bingham was correct. He explained that roll call had been tallied by his holdover assistant, Samuel Clark of Gilford, aided by Republican Representative William H. Hackett of Portsmouth, in error, the vote actually being 162 to 154. So the record was changed to erase the rebuff of the Speaker. Then, at Bingham's suggestion, Hackett and Democrat Samuel B. Page of Concord were formally appointed as roll call aides to Clerk Benton.

Clerk Benton next injected an unusual note to the proceedings by asking Speaker Gove to order the lottery drawing for seats so that scores of unidentified occupants of House seats could be ousted from

Two Decades of Tensions

the chamber. He explained that, because identities were difficult to challenge, dozens of the new lawmakers had been forced to stand around the hall through the long hours of the opening day to obtain seats.

No sooner was the lottery ordered than Republican George A. Cummings of Concord challenged the drawing. He submitted evidence proving that duplicate numbers for some of the choice seats had been distributed before the draw, and Speaker Gove declared the proceedings null and void. Bingham next moved the seating lottery be set over to Friday afternoon. Wadleigh offered an amendment to advance the drawing to Thursday afternoon, but he lost a roll call test, 164 to 162. Republican George A. Ramsdell of Nashua moved to table this Bingham motion, which was denied on a 163 to 161 roll call, after which a luncheon recess was taken.

As the afternoon session opened, Bingham withdrew his motion and the seat drawing was held. Then the proposed election of a Democratic clerk and his aide was taken up, only to run into another Republican challenge. On the question of putting the election to a vote, there ensued a 163 to 163 deadlock roll call, but the Republicans lost out once again, as Speaker Gove voted in the affirmative to make it 164 to 163. Meanwhile, Bingham had agreed to separate votes for the two House aides. Jackson was elected clerk by a 164 to 162 roll call, and Colbath became his assistant by a 163 to 162 roll call.

The Democratic candidates for the other four House positions were next elected on voice votes, after which the session was adjourned to Friday morning. They were Alonzo J. Fogg of Concord, sergeant-at-arms, and doorkeepers Lorenzo Frost of Hampstead, William Yeaton of Pittsfield, and Samuel D. Robinson of Pembroke.

The Friday House session became grimmer than ever. The Republicans launched a last-ditch drive to delay the proceedings over the weekend in hopes that perhaps one or both of their sick members, Scott of Keene and Johnson of Pittsburg, might show up for the second week, beginning the following Tuesday.

As the Democratic leadership prepared to notify the Senate that the House had organized and was ready to sit in joint session for election of a Governor and filling the two vacant Senate seats, Wadleigh moved that three Democratic members be disqualified for various reasons. They were Page of Concord, William W. Messer of Northwood, and William M. Parsons of Bennington. Bingham countered with a motion to substitute the names of Republicans James O. Adams, David B. Varney, Atherton W. Quint, and Hiram K. Slayton, all of Ward 3, Manchester. Democrat George F. Putnam of Warren moved to add the names of Republicans Nathan Whipple of Lisbon, Orren LeBarron of Hill, and Converse Gage of Sutton.

Considerable time was spent arguing the merits of these proposed disqualifications, and Pillsbury then called for adjournment until Monday at 3:00 P.M. He lost on a 163 to 161 roll call, and a recess for lunch followed.

When the House resumed its deliberations on Friday afternoon at three o'clock, Bingham called for action on his pending disqualification of several Republican members and never got it until the next morning. The Republicans launched such a barrage of roll calls that the session continued through the night, in a vain effort to delay filling the Governorship and the two key Senate vacancies until the following week.

After several motions to adjourn or table the Bingham motion had been defeated by close votes, the Republicans developed a new delaying tactic. Various members asked to be excused from voting on the Bingham gambit, claiming they were not acquainted with its merits, and following debate, each such incident wound up in a losing roll call. As the night wore on, the roll calls reflected that more and more members had left and gone to bed. One roll call about midnight totalled 153 to 93, but they picked up somewhat in the early dark hours of Saturday.

Shortly after dawn on Saturday, Wadleigh lost yet another motion to adjourn, this time by a 144 to 128 roll call; on another roll call the main question was put by Speaker Gove, on a 148 to 123 vote; and then the Bingham resolution, with the Putnam amendment, was

Harry Bingham

Two Decades of Tensions

adopted by a 147 to 121 roll call. Then the House recessed at 7:25 A.M. for a breakfast break, to reconvene at 10:00 A.M. Bingham's successful challenge of the qualifications of the Republican legislators was subsequently referred to the House Judiciary Committee and became pigeonholed.

The Senate, meanwhile, had also been beset by unusual organization pangs. The deadlocked ten members had agreed on the opening day upon Republican Charles H. Campbell of Nashua as temporary presiding officer, and then named a committee to report on details of the two vacant seats. It did no business on Thursday, and when the Senate convened on Friday morning, its five Republican members pressed time-consuming delaying maneuvers, like their House colleagues.

Friday's Senate controversy at first centered on the wording of the committee report on the two empty seats and on how it was to be submitted to a joint session for final determination. After two 5 to 5 deadlock votes on that issue, the Senate took a twenty-minute recess. This was followed by five more recesses up to nine o'clock that evening. Next, when the Republicans lost an adjournment motion, and it was twenty minutes after midnight, the Senate agreed to adjournment to nine o'clock that morning.

When the House and Senate finally met in joint session on Saturday morning, the Democrats prevailed on all votes as the Republicans desisted from further procrastinating. Weston became Governor over Pike by a tight 167 to 159 roll call, receiving but 3 more votes than required for election. The two Senate vacancies were filled by Democrats, along with one of the five Council seats, which had not been occupied for lack of a majority candidate.

When the Senate returned to its chamber, Attorney George W.M. Pitman of Bartlett became President, along with a Democratic staff. Pitman was then in his second Senate term, following twelve House terms.

When the Legislature opened its second week of business, Speaker Gove disclosed rewards for the dozen Labor Reform members for their firm support of the Democratic candidates in the hectic first week. Four of them won committee chairmanships. John C. Tucker of Pittsfield, chairman of the Labor Reform bloc, headed the Committee on Insurance; Horace B. Sawyer of Hampstead, clerk of the reform group, got the Military Affairs chairmanship; James Thompson of Bow chaired the Committee on State House and State House Yard;

and Leander W. Cogswell of Henniker headed the powerful Committee on Railroads. The other Labor Reform members were Nathan Nutter and R.B. Wentworth of Rochester, James D. Sanborn of Pittsfield, Daniel E. Tuttle of Barnstead, Daniel B. Austin of Goffstown, Winfield S. Meserve of Danville, John Sanders of Strafford, and Herbert B. Viall of Charlestown.

No sooner had Governor Weston been sworn in than Chairman Tucker won House adoption of the following resolution:

Whereas, we are credibly informed that it has been the usual custom of the Sergeant-at-Arms to give members large quantities of stationery for their individual use;—and

Whereas we are opposed to such schemes of pilfering, therefore be it

Resolved, that the Sergeant-at-Arms be instructed to give the members of this House only such amounts of stationery as are needed for their use while attending to their official duties.

This apparently tied in with a *Concord Monitor* observation of a previous session, which went:

Saturday morning the House and Senate both adjourned and as many as could left for home. Some of them had sundry suspicious looking envelope boxes under their arms, and looked on their way to the station as if they were making way with stationery.

We are glad they are gone and so seems everybody else except the hotel keepers. Concord is a little quiet since their departure but the moral atmosphere is already purer than it was.

Pioneer Women's Suffrage

THE 1871 SESSION produced a pioneering woman's suffrage law. It gave women the right to be elected to local school boards. By 1878 there were members of the female sex on school boards in twenty towns, with such popular acceptance that the 1878 Legislature voted also to permit women to vote in district school meetings.

The democratic aspects of New Hampshire's elephantine House of Representatives were succinctly summarized by Albert R. Hatch of Portsmouth when he became Speaker of the House, in the 1874 session, as follows:

The inconvenience of a large assembly has been deliberately submitted to, that every man in New Hampshire can have in the Legislature some Representative with whom he is personally acquainted. The wisdom which gave to our state this near approach to a pure democracy, will influence us to listen attentively to every grievance and every expression of public sentiment from however obscure or humble a source it may come.

The Legislature Is Reformed

L EGISLATIVE OPERATIONS were sharply reformed by amendments to the state Constitution in 1877. They resulted from a series of General Court political shenanigans by both the Republicans and the Democrats over a period of years.

During their long control of the Legislature, the Republicans had fostered the padding of House representation in the smaller towns so flagrantly that even their own party leadership finally denounced the practice. When the Democrats suddenly took over the Legislature and the Governorship in 1874, they ousted the Republican judges and other state officials and replaced them with party favorites. Before leaving office in June 1875, Democrat Governor James A. Weston of Manchester and his Council manipulated the 1875 spring election returns, which restored the Republicans to power, giving the Democrats continued control of the State Senate for another year. Finally, when the Republicans regained state government controls in 1876, they promptly removed the Democratic incumbents of 1874 and returned Republicans to these appointive positions.

The legislative tit-for-tat political gambits aroused such public censure that when constitutional amendments to improve legislative conduct were proposed by the Constitutional Convention of December 1876, and submitted to the voters at the annual March town meetings in 1877, they were readily approved. The reform amendments launched biennial legislative sessions, shifted state elections from March to November, increased the Senate from twelve to twenty-four members, and changed the formula for House representation from taxpayers to population. In addition, the three county positions of sheriff, solicitor, and register of probate were removed from Governor and Council appointment—and legislative manipulations—and were put up for election by the voters.

The 1877 constitutional adjustments even improved the voters own conduct, in a historic manner. They abolished the traditional restriction that only Protestants could become Governor or serve in the Legislature. Termination of this anti-Catholic prejudice came by a virtually breathless margin of only 5 votes, or 28,477 to 14,231, for the necessary two-thirds referendum approval. But it still chalked the second Tuesday of March 1877 as a historic display of ecumenical progress for New Hampshiremen.

The legislative purges of 1874 and 1876 were admittedly political, with no regard for the character of the ousted officials or for the public welfare. The Legislature utilized its constitutional right to "address" the Governor and the Council to dismiss the officials "for the public good," and no charges were read or required. To expedite the ousting of the Judges, the Legislature used the simple expediency of changing the names of their courts.

When he took office in 1875, Governor Person C. Cheney of Manchester rapped his own Republican legislative leadership for having sponsored substantial increases in House membership from the smaller towns to maintain majorities over the Democrats. He said it was wrong and urged that the House size be cut back to conform with population measurements. Governor Cheney vainly urged repeal of the towns' authority to set their own "ratable polls,"—the denominator then used for House apportionment. He also denounced an 1871 law which changed the definition of ratable polls from poll tax payers to adult males, which he emphasized was contrary to the state Constitution (as ruled by the Superior Court of Judicature in 1834).

Finally, Governor Cheney warned the Legislature that it had fallen in public esteem by permitting the House membership to increase by 25 percent over twenty years, while the population remained virtually unchanged. The number had soared from 288 in 1850 when the census was 317,976, to 373 under the 1870 census of 318,300 (population increases having been curbed by the ravages of the Civil War).

While the towns padded their polls, the Legislature itself had swollen the House membership by special grants of seats to towns lacking the minimum requirement of 150 polls for a full seat, rather than forcing them to merge for legislative representation. By 1874, twenty-six unqualified towns boasted full representation, though they were supposed to be classified for that purpose. These abuses became so prevalent that the Democratic Legislature of 1874 passed a law to curb such "fraud." It imposed a fine of $1,000 upon any person who accepted a House seat without proper entitlement, and a fine of

$2,000 upon any town which countenanced such a constitutional violation.

Governor Cheney exhorted in vain. The 1875 session added three more towns—Dummer, Bridgewater, and Groton—to the questionable group given House seats. And the towns continued their poll paddings, to boot, so the 1876 House of Representatives had 391 members, a gain of 20 in two years.

Governor Cheney joined in denouncing Governor Weston's Senate "steal," even as he agreed the election laws required use of a Christian name on the ballot. But he said that Weston's manipulations constituted a miscarriage of voter intent, and he urged clarification of the law so that such manipulations could not occur again.

Governor Weston's reversal of the 1875 Senate elections outcome was without equal in legislative annals. Republican Natt Head of Hooksett polled 3,771 votes to 3,834 for Democrat James Priest of Derry, but because 101 other ballots were cast in this contest, neither man had a majority, so the Senate was supposed to determine the winner. Weston and his Council invalidated the Head votes because his Christian name was Nathaniel Head, and they blandly gave the seat to Priest, in proclaiming the results of the March election returns.

Governor Weston and his Council next gave another Senate seat to Democrat John Proctor of Andover (for whom Proctor Academy was named), although he did not muster a majority in the election. He received 3,495 votes to 3,457 for Republican George E. Todd of Concord. But 64 votes were cast for other names, so this stalemate was also scheduled by custom for final Senate decision. But Weston and his Council disqualified 46 votes for prohibition candidate Arthur Deering because he had not lived in the state for seven years, and 9 votes for Abraham Thorpe because he was not a district resident. This summary action left Proctor with a majority, so he was also proclaimed a winner.

The Republicans expressed fury, and their partisan newspapers vented unbridled wrath upon Governor Weston for his executive upsets, which gave the Democrats continued control of the Senate by a 7 to 5 majority. The Republican minority refused to participate in organization of the Senate when the Legislature convened on June 2, 1875. So the seven-member Democratic majority elected John W. Sanborn of Wakefield as President and unanimously approved the Weston ploy.

Meanwhile, the Republican minority met in a rump session. It elected George H. Stowell of Claremont as President and appointed Tyler Westgate of Haverhill as clerk. Purpose of this maneuver became readily apparent, for within the hour the rebel group filed a protest with the House of Representatives, claiming that the Senate Democrats had refused to submit the dispute to the Superior Court of Judicature for a ruling. The House, Republican by 192 to 181, rose to the cue. Representative Levi W. Barton of Newport moved that the House challenge the Senate about its own business and request the high court for a ruling. The Democrats lost a roll call maneuver to delay the question but won its postponement until the following morning.

The House convened again on Thursday (the second day of the session), and the Democrats launched a series of parliamentary maneuvers to delay the court test vote to give the Senate majority the opportunity to ask for the ruling first. But after six roll calls lasting more than two hours, the Republicans won out by a 180 to 153 showdown, and the House hustled the issue to the court. The Senate, however, beat the House to the punch, so to speak. It voted to send the dispute to the court, even as the half-dozen roll calls were grinding through the lower branch. Records show the House resolution actually reached the court chambers first, however, and the eventual decision went to the House rather than the Senate.

The three Justices of the high court heard the Senate snarl arguments the following Monday afternoon. They informed the House the next morning that the dispute had been irrevocably decided when the Senate approved the seating of the two upsetting Democratic members. The court emphasized that the state Constitution provides that each legislative branch is final judge of its own membership. Then the court informed the Senate of its reply to the House.

The court declined to rule on what Governor Weston and his Council had done. It wrote that this issue had become moot by the Senate's approval of their actions. Thus went into history what was undoubtedly the only time in General Court history that one branch ever questioned the authority of the other as to its membership. But the furor flared on. The court was denounced by the Republicans because its Democratic members had been appointed by Weston less than a year earlier. And Democrat Attorney General Lewis W. Clark of Manchester, also a Weston appointee, was vilified for alleged failure to present a stronger case for the Republicans before the high court. Critics overlooked the fact that Clark had been proven correct in his contention that the die had been cast when the Senate approved the

Two Decades of Tensions

disputed Senators.

Governor Weston generated other history. He is the only man who ever served as a municipal mayor through his two terms as Governor. Natt Head later became flatteringly vindicated. The Hooksett manufacturer (whose brick residence still adorns Head's Hill in Hooksett) was reelected to the Senate in 1876 and again in 1877, under that name. In 1878, at fifty-one years of age, he was given the honor of being elected as the state's first biennial term Governor.

The constitutional legislative reshuffle paid off. The House membership fell to 280 under the new population formula, which set the apportionment at 600 inhabitants for an initial seat and 1,200 for each additional seat, while the classification of the smaller towns was continued. Proponents successfully argued that the 600 to 1,200 yardstick was the equivalent of the old 150 to 300 ratable polls formula and said the House membership would drop below 290 simply by cancelling the seatings in excess of what the old formula allowed, if it had been strictly adhered to.

The constitutional shift to a biennial state government gave New Hampshire two elections in 1878. The traditional March election named officials for one more period of annual service, starting in June. Then in the first November biennial election, a Governor and legislators were chosen to start biennial service in June 1879.

The switch to November elections cost New Hampshire considerable national prestige. The country's politicos had come to watch the state's first-in-the-nation annual March elections as a barometer of upcoming citizen sentiments in national affairs. Seventy years later this national spotlight role for New Hampshire was resurrected by the 1949 Legislature. As Speaker of the House in that session, youthful Attorney Richard F. Upton of Concord sponsored a "Presidential Preference Primary," tied to the March town meetings, to restore the state's glamour spot in the national political sun.

After a quarter of a century of operation, the quadrennial Presidential popularity primary has yielded beneficial nationwide publicity exceeding the most optimistic Granite State expectations. Presidential aspirants have avidly paid respects to New Hampshire voters far in excess of the value of their handful of electoral votes, because of the prestige of this first-in-the-nation preference primary. The news medias' massive focusing on these first-test Presidential campaigns has also bloomed New Hampshire's recreation and rural images virtually beyond monetary measurement.

1883 Marathon and Woodchucks

THE THIRD BIENNIAL SESSION of the General Court in 1883 turned to woodchucks to alleviate the monotony of a record balloting marathon. With both branches overwhelmingly Republican, the session took six weeks to dump United States Senator Edward H. Rollins, founder and principal pilot of the party for a quarter of a century, and agree upon his successor. This required a record forty-three ballots from June 19 through August 2, during which the vote-weary legislators gave the woodchucks more attention than bargained for.

Rollins, the onetime Concord druggist, sought a second Senate term, following three Congressional terms, and ran into a surprise defeat. His firm controls of party patronage through the years had so alienated several party groups that they influenced the 1883 Legislature to retire him to political oblivion.

This Republican family fuss drew national attention because the national Senate was then so evenly divided, politically, that a single vote often turned the tide on important issues. One local newspaper boasted that the balloting marathon had attracted "reporters from Philadelphia and New York, as well as the Hub."

The fifty-nine-year-old Rollins suffered an initial surprise setback when the Republican legislators were called into caucus before the June 6 session opening, to act on the Senatorial nomination. Such action had become party custom and of a binding status. But only 130 of the 206 Republican legislators of both branches participated, and even though Rollins won the caucus endorsement with 98 votes, the net result made plain he was in more trouble than anticipated.

The 1883 Senatorial election did not start until the third week of the session, by federal law. The 1866 Congress set rules by which members of the United States Senate were chosen by a state Legislature, with a proviso that such elections began on the second Tuesday of a session. Then, if the House and Senate separately failed to muster a majority for a candidate on an initial vote, they were required to convene jointly at high noon on the following day to vote on a pending Senatorship. If this joint vote failed to produce a majority for any candidate, the two branches were required to repeat that unusual action on each ensuing legislative day until someone was elected or final adjournment prevailed before that objective was fulfilled.

The Democrats posted Attorney Harry Bingham of Littleton, a new

Two Decades of Tensions

state Senator, following seventeen House terms, as their candidate. The House and Senate failed to agree on Rollins, or anyone else, on the initial June 19 separate votes. The first joint roll call the next day gave Rollins a 117 to 115 edge over Bingham. But three former Republican Congressmen, James F. Briggs of Manchester, James W. Patterson of Hanover, and Aaron F. Stevens of Nashua, split another 62 votes.

The Legislature voted for forty-two days before achieving a compromise decision. After the twenty-second tally, on July 12, Senator Rollins withdrew his name, in a personal letter to each Republican legislator, for party harmony. But another twenty-one days of voting were required to achieve it. Former Congressman Austin F. Pike of Franklin, who entered his name on the thirty-fifth roll call, became the eventual Republican victor on August 2. He died in office, at sixty-seven, three years later.

It was a bright young Concord lawyer who injected the woodchucks into the 1883 session. He took the House floor one morning and suggested that something be done about farmers' complaints that the waddling field animals were increasingly damaging their crops and clover stands. The solons promptly rose to the challenge and ordered a study committee to ponder a solution. Charles R. Corning, the sponsor, was appointed chairman.

Corning, who later became mayor of Concord and one of its most noted historians, rose to the occasion with all his twenty-five tender years. He was given nine committee associates: Silas M. Morse of Effingham, David Urch of Portsmouth, Silas M. Spalding of Hollis, John C. Bartlett of Lee, George W. Mann of Benton, William R. Robie of New Hampton, John L. Streeter of Chesterfield, Daniel Ide of Croydon, and Henry O. Kent of Lancaster.

Records indicate that Corning did most of the studying. And he filed a report which remains to this day a legislative gem. It is a delightful document of five and one-fifth pages. There being nothing equal to it in Granite State annals, a copy is carefully preserved in the fireproof vaults of the State Library.

The report stressed that woodchucks apparently stemmed from an origin of simplicity. Their color was described as "not red nor auburn, but more like Derry, which is next to Auburn."

Corning's corny report said the woodchuck enjoys corn and even pumpkins and added: "Your committee is very much impressed with the similarity existing between woodchucks and office holders; they both prefer to live in clover." The committee also said:

The average age of the woodchuck is too long to please your committee but the population estimate can only be approximated. One of your committee, however, counted 72 of these creatures in going only a short distance. In some parts of the state it is found necessary to shovel a path through the woodchucks in order to reach the barns. This is not right.

The animal, as they say, takes its bed about October 1 and forthwith rolls itself into a ball, becomes torpid, and to all appearances dead. Unfortunately for the farmers, this interesting habit goes into effect at that season of the year when nobody cares a snap about the woodchuck or the clover crop. Therefore, aside from the scientific value, this does not amount to anything. . . .

As an illustration of the utter want of grace in the animal, the committee would ask the attention of the House to the fact that the woodchuck is fond of sitting on its haunches and letting its fore paws hang loosely down. It also has a very comical rotary movement of the head while engaged in feeding. Your committee is unable to account for this.

Corning's report concluded with a bounty recommendation as follows:

Your committee has given this important subject a most thorough examination, and finds the woodchuck is one of the worst enemies ever known to the farmer; and unless the Legislature will do something to rid the state of these animals, the chances are the woodchuck will have his own way. Your committee is confident that a small bounty will prove of incalculable good,

Charles Corning

Two Decades of Tensions

The New Hampshire Legislature of 1873 as photographed
by W. H. C. Kimball of Concord.

at all events, even as an experiment, it is certainly worth trying; therefore
your committee would respectfully recommend that the accompanying bill
be passed.

The woodchuck report became a House hit, and the bounty bill
was passed and sent up to the august Senate in August, where it ran
into a holy snag. Another bright young lawyer, Senator Irving W.
Drew of Lancaster, agreed to the bounty, set at ten cents, but insisted
it should not soil the sanctity of the Sabbath. So he tacked on an
amendment, by a squeaky 10 to 9 Senate vote, denying the bounty for
any woodchuck tails taken on Sunday. The bill then became law.
Selectmen were told to pay a dime for a woodchuck tail, to be reimbursed from the State Treasury.

The Drew dictum seemed harsh. For the Sabbath in those days was the only time farmers had to relax from their customary dawn-to-dusk husbandry chores. But fears that this restriction might benefit the unsuspecting groundhog proved fruitless. For the woodchucks began to die in droves and drove selectmen to desperation.

Interestingly, there's no earthly record that anyone ever paid attention to the Sunday bounty ban. The statute merely stated it should not be paid on woodchucks killed on Sunday and did not mention enforcement or penalty for possible fraud. So apparently neither the selectmen nor the bearers posed that point on the tails.

Within a few months the town officials became so inundated by the tails that their wails welled to historic proportions. Never before in New Hampshire lore had a bounty wreaked more havoc than it was supposed to suppress. The woodchucks were being wiped out beyond expectations; but the trouble was that so was the State Treasury.

State Treasurer Solon A. Carter sounded the alarm when the 1885 Legislature convened. He disclosed that the selectmen's reimbursement claims were assuming devastating proportions and urged immediate repeal of the bounty to protect the state's solvency.

Carter reported that while his office had paid for only 339 tails as of June 1884, the total had zoomed to 122,065 in the following year. Repeal of the bounty followed. But the payments went on and on. Another 97,656 claims were paid off by June 1886, along with 193 the following year, and a final 41 dimes were recorded for the 1888 fiscal year.

Finally, this tale of the woodchuck tails was given permanence by Winston Churchill of Cornish, noted political crusader and author, in his 1906 book, *Coniston*, with a chapter entitled "The Woodchuck Session."

Another historic event of the 1883 session gave Mrs. Mary Jenness of the seacoast town of Rye the distinction of becoming the only mother ever to have three sons serve in the Granite State General Court. She was ninety years old when her eldest son, Joseph J. Drake, by a previous marriage, served a single term in the 1883 House at the age of sixty-six. Two other sons served in the House—Orin Drake in the 1865 House, at the age of forty-one, and Advid Jenness, who was thirty-eight when elected to the 1871 House (he was also reelected for a second term).

The clock in Representatives Hall is of rare vintage but is still going strong, far beyond its guarantee. It continues to keep accurate time, even though it is often stopped and started during legislative sessions, to reflect the parliamentary maneuvers and gyrations of law-making conduct.

Its origin was reported by the *Concord Monitor* on March 31, 1885, as follows:

A new hanging clock for Representatives Hall has been purchased by authority of the Governor and Council of Norman G. Carr, jeweler of this city, to replace the old one, which was too small to be distinctly seen across the hall.

It is 42 inches in height and has a 24-inch dial, which effectually obviates the difficulty complained of.

The makers, E. Howard & Co., of Boston, have furnished a written guarantee that the clock will run for five years, with proper care, with a variation of not more than one minute per month.

The front of the clock is of pure white marble, and although of plain design and free from ornamentation, is very handsome, and presents a solid and reliable appearance.

Nine days later, on April 9, the Governor and his Council instructed Major Stokes, the "State House Keeper," to procure 144 spittoons "for the Hall of the House of Representatives."

Part 3

The Second Free Century

The 1945 House of Representatives which, chaired by Norris Cotton, enacted "Live Free or Die" as the state motto.

THE RAILROAD SCANDALS

Early Developments

THE LEGISLATURE began railroad supervision in 1838 when New Hampshire got its first line from Lowell, Massachusetts, into Nashua. A county board was created for that purpose. Four years later the Concord Railroad was organized to extend this line into Concord, whereupon a State Railroad Commission was established. It comprised three men, appointed by the Governor and the Council, with a $3 per diem and allowance for expenses.

The 1851 Legislature ordered the commission members to be elected annually, with stockholders and officials of railroads barred from such positions. This policy was rescinded by the 1883 Legislature, in what became a futile reform attempt to rid legislative sessions from manipulations by the corporations.

The Legislature vainly sought to control excess railroad profits. It restricted net profits to 10 percent. For a brief period there was even a statute requiring the corporations to give excess profits to the state, but it failed of enforcement. The Legislature also tried to curb excess profits by requiring reduced freight and passenger rates to offset them. But this policy was also unsuccessful. The railroads deliberately curbed excess profits by siphoning them into handsome and elaborate stations, some of which have become historic shrines since their rail lines were abandoned.

The Legislature strove to restrict and even outlaw free railroad passes, used to curry the favor of citizens and their organizations. But

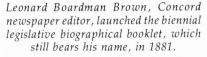

Leonard Boardman Brown, Concord newspaper editor, launched the biennial legislative biographical booklet, which still bears his name, in 1881.

Hosea B. Carter of Hampstead launched the General Court manual in 1889, while manipulating political districts for the Republican party.

enforcement failed, for the General Court carefully avoided imposing penalties for such violations. History has recorded that free passes were so generously doled out, and so well received by most persons within reach of them, that public officials, and even legislators, consistently made use of them.

The 1883 Legislature launched a two-pronged program to get railroading out of the legislative arena. This followed creation by the 1878 Legislature of a Board of Equalization, to set increased railroad taxes, which ran into adverse court rulings sponsored by the railroad corporations.

First, the 1883 session returned Railroad Commission appointments to the Governor and the Council, with handsome salaries, and gave them stronger controls over rates, profits, and operating procedures. The remuneration for the chairman was set at $2,500, with $2,200 for the clerk and $2,000 for the third member. This scale compared with the Governor's salary of $1,000 and was in excess of what most other full-time state officials were paid. As one result, Editor Henry M. Putney of the *Manchester Mirror* held the coveted chairmanship from 1886 through twenty years of protracted criticisms.

Second, the session enacted a general law permitting restricted railroad leases and formation of new corporations, without specific legislative approval in each instance, as in prior years. But early in 1887, a few weeks before the Legislature convened in June, the State Supreme Court ruled the 1883 general law was illegal because it did not provide sufficient protection of the interest of minority stockholder groups. It was this surprise decision that sparked the longest legislative session ever recorded up to 1937.

The Bitter 1887 Battling

BANKER MOODY CURRIER of Manchester reflected the general public attitude concerning railroad domination of public affairs when he became Governor in 1885. He told the Legislature in his inaugural address:

At the last session of the Legislature the railroad laws of this state were materially and radically changed by two enactments,—one creating a Railroad Commission with novel and greatly enlarged powers, giving the board a general supervision of all railroads in the state, with power to examine their affairs, and to regulate their trains, fares, freight, stations, and accommodations; the other, a general law authorizing the formation of railroad corporations for the construction of new roads, and the union of existing roads by lease, sale or contract.

No new road has been constructed under this law, but important unions of old roads have been effected. These consolidations have not, however, been in operation long enough to warrant a positive conclusion as to the results to the people of the state. So far as I can judge, the new policy is generally approved by the people, with a hope that it will put an end to the rivalries and controversies of our roads, and relieve the Legislature from the vexatious contests that have occupied so much time in former years.

From another angle, the Railroad Committee observed in its 1888 annual report on the 1887 court ruling upsetting the so-called Colby Act of 1883:

This decision precipitated a railroad war in the Legislature more expensive, more demoralizing and, in its results, more unsatisfactory to all the contending parties than any other that ever destroyed the substance and sacrificed the dignity of the state.

The Railroad Scandals

Many years of legislative influence by railroad operators was spotlighted by a scandalous General Court session in 1887. Charges of legislative bribery and corruption became so rampant that Governor Charles H. Sawyer of Dover vetoed three bills which would have given the Boston & Maine Railroad, then based in Massachusetts, control of New Hampshire's most profitable lines.

Details of the session were unparalleled in Granite State annals. The controversy became such a heated public issue that dozens of House and Senate members filed petitions signed by thousands of their constituents, denouncing the so-called Boston & Maine grab.

Activities of the railroad lobbyists prolonged the session into a record 158 days, from June 1 through November 5. Each legislator collected an all-time record of $474 in wages. They then paid themselves $3 per day, including Sundays, although they actually worked only three or four days weekly. This was so shocking that eighteen months later the voters permanently pegged the legislative pay at $200, by a constitutional amendment, which has remained in effect to this day.

The session lasted so long that four newspapers, which had each agreed to service the Legislature for $1.00 per member for the entire session, petitioned for a fee increase, and the lawmakers raised it to $2.50 in the final adjournment hours. It also became so prolonged that stoves were ordered by the legislators for protection from the chilly fall weather. In yet another feature of the marathon meeting, the Legislature doubled its customary $50 reward for each newspaperman reporting its proceedings, and the $100 emolument continued another twenty years until the policy was abolished in 1907.

There was an unusual setting for the 1887 railroad melee. The biographical *Brown Book* reported that only 42 of the 307 House members had previous legislative experience, along with a Republican majority of 165 to 134. Thirteen were under thirty years of age, the bulk of them were under fifty, and only four were more than seventy years of age. The House membership included 84 farmers; 30 merchants; 19 manufacturers; 15 lawyers; 6 doctors; 2 clergymen; and 4 each of carpenters, clerks, grocers, machinists, and mill overseers.

The Senate was also of unusual makeup, while 15 to 9 Republican. Nineteen of the 24 members had previously served in the House, but none had ever before sat in the upper branch. Only five were college graduates.

The record 158-day session was sparked by two bills. Louis T. Hazen, fifty-one-year old Whitefield farmer who had never before

To This Day

Legislators joined in this dedication of the Daniel Webster statue on June 17, 1886 in the State House yard.

held public office, filed a measure giving the Boston & Maine opportunity to lease various New Hampshire railroad corporations on ninety-nine-year terms. It was sweetened by provisions forbidding rate hikes except with legislative approval, and sale of mileage books at reduced rates. Henry B. Atherton of Nashua sponsored an opposing bill to give the Concord Railroad authority to merge with its connecting lines and to bar out-of-state railroads from further attempts to dominate the in-state carriers.

There were several other railroad bills in the 1887 session. Some authorized new lines; others permitted reorganization or enlargement of present lines. Most of them were enacted into law. But it was the Hazen and Atherton bills, as they came to be called, that led to the hectic doings of the scandal-ridden 1887 General Court.

The state's top political leaders clashed in this railroad ruckus. Congressman Jacob H. Gallinger of Concord, also chairman of the Republican State Committee, became the foremost partisan for the Atherton bill. Top advocate of the Boston & Maine's Hazen measure was former Congressman Frank Jones, the wealthy Portsmouth brewer and railroad promoter, who was longtime kingpin of New

The Railroad Scandals

Frank D. Currier

Hampshire's Democratic party. In contrast, Attorney Charles F. Stone of Laconia, veteran chairman of the Democratic State Committee, served in the 1887 House and opposed the Hazen bill.

Gallinger was later reputed to have been well paid by the Concord Railroad for his efforts, and four years later the Legislature elected him to the United States Senate, where he served for a record twenty-seven years until he died in 1918. Both Gallinger and Jones were surrounded by fellow lobbyists of varied political reputation and influence beyond any recorded tabulation. And the conduct of the Boston & Maine clique became so brazen that Hazen eventually refused to support his own bill.

It took more than four months to engineer the Hazen bill through the Legislature, after which it was quickly vetoed by Governor Sawyer because it had become tainted with bribery and corruption. But the Governor was forced to kill it twice more. The Senate resurrected the Boston & Maine power grab in different wording in another railroad bill to control rates, which ran into a second veto. Finally, the House incorporated the Boston & Maine power play in yet another supposed railroad control measure, which the Senate readily concurred in, and Governor Sawyer gave it a third veto.

Attorney Alvin Burleigh of Plymouth, forty-five-year-old tanner turned lawyer after Civil War service, became House Speaker in his first legislative term, and Attorney Frank D. Currier of Canaan, Senate clerk for two sessions, became President of the upper branch, to preside over the memorable 1887 session.

Both branches were strongly Republican, but the nefarious railroadings intertwined party lines. Governor Sawyer, self-made wealthy woolen manufacturer, was also Republican. He failed to muster a required majority vote in the previous November election over Democrat Attorney Thomas Cogswell of Gilmanton, so he was elected by the Legislature on a 178 to 146 vote.

Debates and arguments became so bitterly sprinkled with allegations, and the lobbyists became so crassly corrupt, that both the House and Senate conducted their own bribery investigations. Each branch found lobbyists guilty of bribery attempts. But both carefully refrained from pressing charges of corrupt practices against any of them.

The 1887 embroilment culminated half a century of legislative efforts to supervise railroad corporations. Controls became increasingly complex and controversial through the years as dozens of new lines spread through the state. To share the booming profits produced by this welcome new type of transportation, and interlocking leases and stock ownerships, railroads skirted and flirted with supervisory regulations.

The Hazen bill was filed on June 9 and was referred to the House Railroad Committee on June 14, after having been printed. On June 22 the House allowed the committee to hire a stenographer and to use Representatives Hall for day and evening hearings when not otherwise in use.

The committee submitted its recommendations on August 24. The twelve members split 8 to 4, the majority urging passage of the Hazen measure and the minority favoring the Atherton bill. Political party lines disintegrated in this report, and this feature continued through the entire session. Republican Chairman Chester Pike, Cornish farmer, and seven associates favored the Hazen bill. Joining in the majority were Republicans Thomas P. Cheney, Ashland manufacturer; farmer Warren Brown of Hampton Falls; Dr. Henry Marble of Gorham, and Keene Publisher Clement J. Woodward of the *New Hampshire Sentinel;* the Democrats were Attorney George E. Hodgdon of Portsmouth, merchant Josiah R. Calef of Barrington, and manufacturer Henry B. Cotton of Conway.

Republican Editor Orren C. Moore of the *Nashua Telegraph* headed the minority report for the Atherton measure, which never came close

to victory. His associates were Democrat farmer George S. Philbrick of Tilton and Republicans farmer John C. Pearson of Boscawen and Attorney David F. Clark of Manchester.

The Hazen bill hit the House floor for debate on September 7. The arguments became sandwiched into routine daily business and parliamentary maneuvers for two weeks and ran into evening sessions.

Meanwhile, Governor Sawyer began enjoying a 100 percent pay raise. Youthful Joseph E. Porter, Dover bookkeeper and personal friend of Sawyer, won easy approval of a bill to hike the salary to $2,000, from the $1,000 level which had held for more than half a century. The measure was placed upon the Governor's desk on August 24 and became effective five days later without his signature. In retrospect, it seems the Legislature would never have approved the complimentary measure if it had known the three railroad bills vetoes were to follow.

As the Hazen bill oratory developed, its author repudiated his sponsorship. After Cyrus A. Sulloway of Manchester, destined to become the "Tall Pine of the Merrimack" Congressman, had held the floor for two days against the bill, and testified that Hazen had filed his bill without knowledge of its contents, upon promises of a railroad extension into Whitefield, he suddenly yielded to Hazen. The latter asked that the clerk read his statement, in which he shifted his allegiance to the Atherton bill. Hazen explained the sponsors of his bill had reneged on their promise of a railroad extension, and the Concord Railroad spokesmen had given him another promise that the line would be built.

By September 22, delaying oratory and parliamentary procrastinations were in full sway. It was also about this time that two unrelated Haverhill lawmakers with the same name, the same profession, and the same political affiliation swung into opposing sides. They were Attorneys Samuel Berkeley Page, former Democratic state chairman, in his eighth legislative term, who supported the Hazen bill, and Samuel Taylor Page, a third-termer and onetime editor of the *Concord People and Patriot*, who vigorously opposed it.

S.B. Page created a brief sensation by displaying a telegram to Andrew Jackson of Stark saying that his wife was dying. He charged it was designed to induce Jackson to rush home and miss voting for the

Hazen bill in the approaching showdown. Editor Moore took the floor in rebuttal and testified that Concord Railroad officials were not responsible for the fake message.

S.T. Page maneuvered a novel delay, in futile efforts to defeat the measure. He won time for opponents to submit last-minute amendments. They totalled eight in number, and another week of arguments and roll calls followed before they were dumped into oblivion. Meanwhile, S.T. Page's tactics paid off in another manner. Petitions began to pour into the House from some four dozen cities and towns, with more than 7,000 signatures, denouncing the Hazen measure. They included five from Concord, and other petitions bombarded the Senate.

Stoves were ordered to heat the House, during a skeleton session on Monday evening, September 26, with but a token handful of legislators present. William C. Todd of Atkinson, wealthy former educator, sponsored the following:

Resolved, that the Sergeant-at-Arms be instructed to procure stoves for the purpose of heating the Representatives Hall.

No number of stoves was listed, but the original Capitol had four corner chimneys for fireplaces, and the chimneys had remained in place after the 1865 enlargement of the building. Concord's Steven & Dunklee Company was later paid $170.47 for the stoves.

On September 29 the oratory continued after midnight and brought agreement on a showdown vote on October 5. Editor Moore next created a sensation on October 4, a Tuesday, when he won an investigation of alleged corruption.

Tinges of Corruption

THE HOUSE AGREED on a voice vote to have its Judiciary Committee handle the probe, in the following resolution:

Whereas, it has been charged on the floor of the House that members have been improperly approached and corruptly solicited to vote and act on the railroad bills now pending, and

Whereas, it is due to the dignity and integrity of this body that all such charges should be substantiated or dispelled; therefore

The Railroad Scandals

Resolved, that the Judiciary committee be instructed to proceed forthwith to investigate all charges brought by any member of this House of any attempt to corruptly influence the action or vote of any member on the pending railroad bills; and said committee, in order to prosecute said investigation promptly and thoroughly, may sit during the sessions of the House, employ a stenographer, and have full power to send for persons and papers.

This Tuesday session lasted into the night. During the evening the House killed amendments to put the Hazen bill up to a referendum of the people; for a ten-hour workday for railroads; and to impose a $500 fine upon any railroad official who illegally distributed a free pass.

The following day, October 5, Governor Sawyer sent a message into the House stating that legislative funds had become exhausted, because of the protracted deliberations, and asked that additional funds be appropriated. Before nightfall, the House passed the Hazen bill on a 167 to 131 roll call vote and sent it to the Senate, where it was given 15 to 9 roll call approval on October 12.

As the House Judiciary Committee held hearings and heard several legislators testify to improper advances by the lobbyists, the Hazen bill landed on Governor Sawyer's desk on October 18. It was sent back to the House the same day, with the most sensational veto message in legislative history. The gist of the veto was as follows:

Without entering upon the intrinsic merits of the measure, to express any opinion upon a question of such vital importance to the state, and upon which the people may wish to be heard, I am moved to object to this bill for the reason that corrupt methods have been extensively used for the purpose of promoting its passage. The two powerful railroad corporations which have antagonized each other in the contest have had in attendance a paid lobby of unprecedented magnitude, and as a consequence the representatives have been persistently followed and interfered with in the free performance of their legislative duties.

The widespread rumors and scandalous tales of bribery and corruption, which have been freely current during the progress of the contest, finally materialized through charges preferred in the Senate and also the House after the passage of the bill. By the courtesy of the chairman of the Judiciary Committee of the House, upon my request, I have received the official records of the testimony thus far taken by that committee in their investigation of the charges. . . .

While I am glad to be able to say that no evidence has yet been produced to show that any member of the Legislature has been unfaithful to his trust and oath of office, yet, to my mind, it is conclusively shown that there have been deliberate and systematic attempts at wholesale bribery of the servants of the people in this Legislature. It matters not that both of the parties are probably equally guilty.

Plainly upset by the veto, the House referred it to the Judiciary Committee for later action. The next day the Judiciary Committee recommended that the veto be upheld. This report was signed by Chairman Gilman Marston of Exeter, seventy-five-year-old Exeter lawyer serving his thirteenth House term, along with Republicans Cyrus A. Sulloway of Manchester, William F. Nason of Dover, and Luther S. Morrill of Concord, all lawyers, and Henry B. Atherton of Nashua, along with Democrats Charles F. Stone of Laconia and Denis F. O'Connor of Manchester, both lawyers.

A minority of the Judicary Committee filed a surprise report the following day, October 20. It said, in part:

We believe that the provisions enacted in the Hazen bill are vital to the best interests of the state; that the failure to become law will be a public calamity. . . . We fully agree with the conclusion reached in the veto message, that there is absolutely no evidence that any member has been untrue to his trust, or violated the obligation of his oath.

Censuring the veto were Democratic lawyers S.B. Page, Oliver E. Branch of Weare, and George W. Stone of Andover, along with Republicans banker Newton S. Huntington of Hanover and Attorney Ira Colby of Claremont, seventh-termer and sponsor of the ill-fated 1883 railroad Colby Act.

After brief arguments, the House rejected the majority recommendation and endorsed the minority report by a 159 to 125 roll call. Then it tabled the veto for later action.

Concord citizens staged a gala celebration for the veto, which Governor Sawyer handed to the House late in the afternoon of October 18. A newspaper report said: "There have not been so many people on Main street of an evening for many years as was gathered there between the hours of seven and nine last night." An estimated 1,000 persons joined in a march, with music by the Lake Village band of West Concord. A Governor's salute was also fired by the "Independent Battery."

The Railroad Scandals

The capital city's partisanship for the Concord Railroad was reflected in the House vote on the Hazen bill, which the city's legislators opposed 10 to 2, while the Merrimack County delegation opposed it 28 to 12.

After the House Judiciary Committee had devoted three weeks to its bribery probe, the House voted on October 26 to have 5,000 copies of its report printed. The next day it was reduced to 2,000 copies. The committee formally filed its report on November 2, three days before final adjournment. The next day copies were distributed to each legislator.

The twelve-member committee submitted four reports. All agreed that lobbyists on both sides were guilty of bribery attempts involving several legislators. All of them also agreed that none of them was legally guilty of any misconduct.

Ten legislators, including one Senator, were summoned before the committee and testified to alleged bribery offers. They were William A. Morrison of Lempster, William J. Reed of Westmoreland, Joseph W. Bean of Derry, Frank E. Cram of Pittsfield, James W. Lathe of Manchester, Alonzo B. Lang of Alton, Edward A. Watkins of Walpole, Stillman Merrill of Dorchester, Moses Spofford of Danville, and Senator Franklin Worcester of Hollis.

Chairman Marston and four committee associates opposed to the Hazen bill reported that eight of the ten legislators had proven bribery attempts. Five other committeemen led by S.B. Page, all Hazen bill proponents, said only four bribery attempts had been proven. The two other committee members filed qualifying findings, each agreeing in part with their colleagues.

Marston's group completed its report by saying:

Your committee have fully investigated all charges brought by any member of the House, but have not felt authorized to do more under the resolution.

Page's group recommended more vigorous penalties to curb free passes and promiscuous lobbying, and the Legislature enacted them. This group reported:

There was evidence before the committee that passes have been distributed by both parties to the railroad contest to members of the House and others without concealment and in large numbers. This seems to have been done by each side under the impression that it was necessary to protect itself against the influence of the other. We believe the practice to be highly improper and demoralizing in its tendency, and that it should be prohibited under severer penalties than now exist.

We do not believe that bribery or attempts at bribery have changed the result on any measure, but we do believe a law should be passed defranchising any member who accepts a bribe, and providing for the severest penalties upon all others concerned.

This historic committee report went into the record without challenge or comment on the House floor, through the final two days of the session.

Senate Bribery in Action

A S THE HOUSE wrangled over the Hazen bill, the Senate conducted its own investigation of bribery. This was precipitated on September 6 when Senator Oliver D. Sawyer, Weare Quaker merchant, took the floor and said:

It becomes my duty, to myself and to the Senate, to place before this body the facts of a transaction that took place in this State House last week. On Wednesday I was called from this Chamber by the Sergeant-at-Arms and met Kirk D. Pierce. During the conversation, he proposed to me that I make a speech for the Boston & Maine railroad, for $500. I need not say that the proposition was indignantly declined.

Senator Ezra S. Stearns of Rindge, editor, teacher, and historian, demanded that a five-member committee investigate the incident, and President Currier immediately named the group, with subpoena powers and Stearns as chairman. The other members were merchant Benjamin F. Nealley of Dover, druggist Lycurgus Pitman of North Conway, merchant Nathan C. Jameson of Antrim, and Attorney Charles F. Hersey of Keene.

The following day the Senate authorized the committee to employ a stenographer, and two days later the Senate voted to have the testimony printed for general use. Stearns's committee filed its findings on September 21. It said:

Upon our construction of the testimony, and in our opinion, Honorable Oliver D. Sawyer is justified in the conclusion that it was the intent of Mr. Pierce to tender a bribe.

The Railroad Scandals

Hersey submitted a one-man minority report. He said the case centered on one man's word against another, and the bribery claim was not proven beyond reasonable doubt. Attorney Hersey's findings read, in part:

I am forced to say that, in my opinion, the Honorable Senator has not sustained his allegations against Mr. Pierce. . . .

I consider it exceedingly unfortunate that the Honorable Senator, in presenting this matter to the attention of the Senate, allowed himself to be urged on against his better judgment by the advice of over-zealous partisans in the bitter struggle now raging before the Legislature, and was thus impelled to pursue a course which, in any event, I am forced to believe is contrary and inimical to his own best interests.

Hersey also emphasized that Pierce was a lard industry lobbyist, rather than a railroad advocate, and there was no proof that any railroad had authorized him to make such an offer as Senator Sawyer reported. It is recorded, in this connection, that on the same day that the Senate probe was ordered, the Senate killed a House-approved bill to prevent adulteration of lard, which Pierce supported.

The findings of the majority of the committee, apparently written by Chairman Stearns, denounced the railroad lobbyists at great length. The report even said that some of the lobbyists collected fees for claiming having bribed House members who voted for either the Hazen or Atherton bills, when such members were not even approached with such corruption.

The committee report painted the following details:

Amid ample surroundings, the committee has labored in a limited field. This case will be justly regarded by the public as a representative expression of the baneful and illegitimate influences surrounding the Legislature at the present time.

It is painfully admitted that mercenary men, denominated the lobby, equal in ability, superior in number, and exceeding in activity the Legislature itself, have gathered about the Capitol like carrion birds, to fatten on the decay of public morals. Ignoring their duties as citizens, spurning the interests of the state, and heeding only with sickening alacrity the proffered promises of a paltry reward, they hang around the Capitol, penetrating the corridors, boldly entering the halls of legislation, and clinging like barna-

cles upon the ears of a wearied and persecuted audience.

*The influences, the inspirations, and the methods of the lobby work havoc
and desolation upon honest intentions, and worse, to any unfortunate and
vulnerable man who falls within the greedy power. For a vote, the good
name of an honest man is freely exchanged; and for an advantage to their
cause, a well-earned character is assailed.*

*The assembled lobby is not only a disgrace to the state and a perpetual
irritation to all honest men, but it is as well a cancerous sore upon itself. It
breeds corruption and dishonorable practices within itself. Even when
joined in a common cause, a reasonable confidence is not maintained
between the principal and his cohorts. For money fraudulently obtained,
the lobby sells the reputation of an honest man. They bank upon the even
chance that a certain member will vote for a pending measure, and, if that
member, with purest motives, by his vote unconsciously sustains the
scheme, the lobby secures the money upon the wicked allegation that the
honest member has been bribed. At once the master and the victim have
been betrayed. The lobby has been enriched, but an innocent man has
suffered an irreparable injury.*

Senator Jameson agreed with the committee report but filed the
following qualifying statement:

*I agree with the above findings as to the main question; and, while heartily
in accord with the general sentiment expressed in the latter part of this
report, dissent from the superfluity of language and expression.*

The committee report was indefinitely postponed on October 13, a
few minutes after the Senate approved the Hazen bill, 15 to 9.

The House labored deep into the night on both Thursday and
Friday to insure November 5 final adjournment late Saturday morning. Governor Sawyer meanwhile had vetoed a Senate bill on
November 1, because it included features of the objectionable Hazen
bill, which he vetoed October 18. This second veto included a copy of
the first veto message. The Senate summarily tabled the veto and
never voted on its merits.

The House approved the most unusual veto rebuff in New Hampshire annals, on Friday night. Attorney Colby sponsored this gambit.
After winning House approval to taking the October 18 veto message
off the table, he offered a lengthy resolution which said the veto

The Railroad Scandals

violated the state Constitution and therefore the message was invalid and the Hazen bill had become law without the Governor's signature. Colby told the House that Governor Sawyer had failed to discuss the merits of the bill in his veto message, and that he had gone beyond his constitutional prerogatives in censuring the environment in which the bill was enacted. Colby insisted that the Governor had no right to question the conduct of the Legislature and said that concern rested only with the General Court itself.

The Colby resolution said, in part:

That inasmuch as the only reasons which appear in the aforesaid communication of His Excellency, the Governor, why he returned the said bill without his signature, are such as necessarily imply that the Governor is invested with power to inquire into the conduct of the two Houses of the General Court, and further imply that the Governor is charged with the duty of protecting the integrity, honor, and dignity of the two Houses of the General Court and their members. Those reasons are not such as are contemplated and required by the Constitution, and are, therefore, of no validity or legal effect. . . .

Whereas, It is the sense of this House that the omission of the Governor to examine and consider the aforesaid bill, and thereupon to determine whether he approved or disapproved it, and his omission to return with said bill a statement of his objections thereto, where omissions of acts made indispensably necessary by the Constitution to the withholding of his signature therefrom, and that, inasmuch as more than five days (Sundays excepted) have elapsed since said bill was presented to the Governor, and the same has not been returned by him to the House in which it originated, with his objections, according to the true meaning and intent of the Constitution, and the Legislature has not in the meantime adjourned, said bill has become and is a law without the signature of the Governor; therefore, be it

Resolved by the House of Representatives, That no further action be taken by this House upon the bill entitled "An act in amendment of Chapter 100 of the laws of 1883 entitled An act providing for the establishment of railroad corporations by general law," but that said act and this resolution be transmitted to the Secretary of State to the end that said act be published with the other laws passed in this session.

Following a flurry of parliamentary questions, the House approved the resolution by a 134 to 115 roll call vote. For obvious reasons, neither the resolution nor the vetoed bill ever got printed in the volume of the 1887 session laws.

Quiet After the Storm

BITTER PARTISANSHIP gave way to gift giving for a spell on Saturday morning. Warren Brown of Hampton Falls presented Speaker Burleigh with a gold watch and chain and charm, on behalf of the House members. Clerk George A. Dickey of Concord received a purse of money, and his assistant, Stephen S. Jewett of Laconia, was given a marble clock. The pages, Louis M. Patterson, Edward K. Woodworth, Harry O. Coleman, and Leverett N. Freeman, all of Concord, received silver watches and chains. The three doorkeepers, Hiram E. Currier of Littleton, George W. Varnum of Manchester, and Harry O. Coleman of Concord, were given gold-headed canes.

By their petition, publishers who furnished daily newspapers for the marathon session were voted a 150 percent increase in the payment they initially agreed to. They had agreed to each provide 350 copies daily for $1.00 each, as all concerned anticipated the session would last for two months. The final payment was boosted to $2.50. The papers were the *Concord Monitor, Concord People and Patriot, Manchester Mirror,* and *Manchester Union.* Their reporters were also each given a 100 percent emolument increase by the Legislature for their work, because of the protracted deliberations. The House had adopted a policy of paying newsmen $50 a session, since the Legislature went biennial in 1879, but the gift was raised to $100 for the 1887 session, and that rate continued until the practice was terminated twenty years later.

Governor Sawyer submitted his final veto of a third version of the Hazen bill to the House just before final adjournment Saturday morning. He attached copies of his two previous vetoes and wrote he need not say anything more. All his vetoes, incidentally, were transmitted through the Secretary of State, Ai B. Thompson of Concord.

The scandalous 1887 session produced two reform railroad regulations. In the final hours, new laws were enacted to curb bribery and railroad lobbying. One of them read:

Section 1. That whoever gives, offers, or promises to an executive or judicial officer, or any member of either branch of the Legislature, before or after he is qualified or takes his seat, any valuable consideration or gratuity whatsoever, or does or promises to do any act beneficial to such officer or member, with intent to influence his action, vote, or opinion, or judgment in any matter pending, or that may come legally before him in his official capacity, shall be punished by imprisonment for not more than five years or by fine not exceeding three thousand dollars; and whoever accepts such bribe or beneficial thing, in the manner and for the purposes aforesaid, shall forfeit his office, be forever disqualified to hold any public office, trust, or appointment under the state, and be punished by imprisonment for not more than ten years or by fine not exceeding five thousand dollars.

The statute to curb lobbying by railroads read:

Section 1. Railroads being public trusts, any officer, stockholder, or agent of any railroad corporation in this state, or of any railroad outside the state operating any railroad in this state, who shall use any of the income, funds, or property of the corporation of which he is an officer, stockholder, or agent to secure or oppose legislation, except as hereinafter provided, shall be deemed guilty of a misdemeanor, and be liable to punishment by a fine not exceeding one thousand dollars or by imprisonment in the state prison for a term not exceeding one year, or by fine and imprisonment in the discretion of the court.

Section 2. Any railroad corporation having business before the Legislature may employ counsel not exceeding three in any cause, and may be represented by any citizen and by its own officers and agents as actual witnesses and experts only, the expense of which shall appear as a distinct item in the annual returns of every railroad under the item of "Legislative Expense," as required to be made to and published by the railroad commissioners.

The 1889 Legislature wasted no time about railroad leases and mergers. It quickly passed a law granting the Boston & Maine carrier permission to take over New Hampshire lines, but with a guarantee not to increase any rates after doing so.

Creation of a Bureau of Immigration was an unusual feature of the 1889 session. It was charged with publicizing vacant farms and attracting people from other states to settle on them or use them for vacation retreats. It was given an initial appropriation of $2,500, and Secretary of Agriculture Nahum J. Bachelder of Andover was given this extra chore without any more pay. This agency proved such a success it continued in existence for a quarter of a century, and the annual illustrated pamphlets issued by Bachelder, who also became Governor, were distributed through the nation, free of charge, and have long since become collectors' items.

The 1889 session also passed a law requiring school districts to give all pupils free books and pencils, a policy which still continues.

The Railroad Scandals

PROGRESS AND REFORMS

Secret Voting Launched

W HEN THE LEGISLATURE
staged its first January opening in 1891, an array of armed
policemen was on hand because of insurrection fears. Retiring Governor David H. Goodell of Antrim, asked the Concord City government to safeguard the Capitol, and the legislative chambers in particular, for the January 7 convening. He took that action as Democratic
newspapers reported the minority party members might stage a revolt
if they lost a parliamentary fight over the seating of some six dozen
questionable Representatives-elect. Newspapers listed seventeen
policemen present, with some in plain clothes, but all of them armed,
and Mayor Stillman Humphrey seated on the rostrum as the session
was called to order.

The dispute concerned the manner in which many legislators had
been elected two months earlier. When an 1889 constitutional
amendment shifted legislative sessions from June to January, another
amendment abolished the grouping of small towns for legislative
representation and gave them individual part-time representation,
based upon their respective census population.

Nearly three dozen men were elected to the House under the old
grouping system, as their town officials claimed the new formula had
not yet been authorized by the Legislature, and most of them were
Democrats. Another forty-odd men, mostly Republicans from cities

and the larger towns, were in dispute because their elections were based upon the 1890 federal census; and their increased seat entitlements, based upon population gains from 1880, had not been approved by the Legislature.

A month earlier Governor Goodell sponsored a four-day special session of the Legislature to act on this seating dispute, which landed in the state's highest court. (See Chapter XV.)

The Democrats envisioned a chance of winning control of the House of Representatives if the obsolete system of grouping the smaller towns was legal until the new formula had been given formal legislative approval. So they appealed for, and won, a special session of the State Supreme Court to press their case. On the eve of the legislative opening, the court ruled that only each branch of the General Court could determine its own membership.

As the January 7 session convened, Stephen S. Jewett of Laconia, assistant clerk of the 1889 House, read off the names of the new members as elected under the disputed new representation formulas, and they were seated by the Republican majority of the House members who had first been sworn in without challenge. The Democrats then quietly bowed in defeat, and Mayor Humphrey and his policemen departed in peace. Of historic interest, this same 1891 Legislature later passed a law that population adjustments for legislative representation by local communities would not be legal, thenceforth, until first approved by the Legislature following a federal census. This policy was permanently tied into the state Constitution in 1942.

An initial act of the 1891 Legislature was to order ventilation systems for the House and Senate chambers to cope with winter weather. A State Board of Health survey had declared this was necessary to safeguard the solons' health. It also voted a $125,000 bond issue to build the present granite State Library building, into which the state library was moved in 1895 from Room 100 in the State House, where it had been located for thirty years.

The 1891 session produced a historic election reform milestone. New Hampshire became one of the first states to legalize use of the Australian ballot, to insure secrecy and eliminate fraud, in election of public officials. Until then, political parties and candidates produced and distributed their own ballots, of various colors, shapes, and sizes. This led to promiscuous fraud, and vote buying, as ballots could be readily identified by observers when extended by voters as they

Tranquillity marks this 1891 State House winter scene, taken the year the Legislature shifted its biennial session from June to January for the first time.
Courtesy Concord Library.

were dropped into the polling boxes.

Further Improvements in the 1890s

THE 1893 LEGISLATURE met with a surprising development as it voted a twenty-five-cent bounty on hawk heads to protect henyards. In the following year, residents of the inland town of Hudson turned in 643 heads for the bounty.

State Treasurer Solon Augustus Carter became so amazed when the Hudson town officials asked for reimbursement for their payment of the bounty that he submitted a special report on that development to the 1895 Legislature. He suggested that perhaps the Hudson heads included those of sea gulls, which then, as to this day, liked to float up the Merrimack River to guzzle garbage at town dumps. Carter also stressed that town selectmen, who paid the bounty, were not required to be ornithologists and were not supposed to know the difference between the heads of hawks and sea gulls. So he recommended repeal of the hawk bounty as the best solution for the Hudson hawk heads hustling, and the legislators heeded his advice.

The 1893 Legislature voted an additional $75,000 bond issue to complete, and furnish, the State Library structure, and a requirement that town clerks report to that agency the names of officials of their libraries. This session also created a State Forestry Commission and a Bureau of Labor.

The House of Representatives adjusted its fiscal controls in the 1895 session. It established a Committee on Appropriations, to replace the House Finance Committee, which had served since 1824. Frank Elmer Kaley of Milford, thirty-nine-year-old thread manufacturer, became the new committee's first chairman. His name, incidentally, continues to live in Milford because of substantial trusts he left in 1935 to benefit its townspeople. Kaley's committee associates were William H.C. Follansby of Exeter, Newton S. Huntington of Hanover, Fred W. Towle of Meredith, Fred C. Gowing of Dublin, A. Crosby Kennett of Conway, Daniel C. Westgate of Plainfield, Ephraim H. Whitehouse of Dover, Richard M. Johnson of Bath, Benjamin Gathercole of Colebrook, and George W. Abbott and William G. Ahern of Concord.

The 1899 Legislature financed permanent preservation of the eighty-five Civil War flags on display in the State House Hall of Flags. The emblems are in memory of New Hampshiremen who served in eighteen regiments and two artillery units in that conflict. Details of the flags were listed in the 1901 edition of the legislative *General Court Manual*.

New Seats; Local Option

THE 1901 LEGISLATURE voted $2,850 for new seats for members of the House. The old one-legged stools and crowded desks of 1864 vintage were replaced with handsome stuffed leather chairs embossed with the state seal, and with sturdy arm rests. This session also voted $250 for a portrait of the first woman to be displayed in the State House. She was Miss Harriet P. Dame of Concord, a Civil War nurse heroine, who died the previous year.

The 1903 Legislature repealed the state's 1855 prohibition law, which had never been fully enforced, and enacted a local option liquor system, under state supervision. It also served with New Hampshire's only Governor who collected two state salaries while in office. He was Nahum J. Bachelder, Andover farmer and longtime secretary of the State Board of Agriculture, with a $1,500 annual

Stephen S. Jewett

salary. When he became Governor in 1903, with a $2,000 yearly salary, Bachelder filled both positions through his biennial term as Chief Executive.

The 1905 Legislature enacted the state inheritance tax, following a 1902 constitutional amendment permitting such a selective levy. The 1905 House established a Committee on Ways and Means, for a first time, to complement the House Appropriations Committee in financing state government operations.

The Bass Reforms

THE 1911 LEGISLATURE terminated a half-century of railroad domination of the state government, upon the insistence of thirty-seven-year-old Governor Robert Perkins Bass of Peterborough. This was the culmination of struggles by the "Progressive" bloc of the Republican party, sparked by Bass and Winston Churchill of Cornish, famous author and two-term legislator, through three legislative sessions, for major government reforms.

Bass's initial reform achievement occurred in the 1907 session, as he served a second House term under Speaker Bertram Ellis, Keene newspaper editor and archconservative. Bass engineered a surprise reorganization of state spendings, including elimination of legislative subsidies for newspapermen. (See Chapter XVIII.) Bass next served in the 1909 State Senate and helped Governor Henry Brewer Quinby of Laconia sponsor substantial reforms into law. They included the direct primary to replace state political conventions for nomination of party candidates, the abolition of free railroad passes, and the registration of legislative lobbyists.

The 1909 Legislature's state government improvements became so impressive that when the 1911 session convened, it voted to invite retiring Governor Quinby to present a special report on his administration's achievements. Quinby said, in part:

Althought not the usual custom in this state for a retiring Governor to communicate by message with the incoming Legislature, yet I feel justified in acceding to the suggestion of your joint resolution by reason of the progress made and the things of importance accomplished during the administration now drawing to a close.

Assuming the oath of office as Chief Executive in January, 1909, a constant and conscientious effort was immediately begun by me and those associated with me to redeem the pledges made to the people prior to the election, the results of which, with my approval, placed laws upon our statute books fulfilling every promise and which abolished the railroad pass, restricted the influence of the lobby, established the direct primary, equalized the tax rate of corporations and individuals, reduced yet further the traffic in intoxicants, and greatly enlarged the scope of our educational system, making increased appropriations therefor with a view of giving to the children of the country districts, especially, better facilities for securing an education.

Governor Quinby also cited a $400,000 enlargement of the State House (See Chapter XX.); creation of a State Auditor to supervise state spendings; reorganization of the National Guard and the State Forestry Department, along with the launching of three major east, west, and central highways northward from the Massachusetts border, as state-financed projects, which continue to this day as principal traffic arteries.

The 1909 session went into history with another distinction. It abounded with friendly ejaculations. The legislators freely dispensed

Progress and Reforms

The Governor and Council Chamber in the northeast corner of first floor of the State House in the 1890s, before its enlargement in 1910.

Dedication of the Perkins statue at the rear of the State House in 1902. The wooden canopies over the entrance were eliminated in the 1910 revisions to the building.

the phrases "Good Lord" and "Great Scott" and "Holy Moses." This was good-natured banter aimed at Senate President Harry Lord of Manchester; House Speaker Walter Scott of Dover; and George H. Moses of Concord, the enterprising newspaperman and chief aide to Governor Quinby, who later became a famous United States Senator.

As New Hampshire's first Governor resulting from a direct primary, Bass sponsored into law several major government reforms in the 1911 legislative session, by which railroad corporations were barred from the political arena. These reforms, pledged in the Republican platform of the 1910 election campaign, included two state agencies which had long been criticized for improper supervision of railroad activities. A Public Service Commission (now the Public Utilities Commission) replaced the Railroad Commission, and a State Tax Commission (now the Board of Taxation) replaced the Board of Equalization. Another reform law barred all corporations from making political contributions and required political committees and candidates to publicly report their contributions and expenditures, all of which continue to this day.

The Boston & Maine Railroad, which then controlled all of New Hampshire's sprawling rail lines, battled Governor Bass's reforms to the bitter end. The House readily approved them. But the Senate refused, by a 15 to 9 standoff, to approve the reform bills until the eve of final adjournment on April 15. The upper branch bowed in concurrence only after Governor Bass had threatened to recess the session and tour the state to denounce the Senate dissidents for failure to adhere to the reform pledges, which bore the endorsement of the Democrats as well as the Republicans, in the 1910 election campaign.

Governor Bass Blasts Arrogance

GOVERNOR BASS bluntly blasted railroad arrogance in his inaugural address. He told the Legislature, in part:

By statutes passed in 1883 and 1889, the state authorized railroad consolidations, but only on condition that rates for fares and freights should not be increased beyond those then existing.

The Boston & Maine Railroad availed itself of the authority thus conferred, and thereby accepted the conditions upon which the authority was granted. The conditions were observed until 1903, when many rates were increased without legislative authority. In 1908, the Attorney General

Gov. Robert P. Bass

instituted legal proceedings in behalf of the state to enforce the statutory provision against such increases. The Supreme Court held unanimously that these conditions were binding upon the railroad. These illegal rates are still in force.

There is a universal demand on the part of the people of our state that corporations get out and keep out of politics. Heretofore, they have been in politics for their own selfish ends, and to a degree that was highly injurious to the interests of our citizens.

The President of the Boston & Maine Railroad has recently emphatically expressed his intention of taking his corporation out of politics. He has declared his purpose of coming openly and frankly before the Legislature to ask for such action as in his judgment is needed by his corporation. It is most desirable to bring about a proper relation between corporations and the people whom they serve and from whom they primarily derive their privileges.

The Boston & Maine proceeded to petition the Legislature to legalize its illegal rates, but the House sidetracked the plea, as Governor Bass announced refusal to concur with the bill. He insisted that the proposed new Public Service Commission judge the merits of the request first.

While the Senate stalled the two key reorganization bills, other reform measures became law. Besides enactment of controls and restrictions of political financing, they required employers to pay weekly wages in cash, unless workers agreed to accept checks, and set a fifty-eight-hour workweek for boys under sixteen and girls under eighteen years of age.

Considerable behind-the-scenes maneuvering prevailed as the Senate held up the antirailroad bills. Governor Bass later reported that as he strove to pry the reform measures through the Senate, he was repeatedly informed in private that if he approved the disputed railroad rates increases, the Senate would lift its embargo. Bass refused such a concession, and the session became the first to last into April (it adjourned April 15), since winter sessions began in 1891.

As the Senate stalemate continued, Governor Bass served an ultimatum. He let it become known that he would recess the Legislature for two months, to personally carry his reform crusade into the districts of the recalcitrant Senators, and publicly challenge their integrity. When some of the prorailroad Senators began to waver from this threat, a Boston & Maine lobbyist arranged a private party at a Portsmouth hotel to bolster their friendliness.

The railroad's party developed into a gala affair, and all present reportedly thoroughly enjoyed themselves. But it boomeranged. A *Boston American* newspaper reporter learned that several lady dancers from Boston had graced the gathering with such demonstrations of talent that the festivities continued much longer into the evening than originally planned. The newsman interviewed the entertainers, who elicited graphic boasts about how they had titillated some of the Senators, whom they named, into startling and surprising reactions.

The *Boston American* flooded Concord and other New Hampshire areas with extra copies of its edition presenting the firsthand accounts of the railroad party. The details spread through two full pages, with pictures of the dancers in scanty attire, as they said they had appeared to pleasure the Senatorial guests. It was later reported that railroad employees and friends of the dismayed Senators purchased and destroyed most of the copies. But the Bass administration obtained some of the copies and let it become known that the Governor planned to use them on his threatened speaking tour unless his Senate opponents capitulated.

Exposure of the sensational party netted quick results. The Boston

& Maine Railroad President notified Governor Bass through an intermediary that his corporation had withdrawn its opposition to the reorganization bills, with a hope that the new Public Service Commission would approve the illegal railroad rates upon viewing their need. The Senate then promptly approved both measures, after tacking a surprise amendment to the Tax Commission bill. The amendment placed appointment of its three members in the State Supreme Court rather than with the Governor and Council—and this policy continues to this day. The Senate also concurred on a House-approved measure, sponsored by Bass, which created a state workmen's compensation program, to benefit employees (or their families) injured or killed in the line of duty.

Interestingly, one of the initial acts of the new Public Service Commission was to review the disputed railroad rates, and rule them justified. Governor Bass had told the Legislature in his inaugural address that he favored such action if the railroad could prove need for the higher charges.

Governor Bass, who inherited wealth from his father, Attorney Perkins Bass, who helped pioneer Chicago into a metropolis, did not seek reelection. It had become custom to limit the Governorship to a single term after the state went on a biennial basis in 1879, and this policy continued until 1930. But Bass continued active in politics, and in 1926 he lost a bid for the Republican nomination to the United States Senate, being defeated by his longtime political foe, Senator George H. Moses of Concord, who won reelection to a third term.

Governor Bass was one of the youngest men ever to serve as a New Hampshire Governor. A son, Perkins Bass, liked to recall that his father took unusual steps to lend maturity and dignity to his administration, in dealing with his Councilors, legislative leaders, and state officials in general, because most of them were much older in years. After a few months in office, Governor Bass grew a beard and donned glasses, made of plain window glass, for that purpose.

Perkins Bass, a lawyer like his grandfather for whom he was named, followed his father's political footsteps. His Republican liberalism carried him through five legislative terms, including service as Senate President, followed by three terms in Congress. Another son, Attorney Robert Perkins Bass, Jr., served as Republican National committeeman for two quadrennial terms, beginning in 1972, following a two-year term as chairman of the Republican State Committee.

FINAL MARATHON, WAR, AND THE 1920s

The 1913 Voting Snarl

THE 1913 LEGISLATURE produced a galaxy of historic episodes. It was the last to elect a Governor or a United States Senator and the only session ever to expel a member for corruption. It also voted $12,000 to build and name a road for a President of the United States.

The session produced the first Democratic Governor in thirty-nine years. He was Attorney Samuel D. Felker of Rochester, who failed to gain a majority over Republican Franklin Worcester of Hollis, a Senator in the scandalous 1887 session, in the 1912 election. Felker became the last Governor to be elected by the Legislature, because of 1912 approval of a constitutional amendment which permitted biennial elections of Governor by a plurality, rather than majority, margin. The Democrats won 14 to 10 control of the 1913 Senate, and the House was officially tabulated as Republican by 207 to 195 over the Democrats. But newspapers listed 26 of the Republicans as of the "Progressive" bloc, and most of them voted for Felker, as he became Governor by a 222 to 191 roll call vote over Worcester. In return, William J. Britton, forty-one-year-old Wolfeboro attorney and veteran Republican leader, was given the House Speakership, following his election on the Progressive, or "Bull Moose," ticket.

The session became deadlocked in a voting spree over election of a federal Senator, which lasted a record two months, from January 14 through March 13, and totalled forty-two ballots. Unlike the 1883

William E. Chandler
Henry F. Hollis

Senatorial stalemate among Republicans, this one pitted Republicans against Democrats, with the Progressive minority manipulating the balance of power. This became the final legislative election of its kind because the federal Constitution had been amended to let the people elect United States Senators, effective in 1914.

When the Senatorial voting began on July 14, the second Tuesday of the session, as required by federal law, two House members sparked a historical incident. The only twins ever to serve together in the Granite State Legislature voted for Democrat Henry F. Hollis of Concord, on the first vote, to mark their fifty-ninth birthday anniversaries. They were William H. Willey, Jr. (firstborn) of Wakefield, known as "Potato Bill" because he wholesaled potatoes, and Joseph D. Willey, Milton merchant.

The voting continued on a daily basis, at high noon, by roll calls, as required by federal statute. But they were often invalidated because of the lack of a quorum. The voting became so monotonous that it generated an interesting vignette, as reported by newspapers. When Alonzo D. Barrett of Gorham went home one weekend, and as his train approached what had been the North Lisbon station, the brakeman roared "Barrett!" Prompt as he had become to such a call, Representative Barrett rose from his doze and replied "Hollis." The railroad had just changed its North Lisbon stop to Barrett, to avoid

To This Day

telegraphic mixup with Lisbon, and Barrett voted for Democrat Henry French Hollis, debonair young Concord lawyer, throughout the marathon.

Hollis finally won by 4 votes on the final tally. He was top man throughout the voting but lacked a majority over a disarray of Republican contenders, since most of the Progressives clung to former Governor Bass. Secretary of State Edward N. Pearson of Concord, a popular state official who was "drafted" as the Republican Senatorial nominee, held Hollis in check through most of the voting. But when Col. John H. Bartlett of Portsmouth, later to become Governor, became the Republican candidate, Hollis squeaked to victory.

Hollis was a political nonconformist. Trimly athletic, brimming zeal, and sporting a russet mustache, he told the Legislature in an appreciation speech that he was a "radical Democrat" and proud of it; that while not a formal churchgoer, he tried to practice Christian principles; and that he believed that human rights should at least share equally in rank with property rights. Hollis made history even before taking office at Washington. His election gave Concord's Ward 4 the distinction of being the only New Hampshire voting precinct ever to boast two federal Senators simultaneously. Senator Jacob H. Gallinger, then in his twenty-third year at Washington, resided in the same area.

Hollis, who became the state's first Democratic Senator since his party lost domination of state government affairs in 1855, chalked a unique mark in his Washington career. During World War I he went to Spain on a special mission for President Wilson and persuaded that government to lift an embargo on mules, sorely needed by the Allies to haul field guns through French mud, to defeat the Germans.

Interestingly, only 371 of the joint House-Senate membership of 426 voted in the forty-second ballot. It gave Hollis 189 votes, 3 more than a required majority. Bartlett received only 121 votes, as 12 Progressives stuck to the last with Bass. Former Governor Henry B. Quinby of Laconia got 18 votes, to 14 for Pearson, while 17 other votes went to nine other also-rans.

A following legislative investigation led to the ouster of a young House member on corruption charges. This incident, while unique to the Granite State, had become a widespread development in other states, according to the 1906 book on *The Election of Senators* by Dr. George H. Haynes. He wrote that seven states had experienced legislative corruption scandals of national proportion, up to 1906, in election of federal Senators.

Final Marathon, War, and the 1920s

The durable William E. Chandler was the only man to garner votes in both the 1883 and 1913 Senatorial marathons, and served two Senate terms in the interim. He had become a bearded Republican patriarch at seventy-eight, as Governor Felker took office, and frequently expressed editorial frownings upon his doings. But he capped his half-century public career by sponsoring a statue of President Franklin Pierce in the State House yard, after Republican legislatures had firmly denied such tribute to New Hampshire's only President, because he was a Democrat. Interestingly, those voting for the Pierce monument included Franklin Pierce Curtis, fifty-seven-year-old Concord railroad clerk, and a Democrat born on Lincoln's birthday anniversary.

The 1913 Legislature also renamed Mount Clinton in the White Mountains to Mount Pierce, a change which was officially ignored by the state government until 1971 when a group of Belmont grammar school pupils noted the omission on state maps and won a belated correction. To this day, markers on Mount Pierce continue to mention Mount Clinton.

Governor Felker at fifty-four was the state's last mustached Chief Executive. He took office before the General Court at 10:15 P.M., rather than the traditional high noon, so workingmen could attend. And he became a national celebrity, according to newspaper stories, as the only Governor inaugurated that year without wearing a silk shirt.

Felker and his coalition Legislature voted wholesale oustings of Republican officials in the judiciary and executive departments and replaced them with Democrats, a deed which was promptly reversed when the Republicans returned to power two years later.

Governor Felker's most lasting achievement concerned agriculture. He sponsored reorganization of the State Board of Agriculture into the present Department of Agriculture, and headed it with his cousin, Andrew L. Felker, Meredith farmer and prominent Grange leader. This paved the ouster of former Governor Nahum J. Bachelder (1903-5) of Andover, who had served as secretary of the old agency for twenty-six years. Felker was heaped with editorial censure for this act, and even his own Democratic Executive Council hedged for a time on the replacement.

Cousin Felker took office in January 1914, with a $3,500 salary, a rather impressive emolument for that period. He then proceeded to outdo Bachelder, who retired to his 700-acre farm. Commissioner Felker served as promoter and champion of New Hampshire agriculture for thirty-four years, with such self-effacing determination and dedication that he became known as the most revered public servant in State House history. He died in office at seventy-eight, in 1947, having been repeatedly reappointed by Republican Governors.

Speaker Britton was a handsome, square-jawed lawyer who became Speaker by chance. He had become an ardent Progressive of the famed Teddy Roosevelt era, and he considered it useless to seek office with that label in Wolfeboro. He received two Republican primary write-in votes and had to be coaxed, he liked to recall, to accept the nomination, which led to his election. After becoming Speaker, Britton vainly sought the identity of his two townsmen who launched him to that high position, to express suitable thanks.

Expulsion of a Legislator

A YOUTHFUL MANCHESTER PAPERHANGER was stripped from the 1913 session for trying to peddle votes. He was twenty-nine year-old Clifford L. Snow, chairman of the Progressive party's legislative bloc, who testified he was married, earned from $18 to $22 a week, and led an industrious life. Snow was expelled from the House of Representatives by a 177 to 119 roll call vote, following extensive public hearings. He was declared guilty of trying to negotiate payments for his vote, and those of other lawmakers, in Republican circles. He denied the charges under oath. But he admitted taking $100 from Worcester, the losing Republican gubernatorial candidate, and said he used it as expenses in soliciting votes for him.

Snow was a political novice who became victim of a legislative investigation which was not even aimed at him. A joint House-Senate committee had been named to probe bribery rumors connected with Senator Hollis's election. The committee gave Hollis a clean bill of political health. But Snow became buried in an avalanche of guilt, which developed to the amazement of all concerned. So he became the only person ever expelled from the Granite State Legislature in such disgrace.

White-bearded Ezra M. Smith, retired Peterborough town judge and in his twenty-fourth year as selectman, was chairman of the probe committee. Other House members were Harold A. Webster of Holderness and Albert DeMeritt of Durham. The Senate was represented by John W. Prentiss of Walpole, James O. Gerry of Madison, and James B. Wallace of Canaan.

Imposing legal talent dominated the hearings. Former Mayor Nathaniel E. Martin of Concord, glib-tongued veteran Democratic spark plug, represented Snow. Major Thomas H. Madigan, Jr., of Manchester represented the Senate, while Judge William M. Chase of Concord, retired from the Supreme Court, and Attorney Robert P. Burroughs of Manchester, were House counsel.

The committee filed two reports. The House and Senate respectively accepted unanimous reports declaring that no bribery or other corruption had been uncovered relating to the Senate contest. But Chairman Smith and Webster, clerk of the committee, recommended Snow's expulsion, with a detailed indictment of guilt, while DeMeritt declined to sign or oppose the report. Snow was tossed from the Legislature on April 17, 1913, but not before a few lawmakers had risen to his defense. William J. Ahern, Concord Democratic chieftain, said, "Snow is a hot air artist who has used his tongue here, there and everywhere but is not guilty as here charged."

Raymond K. Stevens of Landaff, the silver-tongued Democratic Congressman-elect, suggested the probe committee had possibly exceeded its authority in shifting attention from its primary objective, but agreed that if Snow was guilty he should be ousted. Republican Pardon W. Allen of Haverhill called the penalty too harsh because Snow was a political neophyte who failed to realize the enormity of his transgression. Democrat Charles J. O'Neil of Walpole said:

This whole investigation has been the meanest kind of political chicanery from the beginning and this recommendation is made by men no better than the man at whom it is aimed. Let him who is without sin cast the first stone at this poor, vain, vapid creature here accused.

Both the *Manchester Union* and the *Concord Monitor*, which traditionally seldom agree about any issue, joined in commending the House for the expulsion as a deed deservedly done.

Snow apparently became smothered in his own inexperience and too much boasting. His cross-examination about a visit to a Franklin "road house," in the unsuspecting company of two detectives employed by a Republican source, was so unsavory that newspapers reported it unfit to print. When confronted by testimony from a fellow legislator that he had "flashed" a roll of bills aggregating $300, Snow insisted he had borrowed it from a Manchester moneylender, whom he declined to identify, without signature.

The Smith-Webster expulsion recommendation was embodied in

a written report, which was tabled for weekend study before being put to April 17 vote. It said:

Your committee upon a consideration of all the evidence finds that on or about Feb. 1, 1913, Clifford L. Snow, being at the time a member of this House from Ward 3, in the city of Manchester, offered to dispose of his vote, and that of four other members of this House, whose names he did not divulge, for United States Senator to Gordon Woodbury of Manchester for a pecuniary consideration, to wit, for the sum of $1,000.

Your committee further finds that on or about Feb. 1, 1913, said Clifford L. Snow offered to dispose of his vote, and that of two other members of this House, whose names he did not divulge, for United States Senator to Gordon Woodbury, said offer being made directly to said Woodbury's agent, W.D. Young of said Manchester. This offer was made for a pecuniary consideration, to wit, for the sum of $200.

Your committee further finds that on or about Jan. 15, 1913, said Clifford L. Snow made an offer to Elmer S. Tilton of Laconia—said Tilton being a candidate before the Legislature for election as a member of the Governor's Council—to obtain votes for said Tilton for said office of Councilor, provided said Tilton would "do the right thing" by said Snow.

Your committee further finds that said Clifford L. Snow on or about the date of the convening of this Legislature made an offer to Phillip H. Faulkner of Keene, he being at the time secretary of the Republican State Committee, to obtain the votes of nine Democrats, members of the Legislature, for the sum of $900, or $100 each vote, said Snow to conduct all negotiations and to handle said funds.

Your committee further finds that on or about Feb. 17, 1913, said Clifford L. Snow made a trip to Franklin, and while there visited a so-called "road house."

Your committee further finds that the conduct hereinbefore specifically referred to on the part of said Clifford L. Snow while a member of this House was highly discreditable and disgraceful, and constitutes a stigma upon his own reputation as a member of this House, and likewise constitutes a stigma upon the reputation and dignity and honor of the House itself.

Final Marathon, War, and the 1920s

Wherefore, the undersigned, a majority of your (House) committee, present the following resolution and moves its adoption:

Whereas, Clifford L. Snow, while a member of this House, from Ward 3 in the city of Manchester, has been found guilty of conduct discreditable to himself and highly disgraceful to this House, and constituting a stigma upon the reputation and dignity and honor of this House, therefore,

Resolved that said Clifford L. Snow be and he is hereby expelled from membership in this House and the clerk is hereby instructed to strike his name from the list of members.

A few weeks after Clifford's expulsion, the House voted without comment to allow him the full salary of $200 for the session, which ended late in May.

President Wilson's Visits

OTHER DRAMA WAS LINKED to the April 17 ouster. An hour or so earlier, the General Court dropped everything to rush $12,000 into law for speedy improvement of a three-mile highway section at Cornish, as President Woodrow Wilson announced plans to vacation there.

The new road ran from the old Cornish toll bridge, out of Vermont, up the Connecticut River Valley to Harlakenden House, residence of Winston Churchill, noted author and political Progressive, where the President was to spend the summer. As recommended by Governor Felker, the lawmakers voted to name the improved stretch Wilson Road, in tribute to the honor conferred by President Wilson in shifting the nation's Capital to New Hampshire for the summer season, for the only such instance in the state's history. It proved such a mutual success that Wilson spent two summers there, much to the economic delight of that section of the state.

The Wilson road label was superimposed upon River Road, which skirted the river northward to Lebanon. But it did not stick. Fire destroyed Harlakenden House ten years later, and the site has an appropriate marker sponsored by the State Historical Commission. In contrast, Wilson Road, as such, has become forgotten, though it legally retains that name. Long since, it has become part of Route 12-A.

Congressman-elect Stevens chalked a legislative precedent by sitting in the Legislature while entitled to share more prestigious company at Washington. He remained in Concord to help Senator Hollis snatch victory, and then to safeguard him against possible besmirchment from the bribery investigation. The Republican leadership forced a Stevens showdown the day before Snow fell. It argued that Democrat Stevens had become a legal part of Congress when it convened on March 4, because he not only had accepted a certificate of election but had participated in a Democratic Congressional caucus at the time.

The Republican challenge also stressed that others before Stevens in somewhat similar circumstances had not dared his temerity. What it referred to was that Dr. Jacob H. Gallinger of Concord had served in the 1891 Legislature after being elected to the United States Senate and then resigned on March 4 when his Washington post went into effect, and Henry E. Burnham of Manchester did the same in the 1901 session.

Stevens kept it simple in a floor debate on the Republican threat to oust him. He said he had not taken a Congressional oath and therefore chose to remain in the Legislature and won his point. The House endorsed his stand by an overwhelming vote and added thunderous applause for emphasis. The *Concord Monitor* observed the outcome was not unexpected because "Stevens is one of the most magnetic speakers who ever took the floor in the New Hampshire Legislature." On April 22 Stevens resigned and went to his Washington duties.

The 1913 session was not all grimness. The old *New York Sun* flashed this ray of illumination in late January:

New Hampshire Outrage—In one House of the New Hampshire Legislature lurks a proposal to desecrate a great, natural, New Hampshire monument, to plant a blister on the cheek of New Hampshire poetry, to deflower and ravage the very soul of New Hampshire nomenclature, to kick out the honorable custom of immemorial years, to swat the nose of history and decency.

Then the *Sun* elucidated. It explained that House Bill 269 had been filed to change the name of Hit Tit, or Hitty Titty Pond, in Salem and Windham, to Shadow Lake. The bill became law despite the *Sun's* conniption—and possible argument that regardless, Shadow Lake no longer reflected the image it once cast.

The 1913 Legislature developed still other distinction. It was the first session to convene on New Year's Day. This was caused by the

Final Marathon, War, and the 1920s

1889 constitutional amendment ending summer sessions, which convened on the first Wednesday in June, and requiring the General Court to meet on the first Wednesday of January in the odd-numbered years. This rarity occurred again in 1919 and 1947, along with 1969 and 1975. But it can happen no longer, because a 1974 constitutional amendment now permits the Legislature to organize on the first Wednesday of December, biennially, and then convene for lawmaking on the first Wednesday after the first Tuesday in January.

Perhaps one of the oddest observations ever made relating to legislative affairs was prompted as the 1913 session considered the effectiveness of local option liquor controls. The *Concord Monitor* observed:

The shortest sentence in the English language containing all the letters of the alphabet is "Pack my box with five dozen liquor jugs," but the New Hampshire Legislature has in mind to decrease its epistolary use in this state.

The War Years

THE 1915 LEGISLATURE imposed a ban on members of the Executive Council from state appointments while still in office. This law resulted from appointment by Governor Felker and his 1913-14 Council of Councilor William H. Sawyer of Concord to the Superior Court.

The 1915 session shifted the quadrennial primary for election of delegates to the national Presidential conventions to annual town meeting day, the second Tuesday in March. The 1913 Legislature had set it for the third Tuesday in May. It also reorganized the municipal courts system, for appointment of Republican Judges to replace the Democratic incumbents who took office when the 1913 Legislature reorganized these Republican-dominated tribunals and filled them with Democrats. The 1915 session granted State House agencies permission to close on holiday and Saturday afternoons.

Several hundred legislators poured into Concord on June 8, 1915, for a Second Legislative Reunion, as a final feature of the Capital's observance of the 150th anniversary of its being named Concord by the 1765 provincial Assembly. Hosea W. Parker of Claremont, who served in the 1859 and 1860 sessions, presided over a Representatives Hall program, in which veteran legislators recalled experiences of the previous half-century. The details of this were published in the November 1915 issue of the *Granite Monthly* magazine.

Representatives Hall after its enlargement in 1910. The State House roof was raised to permit removal of the south or rear wall and the chamber's enlargement to its present size. The seats shown were installed in 1900, rearranged in the 1910 renovation, and replaced in 1958.

A First Legislative Reunion was a two-day affair, on June 30 and July 1, 1896. Former Governor Person C. Cheney of Manchester was president of this reunion, which was arranged by Joseph Webster Robinson, sixty-four-year-old Concord telegrapher then serving a first term in the House. Former Mayor Moses Humphreys of Concord, aged eighty-three, was the oldest ex-legislator in attendance, and luncheons, banquets, and a Grand Ball were held in Phenix Hall and the Opera House, along with State House events.

The 1919 Legislature featured expressions of appreciation for New Hampshire's returning veterans of World War I. The legislators imposed a $400,000 tax upon the cities and towns to finance a $30 bonus for each veteran. In a September special session, they authorized an additional $70 bonus, which was financed by boosting the $3 annual poll tax to $5. The joint $100 appreciation payment went to 19,425 veterans.

Several other appreciation actions were voted for the homecoming soldiers and sailors. The Legislature gave a $10,000 appropriation to

The State Department of Education was sponsored in the 1919 legislative session by a 1917 interim commission of house members named by Gov. Henry W. Keyes. Clarence M. Collins of Danville (center) was chairman. His associates were (from left top) Benjamin W. Couch of Concord; James S. French of Moultonborough; youthful Richard H. Horne of Manchester, who later became the agency's business manager for 40 years; and veteran Attorney James F. Brennan of Peterborough.

Governor John H. Bartlett of Portsmouth and his Council to sponsor welcoming programs, and voted local communities special authority to finance similar parties and memorials, as the veterans arrived home. The Governor was given a $15,000 allotment to present each honorably discharged veteran "A certificate of honorable service, to be signed by the Governor and to bear the seal of the state, and also a medal of honor, which shall be a badge of such honorable service."

The 1919 legislators voted a $500,000 bond issue, to be matched by the Maine Legislature, and supplemented by the federal government, for construction of the large bridge over the Piscataqua River at Portsmouth, as a memorial to the veterans of both states, which was opened in August 1923. Governor Bartlett and his Council were also authorized to erect a memorial tablet in the State House to perpetuate the memory of the New Hampshiremen who gave their lives in the recent war. This became a huge bronze tablet, which continues to grace the Hall of Flags, at a cost of $4,100. It contains 697 names, as listed in Secretary of State Hobart Pillsbury's 1927 *New Hampshire History*; it was not hung until the fall of 1924 because of problems in compiling the honored names.

Governor Rolland H. Spaulding of Rochester vainly tried to initiate more detailed budget supervision in the 1915 Legislature. But he was successful in inducing the legislators to impose a uniform fiscal controls system upon the cities and towns.

In his zeal for better government, Governor Spaulding, a millionaire industrialist, continued to press for improved state fiscal controls even after leaving office in January 1917. He published his views in the January 1919 issue of the *Granite Monthly*, for the attention of the members of the 1919 Legislature. Spaulding stressed that annual state government costs had increased from $1 million in the previous decade to $2.5 million. He pointed out that in 1916 Maryland had become the first state to impose executive budget controls, as it was threatened with bankruptcy. He also reported that both Massachusetts and New Jersey had adopted strong budget supervision in 1918.

In emphasizing need for better state budgeting practices, Spaulding graphically cited a budget crisis which faced his successor, Governor Henry W. Keyes of Haverhill, in the 1917 session, as follows:

"How much do you want?" and "We'll give you so much" have been as characteristic of legislative appropriations as of horse trades, in New Hampshire in the past.

Final Marathon, War, and the 1920s

This undignified, to use a mild word, relation between state departments and legislative committees is disliked by the former for another good reason. Even the department head who has shrewdly and with forethought swelled his estimates to take care of the inevitable cut often finds himself and his work sorely wounded by having the legislative committee do its operating on a part of this schedule which he had not anticipated. The pound of flesh sometimes is taken from too near the heart of the subject.

To such an extent was this the case at the legislative session of 1917 that when the House Appropriations Committee was ready to report and the worst was known in regard to what it had done, the heads of the state departments formed in a body, moved in a procession to the executive chamber, and pleaded with the Governor to save the financial lives of some of their projects and lines of work.

This the Governor was able to do to some extent, unofficially; but so far as his power in the matter under the laws and constitution extends, all he could have done would be to veto the entire appropriations bill and to withhold his approval until the various items in it had been adjusted in accordance with his wishes.

There have been times when the governors have been sorely tempted to do that very thing. But it never has been done, and with the adoption of an up-to-date budget plan it never need be done.

Soon after the 1919 Legislature convened, it was presented a unique seminar on the history of state finances. It was sponsored by House Speaker Charles W. Tobey of Temple, who subsequently became the only New Hampshireman ever to preside over both branches of the General Court and be elected as Governor and to both branches of the national Congress.

The fiscal résumé was presented at a February 5 evening session in Representatives Hall by Bank Commissioner James O. Lyford of Concord, a noted historian. He documented details of legislative spendings through the fifty-three-year period following the Civil War. He explained that in the twenty-seven-year period up to 1892, the Legislature's major fiscal problem had been paying off state war debts (largely for enlistment bounties), of about $4 million, along with some $2 million of similar town obligations, which the state took over by legislative decree in 1871. Lyford observed that "It was almost impossible during this period of debt payments to create a new state agency or to increase a state salary."

Lyford's documented report (a copy of which is preserved by the New Hampshire Historical Society) disclosed that the Civil War indebtedness was not completely paid off until 1905. Then he listed basic increases in general state government spendings for the 1905-18 period, as compared with the 1892-1904 years. Interestingly, in retrospect they showed public health up from $117,353 to $625,878; public improvements, including highways, up from $231,786 to $4,731,337; education up from $511,351 to $2,579,000; support of the poor up from $794,185 to $4,623,390; and penal costs up from $192,345 to $1,028,300.

Commissioner Lyford concluded his presentation by emphasizing that state government spendings had increased to $16,344,000 for the 1904-18 period, or five times the $3,250,000 total for the previous dozen years. Turning to the 1919 Legislature's need to increase revenue because of pending spending increases, Lyford philosophically told the legislators:

You are face to face with the same problem that has confronted your predecessors, namely—to select the more pressing demands and defer action on the others.

The millennium is not to be brought about by the acts of one session of the Legislature. One hundred years hence, if the New Hampshire Legislature continues to show the same liberal spirit that it has for the past thirteen years, there will still be opportunity for improving the condition of the people.

There were other memorable events in the 1919 legislative session. It created a State Board of Education with broad supervisory powers over municipal school districts, which continue to this day. It also indulged in a colorful hassle over adoption of the official state flower, the details of which are contained in a 1975 legislative commemorative booklet by this writer.

The 1919 session, which adjourned on March 28, as the shortest since 1905, approved ratification of the national prohibition amendment, but it failed to endorse woman suffrage. So Governor Bartlett called a brief special session for September 9, when the legislators promptly voted approval of the federal constitutional amendment granting women the right to vote and hold elective office, which became effective in August 1920.

More Change in the 1920s

THE 1923 LEGISLATURE came up with a first Democratic House since 1874. It was tied to Democrat Governor Fred H. Brown of Somersworth, New Hampshire's first Chief Executive of that party ever elected by popular vote since the Republicans first took over the General Court in 1857.

The Republicans remained in control of the State Senate for the 1923 session, but the upper branch joined in enactment of one of the most unusual taxes ever developed in this state. It was entitled "An Act For The Taxing Of Income Derived From Intangibles." This was a compromise levy on interest and dividends, to replace the traditional classification of money as property, and subject to the local property tax of each community. The adjustment was made because citizens were declining to report their investments in stocks and bonds, and municipal assessors did not have the means to discover such "property," and impose stiff penalties for such evasions.

In proposing this tax adjustment in his inaugural address, Governor Brown observed:

The present method of taxing securities, such as bonds, notes and money at interest, has proved a complete failure. It produces comparatively little revenue and is unjust in its operation.

Bonds and money on hand or at interest are subject to the general property tax and assessed at full face value, and taxed at the full local rate. This method takes such a large part of the income from such securities that it has resulted in wholesale evasion of the law in spite of drastic penalties.

What became known as the state interest and dividends tax quickly proved its worth. In its first full year of operation it produced $424,000, compared with only $175,000 in 1922 from the old taxing formula on money. By 1931 it had increased to $641,000. This gain in revenue, collected by the state and returned to the towns and cities in which the respective taxpayer resided, materialized, despite a proviso exempting the first $200 of interest and dividends for each person.

The 1929 Legislature voted $25,000 for a New Hampshire building at the Eastern States Exposition in Springfield, Massachusetts. It also established "Armistice Day" (now Veterans Day) as a holiday.

THE LAST FIFTY YEARS

Winant and Budget Controls

CENTRALIZED BUDGET CONTROLS for New Hampshire's state government were launched by the 1931 Legislature, as a massive economic depression swept the nation. This was accomplished as supervision of state finances was transferred from the State Treasurer to the Governor, through a new Comptroller agency.

Governor John Gilbert Winant, Concord schoolmaster who rose to international repute as American ambassador to Great Britain during World War II, sponsored this wholesale revision of the state's fiscal affairs. State spendings had traditionally been supervised by the Treasurer, a legislative appointee. The Comptroller became an appointee of the Governor and the Council and operated under their supervision. The Comptroller was given general supervision of the fiscal affairs of the state agencies and processed their biennial budget requests for the Governor. The Chief Executive, in turn, was charged with evaluating the budget requests and then submitting finalized spending recommendations to the Legislature.

This historic adjustment of state fiscal controls included the shifting of the state government's fiscal year from August 31 to July 1. The 1931 Legislature also established a "sinking fund" to finance bond issues and capital improvements, for creation of jobs to combat soaring unemployment. At Governor Winant's suggestion, the session voted a franchise tax upon public utilities to finance the fund and

Gov. John G. Winant

assigned the state's annual share of the federal estate tax, newly voted by the Congress, to the same purpose.

The first centralized budget, as submitted by Governor Winant to the 1933 Legislature, was adjusted to the economic depression. It showed a 10 percent reduction in the pay of all state personnel, including the Governor himself, and all other executive spendings. This austerity budget, which the Legislature readily approved, totalled about $6.5 million for the ensuing biennium. It contained a significant proviso that no state worker's salary would be reduced to less than $1,500 a year. This first gubernatorial budget did not include the Highway Department and the Fish and Game Department, for they were self-supporting from their own revenue sources.

This Winant-sponsored improvement in state fiscal controls was the culmination of repeated demands for such action through the previous forty years. State Treasurer Solon A. Carter of Concord had first suggested formal budget controls to the 1893 Legislature. He said in his annual report that the few state agencies of that period should be required to submit biennial estimates of their fiscal needs and be prepared to justify them before the Legislature. The recommendation went unheeded.

Governor Henry B. Quinby of Laconia had induced the 1909 Legislature to enact modest fiscal supervision. State officials were then required to file budget requests with the State Treasurer before the Legislature convened, and he then submitted them to the House Appropriations Committee. This 1909 Legislature also had repealed all traditional annual appropriations, with which some agencies had long been in the habit of operating.

The 1933 Legislature gave Governor Winant more than he bargained for. It produced two major new sources of revenue against his wishes, but to which he bowed.

This session pioneered race track gambling for the New England area, and a year later a special session of the 1933 Legislature produced the nation's first State Liquor Monopoly System. (See Chapter XV.) The pari-mutuel gambling, launched at Rockingham Race Track in Salem, became law on April 23, 1933, without Governor Winant's signature. The state liquor program bill was signed by Governor Winant on June 5, 1934, with a unique reservation. He told the Legislature that while he continued to believe that prohibition was better in the public interest, he also felt that the Legislature was more representative of the people's wishes than a Governor.

Governor Winant won a legislative concession on the new gambling and liquor revenues. The Legislature agreed to siphon it into the sinking fund, for retirement of state indebtedness, as Winant successfully argued it was contrary to public prudence to support general state services from such revenue sources. But Winant's restriction was soon abandoned by subsequent Legislatures. Income from liquor and gambling boomed beyond expectations and developed into a principal source of support of the state government, which continues to this day.

Federal Influence Imposed

A S THE FEDERAL GOVERNMENT poured millions of dollars into New Hampshire to help the state create jobs and launch programs for the care of the needy, state activities expanded to such degree through the 1930s that the Governorship became a full-time position for a first time. When Governor Francis Parnell Murphy of Nashua became New Hampshire's first Catholic Chief Executive in 1937, he won a protracted legislative battle to merge county and municipal welfare activities into a state agency. This was done to qualify for massive federal subsidies for new welfare programs.

State finances underwent another adjustment when Governor Murphy, in   ?cond term, won another legislative battle in the 1939 session for enactment of the tobacco tax to replace the traditional annual direct state tax upon the cities and towns. Opponents, including the State Tax Commission, argued that the tobacco levy would not produce sufficient revenue to offset the direct tax, which then totalled more than $1 million a year. But the tobacco tax developed into yet another lucrative state income source.

Dr. Robert O. Blood of Concord, a decorated World War I veteran, became Governor in 1941, and the stresses of World War II curbed state government affairs through his two terms in office. The state was forced to cope with a manpower shortage and with wartime restrictions on travel and supplies to such a degree that his administration produced an approximate $6 million Treasury surplus.

The wartime 1943 Legislature produced several historic incidents. Its House membership rose to an all-time record 443 men and women, Speaker Sherman Adams of Lincoln sponsored daily legislative mileage payments for a first time, and a handsome silver water set was given to the House of Representatives for permanent use on the Speaker's rostrum.

The House seating facilities became so overcrowded by the 1943 membership increase resulting from population gains in the 1940 federal census that a recessed Constitutional Convention was promptly reconvened to resolve the emergency. The convention passed an amendment which restricted the House membership to not more than 400, and the voters gave subsequent referendum approval to the limitation, which continues to this day.

Speaker Adams proposed the daily mileage payments to bolster House attendance. The Legislature had long operated with a weekly mileage allowance of ten cents per mile, to and from a member's home, and an increasing number of Representatives reported for duty on Tuesday of each week, to sign the mileage roster, and then were absent from the customary Wednesday and Thursday sessions. Adams won approval of a daily five cents per mile allowance, and the adjustment substantially improved attendances.

The water set gift resolved a House wartime problem. The House had traditionally purchased water equipment for each Speaker, and he was permitted to retain it upon leaving office. But when the 1943 session convened, the State Purchasing Agent reported a new set was unavailable because of wartime restrictions. When this dilemma became public, Miss Avis W. Robinson, last survivor of a pioneer Concord family, contributed a rare silver set of a pitcher and goblets. This gift has ever since permanently graced the Speaker's rostrum, 217 and has been carefully guarded when the House goes into recess. Engraved on the pitcher bottom is: "Presented by The Family Of Edwin Putnam Robinson, January, 1943," along with "Rogers Smith & Co., New Haven, Conn., June 8, 1858."

The 1943 Legislature enacted Governor Blood's suggestion for a $100 bonus for World War II veterans, even before that conflict neared termination. It also tacked an extra $3 assessment to the annual municipal poll tax (now a residential tax) to finance the payments.

The 1945 Legislature produced several historic events. It paid fresh homage to Gen. John Stark, New Hampshire's hero of the Battles of Bunker Hill and Bennington by adopting his slogan of "Live Free or Die" as the state motto. Then it adopted the Old Man of the Mountain as the state emblem, which included the motto. It voted $5,500 to erect a granite monument on the grave of Franklin Pierce, the Granite State's only United States President (1853-57). The 1945 session also established the present State Retirement System, which provides pensions for state and municipal employees.

State fiscal controls, sponsored by Governor Sherman Adams, were reorganized in a special session of the 1949 Legislature in the spring of 1950 (See Chapter XV.)

Features of Recent Years

THE LEGISLATURE HAS BOOSTED its own mileage allowances several times in the past quarter of a century, and it has twice suffered adverse State Supreme Court rulings in doing so. It voted on two occasions to set minimum payments of $4 or $5 for daily attendance, to benefit the Concord solons and others residing close to the capitol, and each time the high court declared them unconstitutional.

The 1949 Legislature first came up with a mileage formula of $4 for the first mile or fraction thereof, and five cents per mile for additional daily travel. The *Concord Monitor* challenged the formula, and the high court agreed that the $4 proviso exceeded the constitutional restriction that only reasonable mileage payments, and no other form of remuneration besides the $200 biennial salary, could be given to any legislator. So the 1949 Legislature enacted a plan of ten cents for each of the first forty-five miles, eight cents for the following twenty-five, six cents for the next twenty-five miles, and five cents for all additional mileage, on a daily basis.

The 1957 session adjusted the mileage law to twenty cents for the first forty-five miles, eight cents for the next twenty-five miles, six cents for the following twenty-five miles, and five cents for additional travel.

The 1961 Legislature ran into court trouble with a new formula of twenty-five cents for each of the first forty-five miles, eight cents for additional miles of daily travel, and each member to be paid for a minimum of twenty miles per day. The *Concord Monitor* quickly challenged the minimum proviso, for it meant $5 per day, whether traveled or not, and the State Supreme Court ruled it unconstitutional.

The high court's 1961 mileage decision was virtually apologetic. The Judges wrote the Legislature that they sympathized with the legislators' efforts to offset their low pay. But the court explained, in this most unusual opinion, that the state Constitution was crystal clear on the subject of legislative mileage, and should not be circumvented. The Supreme Court went so far as to tell the Legislature:

In this state compensation of legislators for a legislative term was fixed at $200 in another century. Under present conditions it is grossly inadequate. This antediluvian standard for compensation of the legislators has been almost universally criticized by both experts and laymen alike.

When the 1963 legislature convened, it voted another mileage formula for its membership. This one allowed twenty-five cents for each of the first twenty-five miles, twenty cents for the next twenty miles, eight cents for the following twenty-five miles, six cents for the next twenty-five miles, and five cents for all mileage over ninety-five miles per day of travel.

The 1965 Legislature boosted the mileage formula to benefit a majority of the membership. It voted twenty-five cents for each of the first forty-five miles, eight cents for the next twenty-five miles, and six cents for all additional mileage. The 1975 Legislature voted yet another mileage increase. This formula, effective on January 1, 1977, allowed thirty cents for each of the first forty-five miles, fifteen cents for all additional miles of daily travel, but with a daily maximum of $40.

Schoolings for freshmen legislators were started by House Speaker Richard F. Upton of Concord, as the 1949 Legislature convened. He arranged with University of New Hampshire officials to sponsor four informational sessions on January 11-12 and January 18-19, in Representatives Hall, which were labeled a "Legislative Institute." Director George Deming of the UNH Bureau of Government Research, and Professor Norman Alexander of the UNH Department of Government, were in charge.

Four years later the UNH Bureau of Government Research arranged a three-day seminar, January 13-15, in Representatives Hall for all legislators, including the first-termers. In recent sessions, the legislative leaderships have utilized the General Court's own personnel and facilities to inform incoming lawmakers regarding their duties and responsibilities.

The custom of opening daily legislative sessions with a Pledge of Allegiance to the American flag, in addition to the traditional brief invocation, began in the 1955 session. Representative Harry A. Bishop, Sr., of Gorham, fifty-nine-year-old World War I veteran and a first-termer, sponsored this policy. The House voted approval, and Speaker Charles Griffin of Lincoln launched the practice of designating different members to lead each pledge, a practice that is still in effect.

Seats No. 13 Abolished

BECAUSE OF ONE MAN'S SUPERSTITION, there have been no No. 13 seats in New Hampshire's Representatives Hall since 1958. This novelty developed when Governor Lane Dwinell of Lebanon and his Council became deadlocked over purchase of new House chairs in the fall of that year. The dispute centered on the merits of various bids for them.

The stalemate assumed alarming proportions as it dragged through September. This developed because when the 1957 Legislature authorized the replacement of the old chairs, installed in 1900, the members had been permitted to possess their respective seats as historic relics, and the next biennial session was to convene in three months.

The late Representative Joseph H. Geisel of Manchester, banker and veteran legislator, breached the dilemma in a dramatic manner on September 30, as Governor Dwinell was vacationing in Europe. With the advice of Attorney General Louis C. Wyman of Manchester, Geisel presented a check for $23,134 to Acting Governor Eralsey Ferguson of Pittsfield to purchase the new chairs from the company which

George E. Spofford

Dwinell had favored. Wyman promptly ruled the transaction legal, and Representative Geisel announced that he would never seek reimbursement for his unique generosity, but would accept it if voted by the incoming 1959 Legislature. When the 1959 legislators convened in the comfortable new seats, Geisel was promptly reimbursed, with thanks.

Meanwhile, the eighty-seven-year-old Representative Geisel, native of Castalia, Ohio and born on St. Valentine's Day in 1871, unobtrusively had the numeral 13 eliminated from each of the five divisions of seats, which had been separately numbered ever since Representatives Hall was first enlarged in 1865. This deletion was privately agreed to by the legislative leadership as Geisel insisted upon this concession to his superstition, as a modest reward for his generosity.

Mrs. Greta M. Ainley of Manchester, past president of the National Order of Women Legislators, and a twelfth-termer in the 1981 House, often recalled this Geisel imprint, as freshman legislators questioned absence of numeral 13 in each of the five seating sections. The Geisel ploy has had special significance for Representative Ainley because she was the last to occupy Seat 13 in Division Four, in the 1957 session, and has since continued to occupy it at her home. Others who were last to occupy No. 13 seats were Emery W. Carr of Wolfeboro; Miss Ellen Faulkner of Keene; Robert L. Galloway of Walpole; and Mrs. Alice L. Ramsdell of Nashua, who filled Seat 13 in Division Three for five consecutive terms.

The 1963 Legislature won worldwide attention by legalizing the nation's first state lottery of the twentieth century. (Details of the manner in which this historic episode occurred are presented in Chapter XVII.)

New Hampshire's legislators staged a gala celebration in Representatives Hall on June 2, 1969, of the sesquicentennial of the opening of the State House in 1819. The oldest living former legislator, who celebrated his own centennial birthday on the same day, was guest of honor. He was George E. Spofford, retired Auburn farmer, who enjoyed cigars so much that a box of 100 of them was presented to him by the 1969 legislators. Spofford died two months later.

The Legislature sponsored the first of a series of commemorative decanters, for sale in the state liquor stores, for the observance of the Capitol's 150th anniversary. It was a replica of the original 1819 State House as it was shaped prior to its two enlargements.

The 1969 Legislature met with considerable editorial criticism for another action. The legislators voted themselves free rides on the state's three toll turnpikes, and one newspaper editor went so far as to call the action "a new low" in legislative conduct. Actually, it was but a resurrection of an old legislative custom. Back in 1680, when the New Hampshire Legislature was first created at Portsmouth, with only eleven members from four towns, one of their first acts was to vote themselves free rides on the two toll ferries in that town.

Service in New Hampshire's citizen Legislature is not legally considered as employment. The State Supreme Court ruled in 1950 that legislators may collect unemployment compensation when on duty if their regular jobs, or a suitable substitute position, continue unavailable. The issue was raised by Representative Joseph J. Roukay of Manchester, a mill worker who became unemployed after being elected to the House. The high court summarized its decision as follows:

No reason for his ineligibility appears in the record other than his membership in the Legislature, which in and of itself does not make him unavailable for work. . . .

The Last Fifty Years

222

Cornelius, Martin, and Richardson.

Joseph and Kendall Cote

Robert Lawton and Doris Thompson

John and Cecelia Winn

James and Howard Humphrey

Katherine Harriman and Shirley Harriman White

To This Day

Commissioner Benjamin C. Adams of the State Department of Employment Security reported to this writer in October 1978, when asked for comment on that 1950 ruling:

Payments have been made to members of the General Court because of that Supreme Court decision. As a result of this ruling, members of the Legislature are treated exactly as they would be if they were not members of the Legislature.

As the nation observed its Bicentennial, the 1975 Legislature produced a display of democratic membership which was undoubtedly without equal elsewhere. The 1975 House of Representatives included the first black man and the first Indian ever to serve in the Granite State Legislature. They were, respectively, Henry B. Richardson of Greenville, a retired army Colonel, and Michael R. Cornelius of Hanover, a Dartmouth College student.

Most remarkable, the 1975 House also included a sister and brother, two brothers, a mother and son, and a father and son. Nashua produced the sister-brother team of Miss Cecelia L. Winn, retired teacher, and John T. Winn, retired salesman, who served his first House term in 1919, in the last all-male Legislature.

The brothers (the third set to sit in the New Hampshire Legislature) were Howard Humphrey, Sr., of Antrim, retired utility company employee, and James A. Humphrey of Andover, retired state trooper. Both were in their third terms, and each was then chairman of his respective town's board of selectmen.

New Hampshire's 1975 House of Representatives boasted a history-making membership. It included a first Indian, Michael Cornelius, a Dartmouth College student; a first black, retired Army officer, Henry Richardson of Greenville; and Josephine Martin of Amherst, a Florida College student and the first 19-year-old legislator in history. In addition there were a father and son, Joseph and Kendall Cote of Manchester; a mother and son, Doris Thompson of Northfield and Robert Lawton of Meredith; a sister and brother, John and Cecelia Winn of Nashua; two brothers, James Humphrey of Andover and Howard Humphrey of Antrim; and a mother and daughter, Katherine J. Harriman of Concord and Shirley Harriman White of Somersworth. Photos courtesy of The New Hampshire Times *and Doug Van Reath.*

The mother-son combination comprised Mrs. Doris L. Thompson of Northfield, retired bookkeeper, in her seventh term, and Robert M. Lawton of Meredith, proprietor of a tourists' center, in his third term.

Manchester produced the father-son duo of Joseph L. Cote, retired commercial pilot, in his fourth term, and Kendall Jeffrey Cote, a first-termer, and they were elected from different precincts.

The youngest person ever to serve in the Legislature, up to 1975, was nineteen-year-old Josephine Coster Martin of Amherst, a college student. She was born on September 26, 1955, and served in the 1975 session. The mother-daughter combination comprised Mrs. Katherine J. Harriman of Concord and Mrs. Shirley White of Somersworth.

Part 4

Special Topics

Speaker George B. Roberts, Jr. presiding over a 1977 House session from the modernized rostrum he sponsored as part of a major renovation of Representatives Hall.

STORY OF THE SENATE

The 1784 Origin

WHEN NEW HAMPSHIRE'S present constitutional government was launched in 1784, the State Senate was created as a legislative restraint. It was designed primarily to weigh the merit of all actions by the populous House of Representatives, with power to revise or veto any of them.

The Senate became the upper legislative branch, in place of the provincial Council, which, in representing the British royal government, had supervised and restricted House actions for nearly a century. The Senate also became representative of property. In fact, when the Constitution was remodeled in 1792, the twelve Senate seats became apportioned on the basis of taxable wealth.

Unlike the royal Councils, appointed by overseas kings, the Senate became elected by the people. It was given the right to initiate legislation. In the overall, the Senate was established as a coequal legislative branch with the House. Each was given negative authority against the other, except for one major distinction. The Constitution barred the Senate from originating "all money bills." It retained for the House the exclusive authority to initiate taxes and spendings, in the following provision:

All money bills shall originate in the House of Representatives; but the Senate may propose, or concur with amendments, as on other bills.

The Senate was different in its early years from its present makeup.

It first had a membership of twelve men, apportioned on county lines. Rockingham, whose wealthy towns of Portsmouth and Exeter had dominated New Hampshire's political, judicial, and economic life for nearly a century, was allotted five seats. Strafford, Hillsborough, and Cheshire counties were each allowed two Senators. Grafton County, scantily populated and largely a wilderness stretching up to the Canadian border, was granted a single seat.

The original Senate qualifications were more rigid than those of the House. Senators were required to possess a worth of £ 200 (twice that of the lower branch), be thirty years of age, and have a seven-year residency. The Senators were also required to be Protestants. The state's Chief Executive, initially called President, presided over the Senate with full voting privileges. One Senator was annually elected to the title of "Senior," to serve as Acting President when a vacancy occurred.

The 1784 Constitution retained the Executive Council but turned it into a curb on the Chief Executive, in contrast to its provincial role of supporting him. It also specified that the five Council members were to be legislators, two from the Senate and three from the House, as elected by the General Court in joint session.

The Senate's first dozen members included distinguished leaders of the Revolutionary period, and they proved hard to come by. In fact, this pioneer Senate for the most part barely mustered a sufficient attendance to function. Only seven of the seats were filled in the March 1784 first annual election; other candidates failed to win required majorities. They constituted the minimum constitutional requirement for a quorum. The seven elected Senators were John Wentworth of Dover, fresh from Continental Congress service; Simeon Olcott of Charlestown, soon to become a United States Senator; John McClary of Epsom; Joseph Gilman of Exeter; Ebenezer Smith of Meredith; Moses Dow of Haverhill; and Francis Blood of Temple.

These first seven Senators were sworn into office as the General Court convened on June 2, 1784, a Wednesday; the following day they convened in joint session with the House to fill the vacant Senate seats. The quintet of additional Senators became Judge Woodbury Langdon of Portsmouth, Continental Congress three-termer; Judge Timothy Walker of Concord; Dr. Matthew Thornton of Merrimack; John Dudley of Raymond; and Benjamin Bellows of Walpole.

Langdon and Walker joined the Senate on Friday, June 4. Dr. Thornton took his seat on June 8, and on that same day, Judge

Langdon was elected "Senior" Senator. This automatically made him Acting President of the state, because President-elect Meshech Weare was confined to his Hampton Falls home by illness. The Senate apparently had considerable controversy over the Langdon election, for the Senate Journal of June 8 recorded:

The President-elect being absent, after several arguments, it was agreed that the Secretary (of State) should take the minds of the Senate, relative to the method of determining the person who should be esteemed and act as Senior Senator; and it being agreed to determine the question by ballot, the ballots were taken and the Honorable Woodbury Langdon, Esq. was appointed by a majority of the votes, who took the chair accordingly.

Senator Langdon, like his brother, John, became wealthy in the wartime sea trade, and he was quite popular, despite bluntness and sarcasm of speech. Six years later, as related in Chapter VI, the House impeached Judge Langdon for misconduct, but the 1790 Senate was blocked from concurrence by a technical hurdle.

When the second week of the 1784 session opened, Dudley declined his seat, to accept appointment to the Superior Court. So the Senate went into another joint session with the House and elected John Langdon of Portsmouth, younger brother of Acting President Langdon, to replace Dudley. But this Langdon did not join the Senate until its fall session opened on October 20 at Portsmouth.

Three days before adjournment of the summer session, Bellows presented himself on June 12 and personally declined his seat. Thus, still another joint legislative session was required, in which Enoch Hale of Rindge, later of Walpole, was elected in his stead. Hale did not take his seat until February 10, 1785, when the 1784 Legislature held its third and final session at Concord. President Weare, who took office at Exeter on June 15, 1784, for a one-day legislative session, presided over the Senate only from October 20 through November 11, when the Legislature met at Portsmouth, and Langdon filled the presidency all through the rest of that annual term.

When Senators Held Other Positions

THE 1784 LEGISLATURE had different remuneration sources for the Senate and the House members. The daily pay scale was set at six shillings, with a single round-trip travel allowance of four pence per mile for each session. The Senators' payments were from the State Treasury; the towns paid their Representatives' allowances.

Members of the Senate, like those in the House, held other public positions while still serving as legislators. Senators McClary and Blood became Councilors. Senators John Langdon and Dow were elected in June 1784 to the Continental Congress, effective in November, but they continued to serve as Senators in the final legislative session in Concord in February 1785.

The Senate's format was changed in 1792 when the people approved wholesale constitutional amendments. The members became elected by districts, which were measured by tax valuations of property; the Chief Executive was barred from Senate deliberations; and the Senate President was designated to serve as Acting Governor, when necessary. The Senate membership remained at twelve for ninety-five years. The requirement that Senators own property was abolished in 1852. In 1877 the people approved doubling the Senate size to twenty-four and repealed the Protestant requirement for members.

In the first ninety-five-year period, five men served nine or more annual Senate terms. Amos Shepard of Alstead was the champion, with fifteen terms, and Ebenezer Smith of Meredith had ten terms. Nine-term Senators were John Orr of Bedford, James Flanders of Warner, and John Waldron of Dover. Shepard was Senate President for seven terms, and Jonathan Harvey of Sutton was President for six consecutive years.

It was a Senate member who sponsored enactment of the historic "Toleration Act" of the 1819 Legislature, which terminated use of public taxes to support churches. The Reverend Dan Young of Lisbon, a Methodist clergyman, first began promoting this separation of church and state when elected to the Senate in 1816, for the start of five terms. He mustered only 3 votes for his bill in the 1816 session and rallied 6 votes in 1817. The Senate passed the Young measure in 1818, but it was not until 1819 that the House concurred with the upper branch on this controversial bill.

After the Legislature moved into its own Capitol in 1819, the House and Senate in the 1820 session began to print their own rules of conduct in pamphlet form. This was for the convenience of their members, and as public information. This policy continues to this day, as the legislative *Black Manual*. The Senate's 1820 rules of conduct specified that the members had to vote in alphabetical order, rather than by their district number. As reflection of comparatively simple concerns of New Hampshire legislators in that period, the Senate's rules listed only four standing committees, as follows:

There shall be a standing committee of three members, to whom shall be 231
referred all petitions for acts of incorporation; also, a standing committee of three members, to whom shall be referred all matters in relation to the militia; also, a standing committee of three members, to whom shall be referred all military accounts; also a standing committee of three members, to whom shall be referred printers' and all other, except military, accounts.

The Senate Chamber

NEW HAMPSHIRE BOASTS the oldest Senate chamber in the nation; it has been in continuous use since 1819. Records indicate it was originally slightly smaller than it now is. But its height of 18 feet remains the same, as does its south-north width of 33 feet. Jacob Bailey Moore, onetime legislative printer, listed the Senate details in his classic 1824 *Annals of Concord,* in which he wrote:

The north wing second floor contains the Senate Chamber, 18 feet in height, with a beautiful ceiling of plaistering, ornamented with stucco work, supported by four Ionic columns and an equal number of pilasters. This room, for its neatness and elegance of finishing, is not perhaps inferior to any in the United States.

The Senate chamber's east-west dimension was slightly widened when the Capitol was first doubled in size in 1864. This occurred as the two wings of the State House were widened to the same depth as the center section of the building. Old records indicate that the Senate President first presided against the west wall and a public gallery hung over the south wall. In the 1864 enlargement, the rostrum was shifted to the east wall, and the gallery was moved to its present site above the west wall. The present rostrum was set in 1910.

Dr. Jacob Harold Gallinger of Concord, a native of Canada, became President of the first biennial State Senate in a most unusual manner. He won over Attorney Charles H. Burns of Wilmot in a Republican caucus, after four men not yet elected to the Senate were allowed to vote. The caucus was held in the Phenix Hotel, the night before the Legislature convened on June 4, 1879, and the historic details were recorded in the newspapers.

Dr. Jacob H. Gallinger

The 1878 biennial election had given the Republicans 16 to 4 control of the Senate, with no winners in four other districts because no candidate won a majority of all votes cast, which was then a constitutional requirement. The four losing Republican candidates were present as the caucus opened, and after a prolonged debate, they were allowed, by a 9 to 7 vote, to participate in the proceedings. But the quartet declined, as their spokesman, Emmons B. Philbrick of Rye, a farmer, explained they had expected a unanimous invitation to join the caucus.

The Presidential voting quickly developed a 7 to 7 stalemate, as both Gallinger and Burns refrained from voting. This led to a suggestion by Orren C. Moore, founder and publisher of the *Nashua Daily Telegraph*, that the quartet join the balloting, to break the deadlock, but this met with strenuous objections from Charles E. Smith, Dover hotelman.

As the stalemate continued through a dozen ballots, Moore was repeatedly rebuffed on motions to have the quartet join the voting; he finally prevailed on the fourteenth ballot. As a result, Gallinger was nominated for Senate President by a 10 to 7 vote, as Philbrick abstained.

Casting the tie-breaking votes were Hiram Hodgden, Ashland

merchant; Dudley G. Coleman, Brookfield grain dealer; and Charles F. Cate, Northwood bachelor farmer. The next day they, with Philbrick, were elected to the Senate by a joint session of the House and Senate.

The four Democrats of this 1879 Senate included the youngest and the oldest members. They were Edward F. Mann, thirty-three-year-old Benton railroad conductor, and Sherburne R. Merrill, sixty-nine-year-old Colebrook starch manufacturer. The other Democrats were Attorney Isaac H. Blodgett of Franklin and Cornelius Cooledge of Hillsboro, who became well-to-do in the California gold rush a quarter of a century earlier.

The dozen other members were: Albert N. Shaw, Lebanon railroad contractor; Albert Fitts, Charlestown commercial traveler; Nehemiah G. Ordway, Warner politico and Sergeant-at-Arms of the national Congress for a dozen years; Luther Hayes, Milton lumberman; Edward Gustine, Keene civil engineer; Charles J. Amidon, Hinsdale wood manufacturer; George W. Todd, Mont Vernon educator; Elbridge C. Hayes, Manchester stonemason; William G. Perry, Manchester mill superintendent; William H. Shepard, Derry farmer; Greenleaf Clark, Atkinson farmer; and John H. Broughton, Portsmouth lumber dealer.

Renovations of 1879

THE SENATE CHAMBER was renovated for its 1879 enlarged membership. The original austere, long, semicircular desks with straight-backed chairs were replaced by individual deep-drawered desks and more comfortable castered chairs. The old furniture was retained, however, for continued use by the State Supreme Judicial Court, which used the chamber as its office when the Senate was not in session, until 1895, when the high court was given quarters in the new State Library building. The *Concord Monitor* reported on February 21, 1879:

Twenty-four chairs and desks for the Senate Chamber have arrived at the State House. The desks are of black walnut, and the chairs are black walnut frame with cane seats, similar to the make and style of those in the City Hall at Boston.

The desks are moveable, and can be placed in any position the Senators may choose. They were made by Stephen Smith & Co., Cornhill, Boston, a firm which has a good reputation for doing first-class work.

The Senate Chamber with the individual desks and seats installed after the Senate was enlarged from 12 to 24 members in 1879.

The present furniture in the Senate Chamber is well adapted to the law terms of the Supreme Court, and can easily be removed when the Legislature is in session. It was from the fact that the Senate Chamber is set apart for the Court, that Governor Prescott ordered the present style of desk for the Senate, so that both the Senate and the Court could be equally accommodated with only slight trouble in moving the furniture.

When the State House was again enlarged in 1909, two dozen portraits of former Senate Presidents had crowded the Senate chamber's walls, and they were moved into the corridors of the new rear section of the Capitol. The chamber was given fresh improvements in 1942, as four linen murals depicting historic highlights of early New Hampshire life were pasted upon the south wall.

The murals were painted by Barry Faulkner of Keene, nationally noted artist. They were financed by a $40,000 grant to the state from the National Academy of Design, custodian of the Edwin Austin Abbey Memorial Trust Fund, to produce historic murals for the original states, and New Hampshire had the distinction of receiving the first such award.

The huge murals depict Dartmouth's first commencement in 1771, with four graduates; Daniel Webster reading the two-year-old Federal Constitution from a cotton handkerchief in a rural store near his Salisbury home, at the age of nine; John Stark hurrying from his sawmill at Amoskeag Falls (now Manchester) to heroism at Bunker Hill; and Abbott Thayer, Dublin painter and scientist, explaining his theory of protective coloring in the animal kingdom at the turn of the twentieth century.

The murals were unveiled by Governor Robert O. Blood of Concord at a special ceremony on January 5, 1943, on the eve of the opening of that year's Legislature. Faulkner spoke briefly and gave the backgrounds of his four handsome paintings.

Details of the Dartmouth, Stark, and Webster murals are rather common knowledge to lovers of Granite State lore. But the Thayer painting is something else, and artist Faulkner took most interesting personal liberties with it. He said at the unveiling:

I was one of Thayer's pupils, and this is my memory of Thayer and his studio in 1900. On the easel in back of the group of figures is one of Thayer's most famous pictures, the memorial to Robert Louis Stevenson. Thayer painted many winged figures, and I think that his intense interest in ornithology influenced him in this expression. For Thayer was not only one of the greatest of American painters; he was an ornithologist of repute and made an important contribution to that science by his theory of protective coloring in the animal kingdom. This theory is the basis of military camouflage.

I have shown Thayer explaining his theory to his friends and family. Thayer liked to explain it by means of the partridge. In his right hand, he shows the lightness of the belly of the bird when turned upwards, and on his lap is the bird in reverse with its dark back. The partridge is the perfect example of concealment for not only is it countergraded (light belly and dark back), but its coloring mimics the background and its pattern is disruptive.

Shown with Thayer in this mural is undoubtedly the most unusual presentation of personages on public display anywhere in the country. They are, from left to right: Daniel Chester French of Exeter, New Hampshire's sculptor who won international fame for carving the pensive Abraham Lincoln Memorial at Washington; Mrs. Thayer; George de Forest Brush, one of Faulkner's associate artists at Dublin; Faulkner himself in the bloom of youth; Alexander James of Dublin, who in 1926 produced the Abraham Lincoln portrait which hangs in Representatives Hall, with hands which some insist are out of proportion but which James steadfastly claimed were true to life; and Miss Thayer, the ornithologist's daughter. All of them were longtime friends, some being portrayed from memory!

Recent research disclosed the identity of the mother and son in the Webster mural. She actually was Mrs. Frances B. Cox of Windsor, Vermont, mother of Archibald Cox of Boston, celebrated Special Prosecutor in Washington's "Watergate scandal" of the 1970s. She recalled posing in a New York studio for her friend, artist Faulkner.

Thanks to Mrs. Cox's memory, it also became known that the boy depicting Daniel Webster on the store floor was eight-year-old Charles A. Platt, whose family was also friendly with Faulkner. He now (1977) operates an architectural firm on Madison Avenue in New York City with his father, William Platt.

Faulkner personally pasted the linen murals upon the paneled walls, and he supervised new colorings for the Senate chamber to blend with them. The Keene artist at the same time was asked to redecorate the Council chamber, at the other end of the State House, and his colorings of the 1910 room were so meritorious that they have also been retained to this day.

The Senate's big desks and chairs of 1879 had become so worn that they were replaced when the murals were installed. The third set of desks and chairs was a replica of the original 1819 furniture, except that there were four long desks in two rows for the twenty-four Senators, compared with but two desks in a single circular row for the original twelve Senators.

It was also in 1943 that the portrait of Woodbury Langdon, the Senate's first presiding officer, became displayed on the west wall, from which the first rostrum was perched.

Historical Details

A MANCHESTER MILL official marked the Senate's centennial in 1884 by producing a booklet listing the 579 men who served in that body from 1784 into the 1883 session. He was George C. Gilmore, an 1881 Senate member, who became a prominent historian. The pocket-sized booklet, entitled *Manual of the New Hampshire Senate*, became so popular that Gilmore continued its biennial publication through the following decade.

Gilmore recorded that the Senate formed its own association on July 12, 1878, the final year of annual legislative sessions. The New 237 Hampshire Senate Association was dedicated "To promote acquaintanceship and fellowship" among past and current Senate members. Gilmore's booklet reported that Hiram K. Slayton of Manchester became association president in 1883, as the Senate observed its 100th anniversary. Jacob H. Gallinger of Concord was secretary-treasurer, and Orren C. Moore of Manchester was historiographer.

The Senate Association was reorganized as the 1889 session adjourned on August 16. Senator Ezra S. Stearns, Rindge historian, became president, along with Senator Charles R. Corning of Concord as secretary, and President David A. Taggart of Goffstown as treasurer. Senator Charles A. Sinclair, wealthy Portsmouth Democrat, was given a rousing vote of thanks as he invited the rejuvenated association to a seaside outing at the Hotel Wentworth in New Castle.

The association became inactive after a few years. Then it was revived in 1951 by Senator Suzanne Loizeaux, Plymouth weekly newspaper editor, as six women served in that Senate session. Biennial association parties followed for a dozen years, and Senator Edith B. Gardner of Gilford served through this period as secretary.

Attorney Harry Hibbard of Bath was the youngest ever to serve in the New Hampshire Senate, and did so illegally in the 1846 session. Following two terms as Speaker of the House of Representatives, he won a Senate seat in the March annual election of 1846, and was sworn into office when the Legislature convened on June 3, just two days after his thirtieth birthday anniversary.

The state Constitution specifies that a person must be thirty years of age at the time of election as Senator but records show that Hibbard's age discrepancy was never challenged. He became chairman of the 1846 Senate's Judiciary Committee, then served as Senate President in the following two sessions, after which he was elected to three terms in the national Congress. Hibbard was a Democrat, and that party dominated legislative affairs in this period.

Henry Robinson of Concord served in the 1883 Senate as the youngest to sit in that chamber since the Legislature went on a biennial basis in 1879. Fresh from two House terms, this Republican lawyer and journalist reached the constitutional requirement of thirty years of age on July 14, or 115 days before his November 7, 1882, election. Robinson was son of prison warden Nahum Robinson. In

Henry Robinson

1878, at the age of twenty-six, he married Helen Rollins, only daughter of wealthy Edward H. Rollins of Concord, just elected to the United States Senate, and they had seven children. Robinson later became postmaster and mayor of his native city and a prolific journalist.

Richard H. Horan, Manchester Democrat, was the third youngest Senate member, serving in the 1919 session after two House terms. He became thirty years of age on June 29, 129 days before his election on November 5, 1918. Horan, a factory manager, soon thereafter moved to Concord to become business manager for the State Department of Education (which he helped create in the 1919 session) for forty years. Upon retirement, he returned to the House as a Republican member in the 1969 session.

Congressman James C. Cleveland of New London won rank as the fourth youngest member of the Senate, in its 1951 session. He became thirty years of age on June 13, 146 days before his election on November 7, 1950. Cleveland, a decorated World War II veteran, went on to serve six terms in the Senate, as a Republican leader, and then went to the national Congress, to which he was reelected in 1978 for a ninth consecutive term.

One brash Tilton youngster of twenty-nine was elected to the

Senate in 1940 and tried to delay taking his seat until January 9, 1941, his thirtieth birthday anniversary, but, unlike Harry Hibbard, he was ruled out of order. He was Arthur K. Smart, a National Youth Administration official of the depression era of the 1930s, who never sought the Senate seat. He was a write-in Democratic candidate who nosed out the venerable Dr. Anson L. Alexander of Boscawen, the 1937 Republican Senate President, by 63 votes in the November 5, 1940 election, and then survived a recount challenge.

No one had recognized that Smart did not meet the legal age qualifications. It was not until the Legislature convened on New Year's Day that this writer, then a *Concord Monitor* reporter, discovered the discrepancy. When the Tilton man was absent from the opening ceremony, he was reached by telephone. It was then that young Smart disclosed his exact age and confided that he would wait until he became thirty years of age, on January 9, to be sworn in as a Senator.

When Smart's true age became known, Senate President William Cole of Derry swung into action and asked Attorney General Frank R. Kenison for a ruling. Kenison (who retired in 1977 as Chief Justice of the State Supreme Court) promptly declared Smart's ineligibility. He pointed out that the state Constitution requires the thirty-year attainment by the time of election, rather than when seated. The Senate then voted to seat the seventy-nine-year-old Dr. Alexander for a fourth term. But Smart's audacity was never erased from the record books. The Legislature's *General Court Manual* still lists him as elected, as does the legislative biographical *Brown Book* of that session.

Senatorial Scholarships

SPECIAL SENATE SCHOLARSHIPS began in 1890 and were the vogue for more than half a century. They were offered by the New Hampshire College of Agriculture and Mechanic Arts, as the 1891 Legislature prepared to authorize its removal from Hanover to Durham. Trustees of the then tiny institution (which became the University of New Hampshire in 1923) offered each Senate member a free scholarship in each biennium, as a goodwill policy, and to help recruit students. The trustees voted at the same time to admit women, for the same reasons.

There are no records about how the Senators made use of their

Joseph P. Chatel

gratis scholarships through the ensuing years. Representative Everett S. Sackett of Lee, retired UNH dean and author of the 1974 *New Hampshire's University* history, recalled that when he became chairman of the UNH Scholarship Committee in 1938, "reasonable need" was a qualification for the Senatorial scholarships. He said they continued to a lessening degree for another decade, and then the policy faded out.

Dean Sackett also explained that through the early years of this century, similar courtesy scholarships were granted to Pomona Grange units and the State Federation of Women's Clubs.

Attorney Samuel D. Felker of Rochester in 1891 became the only Senate member ever seated by a pre-session State Supreme Court ruling. Then only thirty-one and destined to become Governor twenty-two years later, Democrat Felker got the most votes in the 1890 biennial election, beating out Republican Augustine S. Parshley in the twelfth Senatorial district, 2,100 to 2,031. But Frank R. Bean, prohibition candidate, was listed with 68 disputed votes, along with 9 scattered, so Felker failed by a reported 5 votes to win a majority, then a legal requirement.

The election night tally reported 34 votes for Bean from Rochester, but when Town Clerk Fred L. Chesley (Rochester became a city in the

1891 session) reported the official returns later to the Secretary of State, he announced that Bean's vote in that community had been 44, or 10 more than originally stated.

Governor David H. Goodell of Antrim and his Republican Council certified the revised returns, which showed no victor and automatically turned the final decision of the election over to the incoming Republican Legislature. But Felker took his case to the high court and won a ruling that sustained the original election night tally, which gave him a majority victory by a single vote. The court said Chesley had no legal right to change the returns, in the following words:

The defendant's duty is not an open question. The arithmetical error could have been corrected by the moderator in a supplementary public declaration before the close of the meeting, but could not be corrected by the clerk in his record and return without such corrective action taken by the moderator.

Farmington, Milton, and Somersworth were then a part of Senatorial district 12.

Republicans won record-making majorities in the State Senate when New Hampshire Democrats became fragmented in the 1896 biennial election, as their Presidential nominee, William Jennings Bryan, and his controversial silver platform, won only a 25 percent vote total. The 1897 Senate came up with an unprecedented 22 to 2 Republican majority. Its sole Democratic members were Attorney Timothy J. Howard of Manchester and John W. Emery of Portsmouth, an insurance company executive. The 1899 Senate also constituted a 22 to 2 Republican majority. The only Democratic Senators were Dr. Charles A. Morse of Newmarket, former Concord resident and Salisbury native, and Joseph P. Chatel, Manchester liquor store proprietor. And Chatel made history with a boast that he was the first man of French-Canadian origin ever to be elected to the Senate of any of the six New England states. Chatel presented this legislative milestone in the 1899 legislative biographical *Brown Book* as follows:

District 18—Joseph P. Chatel, Manchester, Democrat, Catholic, liquor dealer, married, aged 44, born in Stokely, P.Q., January 14, 1854. He removed to Biddeford, Me., at the opening of the Civil War, and to Manchester in 1868. Although having received no college education, he had had the benefit of special library studies under private tutors, among whom was G.I. Hopkins, submaster at the Manchester High School. After

Story of the Senate

spending a few years on the road as a travelling salesman, he opened a store of his own in 1894, and is doing a very successful business. Mr. Chatel enjoys a wide acquaintance and popularity, and is the first French-Canadian to be elected to a state Senate in New England. He has never before held public office and has always been a Democrat.

As New Hampshire moved into the twentieth century, the 1901 State Senate set an all-time record, with a 23 to 1 Republican majority. The lone Democrat member was John Leddy, Epping merchant, and he promptly and unwittingly carved a niche of historical import for himself.

Senator Leddy said in the 1901 legislative *Brown Book* that he was a Catholic who had served two terms in the House in 1874 and 1875, which was prior to the 1877 repeal of the state's constitutional Protestant proviso, barring Catholics from election to the General Court. While Granite State historians have generally agreed that the Catholic ban had not been strictly enforced by the Legislature since the Civil War, Leddy's *Brown Book* biography is considered the only official recording of that fact in legislative annals. Leddy reported of himself in the *Brown Book:*

District 23–John Leddy, Epping, Democrat, Catholic, merchant, married age 60. Born in Oldcastle, Ireland, and has resided for 51 years in Epping, having received his education there. Has served as town clerk, supervisor, selectman. Member of the House in 1874 and 1875. Always a Democrat.

The 1901 Senate had twenty-four standing committees, and President Bertram Ellis, Keene newspaper editor, appointed Senator Leddy as chairman of the Senate Committee on Labor.

The Taggart Presidency

ATTORNEY DAVID ARTHUR TAGGART of Goffstown produced historic incidents when he became a member of the 1889 Senate, the last June session before the General Court shifted to January openings two years later. He became the Senate's youngest President of all time, in a Republican caucus which snagged into a record eighty-two ballots with questionable results. Then he later forced a State Supreme Court ruling before he would serve as Acting Governor. Taggart's thirtieth birthday occurred on January 30, 1888, just 279 days before his November 6, 1888, election.

There were eighteen Republicans in that memorable caucus, staged on the eve of the June 5 General Court opening, in the old Republican Club Room, over what was then the Blue Front Clothing Store on Main street. It lasted from 9:00 P.M. to 12:50 A.M. the following morning. One newspaper labeled it "The most spirited and stubborn ever known." The *Concord Monitor* reported with its Republican bias of those days: "The eighty-two ballots were characterized by the utmost courtesy on the part of the rivals and their friends, with a dignified decorum appropriate to the senior branch of the Legislature." But this marathon caucus did not entirely drip honey. It featured colorful manipulations, according to newspaper accounts.

Ezra Scollay Stearns of Rindge, fifty-year-old veteran legislator, editor, and historian, was Taggart's principal opponent. He collected 6 votes most of the time and 5 on other occasions, as eight Senators stuck solidly with Taggart, who also infrequently tallied 9 votes. Attorney Frank G. Clarke of Peterborough clung to 2 votes. And Attorney Charles R. Corning of Concord voted for himself throughout because he did not favor either Taggart or Stearns.

George H. Stearns of Manchester, a Taggart supporter, was caucus chairman. James B. Tennant of Epsom and Charles T. Means of Manchester were the first tellers. There was a five-minute recess after the forty-ninth ballot. After the sixty-sixth, Thomas P. Cheney of Ashland suggested the tellers should be allowed mileage payments! And after the sixty-seventh ballot, Ezra Stearns lost an attempt to recess the marathon until eight o'clock the following morning. Then, following the sixty-eighth tally, Taggart suggested that the tellers appeared too tired to carry on, so they were replaced by John H. Nute of Dover and Edward T. Willson of Farmington.

The eightieth ballot struck a surprise snafu. As the tellers reported yet another 18-vote stalemate, Senator Means popped a shocking development. Means announced that he had purposely refrained from voting to see what would happen. He gained his point and this ballot was ruled invalid. Two ballots later, on the eighty-second tally, Taggart was declared the winner, with a majority of 9 votes out of 17 cast.

The *Manchester Union* reported the following day that all eighteen Senators had individually said they had voted on the final ballot. While the identity of the missing vote was never officially disclosed, newspaper accounts indicated it was a Stearns supporter. But the omission did the trick, and Taggart got his victorious majority. The *Concord Monitor* subsequently agreed with the *Union* that this was an

David Arthur Taggert

unsavory termination of the nocturnal marathon. But the eighteen Republicans closed ranks, kept the party faith, and Taggart became a competent and honorable Senate President. The Senate gave him a gold watch at adjournment in esteem for his leadership.

The Goodell Ruling

PRESIDENT TAGGART'S Senate leadership produced another historic event. When Governor David Harvey Goodell, fifty-four-year-old robust Antrim manufacturer, became seriously ill in the spring of 1890, Taggart held out for a court ruling before he would serve as Acting Governor. Goodell was stricken on March 10 by "acute nervous prostration," and confined to his home. A week later, Taggart declined to preside at an Executive Council meeting, and Councilor Charles H. Horton of Dover, seventy-two-year-old senior member, chaired the session, during which routine business was transacted.

Secretary of State Ai B. Thompson of Concord submitted to the Council a letter from Governor Goodell, signed by three physicians, which stated that he was suffering from a spinal disorder, that he did not have a "shock," and that he would remain incapacitated for several weeks. On March 31, Governor Goodell wrote to Attorney General Daniel Barnard of Franklin:

Dear Sir: Please take such steps as you think necessary to cause the President of the Senate to exercise the powers of the office of Governor during the vacancy caused by my illness. I am not able to perform the duties of the office and the public service should not suffer from my inability.

Barnard submitted the dilemma to the high court, which posted an April 7 hearing at its spring session in Manchester. President Taggart was ordered to appear, and he testified that he was willing to fill in for Governor Goodell, but feared a legal challenge if he did so without judicial clarification. Barnard argued that the constitutional provision that a Senate President must fill a gubernatorial vacancy caused "by reason of his death, absence from the state, or otherwise," included an incapacitating illness. He also asked the court to determine the title for such substitution.

Dr. S.G. Dearborn of Nashua, one of Goodell's physicians, told the court that the Governor "lacks the power to walk" and that while "one rarely recovers" from his ailment, he expected that Goodell would regain his health. On April 8, 1890, the Supreme Court issued a terse "judgment for the plaintiff" decision and said a written opinion would be issued later. Newspapers reported that Taggart was informed by the court that he should at once replace Goodell, and use the title "President of the Senate, acting Governor."

President Taggart became Acting Governor on April 22, 1890, at a brief State House ceremony. Councilor Horton called the Council to order and appointed Councilors Edward C. Shirley of Goffstown and William S. Pillsbury of Londonderry to escort Taggart to the Governor's chair. Newspapers reported that Taggart read a formal statement, in which he stressed his youth and lack of political experience, and said he would "depend heavily" upon the Executive Council for "counsel and assistance." Then he was administered the oath of office by Secretary Thompson.

Chief Justice Charles Doe of the high court wrote a voluminous opinion on the case which was later issued. It went back to the 1784 constitutional beginning, for an example to bolster its ruling that a Senate President has no choice, when a gubernatorial vacancy occurred, and must automatically fill it. The opinion also stressed that when a Senate President becomes an Acting Governor, he cannot also be part of the Senate. The ruling said, in part:

When the Constitution took effect, and the Legislature met for the inauguration of the new government, June 2, 1784, Meshech Weare, the Governor-elect, was unable to be present.

In brief periods of his illness and absence, in June, 1784, and February, 1785, his duties were performed by Woodbury Langdon, senior Senator, acting as Governor pro tem.

On both occasions, Langdon presided in the Senate by virtue of his position as acting Governor; and on the 8th of June, 1784, as acting Governor, he sat with the Council, and exercised the Governor's power (with the required advice and consent of the Council) of signing warrants for the payment of money out of the state treasury.

The authority of this precedent has not been shaken, and it does not appear that the soundness of the contemporaneous construction has ever been doubted.

Acting Governor Taggart presided over the National Guard's annual review at the Concord camp grounds on June 19, 1890, and, interestingly, newspapers reported that Governor and Mrs. Goodell were among those present. Governor Goodell resumed his State House duties on July 1, with a friendly welcoming ceremony headed by Taggart.

Taggart's Senate also produced a "mistake" law, which is still in the records. The upper branch killed a House-approved bill relating to cemetery legacies; a week later it approved the measure in engrossed form; and Governor Goodell signed it into law. The Senate's 1889 Journal has this "Addenda":

HB 38—An act to amend Sect. 7 Chap. 49 of the General Laws, and Chap. 46 of the laws of 1887 relating to legacies left for care and protection of lots in cemeteries, and HB 265, inadvertently engrossed by engrossing clerk, signed by Governor and not passed by the Senate. The mistake was not discovered until after the Legislature adjourned.

Twentieth-Century Adjustments

GOVERNOR HENRY W. KEYES of Haverhill resigned in an unusual manner on December 31, 1918, the day before his term expired, and Senate President Jesse M. Barton of Newport took his place in a rare ceremony. Keyes, fresh from election to the United States Senate in the previous month, telegraphed Secretary of State Edwin C. Bean of Belmont that he was ill and suggested that Barton preside over that day's Council meeting. Bean administered the gubernatorial oath to Barton (an action never recorded for other Acting Governors), and then Barton joined with the Council in voting thanks to Keyes for his service as Governor and expressing hopes for his speedy recovery. The next morning Governor Barton officiated as the Legislature convened on the New Year's Day holiday.

Senate President Blaylock Atherton of Nashua served extensively as Acting Governor in 1952, since Governor Sherman Adams of Lincoln devoted most of that final year of his two terms to spearheading the election of Gen. Dwight D. Eisenhower as President of the United States. Atherton presided over about fifteen Council meetings, from May to December, as Adams toured the nation as chief promoter of the Eisenhower candidacy, and returned to New Hampshire only infrequently to officiate as Governor, before accepting appointment as President Eisenhower's principal assistant when he took office.

The 1957 Senate staged an abortive attempt to censure an editor. It was aimed at Publisher William Loeb of the *Manchester Union Leader,* for calling President Eisenhower a "stinking hypocrite." On May 7, Senator James P. Rogers of Laconia offered the following resolution:

Whereas, the publisher of the Manchester Union Leader *has on many occasions referred to the President of the United States in terms which are not consistent with good ethics or common decency; and*

Whereas, the repeated and malicious abuse of the President is an unhealthy influence, akin to subversion; and

Whereas, on page 3 of the Union Leader *of Friday, May 3, the said publisher, William Loeb, has referred to the Chief Executive in a manner which is repulsive to all good citizens; now therefore*

Be it resolved, that the New Hampshire Senate condemns the unbridled use of such vicious and irresponsible language in the public press; and

Be it further resolved, that a copy of this resolution be mailed forthwith to the editor of each daily and weekly newspaper published within the state of New Hampshire.

After the resolution had been read, Rogers moved that it be made a special order of business a week later, and heated arguments ensued. Republican majority floor leader James C. Cleveland of New London supported the censure and Senator Cecil C. Humphreys of New Castle said the Senate had as much right as editors to criticize or praise.

When President Eralsey C. Ferguson of Pittsfield put the vote, Rogers's proposal was endorsed, 15 to 8, with Republicans Benjamin C. Adams of Derry and Norman A. Packard of Manchester siding with the united Democratic minority against it. The issue centered upon a Loeb editorial criticizing Eisenhower for having barred Senator Joseph McCarthy, who had been censured by the United States Senate for claiming communist infiltration into the American government, from his second-term White House reception.

A week later, after copies of the anti-Loeb resolution had been mailed to the editors, the Senate reversed itself and killed it. Cleveland vainly tried to have the resolution referred to the Attorney General for a ruling as to whether freedom of the press was involved. But this maneuver was killed, 16 to 7, and then the resolution was shelved on a voice vote. Publisher Loeb had the last word the following day. He wrote:

In my opinion it just represents the continued anger and frustration of the Republican party that the Union Leader *is no longer the Republican party's mouthpiece. It's an independent newspaper.*

Senate procedures were given judicial clarification in the 1959 session, to settle a bitter battle over a departmental reorganization bill. The dispute ran into a 12 to 12 stalemate, and then the measure was passed in such a sensational manner that the State Supreme Court ruled the action unconstitutional.

The House-approved bill to create a Department of Commerce had generated such Senate dissension that on June 24, a Wednesday, it was referred by a majority vote to a special joint committee for conciliatory consideration.

With the measure seemingly shelved for a spell, Senator Neil C. Cates of North Conway, an opponent, took a Thursday leave of absence for a weekend fishing trip. But when the Thursday session convened without Cates, Senator Benjamin C. Adams of Derry, the Republican majority floor leader, sprang into action. He moved that the bill be summarily recalled from the committee and immediately passed.

Senator James C. Cleveland of New London blasted Adams's maneuver. He charged it was a breach of faith and Senatorial courtesy to take such advantage of Cates's absence. Cleveland vainly argued to have Senate President Norman A. Packard of Manchester rule Adams out of order.

With a 12 to 11 majority seemingly assured, Senator Adams pushed for enactment of the measure for Governor Wesley Powell, its sponsor. Then, when other Senators joined in the floor arguments and parliamentary motions, Senator Cleveland requested a brief recess, which President Packard approved. The Senate Journal then significantly recorded:

The Senate reassembled. The Chair stated: "Every effort has been made to round up every Senator following a short recess."

The Senate then proceeded to pass the Department of Commerce bill without argument or a recorded dissenting vote. As this was done, Senator Nathan T. Battles of Kingston took the floor and said:

I feel that these tactics are no different than what has been used by our national Congress. I don't believe in them. I think they are despicable, unethical and without precedent. I also believe in the Commerce bill and in reorganization. I feel that these tactics are the only ones that could be used to pass this bill. I also feel that these tactics would have been used by the opposition if they had had the chance. It is for these reasons, and for these reasons only, that I am going along with this procedure.

The bill was rushed to Governor Powell without a customary engrossing committee report and was signed into law early that evening. By the following morning, this Senate action had become a public sensation. Newspapers reported that Cleveland and his ten Senate associates opposed to the measure had gone into hiding within the State House during his requested recess, so there would be no quorum (of thirteen members) when the Senate went back into session. But there was no evidence to that effect in the official Senate recordings.

Senator Cleveland and his opposition associates devoted the weekend to consideration of possible legal steps, including a possible court challenge. Then when the Senate reconvened the following Tuesday morning, on June 30, a startling surprise developed. As Senator Cates returned to duty, Senator Cecil C. Humphreys of New

Castle, who had joined with President Packard in supporting passage of the Powell reorganization bill, was absent because of a serious illness. Cleveland was quick to take advantage of this sudden reversal of the previous week's 12 to 11 lineup for the measure. He proposed corrections in the Thursday Senate Journal to show lack of a quorum when the Commerce bill was passed. President Packard time and again vainly ruled Cleveland's gambit out of order, as his decisions were overruled by rigid 12 to 11 roll call votes.

Senator Edward J. Bennett of Bristol became sponsor of the correction, which comprised a statement signed by himself and the eleven other Senators opposed to the disputed bill, stating that they had been absent when it was passed and given to Governor Powell. Senator Adams staged a futile floor fight to stem the reversal tide, and Senator Battles lost a motion to postpone the onslaught until Senator Humphreys could be present.

On July 9 the Senate sent the dispute to the high court, and on July 21 the judges declared the bill had been improperly enacted and was not a law. The court ruled not only that the Senate must have a quorum of thirteen members present to do business but that "a legislative body has an inherent right to correct its own journal . . . [and] . . . the corrected journal becomes the only authorized journal of the day's proceedings." The court told the Senate, in part:

Limiting ourselves solely and exclusively to the journals of the Senate and the facts disclosed thereby (N.H. Const., Pt. 11, Art. 24th) the following entries appear in substance:

On Thursday, June 25, 1959, the Senate ordered to third reading and to passage, House Bill 348. On the next legislative day which was Tuesday, June 30, 1959, the Senate journal for June 25 was corrected and amended to show that the action taken on June 25 with respect to House Bill 348 was taken when 12 Senators only were present. The Senate journal of July 1, 1959, shows that with 23 Senators present it was voted to accept the journal of June 30, 1959. In the meantime on June 25, 1959, House Bill 348 had been signed by the Speaker of the House, the President of the Senate and the Governor and engrossed.

. . . In the present case the journals clearly demonstrate that a constitutional quorum of 13 members of the Senate (N.H. Const., Pt. 11, Art. 37) was not present when the Senate purported to act upon House Bill 348. Therefore House Bill 348 which was purported to be engrossed as Laws

1959 c 166, was not validly and constitutionally enacted and never became law.

The Shift to Population

BECAUSE OF UNITED STATES SUPREME COURT RULINGS, the traditional measure for New Hampshire's Senate districts was changed in 1964 from taxable wealth to population, which had been the House denominator since 1877. The Senate also filled its own vacancies up to 1968, when a constitutional amendment required a special election for that purpose.

The first man to be reelected as Senate President since biennial sessions began in 1879 was Stewart Lamprey, Moultonborough realtor. He was President for three terms from 1965 into 1969, following a record three biennial terms as House Speaker. He resigned in his third term as President in 1969 to accept a federal appointment, and was succeeded by Senator Arthur Tufts of Exeter for the remainder of that term.

The numbering of Senate seats was completely reversed when the membership was doubled to twenty-four in the 1879 session. From 1784 until that enlargement, the No. 1 district had been Portsmouth and surrounding towns. Since 1879, the No. 1 district has centered in Berlin, and the twenty-four Senate districts have since been numbered from the north to the south, rather than the other way around as was the original custom.

Several innovations marked the 1973 session of Senate President David L. Nixon of New Boston. It became the first Senate to create the position of Vice President, which was filled by Democrat Harry V. Spanos of Newport. This resulted from a prolonged Republican 7 to 7 caucus deadlock on the presidency, which Nixon finally won by an unprecedented coalition with the Democratic minority members.

Nixon's Senate sponsored a novel series of "hometown" sessions, in observance of the state's 250th anniversary of its 1623 settlement. Never before had a New Hampshire legislative branch convened except within the proximity of its counterpart. The meetings were staged each Thursday in most of the twenty-four Senatorial districts, and the respective Senators presided. President Nixon styled this innovation "to bring government closer to the people it serves"; some of the sessions attracted more than 300 citizens, and the final program at Durham was televised in its entirety.

The Nixon Senate became the first legislative branch to sponsor

Laurier Lamontagne

"The State of Departments" weekly programs, in which officials of the major state agencies presented reports of their activities, which were printed in the Senate's daily Journal for general public distribution.

The 1973 Senate was also the first to have its own chaplain. By tradition, the upper branch traditionally met jointly with the House for brief daily opening prayer by the House-employed chaplain. But this was terminated as the Nixon Senate streamlined its operations around a 1:00 P.M. daily starting time, compared with the 11:00 A.M. opening of the House sessions. The Reverend Dr. Vincent Fischer of Concord, a semi-retired Episcopal clergyman, became the Senate's first chaplain, and continued in that role through the 1979 session. Nixon's Senate also published a sixteen-page booklet history of the New Hampshire Senate, which featured pictures of all its twenty-four members.

As the 1975 Senate convened with Alf E. Jacobson, New London college professor, as President, it was greeted with a $40,000 renovation of its historic chamber. A special committee headed by Senator Ward B. Brown of Hampstead sparked the improvements. They included new carpeting, a recording system with microphones at each desk, renovation of the President's rostrum, improved overhead lighting, and painting of the entire chamber. Serving with Brown, who went on to become majority leader of the 1975 and 1979 sessions, and Vice President of the 1977 Senate, were Senators Clesson J. Blaisdell of Keene, Roger Smith of Concord, C. Robertson Trowbridge of Dublin, and Robert F. Preston of Hampton.

Jacobson served two terms as President, with historic episodes. He sponsored an elevated rostrum chair to permit the President to preside while seated. He also served as Acting Governor, with the Executive Council, for two-score days of hearings spread through an entire year, on proposed dismissal of state Probation Director John A. King. Governor Meldrim Thomson, Jr., had disqualified himself from the case, and the State Supreme Court ruled the Senate President should preside as Acting Governor over the hearings, even as Governor Thomson continued to otherwise officiate. Because of the uniqueness of the case, in which the Executive Council voted to continue King in office, the Legislature voted Jacobson a $60 per diem allowance for this special service.

Robert B. Monier, Goffstown college professor, became President of the 1979 Senate, following two terms in that body, which was politically deadlocked with twelve Republicans and twelve Democrats. Republican Monier won out in a coalition vote, whereby Democrat Louis E. Bergeron of Rochester became Vice President.

Laurier Lamontagne of Berlin set a Senate record in the 1980 biennial election by winning reelection to a fourteenth consecutive biennial term. This sixty-three-year-old trucking company owner proudly boasted that he never missed a single day's attendance throughout his first eleven terms. Then in February 1977 he was absent one day while in Washington on official Senate business, and the Senate later voted to have its Journal list his presence on that occasion. Senator Lamontagne served three terms as mayor of Berlin and was Democratic minority floor leader in the 1957 session.

Robert English of Hancock served nine consecutive biennial terms in the state, through 1972.

New Hampshire's Senate has the fourth smallest membership among the fifty states of the nation. The Delaware Senate had twenty-one members (as of 1977), and Alaska and Nevada each had twenty. The Granite State's Senators are restricted to a biennial salary of $200, as constitutionally set in 1889. But, like the House members, they have been voting themselves frequently increased daily mileage allowances, to partially offset the antiquated pay scale.

Minnesota has the largest State Senate, of sixty-seven members. Senate memberships in the five other new England states have been: Maine, thirty-three; Vermont, thirty; Massachusetts, forty; Rhode Island, fifty; and Connecticut, thirty-six.

The Senate has redistricted itself on several occasions since 1792, with required House concurrence, for political gain, by both Republican and Democratic majorities. Election to the Senate required a majority vote total up to 1914, when a constitutional amendment became effective, permitting election by a plurality margin.

SPECIAL SESSIONS

First in 1813

NEW HAMPSHIRE'S GEN-
ERAL COURT has had nine-
teen special sessions since it
began holding annual sessions in 1800. Governor John Taylor Gilman
of Exeter called the first one in 1813, to quell a revolt in the courts. And
they include an unprecedented two special sessions, linked together,
sponsored in 1977 by Governor Meldrim Thomson, Jr., of Orford, to
resolve budget problems.

Up to 1800, this Legislature, first formed in 1776, met so frequently
that special sessions were unnecessary. While elected on an annual
basis, it convened from three to six times yearly during the
Revolutionary War period. Even after the Legislature went on a permanent constitutional basis in 1784, frequent sessions continued
until 1790 when, for a decade, the lawmakers settled into summer and
fall meetings.

After 1800, annual June sessions prevailed until 1879, when the
Legislature and its state government shifted to a biennial basis. Except for the first half of the nineteenth century, the Legislature held
regular November sessions every fourth year, to reapportion state
taxes on the towns, and to supervise the Board of Presidential Electors. Then in 1852 these quadrennial fall meetings were abandoned,
as the Governor and the Council handled the Presidential election
details, and the tax assessments were adjusted in the regular June
session on a quadrennial basis.

Governor Gilman presented a remarkable charge as the first special session convened on October 27, 1813, for a ten-day period. He told the legislators that two ousted high court Judges had refused to leave their benches and that sheriffs had upheld their surprise behavior. As a result, Gilman said, new Justices sat in mortification as the dismissed Jurists persisted in presiding in the same courtrooms. The crisis was precipitated by a legislative court reorganization in the 1813 June session. Governor Gilman sponsored it, to replace Republicans (as Democrats were then called) with members of his Federalist party. To achieve this political manipulation, the Superior Court of Judicature was replaced by a Supreme Judicial Court and a Circuit Court of Common Pleas.

Governor Gilman told the legislators that former Justices Richard Evans of Portsmouth and Clifton Claggett of Litchfield were the culprits. He explained that they forcefully held sway in fall court terms at Exeter, for Rockingham County, and at Amherst, for Hillsborough County, even as the new Chief Justice Jeremiah Smith of Exeter, and an associate, Justice Caleb Ellis of Claremont, tried to preside in the respective tribunals. Gilman declared that the county sheriffs had been particularly offensive to the new Judges. He explained that they had refused to recognize the new presiding officials and had defied them to do anything about their allegiance to the ousted Jurists.

The Legislature voted speedy solution to the quandary. It addressed the two sheriffs out of office, and suggested to Governor Gilman that new sheriffs had sufficient authority to remove the old Judges from the court premises, if necessary. Summarily dismissed were Sheriff Benjamin Pierce of Hillsborough County (who later served two terms as Governor, and who was the father of President Franklin Pierce), and Sheriff Josiah Butler of Rockingham County.

Gilman told the special session that the new Justices would more than offset the increased costs of the enlarged judicial system by expediting long-delayed cases, with substantial monetary benefits for litigants. This first special session processed two other items. It allowed Noah Cooke, Jr. (no address), to change his name to Noah Rockwood Cooke, and it chartered the Dunstable Cotton and Woollen Manufactory, with a five-year property tax exemption of $20,000.

Noisiest and Nastiest

IT WAS NOT UNTIL 1864, during the Civil War, that a second special session was held. This one erupted into possibly the noisiest, nastiest, and most noxious legislative deliberations in Granite State annals. It convened on August 9, much against the wishes of the legislators, and ran through three weeks into September 1 adjournment. Governor Joseph A. Gilmore of Concord, fifty-three-year-old rough-and-tough railroad superintendent, incensed the solons by ordering them back to the State House only three weeks following completion of their annual summer meeting. In an opening address, Gilmore charged them with dereliction, said they had insulted his integrity, and demanded repeal of restrictions on his handling of soldiers' bounties and state finances in general.

Insults flew frequently and freely from both sides as the session dragged through August. Animosity burst into unbridled anger. There were even fisticuffs and knife-drawing on August 24, according to newspaper reports, as the House barred a veto message from the Governor. Newspapers stated that on this occasion the ensuing uproar was heard through open windows by farmers almost a mile distant, in their Merrimack River meadows. Needless to add, adjacent Main Street habitants were shocked by the din from the normally decorous edifice.

Governor Gilman berated the solons for failure to support a Constitutional Convention call to consider absentee voting for soldiers and a reduction in the growing House membership, along with state assumption of war-supporting debts of the towns. He also denounced the legislative creation of an Auditor of Accounts to supervise the Governor and the Council's fiscal operations.

The Republican-dominated Legislature paid scant heed to Republican Gilmore, his adamant postures of the June session being still fresh in their minds. Even twenty-eight-year-old House Speaker William E. Chandler, Gilmore's son-in-law, gave the Governor no support. This was surprising, because Chandler had diligently helped sponsor two gubernatorial terms for his father-in-law, despite his railroad affiliation, which even then was becoming abhorrent in the ranks of the new Republican party. Time has disclosed, however, that two weeks before the special session, Chandler asked Governor Gilmore for appointment to the State Supreme Judicial Council, and hot words followed denial of the request.

Flouting Governor Gilmore's warnings that it was illegal, the Legislature took a cue from Vermont and passed a modified servicemen's absentee voting bill. The Vermont Legislature had developed the principle that while voting in state elections constitutionally barred absentee voting, balloting for federal officials was not so restricted. The special session approved a bill permitting soldiers to vote by absentee ballot for President and members of Congress, and it was laid upon Gilmore's desk on August 17, 1864, a Wednesday, while he was absent. It was returned to the House the following Wednesday under such unusual circumstances that they sparked open revolt.

Governor Gilmore later explained he had gone home because of illness when the voting bill reached his office, so he did not personally receive it until the following day. For that reason, he insisted, his veto had been given to the Legislature within the five-day grace period (not including Sunday) then permitted by the Constitution.

Confusion erupted as Representative John G. Sinclair of Bethlehem, spokesman for the Democratic minority, rather than the Secretary of State, tried to deliver the veto message. Speaker Chandler refused to recognize Sinclair, and persistent uproars ensued while he repeatedly attempted to read the Gilmore statement. Another Democrat stalwart, Representative Harry Bingham of Littleton, vainly challenged Chandler's rebuff of the veto. Bingham's efforts became buried in confusing debate and motions designed to block consideration of the veto.

As the midafternoon fracas assumed alarming proportions, a cordon of imposing Republican solons hemmed the rostrum to safeguard Speaker Chandler's decorum, and his frail and bespectacled person. Democrats filled the aisles, ranting and chanting for constitutional rights, and shouting that Sinclair was being unfairly muzzled. Meanwhile, the House gallery overflowed, as a startled citizenry piled into the Capitol to view the raucous proceedings.

Shortly before 7:00 P.M., Secretary of State Allen Tenny took possession of the veto and tried to present it to the House. Prolonged demands for an adjournment roll call had finally prevailed out of the tumult, however, and Speaker Chandler refused to recognize Tenny while the vote was in progress. So Tenny deposited the veto message upon the Speaker's desk, and the hectic session came to an abrupt end a few minutes later on a 142 to 88 adjournment tally.

Newspapers gave colorful reports of the dramatic details. Said the *Nashua Gazette:*

One of the most extraordinary and disgraceful scenes occurred in the House of Representatives on Wednesday that ever took place in a deliberative body. On that day the Republican majority . . . undertook to inaugurate revolution and overthrow the Constitution. . . . As the yeas and nays were demanded, intense excitement prevailed. Shouts and yells were heard by persons at great distance from the State House. Two members drew knives on each other but no blood was spilt.

The *Gazette* reported that Sinclair handled the veto message after Secretary Tenny declined to do so because Governor Gilmore had not personally delivered it to him. The newspaper also said that Sinclair had been asked, during an evening visit to Governor Gilmore's home to give the veto message to Tenny, after finding Gilmore grief-stricken beside his dying twenty-year-old son, Edward Everett Gilmore, who was buried three days later.

The *Boston Journal* reported on Speaker Chandler's rebuff of the veto statement:

The most intense excitement prevailed. Thereupon a scene of great commotion ensued. Disputes arose concerning points of order, which were associated with the wildest confusion and most uproarious disorder. The Republicans demanded that the motion to adjourn be put, while the Democrats shouted at the top of their voices "Message from the Governor—Stand up for the Constitution—No gag rule." This most disgraceful state of things continued till after 7 P.M.

The *Concord Monitor* blamed the Democrats for "the disgraceful tumult," but agreed the "House leadership was equally at fault" for not admitting the veto message as presented.

When processing the voting bill, the Legislature had asked the Supreme Judicial Court to rule on its contents. The day following the veto ruckus, the tribunal rendered its decision, which upheld the lawmakers against Governor Gilmore. It said the Vermont stand was correct, in that voting for federal officials could not be restricted by any state.

There was an anticlimax to the veto fiasco. The Senate sponsored a lengthy resolution censuring Governor Gilmore in perhaps the most critical language ever visited upon a Chief Executive by Granite State legislators. Said the resolution:

It would have been gratifying if it had pleased His Excellency to address to us his own views in his own language. It is extremely embarrassing when . . . it is deemed expedient by a public functionary, charged with responsible duties, to entrust the determination of what duties are, or how they shall be discharged, to an irresponsible agent . . . the Legislature leaves the illustra-

Special Sessions

tion of the crudities and contradictions of the message to some new writer on the curiosities of literature.

The resolution rapped Gilmore for appointing his son-in-law, Edwin S. Barrett, to the new Auditor of Accounts position as follows:

If not misrepresented, the young man who has been summoned to this embarrassing and responsible position was not at the time of his appointment a citizen of the state and has never resided within her jurisdiction, and is without experience or financial ability, or amiable and inoffensive character, and son-in-law of His Excellency, and a member of his household.

The Senate statement concluded:

The Legislature regards the message of His Excellency, Joseph A. Gilmore, under date of August 9, 1864, as discourteous in its language, erroneous in its assumption of facts, and a breach of privilege of the legislative department of the government.

The House declined to concur with the Senate's denunciation of Governor Gilmore. But it joined in a court petition for another opinion, seeking confirmation of the legislative contention that Gilmore's veto was delivered too late, so the voting bill had become law without his signature. The high court ruled both Gilmore and Chandler at fault, but agreed the bill had become law because the Governor failed to meet the five-day deadline.

First, the Justices ruled a bill need not go to a Governor in person, for such a requirement could lead to ridiculous situations, including hide-and-seek complications. They also said there was no set manner for returning a veto message, despite possible custom, and Sinclair's presentation should have been recognized by Speaker Chandler. The court also declared the five-day grace period began the day following presentation of a bill to a Governor, with only Sunday excepted.

The special session repealed some restrictions requested by Gilmore, but it denied most of his demands. And this session of eighteen working days piled up a record forty-five roll calls. A year later, Governor Gilmore was somewhat vindicated by his successor, Governor Frederick Smyth of Manchester. He told the 1865 Legislature that fiscal curbs imposed upon Gilmore's administration continued to threaten the state's fiscal responsibilities, and Smyth won the repeals denied his predecessor.

To This Day

Dispute Over Elections

A THIRD SPECIAL SESSION in 1890 lasted four days—December 2-5— and was propelled by a two-pronged political snarl over House membership for the 1891 session. The dispute flared around two issues. Thirty-two tinier towns had each elected a Representative after a constitutional amendment had declassified them, and substituted proportionate representation, which the 1889 Legislature failed to implement. Second, forty additional House seats were also filled in the 1890 November election, based upon population gains in the decennial federal census a few months earlier, before authorization by the General Court.

The Democrats clamored for justice when the election returns revealed they might capture the House, and even the Governorship, if the legislators-elect in the disputed groups were not seated until after organization of the Legislature. For otherwise, the election tally showed the Republicans with a scant 2-vote House majority, and the Democrats hoped to entice a shift in that balance in showdown balloting.

The arguments swirled upon Assistant House Clerk Stephen S. Jewett of Laconia, who was scheduled to certify the House roll for the 1891 session, because Clerk George A. Dickey of Concord had moved to Maine. The Democrats challenged Jewett's authority to act as clerk without legislative vote to that effect and cited lack of precedent for such procedure. They also threatened a rump session when the Legislature convened on January 7 if the disputed legislators-elect (mostly Republican) were certified before their merits were formally voted upon.

Governor David H. Goodell of Antrim ordered the special session because the controversy "threatened the peace and dignity of the state." He said the tiny towns should not be granted their full representation demands. But he also declared that the forty new census-gained legislators should be certified, because the House had seated a similar group ten years earlier, with Democratic endorsement.

This 1890 special session moved smoothly. It gave the assistant clerk of each branch automatic authority to fill a clerkship vacancy. The House set another precedent. It blocked a dozen new members from being seated, because they had served on the federal payroll as census takers. The Democrats vainly argued that such temporary employment was not strictly contrary to the state Constitution's prohibition against legislators accepting federal remuneration. The

Democrats turned to the courts for redress. They went before the State Supreme Court and demanded that Jewett be enjoined from certifying any disputed lawmakers-elect until after the House had organized and judged their qualifications.

The Senate chamber—then home of the Supreme Court—was jammed for a December 30 (Tuesday) airing of the test case. The audience comprised perhaps the most impressive array ever in the chamber. It included United States Senator Henry W. Blair of Campton and Representative Jacob H. Gallinger of Concord, who was to succeed him ten days later; Col. Hiram A. Tuttle of Pittsfield (Governor within ten days); upcoming federal Judge Edgar Aldrich of Littleton; United States Senator William Chandler and Governor Goodell; and Democratic stalwarts Harry Bingham of Littleton, Attorney Oliver E. Branch of Manchester, and John M. Mitchell of Concord.

The high court Justices arrived an hour late and announced postponement of the hearing until Monday, January 5, 1891, two days before opening of the Legislature. Illness of Chief Justice Charles Doe and Justice George A. Bingham forced the delay. The postponed hearing developed another surprise. Scheduled for 11:00 A.M., the court appeared forty-five minutes late and declared another postponement to 2:00 P.M.

Arguments ended by midafternoon of the following day (Tuesday), after Clerk Jewett testified he had not made up his mind whether or not to certify any of the controversial members-elect. Following a brief recess, the court dismissed the case at 4:00 P.M. the same day, for lack of jurisdiction. The Justices later issued a formal decision that each legislative branch was sole judge of its membership and officers, including their manner of election.

When the Legislature convened on Wednesday, January 7, Clerk Jewett's roll included the forty-odd census-gained members, who became seated without Democratic challenge. The House later seated fifteen others from the smaller towns and voted consolation mileage payments to the remainder in this group who were denied membership. With the Republicans again in firm control, the Legislature elected Pittsfield's Hiram Americus Tuttle as Governor, over Charles H. Amsden, long prominent Antrim Democrat.

The First Half of the Twentieth Century

A 1919 SPECIAL SESSION lasted only three days—September 9-11—to approve a federal constitutional amendment giving women the right to vote. This session boosted the World War I veterans' bonus from $30, voted earlier in the year, to $100, with a $1.5 million bond issue to finance it, and an added $2 poll tax to pay it off.

A 1927 special session of one day, on November 29, floated a $3 million bond issue, on recommendation of Governor Huntley N. Spaulding of Rochester, to repair devastating highway damages caused by a flood earlier the same month. It was financed by a penny hike in the gasoline tax.

A 1930 special session for tax reform lasted eleven days—February 18-28—and adjourned with a newspaper headline epitaph "Futile Session Comes To End." Governor Charles W. Tobey of Temple sponsored enactment of a tax equalization program bolstered by State Supreme Court advisory opinions. But the legislators, who had shown strong tax reform sentiment in their 1929 regular session, completely repudiated it, apparently because of mounting public opposition. This developed after Governor Tobey had induced the Senate to table House-approved tax reform bills, pending court rulings on some of the details.

Up for consideration was a state income tax, with basic exemptions; a franchise levy on utilities and tax exemptions for growing timber to promote reforestation. The program had first been sponsored by a 1927 legislative interim commission, which filed its recommendations with the 1929 Legislature.

Basic legal guidelines came out of this special session. The Supreme Court emphasized that advisory opinions were not binding upon future laws. It said that while reasonable exemptions in an income tax might then be set at $2,000 for a family head and $1,200 for a single person, the definition of what was reasonable for such exemptions, as required by the Constitution, could well change, depending upon economic values.

The House asked Attorney General Ralph W. Davis of Manchester if a special session could operate after the fifteen-day period in which daily pay and mileage payments were allowed, and he ruled in the affirmative. Davis said a special session could continue indefinitely, but all remuneration terminated after fifteen working days. The session adjourned the day after this ruling.

A 1934 special session of twenty-one days—May 14-June 4—created the present State Liquor Monopoly System, following repeal of national prohibition. The 1933 Legislature had repealed state prohibition and legalized sale of beer, but postponed spirituous liquor sales pending an interim study.

Special Sessions

Governor John G. Winant of Concord keynoted this session with a plea that the private profit motive be distilled from the liquor business as much as possible, to curb the evils of avarice. He also urged that revenue from state-supervised liquor sales be devoted to reducing state indebtedness, rather than to direct support of the state government. He said such policy would curb legislative inclination to pry pyramiding profits from liquor users to sidestep more responsible support of public services.

Winant's idealism prevailed, for the most part. Liquor sales became theoretically hinged to retail prices high enough to discourage excessive drinking and low enough to discourage bootlegging, while also sufficiently heavy to yield modest profits and yet light enough to compete favorably with neighboring states.

The legislators labored three weeks to please Governor Winant, then personally a prohibitionist. At his insistence, licensed clubs were forbidden from making a profit on liquor sales (this prohibition was soon repealed). The House voted to bar legislators from distribution or sale of alcoholic beverages until two years after leaving office, but the Senate killed that proposal. While Governor Winant opposed some details of the new control statute, he accepted it and complimented the lawmakers, saying, "You more intimately represent the people . . . than a man holding executive office."

New Hampshire pioneered the nation with this 1934 liquor monopoly law. It was the brainchild of Representative F. Clyde Keefe of Dover, veteran Democratic party leader. As other states copied this liquor control policy, Keefe became employed to organize the present National Alcoholic Beverage Control Association. He helped generate a policy whereby liquor and wine companies doing business with any "control" state (now totalling seventeen) are required to maintain uniform prices for every state, whether large or small. Time has diluted much of Winant's altruistic dedication to the 1934 liquor control program. Its revenue soon was siphoned into direct state budget support, and the profit motive has in recent years increasingly induced the Legislature to promote, rather than modify, liquor sales.

As in 1927, a special session to finance flood damage was held in 1938, for a single day—May 12. Governor Styles Bridges of Concord reported March flood damages of $4,256,900 to highways and bridges and recommended that a $2 million bond issue would suffice for emergency repairs. The Legislature continued the penny per gallon gasoline tax increase for the 1927 flood repairs to finance this 1938 bond issue.

This 1938 session also created a Maine-New Hampshire Bridge Authority to build a giant bridge over the Piscataqua River at Portsmouth; Congress had given its support to the interstate venture in 1937. Thirty years later, the Legislature approved, with Maine, a $40 million outlay, for an even larger span, a short distance upstream on a toll turnpike. The older bridge continues in use for local traffic.

A ninth special session in 1944, of ten days—March 21-30 —advanced the biennial September primary to July 11 to provide time for processing absentee balloting by members of the armed forces in the World War II sectors around the globe, for the November Presidential election. The 1945 Legislature continued this wartime emergency action, but set the primary for August 6 for the 1946 biennial state election.

By this time, a 1942 constitutional amendment had given the Legislature authority to extend all voting rights beyond the state borders. The 1943 Legislature did so, and a 1956 amendment included such voting in biennial primaries.

Reorganization Session

A TENTH SPECIAL SESSION in 1950 equalled the length of the 1864 session, running to twenty-four days—April 25-May 18— and approved a broad state government reorganization program without argument. It featured rigid centralized spending controls, and a State Classification System to insulate state personnel from political patronage shortcomings.

The 1949 Legislature had given Governor Sherman Adams of Lincoln unique authority to implement the fiscal reforms, but the State Supreme Court killed it by a rare 3 to 2 advisory opinion. The Legislature had voted that Adams's reforms would automatically become law twenty-five days after submission to a legislative session, unless rebuffed in whole or in part by both the House and the Senate.

Governor Adams sought the court ruling when a Democratic legislative minority challenged the strange enactment device. A majority of the court ruled that all laws must have direct approval by both the House and Senate, and this requirement cannot be bypassed by advance endorsement of unknown proposals. Adams's reorganization success followed a state contracts scandal, in which State Comptroller Stephen B. Story was imprisoned, along with a private contractor.

There was but one major disagreement as the reform bills were

Gov. Sherman Adams

enacted. Representative Charles A. Holden, retired Dartmouth College professor, vainly denounced placing postaudits in the Comptroller's agency. He argued it would be improper for state officials to audit their own affairs, and three years later Holden won his point. The 1953 Legislature created its own agency, the Legislative Budget Assistant Office, to handle postaudits of executive agencies, and it continues to this day.

A 1954 special session lasted four hectic days—April 6-9— and was the first ever called by the General Court itself. It was sparked by Senator Fred Fletcher, Milford paint manufacturer, in argument with Governor Hugh Gregg of Nashua over a giant highway land damage award. Fletcher demanded a special session to air secrecy which up to then cloaked such payments, and when Gregg refused to call it, the Milford man mustered sufficient legislative votes to convene it.

Senator Fletcher's gambit became possible by a wartime court ruling. The 1945 House of Representatives asked the State Supreme Court if the Legislature could convene itself, during World War II, if the Governor became unable to do so during a possible enemy attack. The court ruled the Constitution permitted such action at any time.

But the court also said the Legislature would have to enact details to implement this "inherent right." The 1945 Legislature promptly did so. The formula required that a minimum of eight Senators and fifty House members (with not more than ten from any county) could petition the Secretary of State to conduct a mail poll on the question of sponsoring a special session, and a majority vote of the joint branches would prevail.

As Fletcher's protests won support and the required initial petition was endorsed, Governor Gregg insisted the action was unwarranted. He also announced that if a special session was forced, he would hand it bills to raise the tax on Rockingham Race Track, to permit liquor sales in first-class restaurants, and to strengthen the wartime Civil Defense program. Fletcher's forces persevered, with the backing of thirteen Senators, and a 231 to 94 House vote. So the special session opened April 6, and Governor Gregg shelved his threatened measures.

The dispute centered on a proposed $174,000 award by a Land Damage Commission on a toll turnpike project at Nashua. Governor Gregg joined State Highway Department officials in defending the commission's integrity and the size of the award. The case went into the courts, and both the Superior Court and the Supreme Court ruled the award could not be challenged, except for fraud or gross misconduct. Attorney General Louis C. Wyman of Manchester told the Legislature no such charge had been filed.

This 1954 session clipped the wings of Land Damage Commissions. It ordered that awards be made public, which they have been ever since. The Legislature also transferred final authority on the awards to the Governor and the Council (who appoint the commissions).

The $174,000 award to the Edgecomb Steel Company was later nullified when the commission reduced the size of the condemned land area. This compromise allowed space for expansion desired by the company and diminished the value of the requisitioned property. The commission posted a revised award of $20,500, and the Edgecomb Steel Company went to court and won a $95,000 verdict, plus a $13,706 interest payment.

The 1954 special session also extended annual observance of Daylight Saving Time from the last Sunday in September to the final Sunday in October.

Franchise Tax Restored

A 1958 SPECIAL SESSION of nine days—February 11-19—reenacted an invalidated utility franchise tax and produced a $7,000 balm for a Manchester man for wrongful imprisonment. Governor Lane Dwinell of Lebanon called the session to resolve a financial crisis, after gas and electric utilities won a $1,358,000 tax rebate, in a State Supreme Court challenge of the tax collection method. Dwinell then obtained the high court's advisory opinion approving a new tax formula, and the Legislature promptly reimposed it. The new levy was also set at higher rates, to recapture the rebate loss.

The retribution payment—the only one in New Hampshire legislative history—went to Henry C. Duke, forty-year-old garage mechanic, for three years of illegal confinement for rape, to which another man finally confessed. The Attorney General's office confirmed the miscarriage of justice, following lengthy investigation by Assistant Attorney General Elmer T. Bourque of Manchester. An unidentified sex psychopath at New Hampshire Hospital admitted the crime in such detail, Bourque reported, that he agreed that Duke had been wrongly convicted and given a prison term of from fifteen to twenty years.

Duke had vainly protested his innocence. He had been arrested in a theater after the rape victim said her assailant mentioned a movie after the dusk attack in a vacant lot. The victim, a nurse, recalled a kerosene smell, and Duke readily admitted having used such fluid to clean up from his day's work. A bloodstain on the victim's clothing matched Duke's blood type, Bourque's probe showed, and this became a strong point of evidence in the jury trial.

Bourque filed a most unusual report to Governor Dwinell and the Executive Council. He disclosed that while the bloodstain matched that of Duke, it also matched the victim's blood type. Bourque also reported that the man who confessed to the rape matched Duke's height; he looked like Duke; he also was a garage worker who had washed up with kerosene on the day of the crime; and he had previously been involved in similar attacks.

Governor Dwinell and his Council approved a pardon for Duke, with official regrets. The special session legislators readily agreed to balm, but briefly argued the payment method because of Duke's drinking record. The $7,000 award was adjusted to a $2,500 cash payment, and a $125 monthly allotment for three years.

A 1966 special session of one day—June 13—was called, by chance, to salvage an expiring part of the state gasoline tax. A one-cent increase in that road toll voted fifteen years earlier would have expired on July 1, but for Representative Stacey W. Cole of Swanzey, an agricultural leader who had just become Executive Director of the New Hampshire Petroleum Council. No one in state government had remembered a 1951 gasoline tax hike had been geared to a fifteen-year expiration date; Cole explained he learned of it by chance. The termination crisis came to light when a gasoline company official mentioned it to him.

Representative Cole soon learned some interesting details. An unusual sequence of subsequent gasoline tax increases had apparently caused all concerned to overlook the 1951 increase expiration tag, because it had been placed in an adjacent section of the law. The 1957 Legislature amended the 1951 penny hike to five cents, by adding a sixth penny, with a forty-eight month expiration clause. Then the 1959 Legislature added a seventh penny on a permanent basis and amended the 1957 boost by repealing its four-year expiration date. Meanwhile, nothing was ever done to the 1951 hike's expiration clause.

Cole measured his conscience, as he later explained. He realized that his new employers would benefit from the pending tax reduction. But Cole went to Governor John W. King and reported the crisis. As the startling development became public, legislative leaders quickly joined with Governor King in expediting the special session to avoid loss of $1 million in revenue, which would have occurred if the July 1 termination date of the forgotten penny tax boost was not restored until the 1967 Legislature convened six months later.

Representative Cole's Good Samaritan role remained private until after the special session adjourned. He recently recalled that some of his Republican colleagues later ruefully observed that if Cole had held his tongue, the onus of the threatened reduction in gasoline tax revenue might have reflected against Democrat Governor King's ensuing successful bid for an unprecedented third consecutive biennial term.

Rulings Change Conduct

TWO RULINGS by the State Supreme Court radically changed the conduct of New Hampshire's special legislative sessions through the decade of 1969-79. A surprise 1967 court decision abolished a recess restraint on daily meetings. And in 1975 the court declared that the Governor and the Council could not restrict special session deliberations.

Up to 1948 the state Constitution limited legislative recesses to two days. As a result, the Legislature met daily, when in session, except for Saturdays and Sundays. Then, about the turn of this century, when the legislators shifted to a three-day workweek schedule, "skeleton" sessions were held on Fridays and Mondays, to conform with the Constitution.

In 1948 the people approved a constitutional amendment which boosted the recess allowance to five days. Then, on January 13, 1967, a most unusual Supreme Court ruling abolished the recess restraint entirely. This ruling was linked to a 1966 amendment approved by the people, which provided for annual legislative sessions, and which the high court invalidated in the January 13, 1967, decision, for being improperly worded on the ballot. The amendment question read: "Do you favor having the Legislature meet in two annual sessions with a total limit of ninety days but no limit on time of adjournment?" The court killed the first part of the question because it did not explain that it referred to biennial sessions. But it also emphasized that repeal of the five-day recess—or adjournment—restriction had been approved.

The 1967 court ruling also loosened another restriction on special sessions. When an 1889 constitutional amendment pegged the legislators' pay at $200 per biennium, it also set special session remuneration at $3 a day, for not more than fifteen legislative days, tied to the recess restriction. So when this was repealed, the fifteen days could be spread at legislative will.

Governor Walter Peterson of Peterborough sponsored a 1970 special session, which ran from March 25 to April 30, to act on proposed state government reforms, as recommended by a $190,000 Citizens Task Force study. It produced the present business profits tax to replace repeal of the municipal property tax on stock in trade, farm livestock and poultry, fuel pumps, and mills and machinery. When the session adjourned, Governor Peterson complimented the lawmakers for enacting seventy-five new statutes, many of them suggested by the CTF study group.

Governor Peterson sponsored a second special session, in his second term, in 1972, which ran from January 6 to March 23. He proposed a 3 percent state income tax, which was earmarked for distribution to cities and towns for the purpose of reducing property taxes on homes and farms. House Speaker Marshall Cobleigh of Nashua endorsed the bill, labeled "An Act Relative To Property Tax Relief," but it failed of enactment. This seventy-six-day special session enacted sixty-four new laws.

A capital budget dispute led to a 1974 special session called by Governor Thomson, which lasted from February 19 to April 11. It produced fifty-two new laws, including a compromise capital budget, overtime pay for certain state employees, and a cost-of-living adjustment formula for retired state personnel.

Governor Thomson launched a 1975 special session, which opened December 1, and continued to June 10, 1976, for repeal of objectionable features of a new compulsory mental health insurance program, which sparked a State Supreme Court ruling. Governor Thomson and his Council sought to specify and restrict the business of this session, and House Speaker George B. Roberts, Jr., induced the House of Representatives to challenge such restraint in the high court. The Supreme Court upheld Speaker Roberts's contention that each branch of the Legislature was sole judge of its own operations. Under Speaker Roberts's guidance, this special session lasted more than six months and produced fifty-nine new laws, including creation of a Legislative Utility Consumers Council, over a Thomson veto.

When the 1977 Legislature failed to enact the traditional biennial operating budget by its July 1 mileage payment deadline, because of disagreements with Governor Thomson, the stalemate produced a special session on top of a special session in a history-making manner. Thomson sponsored a special session for July 12, 1977, and when the House failed to produce a compromise budget after two months, the Governor and his Council ordered a second special session to convene on September 27.

As he convened the second special session, Speaker Roberts roundly denounced Governor Thomson for ordering it without consultation with legislative leaders. Roberts, who was in China with a delegation of American legislative leaders as guests of that nation, when Thomson and his Council voted the second session, told the House in a lengthy opening statement:

As soon as the Governor knew that the Speaker of the House was almost 10,000 miles away, the Chairman of the Senate Finance Committee was recovering from back surgery in a Massachusetts hospital, and other key House members were unavailable because of their business and personal plans, the Governor tried to change the time-schedule of this Legislature. He did so without even having the common courtesy of either writing the majority leader of the House, who was acting on the Speaker's behalf, as Speaker pro-tem, or even telephoning the majority leader who was present every single day during my absence in the House of Representatives.

Speaker Roberts promptly declared the House would not recognize the second special session, after the opening day's requirement, and it subsequently confined its deliberations to within the fifteen days of $3 daily pay, with mileage allowances, of the July 12 first special session. But he avoided a court challenge of the constitutionality of the linking of two special sessions into each other, which had been anticipated by veteran State House observers.

Making use of the 1967 repeal of limitation on legislative recesses, Speaker Roberts spread this historic special session's fifteen working days as follows: July 12 and 19; October 20 and 27; November 3; April 11, 18, 25, and 27; June 6, 15, and 29; July 26; August 12; and October 4. The Senate spread its work into early November before concluding its end of the session.

The 1977-78 marathon special session featured yet another operating precedent. The 1977 biennial session was continued in operation after the July 1 mileage deadline, and regular session and special session deliberations were conducted on the same days. Whenever Speaker Roberts convened a day of the special session, the legislators became entitled to a daily mileage payment, even though that same day became devoted to regular session work, for which mileage allowance was illegal.

This unprecedented policy of avoiding final adjournment of a biennial legislative session before the convening of a special session was initiated by Speaker Roberts in the 1975 biennial session. It was continued in 1977 without possible constitutional challenge.

The 1977-78 special session, the first to spread through twice the normal length of a biennial regular session, produced fifty-eight new laws. They included a pay raise for state personnel, and implementation of a new "Sunset Law," to provide for special evaluations of the Executive Department's functions and services, to eliminate waste and duplication. This special session also financed a new state building on top of Mount Washington, two state liquor stores on the toll turnpike in Hooksett, and creation of a Joint Legislative Committee on Elderly Affairs.

WOMEN LEGISLATORS

House Members

WOMEN began serving in the Granite State Legislature in the 1921 session, as the United States Constitution was amended to grant full suffrage to the feminine sex. First to serve as members of the House were Democrat Mrs. Mary Louise Rolfe Farnum, aged fifty, of Boscawen, a widowed physician who had retired from practice, and Republican Miss Jessie Doe, aged thirty-three, of Rollinsford, daughter of the late Chief Justice Charles Doe of the State Supreme Court.

This pioneer pair of lady legislators, who had never met before, displayed unity as they took office. They sat beside each other, organized themselves into the New Hampshire Association of Women Legislators, and voted themselves all its titles. It is recorded that Miss Doe became president, treasurer, and sergeant-at-arms, of the association, while Dr. Farnum became vice president, secretary, and the entire executive committee. They were excused from the seating lottery, then in use, and given their choice. So they picked Seats 17 and 18 in Division Five.

Each of these first New Hampshire women solons was assigned to two House committees. Dr. Farnum served on the Committees on Normal School and Public Health. Miss Doe was appointed to the Committees on Forestry and Public Health.

In 1971, as the Legislature observed the Golden Anniversary of women legislators, it was recorded that in that fifty-year period, a

Dr. Mary L. R. Farnum   *Jessie Doe*

total of 410 women had served in the House, and twenty-one had served in the Senate. To mark this celebration, this writer compiled a sixty-four-page booklet history of the service of these 431 lady lawmakers, which was sponsored by New Hampshire Savings Bank of Concord and presented to the Legislature for distribution throughout the state.

Three women were elected to the 1923 House, as Dr. Farnum lost a second-term bid and Miss Doe declined to seek reelection. From then on their numbers had steadily increased in each biennial election. As a result, the number of women legislators topped the 100 mark in the 1975 House. They totalled 103, or more than 25 percent of the entire House membership of 400. This is a higher percentage than has ever been achieved by women in any other Legislature in the nation—or the world, for that matter.

Two of the three women in the 1923 session were Democrats, and this was the only time in which they have outnumbered their Republican counterparts. They were Mrs. Emma L. Bartlett of Raymond, sixty-three-year-old insurance agency operator, and Mrs. Gertrude Moran Caldwell, forty-two-year-old Portsmouth housewife. The third member was Republican Mrs. Effie Earll Yantis of Manchester, first woman legislator who declined to reveal her age for the legislative biographical *Brown Book* (she was about fifty-three). The 1923 House had a Democratic majority, and Mrs. Bartlett became the first of her sex to serve as a House committee chairman, heading its Public Health Committee.

There were fourteen women in the 1925 House, and two of them proceeded to produce national history. Mrs. Augusta Pillsbury of Manchester, at thirty-seven, became famous on April 15, 1928, as the nation's first legislator to have a baby while in office. Later the same year, Dr. Zatae L. Straw, also of Manchester, who pioneered hiking as a health measure, became the country's first woman to preside over a state political convention. She served as chairman of the biennial Republican State Convention in Concord.

Ten years after women first joined the General Court, Berlin sent a forty-four-year-old mother of six children to the Legislature, launching an all-time world's record as a woman legislator. She was Mrs. Hilda Constance Frederika Brungot, who proceeded to roll up nineteen terms in the House, and then lost out in a reelection bid in the 1974 election.

The 1977 Legislature joined with Governor Meldrim Thomson, Jr., of Orford in paying tribute to Mrs. Brungot's legislative achievement. A handsome portrait of the ninety-year-old grandmother was unveiled at a joint session of this Legislature, on June 29, 1978, with Mrs. Brungot in a wheelchair as guest of honor. The portrait, now on permanent display in the State House, was sponsored by the Forty-Three Club, a legislative social group formed in 1943, which disbanded in 1977 and contributed a $550 treasury balance to the project. Legislators and other friends joined with the New Hampshire Commission on the Arts in producing the remainder of the $2,300 required for the portrait and its frame. Mrs. Willey Fromm of Sandwich was the artist.

Mrs. Brungot's legislative record is considered without equal by any other legislative body, up to her retirement. Only the late Mrs. Edith Nourse Rogers of Lowell, Massachusetts, came close to equalling her nineteen biennial terms. Mrs. Rogers won an interim election to Congress in 1925, to succeed her late husband, and then was given seventeen biennial terms, before her death, at seventy-nine, in 1960. Mrs. Brungot also served as a delegate from Berlin in five state Constitutional Conventions, also considered a feminine record.

Mrs. Margaret E. Dustin of Rochester won special distinction when

Hilda C. F. Brungot

elected to the 1943 House. She became the first woman to serve with a husband, Representative Miles H. Dustin, a retired teacher. Mrs. Doris L. Thompson of Northfield became the first mother to serve with a son, Robert M. Lawton of Meredith, in the 1971 session. And Miss Cecelia L. Winn, Nashua retired teacher, became the first to serve with a brother, John T. Winn, of the same city, in the 1973 House.

The *Ladies Home Journal* magazine gave the 1951 women legislators national attention. It reported forty-six women in that session, including a dozen widows and five single women. A feature article reported, in part:

The most frequently mentioned criticism of New Hampshire women legislators is their inability to take defeat. House Speaker Lane Dwinell (later Governor) believes "They haven't quite the ability to come through a rough and tumble as easily as a man—they take rebuffs too hard."

Members of the Senate

TWENTY-THREE WOMEN have served in the State Senate since they first joined that body in 1931. Nineteen of them earlier served in the House, and four have served four or more Senate terms.

Mrs. E. Maude Ferguson of Bristol was the first female Senator. She was elected in 1930, a decade following national enactment of woman suffrage. This stately brunette of forty-seven had completed two terms in the House, where she joined in opposing special privilege for women in allocation of seats.

Mrs. Ferguson was greeted by the "august" Senate with flattering homage, which she accepted. She was given the distinction of presiding as chairman of the Senate's Republican caucus for choice of the session's officials. She also became temporary President when the Senate convened, as skeptical newsmen, including this writer, reported she officiated without flaw or miscues.

A bouquet of roses from her Bristol neighbors graced Senator Ferguson's desk on opening day to mark her presence. There was also a single rose, in silent homage to Dr. George H. Calley of Bristol, Senator Ferguson's late stepfather, who filled the same seat in 1909.

Senator Ferguson became so esteemed that the following spring the Republican leadership nominated her for delegate to the party's national convention, and she readily won that election. Three months later, Mrs. Ferguson was stricken with a fatal illness and ended life in her lovely flower garden.

Six years later, Mrs. Lula J.A. Morris of Lancaster became the second woman Senator, in the 1937 session. Then sixty-four and wife of Judge George F. Morris of the federal District Court in Concord, Mrs. Morris served thrice in the House.

Another eight years passed before a third woman was elected to the Senate. The first Democratic woman in the upper branch, she was Mrs. Marye Walsh Caron of Manchester. A House three-termer, she joined the 1945 Senate and rolled up eight Senate terms, following which she became the first woman ever to serve on the state Liquor Commission.

Hampstead produced the Senate's fourth woman member for 1947. She was Miss Doris M. Spollett, girlhood schoolteacher who became a veteran rural mail carrier and internationally famous breeder of prize goats and ponies. Still in business at seventy-five, she attained a fifteenth biennial House term in 1973, after two dozen years as a town selectman, and then retired from public life. She died in 1977.

Senator Spollett waged a colorful battle to make the New Hampshire Red, once a famous hen breed, the official state bird. She lost to the dainty six-inch purple finch, as national headlines featured the episode. Which time has proven was just as well, because this once-

E. *Maude Ferguson*

vaunted Granite State fowl, noted for its poundage and production, has become extinct, being replaced by even more scientifically improved strains.

Mrs. Sara E. Otis of Concord, born on New Year's Day in 1876 in the mountain hamlet of Bartlett, joined the 1949 Senate and served four House terms after raising a family of six children. She championed two memorable laws still in use. One was the ban on public sale or use of fireworks; the other was 1947 creation of the state program against alcoholism.

The "Petticoat Session"

THE 1951 SENATE became known as "the Petticoat session" because six of the twenty-four members were women, and one of them staged the greatest spectacle ever beheld in the tradition-draped Senate chamber. Senator Winifred Julia Wild of Jackson, wealthy fifty-three-year-old widow, became the bride of Senator George Wesley Tarlson, forty-seven-year-old Laconia bachelor businessman, in a sensational October 27, 1951, ceremony.

Governor and Mrs. Sherman Adams headed an overflow array of political luminaries for the gala Saturday afternoon wedding, some

Gov. Sherman Adams congratulates Senate members Winifred Julia Wild and George Wesley Tarlson on their marriage on October 27, 1951.

even straddling windowsills to witness it. And so the Senate got its only husband-wife combination!

Congressmen Chester E. Merrow and Norris Cotton occupied front seats as Dr. Oscar Polhemus of Haverhill, Massachusetts, former Laconia Methodist pastor, officiated, and a small host of photographers popped their bulbs and newsreel crews filmed the colorful details for national distribution.

The *New Hampshire Sunday News* reported, in part:

The Senate Chamber was lavishly decorated with palms and ferns, and large orchid-colored chrysanthemums against a backdrop of evergreens. It was in this same Senate chamber that the couple first met and began their romance. . . .

The bride was ushered to the improvised altar at the front of the room by her son. . . . She wore an ice-blue floor-length satin gown with court train. Bands of imported Alencon lace trimmed with princess lines of the fitted bodice and paneled the full skirt fashioned with unpressed pleats over a crinoline petticoat.

Women Legislators

Edith B. Gardner

Her headpiece, a soft crepe of matching ice-blue satin twined with pearls, was attached to a very short circular veil of imported ice-blue illusion.

The bride wore ice-blue satin slippers to match her gown, and a pearl necklace with diamond and pearl clasp. She carried a bouquet of white orchids with orchid-colored throats encircled with stephanotis, and stephanotis on the short ice-blue satin ribbon drops.

Following the 4:00 P.M. ceremony, the newlyweds and their entourage marched through 2,000 guests and neck-stretching Concord citizenry, down the State House yard to the Eagle Hotel for a reception. They were serenaded by the noted Bektash Temple Shriners band of Concord, of which the bridegroom was a member. In fact, he led the band with a glockenspiel, as the new and second Senator Tarlson skipped joyously by his side, to the delight of onlookers.

Several Senators officiated at the wedding, and Senator Raoul J. Lalumiere of Manchester strutted as self-proclaimed "Cupid," with boasts and toasts that he had promoted the match. President Blaylock Atherton of Nashua was head usher, assisted by Senators Charles Hartnett of Dover, Stanley Brown of Bradford, and John Dole of Bristol.

To This Day

The Tarlsons' reception spilled into evening dancing. After a first fling with Senator Mrs. Tarlson, Senator Mr. Tarlson suggested she share her gaiety with the guests, while he attended the orchestra drums. They went on a world cruise, terminated their legislative life, and have lived happily ever since at The Weirs, Laconia's Lake Winnipesaukee suburb.

The five other women Senators of the 1951 session were Mrs. Otis, Mrs. Caron, and newcomers Miss Suzanne Loizeaux of Plymouth, Mrs. Lena A. Read of Plainfield and Mrs. Margery W. Graves of Brentwood.

Five years later, Miss Ida Horner of Thornton, bookkeeper and veteran town tax collector, joined the 1957 Senate, and later that same year she became the bride of widower Representative Jesse R. Rowell, Newport businessman, then serving a ninth House term. Other women Senators have included single-termers Mrs. Marjorie M. Greene of Concord, Mrs. Katherine Jackson of Dublin, Mrs. Irene Weed Landers of Keene, Mrs. Dorothy Green of Manchester, Mrs. Marion L. Phillips of Claremont, Miss Eda C. Martin of Littleton, and Mrs. Molly O'Gara of Exeter.

Mrs. Margaret B. DeLude of Unity served two Senate terms. Mrs. Nelle L. Holmes of Amherst, onetime Kentucky schoolteacher, was a four-termer, ending in 1963.

Senator Edith B. Gardner of Gilford, an 1899 New Year's Day baby, was reelected to a tenth straight term in the 1979 Senate. This was an all-time female record, and Mrs. Gardner also became the oldest woman ever to sit in the Senate. She previously served five House terms, and the public career of this onetime nurse included two terms as president of the National Order of Women Legislators.

Mrs. Eileen Foley, former Portsmouth mayor, completed seven Senate terms in the 1977 session and then declined to seek reelection. Two freshman Senators of the 1977 session were Mrs. Phyllis M. Keeney of Hudson, college librarian and three-term House member, and Miss Mary Louise Hancock of Concord, retired director of the State Planning Division. Miss Hancock won a second term in the 1979 Senate.

Mrs. Vesta M. Roy, Salem housewife and World War II veteran, was elected to the 1979 Senate.

New Hampshire's women legislators reached a new leadership plateau in the 1977 session. Speaker George B. Roberts, Jr., appointed six of them to House committee chairmanships and another nine to committee vice chairmanships.

The 1977 women chairmen of standing House committees were listed in the legislative *Black Manual* as Elizabeth A. Greene of Rye, Committee on Environment and Agriculture; Roma A. Spaulding of Claremont, Committee on Health and Welfare; Martha McD. Frizzell of Charlestown, Committee on Judiciary; Patricia M. Skinner of Windham, Committee on Labor, Human Resources and Rehabilitation; Elaine T. Lyons of Merrimack, Committee on Legislative Administration; Susan B. McLane of Concord, Committee on Ways and Means.

Ruth L. Griffin of Portsmouth served as vice chairman of both the House Committees on Interstate Cooperation, and Rules. The other women vice chairmen were Judith Ann Hess of Hooksett, Committee on Constitutional Revision; Sara M. Townsend of Meriden, Committee on Executive Departments and Administration; Helen F. Wilson of Manchester, Committee on Health and Welfare; Ednapearl F. Parr of Hampton, Committee on Legislative Administration; Augustine J. Marshala of Keene, Committee on Public Works; Judith M. Stahl of Nashua, Committee on Science and Technology; Donalda K. Howard of Glen, Committee on State Institutions; and Natalie S. Flanagan of Atkinson, Committee on Statutory Revision.

THE OFF AND ON LOTTERIES

LOTTERIES have studded New Hampshire's legislative life throughout its three centuries of existence.

Hobart Pillsbury's 1927 *New Hampshire History* tells of a 1757 legislative lottery to raise £ 6,000 to build a harbor at Rye, and another to erect a bridge in New Castle. In that same period, Portsmouth citizens were granted a lottery to finance road improvements. The Reverend J. Lane Fitts's 1912 *History of Newfields* relates that surveyor Walter Bryant of that town helped manage legislative lotteries to build bridges over the Exeter and Squamscot rivers.

Numerous lotteries were authorized to finance education, and construction of roads and bridges in the first quarter of a century, following 1784 creation of the present state government. Meanwhile, Col. Timothy Walker, Jr., of Concord asked the 1781 wartime Legislature at Exeter for an initial lottery to finance a Merrimack River bridge in his town, but it was denied. Walker then induced the Legislature to shift its sessions to Concord, in 1782, and soon thereafter Henry Gerrish and associates were granted a $1,600 lottery for a timber sluiceway at Garvin's Falls, in Bow, just south of Concord. Col. Walker and General John Stark of present Manchester were among the managers of this project. Claremont was next given a lottery to raise £ 200 for a Sugar River bridge, and another was granted for a Baker River span at Plymouth.

In 1790 the Legislature approved a lottery of £ 450 for two bridges over "rapid streams," as the "Ammonusuck and Wild Ammonusuck" at Haverhill were called. At the same time, a lottery of £ 1,500 was granted to rebuild a bridge "over Little Harbour" to New Castle, apparently first erected with the 1757 lottery. This venture ran into censure. Citizens of Portsmouth complained ticket promotions had become a nuisance. So the Legislature forbade such sales in Portsmouth and ordered the managers to terminate the lottery within four years.

Aid to Dartmouth College

DARTMOUTH COLLEGE vainly tried for several years to utilize lotteries to finance its growth. As the institution plunged into debt for what became known as Dartmouth Hall, the 1784 Legislature granted it a lottery to raise £ 3,000. A dozen years earlier, the colonial Assembly had refused President Wheelock a lottery to raise £ 5,000 for a building program and instead voted the college an outright grant of £ 500.

Dartmouth's lottery life, as detailed in Frederick Chase's 1891 history of the college, was given a supposed impressive launching in 1784. The Legislature appointed five managers for this comparatively elaborate project, and allowed them "reasonable" remuneration and expenses. Interestingly, the appointees were John Parker, Joshua Wentworth, and Thomas Martin of Portsmouth, and Josiah Gilman and Thomas Odiorne of Exeter, all presumably personally known to the legislators, and all distant from Hanover, Dartmouth's location. Before the year was out, the quintet quit in embarrassment. They reported cash was so scarce (because the war had depreciated the value of paper currency) that few could buy the lottery tickets. So they recommended that management of the lottery be transferred to Hanover so that grain, timber, and other materials could be accepted in lieu of money for the tickets. The Legislature readily heeded this advice and named college officials to handle the lottery, with a two-year extension to insure its success.

In 1787 Dartmouth got a new lottery of £ 1,800 "for raising country produce" to help reduce debts. College officials were again the managers. All the tickets were not sold, but historian Chase relates there was a 1791 drawing "in the desk of the college chapel, much to the scandal of some worthy people."

Dartmouth's lottery hopes continued. So in 1795 the Legislature authorized the college to raise $15,000 with a third lottery over a five-year period. This one was different. The Governor and his Council were given personal supervision, along with Jonathan Freeman of Hanover, Benjamin Connor of Exeter, and William A. Kent of Concord as managers. Seven drawings were scheduled and Massachusetts agreed to permit ticket sales. In the first lottery, held in 1796, tickets sold at $4 each; and there were 1,168 prizes totalling $20,000, ranging from $3,000 down to $6. The first drawing was staged in the legislative chambers during a summer session at Exeter and lasted from June 7 to June 16. The six other drawings were held at Concord, the final two in 1800, and historian Chase records that net profits to the college from the five-year affair totalled $4,000.

When the Legislature met at Hopkinton in 1806, a seventeen-member study committee recommended five annual lotteries to raise $5,000 for Dartmouth, but they were denied. Instead, the Legislature imposed a modest tax on banks to support the college, but Governor Langdon vetoed this forerunner of the 1821 literary fund. Finally, Dartmouth President John Wheelock petitioned the 1812 Legislature for a $30,000 lottery to "provide philosophical apparatus and erect a library and repair college buildings," but it was tabled to the 1813 session and was never brought up again.

Other Early Lotteries

THESE PIONEER LOTTERIES, which were popular through the early colonies and boasted George Washington and Benjamin Franklin as sponsors, developed shortcomings. For by 1803, when the Legislature, on Christmas Eve, authorized a $15,000 lottery for repair and maintenance of the Piscataqua bridge at Portsmouth, each manager was required to post a $10,000 integrity bond. The same rigid requirement of honesty was imposed again in 1808 when the academies at Chesterfield and Haverhill were granted lotteries to raise $5,000 and $3,000, respectively.

New Hampshire's most noted lottery of earlier days was granted to Judge Samuel Blodget of Derryfield (Manchester) to finance his giant canal around the rugged Amoskeag Falls, an important project in making the Merrimack River navigable from Concord to the sea, at the turn of the nineteenth century. Blodget had prospered in various enterprises before settling in Derryfield, to launch his bypass in 1793, when soon to become a septuagenarian. The story of his success against uphill odds continues a highlight of Manchester lore. After five years of labor and a $20,000 expenditure, a freshet washed it all away, and Blodget turned to a lottery for succor. The Legislature granted him a $9,000 lottery but forced him to post a $20,000 good performance bond and required him to pay management costs. It was boosted to $10,000 three years later, after the Legislature demanded an accounting, and Potter's 1856 history of Manchester says Blodget realized some $5,000 from the venture.

Soon after the 1802 extension of the lottery, Judge Blodget complained the managers were milking it too heavily for their services. A legislative probe was ordered; the managers counterclaimed that Blodget had built a new home and had otherwise improperly spent the lottery profits; and the management was exonerated.

The aging Blodget's herculean efforts apparently met with general approbation. In 1804 the Massachusetts Legislature gave him authority to run a $10,000 lottery in that neighboring state; New Hampshire's 1805 Legislature extended the 1798 lottery grant; and both proved lucrative, according to historian Potter. And in 1806 the Bay State's General Court voted Blodget its second lottery for his canal. Blodget undoubtedly became the only man ever granted lottery privileges by two states for a single project. And to cap his public esteem, the Granite State's 1810 Legislature granted the heirs of Blodget, who died at eighty-three of a cold shortly after 1807 completion of his canal, a final lottery to pay off his debts. But it was abandoned when the canal was sold to owners of the Middlesex Canal south of Lowell, which linked the Merrimack by water to Boston.

When historian George Waldo Browne addressed the 1910 centennial of the naming of Manchester, he said:

Though a man then in his seventieth year, he entered upon the herculean task of making the river navigable. To do this the bed of the stream had not only got to be made clear, but the rapids must be surmounted.

This the majority believed to be impossible. The most formidable obstruction was at the falls of Amoskeag, and here Judge Blodget, confident of his ultimate success, began upon the morning of May 2, 1793, the mightiest task ever undertaken in this country by a single individual at that time.

The following fourteen years of earnest work; fourteen years of expenditure of what was, for those times, large sums of money; fourteen years of intense anxiety; fourteen years of the persecution of enemies and the faith of friends; fourteen years filled with vexatious disappointments and hardships; fourteen years, any one of which must have discouraged a less

sanguine person than the stalwart projector of this great work; fourteen
years of sacrifice to the upbuilding of the public good; fourteen years—and
then another May morning, 1807, when the conquerer rode in triumph
through the canal of his construction, amid the plaudits of a vast concourse
of people who had gathered to witness this trial.

In 1807 the Legislature seemingly for a first time turned to neighboring Massachusetts for easy revenue. An $8,000 lottery to repair and safeguard a bridge against ice at Hinsdale, on the Massachusetts border, was conditioned upon the Bay State permitting sale of the tickets in that commonwealth.

Massachusetts apparently granted that privilege for the Hinsdale lottery, because the following year the Legislature reciprocated by permitting tickets on a Harvard College lottery to be sold in New Hampshire. Three years later, when Timothy Dix, Jr., was granted a $3,000 lottery to build a "good waggon road" through Dixville Notch, the Massachusetts sales proviso was tied to it.

By 1827 the Legislature voted to suppress illegal lotteries. It required town selectmen to prosecute such offenses, with fines of from £ 25 to £ 50 going to the respective county government. But this law ran into such an uproar of opposition that the Legislature later in the same year voted that the fines could be retained by the town in which the offense occurred. By 1845 the fine for an illegal lottery operation had been boosted to $500, and the same penalty had been included against gambling with cards, dice, bowling, and billiards.

By 1891, as the scandals of the Louisiana State lottery had caused Congress to bar such lottery tickets from the mails, the New Hampshire Legislature had imposed a $100 fine against such mailings, as well as against gambling on railroad trains and steamboats, and exhibitions of fights between roosters, dogs, or other animals.

Drawings for House Seating

NEW HAMPSHIRE'S most durable lottery was enacted by the General Court in 1862, functioned for ninety years, and then was killed in 1953 without any public concern. This lottery law was designed to produce seating equality for members of the House of Representatives, but it was violated for the most part by the very legislators it was supposed to benefit.

It was the Republicans, who had taken control of the Legislature five years earlier after three decades of Democratic domination, who sponsored this unique statute. It placed the House seats up to chance, in place of the traditional custom of seniority grab and prestige. Veteran Democratic legislators thus lost the choice seats they had acquired by the old longevity rule. This lottery, signed into law on July 1, 1862, by Governor Nathaniel S. Berry of Hebron, read as follows:

Section 1. The seats of the members-elect of the House of Representatives shall be selected by lot on the first Wednesday of June in each year.

Section 2. The clerk of the House of Representatives shall prepare pieces of paper in the usual form and size of ballots, equal to the whole number of seats in the hall, including those without desks, and shall write upon such pieces of paper numbers corresponding to the numbers placed upon the seats, and the lots, when thus prepared, shall be placed in a box and well shaken together.

Section 3. The box containing the lots shall be placed upon the clerk's desk, and the roll of members called, and such member, when his name is called, shall come to the clerk's desk and draw from the box one lot, and shall be entitled to occupy for the ensuing year the seat corresponding to the number written on the lot drawn by him.

Section 4. It shall be the duty of the keeper of the State House to number all the seats in the Hall of Representatives, previous to the annual session of the Legislature.

Charles Robinson of Portsmouth sponsored the seating lottery and it was approved without opposition, according to newspaper accounts. *The Legislative Reporter,* jointly sponsored by the Concord newspapers as a wartime economy effort, recorded:

Robinson said it was designed to do away with the present grab system (laughter). The seats in the Halls of Congress, in the Mass. Legislative Halls, and all other places, as far as he knew, were drawn in the manner proposed in the bill.

It was the only true democratic principle by which every man could have his rights. He was driven almost of necessity to this, he said, being himself an intruder on his neighbor.

The very seat before him had three members on it within three feet. The seats were not correctly and properly marked. They were marked, some said, previous to the election, by those who lived nearby.

The bill was intended to place all the members on an equality in this matter. The bill took no effect until the next session. He asked no favor for himself, although he had no seat unless he squeezed himself in with two others in a space of three feet. The bill passed.

The House passed the lottery on June 25, and the Senate concurred without comment or hearing two days later.

Robinson's statement spotlights long-forgotten legislative seating lore. The House members sat on benches from 1819 up to the 1865 State House enlargement, with long desks. After that the members had individual stools, fastened to the floor, with long desks each accommodating several members. This arrangement gave way to "opera" chairs without desks in 1900, to conserve space for the ever increasing House membership. The seating lottery was also a far cry from the provincial custom of assigning seats by town seniority. In 1756, for instance, a five-man committee assigned the eighteen House seats. Portsmouth, as the oldest town, had the choicest seat, in front of the Speaker, with Dover to the front left. Next in the front seats, in two "collomes" were "Hampton and Falls" and "New Castle-Rye" to the right, and Exeter and Kingston to the left.

The legislative lottery developed deviously. Members began peddling prestigious positions for cash, and the integrity of the drawings became suspect. In the 1871 drawing, George A. Pillsbury of Concord charged fraud and won a demand for a second lottery after proving that duplicate tickets were being bandied before the draw.

Concord's *Patriot* reported as the 1881 session convened:

Five dollars was the ruling price for front seats Wednesday afternoon. Those facing the reporters' table were quoted at an advance of this figure. Members are requested to keep their hats off the reporters' table. They are no ornament to the same and interfere with the dissemination of news.

As the 1883 session opened, the *Manchester Mirror* observed:

One of the conundrums of the day is—How did it happen that the old members drew all the front seats? There are many things in this world more uncertain than a well-managed lottery.

The Off and On Lotteries

While the constitutional conventions traditionally used legislative rules of operation, the two following enactment of the seating lottery, in 1876 and 1889, refrained from using it. The 1889 Constitutional Convention even went so far as to display its lack of faith in the legislative lottery by utilizing a different seating lottery used by the national Congress (up to 1913). William C. Todd of Atkinson, veteran bachelor lawmaker, sponsored this departure. Delegate Todd argued the national lottery was fairer, because it allowed a member to choose his own seat and eliminated the possibility that a member might already have a number in his hand when drawing from the box, under the legislative procedure.

The *Manchester Union,* in reporting details of this episode, labeled it "Wheel of Fortune and Lottery." Freight agent Clark F. Rowell of Keene and Attorney John Hatch denounced Todd's proposal, but it won convention approval by a 142 to 96 division vote. The substitute lottery read:

Moved and adopted, that the clerk of the convention, as soon as practicable, place in a box the name of each delegate written on a separate slip of paper; that he then draw from the box, one at a time, the slips of paper, and as each is drawn he shall announce the name of the delegate, who shall thereupon choose his seat, provided, that before the drawing shall commence, the President shall cause each seat to be vacated, and that any seat after having been selected, shall be deemed forfeited if left unoccupied before the drawing is finished.

Todd's lottery included aim against an obnoxious development of the legislative lottery. It seems that some adamant legislators preempted choice front seats as a session opened, and when others of more timid character drew them, there resulted personal embarrassments.

The *Manchester Union's* report of the Constitutional Convention drawing presented interesting details. John H. Sullivan of Allenstown was first drawn and modestly took Seat 22 in Division Two. Patrick E. Mallon of Dover, Charles A. Dale of Lebanon, and James G. Taggart of Goffstown followed, in that order, and they all passed up "Statesman's Row," as the front seats were called.

On the fifth draw, Todd's name came up, and he promptly occupied a front-row seat long filled by Gen. Gilman Marston of Exeter, as a legislator, "amid laughter and applause," according to the *Union.* Last out of the box of the 322 delegates was the name of Charles C. Danforth of Concord, and he inherited a chair stuck beneath a side window of Representatives Hall. Said the *Union:* "The last to be drawn was Mr. Danforth of Concord, who appeared like the reporter's hat after it had been sat upon—slightly crushed."

Surprise Revolt

A S THE TWENTIETH CENTURY UNFOLDED, the House increasingly ducked and dodged its own lottery law, and constitutional conventions followed suit, although not legally tied to the statute. But there was a Democratic minority revolt in the 1909 session. Charles J. O'Neil, called the "Sage of Walpole," led this surprise insurrection against what had become standard lottery manipulations, in a party caucus. One newspaper account went:

Mr. O'Neil was called upon and his brief speech was practical and sufficiently succinct so that the members understood every word of it.

Mr. O'Neil explained some things that the new members would see that they would not understand, but would have a thorough comprehension of before the session ended.

Mr. O'Neil said "This privilege of choosing a front seat was also allowed the aged and infirm, but in the course of time it has come about that a chosen few, at each session by some manner unknown to new members, secure for themselves the front seats, and the country members who come here in good faith to represent to the best of their ability their respective towns and wards, are obliged to shrivel up in the rear of the hall and await the pleasure of the experienced man down front, whose back they must currycomb before they can scratch their own heads.

O'Neil warned he would formally challenge any circumvention of the lottery law. And on opening day, for a change, the Republican House leadership bowed to his threat and the seats were drawn without any favoritism.

There was an aftermath. Concord's Democratic *Patriot* reported:

Negotiations for seats are progressing well and many of the statesmen who were relegated to the back rows on the drawings will be down front when the session opens next week.

Rep. Ahern (of Concord) stated to a Patriot *man last night he had already*

The Off and On Lotteries

made three swaps and expected to have something equally as good to offer when he approached the holder of his old seat with an offer of exchange.

News has also been received that the negotiations conducted by the friends of Rep. Hill of Ward 9 (Concord) for his chair in Division Four have been successful and that he will continue to sit beside the gentleman from Moultonborough (French) on and after Tuesday next.

The House thereafter continued, however, to grant lottery exemptions for its leaders, veterans, committee chairmen, the elderly and disabled, and even women members until they demanded equal rights to take chances on the luck of the draw. The 1921 House bowed to the first presence of women legislators and allowed them to select their own seats. They were Republican Miss Jessie Doe of Rollinsford and Democrat Dr. Mary L.R. Farnum of Boscawen. They modestly chose Seats 17 and 18 in Division Five and sat together despite their political differences.

Four distinguished members of the 1925 House got seating privileges before the draw. They were former Governor Albert O. Brown of Manchester, retired Supreme Court Chief Justice Frank N. Parsons of Franklin, and former Speakers Harry M. Cheney and William J. Ahern of Concord.

The women legislators rebuffed seating courtesies in the 1927 session. Dr. Zatae L. Straw of Manchester denounced a committee recommendation exempting women from the lottery, there being thirteen by then. Mrs. E. Maude Ferguson of Bristol joined in the protest, insisting that the feminine sex did not seek nor want special favors from the males. Never again were the lady legislators offered such special attention.

The 1943 House gave a special seating committee six specific exemption areas to work out. They were the ten major committee chairmen, the majority and minority floor leaders, former Speakers, members with six or more terms, the division tellers, and "those with bona fide physical disabilities." The other members then drew lots for the remaining seats behind the first two rows and off the aisles.

Finally, the House disregarded its own lottery law in its entirety, as it organized for the 1953 session. On motion of Emile J. Soucy of Manchester, a committee was appointed to parcel out all the 400 seats, and he became its chairman by appointment of Speaker Raymond K. Perkins of Concord. No one questioned the legal violation, and there were no recorded complaints from any legislator as to where he or she landed.

On February 12, 1953, Lincoln's birthday anniversary, Governor Hugh Gregg of Nashua signed a law repealing the 1862 lottery statute. It was brief, as follows:

Section 7 of Chapter 9 of the Revised Laws, relative to the method for the selection of seats by Representatives is hereby repealed.

And so this ninety-year-old legislative lottery, which the House long violated as much as it adhered to, went into history without fuss or fanfare. Legislative newsmen, including this writer, did not even report the demise.

The State Adopts a Lottery

THE PUBLIC LOTTERY specter began haunting legislative halls once again after World War II, as increasing state spendings required greater revenue. Representative Joseph H. Geisel, wealthy Manchester Republican laundryman and banker, began championing its merits as an easy income source. Representative Laurence M. Pickett of Keene, veteran Democratic leader, followed suit.

Pickett sponsored lottery proposals in several sessions, and they were regularly voted down. But as the 1955 Legislature drew to adjournment early in August, Pickett pulled the plug. The House had earlier in the session killed a lottery bill as a matter of routine. Then when a substantial appropriation to finance local school construction came up for vote, Pickett tacked a skeleton lottery amendment to the bill.

The Republican leadership denounced Pickett's ploy. Floor leader John Pillsbury of Manchester insisted the lottery would harm "those least able to pay, the working people." Others warned the state "would be heading down the highway to hell," and that New Hampshire would become "the laughing-stock of the nation" if such gambling became law.

Pickett argued his amendment would produce $2 million annually, to subsidize education. He said that Rockingham Race Track officials were prepared to implement it. He also claimed the lottery would replace the illegal Irish Sweepstakes, then admittedly popular throughout New Hampshire, and other forms of unlawful gambling.

The Off and On Lotteries

Laurence M. Pickett

The House approved the lottery on August 2, 1955, by a 166 to 141 roll call vote. The sudden action was a bombshell surprise to most Granite State citizens. The following day, a Wednesday, the sensational measure went into the Senate, where President Raymond K. Perkins of Concord promptly turned it over to three committees for public hearings, an unprecedented maneuver.

Senator James C. Cleveland of New London denounced the lottery as a "sign of moral, political and financial bankruptcy." Attorney General Louis C. Wyman told newsmen that the lottery would not conflict with federal statutes if its operation was confined within New Hampshire's borders.

On Thursday morning, Attorney John N. Nassikas of Manchester, legislative counsel for Governor Lane Dwinell of Lebanon, disclosed the bill would be signed into law if it passed the Senate. That afternoon it won 13 to 10 roll call approval in the upper branch.

Governor Dwinell was expected to sign the lottery late Friday. But pressures avalanched his office. Newsmen reported that former Governor Sherman Adams of Lincoln, top assistant to President Eisenhower, had telephoned Washington opposition, warning the lottery would subject New Hampshire to national disgrace. But

Dwinell later revealed that Adams had no part in his dilemma. It was the in-state Republican party leadership which induced him into reversing his position.

Governor Dwinell vetoed the lottery late Friday, and the Republican-dominated House upheld his surprise action by a 193 to 80 roll call vote. Meanwhile, Editor James M. Langley of the *Concord Monitor* had prepared a blistering denunciation for his Saturday edition, and printed it despite the veto.

Langley blasted "the shallow leadership of the Legislature, including the Governor." He said, "every school built with sweepstakes funds should have a tablet of gratitude to Lou Smith" (Rockingham track operator). Langley also declaimed that the chairman of the State Racing Commission and the president of the New Hampshire Jockey Club should be appointed to the State Board of Education, and that all "superintendents of schools should be given special instruction in sweepstakes ticket salesmanship." The following Monday, August 8, Governor Dwinell apologized. He told his monthly press-radio news conference:

I am frank to admit it was a mistake on my part to indicate I would sign the sweepstakes bill. I have made mistakes before, but this one was right out in public. It was an error of judgment to say I would approve the sweepstakes, and I am sorry about that, but I'm not ashamed to admit my error.

The giant House of Representatives continued to flex its lottery muscle. It voted a 180 to 154 roll call reindorsement in 1957 and again favored the lottery by a 240 to 101 vote in 1961. But Dwinell and his successor, Governor Wesley Powell of Hampton Falls, curbed it in the Senate with repeated veto threats.

Finally, when Attorney John W. King of Manchester became New Hampshire's first Democratic Governor in forty years, in January 1963, the lottery blossomed into law. The Legislature's Republican leadership once again battled the proposal. But the House gave it a 196 to 166 roll call approval on March 13. It squeaked through the Senate by a 13 to 11 vote, with amendments, on April 17, and on the following day the House killed a delaying maneuver to refer the bill to the Supreme Court for a validity ruling. Then Governor King signed it into law on April 30.

New Hampshire thus pioneered the nation's first public lottery of the twentieth century in a dramatic manner. As the lottery bill was readied for Governor King's desk, top officials of the Protestant clergy besieged him with pleas for a veto. And *Concord Monitor* Editor Langley again dripped sarcasm. He wrote of the lottery bill, "It's a lulu . . . and makes bookie joints out of the liquor stores," and suggested that "giant signs" with the word "bookie" be hung upon the state-operated stores "so the gamblers will know unerringly where to join the drunks and others who already patronize these establishments."

Governor King marshalled national and world attention for birth of the lottery. He announced on April 25 that he would make his decision on the bill known five days later before a joint session of the Legislature.

As the fateful hour arrived, one newspaper reported that "A small army of news media crews from New York City and other metropolitan areas jammed all available space in Representatives Hall to speed the lottery enactment through the nation and around the globe."

Governor King, who had twice voted for the lottery while serving in the House, but had maintained a strict hands-off policy as it went through the Legislature a second time, summarized the reasons for his signature as follows:

May I say that I have not been unmoved by the messages from many sincere people in our state who have deep convictions against this legislation.

I have respect for those who have an honest, sincere concern about the morality of this action although I do not agree with them.

As for those who raise the fear of undesirable elements invading our state, I firmly believe this fear is without foundation. I am convinced that we can conduct an honest and respectable operation that will have a tendency to discourage those who seek illegal gain in this field.

Over the past few weeks I have had increasingly heavy pressures on the part of well-intentioned citizens to thwart the will of the majority by a veto of this legislation, but I am convinced that to do so would be to deny the right of the people of the state to embark on a legitimate fiscal experiment.

This is the right of self-government and so long as I am Chief Executive that right will be preserved. I am unwilling to set myself up as a Solomon or a Caesar in the holy assumption that my views are more intelligent or discerning or moralistic than those of our people.

The lottery law included a proviso that it be submitted to a popular referendum in March of the following year. It then won 108,110 to 34,440 endorsement and immediately ceased to be a political issue. In the following decade other states, such as New York, New Jersey, Connecticut, Massachusetts, and Pennsylvania, also turned to lotteries as revenue sources. By 1978, a dozen years after New Hampshire had resurrected this form of revenue, thirteen states had followed suit. They included Maine and Vermont.

The Off and On Lotteries

THE PRESS AND ITS USES

The Two Editors Fowle

NEWSPAPERS and their editors have always played an integral role in the life of New Hampshire's General Court. In fact, the state's first editor launched his tiny newspaper at Portsmouth in 1756, by special invitation to serve as legislative printer. He was forty-one-year-old Daniel Fowle of Boston, who had been jailed by the Massachusetts General Court for criticizing its conduct.

Fowle had been confined in a Boston jail for two days in October 1754 "among common thieves and murderers," as the alleged author of a pamphlet entitled *The Monster of Monsters,* signed by "Tom Thumb, Jr." The Bay State legislators ordered his release on the third day, whereupon Editor Fowle demanded a legislative apology for its affront to "freedom of the press" before he would accept restoration of his personal freedom. But his wife and friends prevailed upon Fowle to return home, after which he issued a blistering indictment of the Legislature, entitled "A Total Eclipse of Liberty." Portsmouth citizens invited Fowle to their town, then New Hampshire's provincial capital, with promises of complete freedom of expression and the lucrative position of legislative printer.

Fowle issued New Hampshire's first newspaper on October 7, 1756. It was a weekly, 8 by 9 inches in size, called *The New Hampshire*

Gazette. He brought three black servants from Boston to run his hand-operated printing plant. One of them, known as "Primus," who could neither read nor write, continues noted in Portsmouth lore for his mechanical efficiency and tart indulgence in freedom of expression.

Editor Fowle wrote on the first page of his first issue:

As the press always claims liberty in free countries, it is presumed that none will be offended if this paper discovers that spirit of freedom which so remarkably prevails in the English nation; but as a liberty ought not to be abused, no encouragement will be given by the publishers to anything which is apparently designed to foment divisions in the church or state, nor to anything profane, obscene, or tending to encourage immorality, nor to such writings as are produced by private pique, and filled with personal reflections and insolent scurrilous language.

Fowle prospered, but so did his independence, and within twenty years he once again was subjected to legislative arrest for printing his mind in the public interest. He was ordered to stand trial for criticizing the Revolutionary Legislature's break with royal rule and formation of a free government on January 5, 1776.

The irate legislators, then meeting in secret sessions at Exeter, minced no words with Editor Fowle for his January 9 censure. They voted on January 17:

Upon reading an ignonimous, scurrilous and scandalous piece printed in the New Hampshire Gazette and Historical Chronicle, No. 1001, of Tuesday, January 9, 1776, directed or addressed to the Congress at Exeter . . . be it voted that Daniel Fowle, Esq., the supposed printer of said January 7 paper, be forthwith sent for and ordered to appear before this House and give an account of the author of said piece, and further to answer for his printing said piece.

Editor Fowle, who had long denounced British tax impositions upon the American colonies, expressed fears that the Legislature had gone too far, in creating a new government, and said it was doomed to failure. His presentation, incidentally, reflected the opinions of the legislators from the Portsmouth area.

Fowle wrote that "Every step towards independency . . . would be ruinous and destructive in its consequences." He pointed out that Great Britain had 500 warships while the colonies had none; that

The Press and Its Uses

Great Britain could muster 500,000 fighting men to but 30,000 in the colonies, and that New Hampshire would be forced to garrison the borders of Canada and Nova Scotia against British retaliations.

The legislators apparently developed second thoughts about hauling Editor Fowle to Exeter for questioning. Legislative records contain no further mention of the incident. But they do show that Fowle continued as legislative printer, and five months later he produced copies of the United States Declaration of Independence for distribution through the towns.

The Legislature subsequently bestowed upon Fowle the title of Justice of the Peace, both an honor and a source of lucrative fees, as he supported the new government until his death in 1787.

Another Editor Fowle did not fare so well with legislative affiliations. He was Robert Luist Fowle, nephew of the childless Daniel Fowle, who learned the printing business from his uncle. The younger Fowle moved to Exeter, where the Legislature had settled for the long war period, and in 1776, shortly after the lawmakers' abortive skirmish with his uncle, he started a newspaper which he labeled *The New Hampshire Gazette or Exeter Morning Chronicle*. This title was an obvious effort to profit from the good reputation the Portsmouth publication had acquired through its twenty years of existence.

In his 1888 *History of Exeter*, Governor Charles H. Bell penned a graphic account of how young Editor Fowle betrayed legislative faith. It went:

Fowle was discreet enough to gain the confidence of the leading men in the popular movement, so that he was at length employed in the delicate and confidential business of printing the bills of credit for the state.

It was not long before counterfeits were discovered, of these, and of the similar paper currency of other states, and suspicion arose, from various circumstances, that Fowle was concerned in issuing the spurious bills.

The Committee of Safety at once ordered him committed to the jail at Exeter. He had the effrontery then to propose to the committee that in case they would screen him from punishment, he would confess what he knew in reference to the offence. If he had done this from principle, in order that justice might be vindicated, it would have been pardonable, if not commendable, but his subsequent conduct forbids such a construction of his motives.

The committee took him at his word, and he made disclosures of his furnishing the types to one or more tories, from which to print the fraudulent paper money. In return for his revelations the authorities were to allow him his liberty on bail. Whether it was that no one cared to be his surety is not known, but he remained in jail until he took "leg bail" and escaped to the British lines. . . .

In 1778 the Legislature . . . proscribed him with many other loyalists who had fled, and ordered his property confiscated; but probably he had little left to confiscate, if his complaint afterwards made of the pillaging of his effects had any foundation in fact.

The errant Fowle returned to Exeter after the peace of 1783, with a British government pension, married the widow of his brother, Zechariah, who had continued the paper in a patriotic manner, operated a small shop for sale of English goods, and died in Brentwood in 1802.

Partisan Preferences

THE LEGISLATURE made use of newspapers throughout its constitutional existence. The 1792 legislators voted free copies of the annual laws to the few tiny weeklies, with permission to print them, but at no cost to the state.

Legislative printing became partisan in the early 1800s, as political parties took form and sponsored newspapers to promote their bias. By 1820 the Legislature was paying editors to print the session statutes, and until 1825 some editors were furnishing their newspapers free to the legislators. The 1825 State Senate voted to purchase two Concord papers for each of its dozen members. The following year the Legislature voted to have the session laws printed in all the weeklies, regardless of political bias.

Franklin Pierce restored political preference to legislative printing when he became a novice lawmaker at twenty-four, in 1829. As chairman of the House Education Committee, he successfully sponsored a law channeling dissemination of the session laws only through Democratic papers, and this policy continued for many years.

The 1844 Legislature lauded newspapers. It memorialized Congress to grant them free postal privileges within their respective states, saying that "diffusion of information" was a vital public func-

The Press and Its Uses

tion. But Congress boosted the rates the following year.

Governor Anthony Colby of New London denounced legislative printing patronage when he assumed office in 1846. This college founder, who was the only Whig to break some three decades of Democratic domination of the state government, said in his inaugural address:

I recommend that whatever sums of money be paid out of the treasury for publishing the state laws and resolves, be justly distributed among all the newspapers, of every political party, published weekly, in this state.

Each citizen is bound to obey the laws, and should have every opportunity to learn what they are, with the least possible trouble or expense to himself, after paying his proportion of the expense for making them.

No one should be compelled to take a newspaper in which he has no confidence; and any party in power which will refuse such equitable distribution, when they speak of their democracy and love of equal rights, should speak softly.

Governor Colby won his point. The 1846 Legislature voted to pay twenty-six weeklies of all political persuasions to print the session laws, but with a limit of not more than $10 to any one paper.

After the newborn Republican party took virtually permanent control of the Legislature in 1857, it became friendlier than ever with the newspapers, and especially their reporters. As the 1860 House convened, it voted:

That reporters for the New Hampshire Statesman, New Hampshire Patriot *and* State Gazette, *and the* Independent Democrat *(all of Concord) be allowed to occupy respectively the same seats in this House which were occupied by them last year. . . .*

This trio of papers in turn sponsored free reading rooms in their respective printing plants, where other papers were also available, for the legislators and their visiting guests. Two years later, as the Civil War skyrocketed newsprint costs, these same three newspapers, of opposing political affiliations, merged their legislative coverage in 1862, and this novel alliance continued through the war years. They labeled their economy project *The Legislative Reporter,* with this pledge:

The Legislative Reporter *will be devoted exclusively to the publication of the proceedings of the Legislature and the news of the day; nothing of a party character will be admitted in its columns.*

Its reports of the proceedings will be full, faithful and correct, and its sketches of debates impartial and as full as the importance of the subject may seem to demand.

This special paper ran to four pages, heavy with advertisements, and was issued each legislative day. It sold for twenty-five cents per copy, or five copies for $1 (an all-time record high price), and the Legislature readily purchased copies for each member. As the session adjourned after twenty-five issues, the editors jointly boasted they had presented "the most detailed reports on the Legislature ever published." They presented stenographic accounts of the House and Senate proceedings, a custom which the newspapers adhered to for the subsequent half-century.

Young James M. W. Yerrinton of Boston earned a niche in Granite State legislative life as one of the first ever to transcribe its deliberations for newspaper use. He was one of New England's ablest "phonographic" experts and was hired by Concord's *Daily Statesman* to record legislative proceedings in the early 1850s. When the *Concord Monitor* was founded in May 1864, its debut boast was that it had hired Yerrinton as "the first full time newspaper reporter" ever to record legislative doings.

Interestingly, the 1864 Legislature purchased three copies of *The Legislative Reporter* for each member and each attaché. The following year the Senate gave each member three *Legislative Reporters* and one *Concord Monitor*, while the House voted each member one copy of each of these two papers. Through the ensuing half-century, the legislators voted themselves two or more papers each session, to keep up with their own affairs. In 1887, for example, they enjoyed four papers, two from Concord and two from Manchester, and this occurred again in 1913.

The Humor of 1876

HUMOR was heaped upon the 1876 legislative session as the nation celebrated its Centennial with a gala Philadelphia Exposition.

One of Concord's many short-lived newspapers, the *Concord Daily*

People, hired a professional humorist to report its doings. He was "Major" George J. Manson of New York City, author of popular joke pamphlets. As the lawmakers convened, Manson warned the new members:

Beware of paper collars. They are a delusion and a snare.

Wear old clothes, sit easy and unconstrained. Carry a big fan.

Pay your board bill weekly, and see that the landlady does not get her accounts mixed up; otherwise you will hear the convincing argument, "Why, Mr. Jones, there it is on my own book in black and white," with a winning smile or an aggrieved expression, and who could resist her?

Look out for summer fruit. Beware the captivating cucumber and the seductive strawberry. Have your little bottle of Jamaica Ginger in your pocket and take it like a man.

Don't go to the drugstore too often and come into the House with a solemn air, chewing cardimon seeds.

Don't flirt with the girls in the gallery if you are a young fellow; and if you are an old fellow, beware of that charming lady boarder to whom you were introduced today.

Be cautious, very cautious when approached by the bewitching book agent of feminine persuasion, who will sell you a fifty cent book for $3.50.

Major Manson's press table associates included John W. Odlin of the *Concord Monitor*, Leonard B. Brown of the *New Hampshire Patriot*, Allan H. Robinson for the *New England Associated Press* and John T. Hulme of the *Boston Herald*, to whom he refers in the following report of an all-night session:

(At 1:30 a.m.) Moore of Nashua is chewing something. Does he use the weed? Cross of Manchester looks cross, acts cross. He is cross. Sinclair of Bethlehem winks with both eyes at once. It is suggestive of trouble.

Patriot Brown asks if it is healthy to sleep with the mouth open, as he gazes at the open countenance of Weed of Sandwich. Bingham of Littleton sits near the clerk during roll call gets an ear-ache and says it is enough to Wear(e) one out to listen to the member from Seabrook.

Herald Hulme moralizes on the saying, "Good children always die young" 305

and can't believe it true as he gazes on Associated Press Robinson's beaming face. O'Connor of Manchester on the front row lying down; paper balls fired at him.

Millers flying around; members creeping up and down the aisle. Ordway of Warner asleep on speaker's sofa, shoes off. Odlin fires paper pellets at him. The "Si-ox" chief takes them for flies and dreamily brushes them away with a fan. Barton of Newport utterly exhausted. . . .

Democratic members growing beautifully less. Someone suggested they had all paired off. Republican members dashing around in great excitement; couriers being sent to wake and bring in sleepy members. Arrivals begin to come in by twos and threes.

Members on the front row eating crackers from small paper bags. It was Mr. George W. Fletcher of Rumney who with his coat off observed the situation. What did he see at this time?

He gazed 'round about and observed the effect want of sleep had on various classes of members. There was the nervous man who hopped around in his little seat like a New England doughnut in a frying pan. There was the solid, ponderous man who sat perfectly still, looking horrible and heavy.

There was the don't-care-a-darn man who put his feet inside his little desk and imagined he was comfortable. There was the respectable man who worried at the demoralized state of his linen. There was the man who wore a paper collar; he put it on in the morning as stiff as a bit of tin, and took it off at noon like a poultice.

There was the fat man who picked up the Daily Patriot and fell asleep two minutes after he struck his seat, and snored like a steam engine in good repair. And there was Brown, who fell asleep writing, with a bit of a stale cracker in one hand, a pen in the other.

Deliberately looking at the speaker, Mr. Fletcher moved to adjourn. Carried at a quarter to six a.m.

The Press and Its Uses

P. T. Barnum's circus came to Concord on July 7, 1876, and Major Manson was not the only one wishing to enjoy it. He reported early adjournment of the House thus:

Bathed in blood, dripping from the gory guillotine, as we were, who was there to rescue us; who, with swift, statesmanlike vigor, a sublime sentiment and honest purpose dancing around gaily on his breast—who was there to do what so few in the world of tears can do, namely, to wit, thus: say "the right word in the right place?"

Ah, the search for such a man was not in vain. The eye did not tire ere it found the object of the wearied reporter's heart, the beacon lights which he would have forever shining on his pathway pointing to rest and ease; that object was Mr. Levi W. Barton of Newport, who promptly, and in unexceptionable English, moved that the House adjourn. The motion was carried just ten minutes, five and eleven-sixteenth seconds before one o'clock, and the circus matinee did not begin until two.

The 1876 session ran hot and heavy as the Republicans recovered from a brief Democratic domination in a depression and sweepingly voted the latter out of the judgeships and all other appointive state jobs. But there were dull days, and Manson devoted one of them to "pen photographs" of his reportorial associates—and himself. He sketched:

Major Manson produces those libelous and temper stirring reports which appear in the Daily People.

He has a military record which was gained in the west. In Louisville he killed 20, Cincinnati 100, but Indianapolis took the palm, for there 250 were slaughtered. All these deeds were done in one night. They were done in hotel bedrooms where he happened to be stopping. The deceased were not men.

His bald-headedness came from trying to make both ends meat; failing in that experiment they have been made fish.

Still there is no denying he is of an affectionate disposition. Though bald, he is young and is president of the "Society for the Better Suppression of Coddling." He is a cheerfully disposed animal and feeds principally on New Hampshire oats, commonly called beans.

He has accumulated great wealth and lives in an elegant mansion on Centre street, just around the corner, a little to the left as you climb the hill. He published the "Joker's Dictionary," without which, and a "People's Political Hand Book," no family can be considered respectable.

Manson described youthful Nat H. Taylor, reporter for the *Boston Globe*, as follows:

Mr. Taylor comes from the Hub and revolves around the Globe office, of which paper his brother is the managing editor.

He is in conversation what Wagner is to music. He is a whirlwind of words; he has been called "Talker the Terrible," or the "Ear Buster of Boston." He is a boomerang of patriotic, sentimental, socialistic and historic suggestion; a wild war-whoop of wondrous wordiness.

It may take nine tailors to make a man, but one talking Taylor like the speciman under examination will furnish a whole centennial with enough chin music.

Mr. Taylor is a medium sized wiry young man. He is unmarried and when he stops at the Eagle takes a suspiciously long while to give his order to those pretty waiter girls. The dignified manner in which he makes cocktails disappear is wonderful to behold; they seem like colored lanterns flying through the air. Mr. Taylor makes Boston happy, that being his home.

Reporter Brown (editor of the *Patriot*) brought his son of seven to the Legislature when two dozen blind youngsters from the Perkins School for the Blind, at South Boston, presented a musical program. So Manson reported Harry, the boy, as writing from the press table:

I would like to be a legislator 'cause then I would have a long pencil and lots of paper to write and draw funny pictoores on.

Legislators, my papa tells me, are of two kinds; those that treet and those that don't treet. Papa tells me he doesn't think much of those that don't treet. Though he takes a glass of sider now and then he says won't hurt any man if you drink it quick on a warm day.

I should like to roll around in those little seets the Reps have. It must be awful uncomfortable for big men to set in such small seets. Big fat men like

The Press and Its Uses

soft seets; then they are happy.

Manson amusingly presented legislative committee assignments to his readers. Of the Committee on Finance, he wrote: "He that has more than enough is a thief of the rights of his brother." The Committee on Towns and Parishes called for "God made the country and man the towns." The Committee on Unfinished Business was tied to "Procrastination is the thief of time." And Manson observed of the Committee on Incorporations that "Corporations cannot commit treason, nor be outlawed nor excommunicated, for they have no souls."

Manson's imported humor did not detract from his veracity as a reporter. New Hampshire courts made use of his "shorthand" talent, and when the sixth Constitutional Convention met in December 1876, he was hired to record its proceedings.

The convention leaders offered Manson $5 per day for this assignment, but he turned it down. He asked twenty-five cents per page. The leadership qualified this demand, with a proviso that a page should contain at least 100 words and that Manson's remuneration could not exceed $500 for the session. The humorist agreed and then performed such an admirable job that the convention voted him $550.

The House Pays Reporters

A S THE LEGISLATURE SHIFTED to biennial sessions in 1879, the House began paying newspapermen for reporting its doings. The 1881 session voted initial payments of $50 each to John W. Odlin of the *Concord Monitor* and John T. Hulme of the *Manchester Union*. By 1887 this largesse had been raised to $100, and this rate continued for twenty years, until it was dramatically abolished in 1907.

Newspaper reporters flourished in this era, as their legislative bonuses compared favorably with their regular pay from their publishers. Never before or since have so many of them devoted so much time and attention to legislative deliberations. Boston newspapers enjoyed full-time representation as Concord newsmen and even editors vied for the $100 emoluments.

By 1891 a record total of fourteen reporters thronged two long press tables located on each side of the House rostrum, and each collected $100. The 1893 House even paid $100 to John Edward Coffin, the *Manchester Union's* talented cartoonist. And by 1897, the State Senate, apparently overshadowed by the reportorial attention devoted to the lower branch, began hiring an official Senate Reporter to disseminate daily copies of its doings to the newspapers!

The 1891 Legislature voted a new wrinkle by requiring that all papers paid for printing its statutes were required to file a complete set of such copies with the State Library "without additional compensation."

Interestingly, when the Legislature held a four-day special session in December 1890, the reporters were paid $10 each.

Even the 1902 Constitutional Convention paid newsmen. Eight reporters were given $50 each for covering the thirteen working days of that session. They were officially listed as J. Ed Coffin and G. W. Fowler of the *Manchester Union*, Fred Leighton of the *Concord Patriot*, H. C. Pearson of the *Concord Monitor*, James M. Cooper of the *Manchester News*, I. E. Keeler of the *Boston Globe*, A. H. Robinson of the *Boston Herald*, and E. A. McQuade (McQuaid) of the *Manchester Mirror*.

The legislative subsidies to newspapermen were abruptly terminated in the 1907 session in a dramatic manner. Representative Robert P. Bass of Peterborough, who was to become New Hampshire's most noted reform Governor of all time, killed this largesse after his fervor for better government was supposedly crimped into obscurity.

This dapper little Peterborough man was in his second House term at thirty-three when the 1907 session convened, and aimed for membership on the important Judiciary Committee. But Editor Bertram Ellis of the *Keene Sentinel* became Speaker and he sidetracked Bass's progressiveness. Speaker Ellis appointed Bass chairman of the House Retrenchment and Reform Committee, which had deteriorated in rank and prestige, and then refrained from referring any bills to it.

But Bass bided and blossomed. With nothing to do, his committee asked permission to study the modest state affairs of that era for possible efficiency improvements. The House readily concurred and attached a $100 operating allowance for good measure.

As Bass battled obscurity, so did a sickly little Concord orphan —but for a different reason. He was sixteen-year-old Edward J. Gallagher, who dreamed of becoming a legislative reporter, to share in the $100 rewards. Bass hailed from Chicago wealth. Gallagher's immigrant parents died in his childhood. Protestant neighbors nursed him through boyhood bedridden years with a tubercular intestinal ailment, as Catholic nuns improvised schooling for him.

Gallagher learned to compose on a toy typewriter. Then his attending physician suggested that a real typewriter might help speed his recovery more than medication, and from it the orphan got compositions published in Boston newspapers and elsewhere, and laid his temerity before the 1907 Legislature.

The drama of Gallagher's daring was gleaned from his recollections as the octogenarian publisher of the *Laconia Evening Citizen* (he died in 1978). He styled himself as representing the F. K. Gilpin Syndicate, to serve legislative news to weekly newspapers. He invented this title for fear his boyhood qualifications would fail to entice the attention of editors.

Gallagher's homespun role was accepted by a legislative clerk, and his name and synthetic syndicate were officially recorded in the 1907 *Legislative Manual*. So it was in this manner that the Legislature greeted its youngest newspaper reporter of all time, and New Hampshire's weeklies were offered a first legislative column from Concord!

Two weeklies accepted Gallagher's novel offer, at fifty cents per column. But not so his new associates. The legislative reporters treated him as an unwanted and unqualified upstart. They denied him a seat, or even elbow room, at the two long press tables in Representatives Hall, then crowded with aspirants for the $100 gifts. So young Gallagher was forced to perch his enterprise upon the steps of the Speaker's rostrum and remain alert to keep from being trampled by hectic legislators scurrying to and from the rostrum for various reasons. After some weeks, however, the boy's reportorial talent won him part-time employment with the *Manchester Union* and press table privileges.

As the thirteen-week session drew to a close, Retrenchment and Reform Committee Chairman Bass told reporters he would disclose his committee's report at a special night meeting at the Eagle Hotel. Young Gallagher was present, and one can only imagine his consternation as Bass revealed a shocking recommendation that the reporters' subsidies be abolished.

The Bass committee also recommended the Legislature stop subsidizing newspapers by paying them special fees for distributing the session laws. It said the state could do the same at one tenth of what the newspapers had been collecting for many years. The committee was polite about terminating the reporters' largesse. It reported:

The practice of voting certain sums to persons other than state employees or appointees, is a generous error which cannot consistently be continued if economy is to play its due part in our financial policy. The amiable weakness of distributing such favors is so human and so prevalent that your committee, being of the same species, appreciates the situation, but as officials we may not becomingly bestow the people's money as gifts.

While the newspapers gave slight attention to the surprise Bass ban, it became a hot issue in legislative circles. As adjournment approached and the catch-all omnibus bill came before the House, a special clause granting the cash favors for reporters was deleted for the first time since 1881.

But when the measure was sent into the Senate for concurrence, the newsmen's names were restored with the $100 payments. Listed were Harlan C. Pearson of the *Concord Monitor,* Fred Leighton of the *Concord People and Patriot,* George W. Fowler of the *Manchester Union,* Winfred D. Davis of the *Manchester Mirror American,* I. Eugene Keeler of the *Boston Globe,* Allan H. Robinson of the *Boston Herald,* Henry H. Metcalf of the *Portsmouth Times,* and Edward J. Gallagher of the F. K. Gilpin Syndicate.

This Senate maneuver, backed by the reporters, led to a House-Senate committee of conference demanded by Bass. He was appointed to it, along with Representative Herbert B. Fischer of Pittsfield and Charles W. Howard of Nashua (later state Adjutant General), and Senators Henry W. Boutwell of Manchester and Charles A. Roby of Nashua. Bass prevailed and the press payments were dumped into the history bin.

More Recent Features

WHEN DEMOCRAT GOVERNOR SAMUEL D. FELKER of Rochester took office in 1913 after a long period of unbroken Republican controls of state affairs, he denounced the continued legislative payments to newspapers for distributing the biennial session laws.

Felker disclosed in a special message to the Legislature that in 1911 it had paid sixty-two newspapers a total of $11,309.40 for this service, or an average of $183.40 to each paper. He then emphasized that the sixty-two papers had the pamphlets containing the new laws printed jointly, so that each made an average profit of $63, after deducting postage and wrapping costs.

The Legislature continued this traditional method of making its new laws easily available to the general public for nearly 20 more years. The 1929 booklet, for example, which was issued by the Secretary of State, under supervision of the Governor and the Council, as had long been the custom, was 6 by 9 inches in size, ran to 96 pages of small type, and contained 193 new laws and 78 joint resolutions.

The 1951 House of Representatives banned free newspapers for its members as an austerity binge crystallized out of mounting governmental costs following World War II. Representative Eralsey ("Frugal Fergie") Ferguson of Pittsfield sparked this parsimony and it continued through the 1953 session.

The Senate continued purchasing two newspapers daily for each member and attaché. The House, meanwhile, voted in 1955 to give each member one newspaper of his or her choice, and this policy became standard practice. This single choice has been dominated by the *Manchester Union Leader,* the state's only morning newspaper, with an afternoon edition.

The Legislature won a journalistic championship in a 1956 national poll. A journalistic fraternity announced a survey had disclosed it was the best reported lawmaking body in the country. This bouquet to New Hampshire newspapers was featured in the March 1957 issue of *The Quill,* the monthly magazine of Sigma Delta Chi, a professional journalistic fraternity. It reported the top honor was produced by a questionnaire sent to legislators in the forty-eight states, conducted by youthful Paul Simon, a publisher and member of the Illinois Legislature.

Simon based his findings on a three-page random sampling of twenty lawmakers in each state, which yielded a 50 percent response. He reported New Hampshire at the top, with Utah. Vermont ranked nineteenth, just above Maine, while Massachusetts landed in the thirty-second spot. At the bottom were Montana and Delaware.

The House passed a resolution of appreciation for the novel citation, saying it was "a tribute to our New Hampshire democracy, which we cherish." It also ordered a reprint in the House Journal of a *Concord Monitor* editorial on the subject, which read, in part:

The comment in Simon's article reads, "In New Hampshire all (members of the Legislature) checked honest reporting except one solon who checked both categories. Committee coverage did not rate high, only one calling it good and one checking both 'seldom' and 'good.' There were complaints about a lack of radio and TV coverage. A Senator was very critical of weekly newspapers, an opinion voiced in many states."

. . . The state by state survey disclosed an amazing number of states where legislative committees do not customarily hold open hearings. There was no such complaint in New Hampshire. Of course, legislative coverage cannot be good where the committees always meet in executive session. . . .

The Quill article should make Leon Anderson of the Monitor and Frank O'Neil of the Union Leader feel pretty good. They are the principal constant reporters of legislative doings. Anderson, in addition to his news stories, writes much of legislative affairs in his daily column, "The State Is My Beat," and O'Neil also writes a column, though not on an every day basis, besides writing news stories.

In their columns, as distinct from new stories, these two express personal opinions, yet members of the New Hampshire Legislature do not condemn them for this, even though the members may not be in agreement with such opinions.

It is possible to cover the Legislature even more fully than is done, but the public interest in such fuller coverage is questionable. The more important committee hearings are covered, and all legislative news is to some extent condensed, rather than being verbatim.

On the whole, as the Simon survey concluded, the Legislature here is covered reasonably well.

The *Concord Monitor* won two high court challenges against the Legislature in recent years. When the 1961 session voted its members a minimum daily travel allowance of $5, the *Monitor* called it unconstitutional, and the State Supreme Court agreed. The tribunal joined the *Monitor* in sympathizing that the antiquated $200 legislative salary was disgraceful but declared that abuse of mileage reimbursement privileges was not the proper method of redress. The high court officially observed:

In this state compensation of legislators for a legislative term was fixed at $200 in another century. Under present conditions it is grossly inadequate. This antediluvian standard . . . has been almost universally criticized by both experts and laymen alike.

The Press and Its Uses

The author, at left, digging out the facts of legislative history on a summer afternoon in 1969 at Rockingham Park with Richard M. O'Dowd of Manchester, and Edward J. Gallagher of Laconia. Veteran race track executive O'Dowd at the age of 14 in 1909 was the youngest page ever to serve the House, and publisher Gallagher was the youngest legislative reporter in Granite State history at the age of 16 during the 1907 session.

The *Monitor* won high court concurrence in 1967 of its claim that a constitutional amendment shifting the Legislature back to annual sessions had been improperly presented to the people. It won a close two-thirds, 109,487 to 53,792 vote approval, but the Supreme Court agreed with the *Monitor* that the manner in which the question was placed on the ballot was both "misleading and obscure." It read: "Are you in favor of having the Legislature meet in two annual sessions with a total limit of ninety days but no limit on time of adjournment?"

To This Day

The court explained that if the words "in each biennium" had been inserted in the question after the words "annual sessions" the proposition would have met legal requirements.

Interestingly, this was the first constitutional amendment ever proposed by the Legislature. Up to 1964, New Hampshire remained the only state in which the Constitution could be changed only by a convention. But in that year the voters approved a convention recommendation that the Legislature be allowed to share in submitting constitutional questions to the people from time to time.

PRAYERS AND SERMONS

Of The Provincial Era

PRAYERS have ever been part of New Hampshire legislative life. When the first colonial Assembly of but eleven men convened on March 16, 1680, at Portsmouth, the session was opened with a prayer and a sermon by the Reverend Joshua Moodey, the town's Puritan (Congregational) pastor.

A year later the tiny Legislature voted Thursday, March 17, 1681, as a day of "public fasting and prayer, to be solemnly kept by all inhabitants," on behalf of ailing President John Cutt, the first Chief Executive. But the elderly Portsmouth merchant died ten days later.

Dr. J. Duane Squires's 1956 *The Granite State of the United States* calls this the beginning of New Hampshire's unique spring Fast Day holiday, which no other state still observes. Originally devoted to prayers for good crops, this holiday has long become popular for spring cleaning, fishing, and Boston shopping sprees, while the Masonic orders use it for colorful annual rituals. In fact, the original significance so changed in this century that the 1949 Legislature shifted the Fast Day observance from the traditional Thursday to the fourth Monday in April, for its more convenient enjoyment by the populace.

Fry's 1908 *New Hampshire as a Royal Province* tells that legislative prayers became routine about 1745, when still based at Portsmouth. In that year there were two chaplains, listed by Fry as "Rev. Mr. Fitch and Rev. Mr. Shirtleff," and they alternated with morning invocations. This dual duty custom continued for some years, and the royal Council, which served as the legislative upper branch, employed its own chaplain at times.

When the state Constitution became effective in June 1784, an "election sermon" featured the Legislature's opening exercises for that historic event. The Reverend Samuel McClintock of Greenland was invited to Concord for this program at the Old North Meetinghouse, and he discoursed for more than an hour. The Reverend Jeremy Belknap of Dover, the state's first historian who had a county and a mountain named in his honor, gave the second annual sermon in 1785 when the Legislature convened at Portsmouth.

The "election sermons" were so named because the Legislature in those early years elected Governors, Councilors, and state Senators, when none of the candidates won election by a majority vote total (rather than the present plurality requirement), and this often occurred in some of the categories. There was also the additional fact that the Legislature elected United States Senators, a custom which continued up to 1914, when the voters began to elect them directly.

Clergymen vied for the distinction of piloting the Legislature with a spiritual start, as well as for the customary $20 emolument for this special service, which was a substantial sum for those days.

These sermons lasted into 1831, and the 1899 *General Court Manual* says all were printed, except for that of 1789 by the Reverend Oliver Noble of New Castle and that of 1795 by the Reverend John Smith of Hanover. There was no sermon in 1793, and while the custom was killed by the Legislature in 1831, it was revived for a single year in 1861, as the Civil War erupted, and the Reverend Henry E. Parker of Concord officiated.

The other election sermon clergymen were: 1786, Samuel Haven of Portsmouth; 1787, Joseph Buckminster of Portsmouth; 1788, Samuel Langdon of Hampton Falls; 1790, John C. Ogden of Portsmouth; 1791, Israel Evans of Concord; 1792, William Morrison of Londonderry; 1794, Amos Wood of Weare; 1796, William F. Rowland of Exeter; 1797, Stephen Peabody of Exeter; 1798, Robert Gray of Dover; 1799, Seth Payson of Rindge; 1800, Noah Worcester of Thornton; 1801, Jacob Burnap of Merrimack; 1802, Joseph Woodman of Sanbornton; 1803, Aaron Hall of Keene; 1804, Nathaniel Porter of Conway; 1805, Reed Paige of Hancock; 1806, James Miltimore of Stratham; 1807, Nathan Bradstreet of Chester; 1808, Asa McFarland of Concord; 1809, William

F. Rowland of Exeter; 1810, Roswell Shurtleff of Hanover.

Also: 1811, Thomas Beede of Wilton; 1812, Moses Bradford of Francestown; 1813, John H. Church of Pelham; 1814, Peter Holt of Epping; 1815, David Sutherland of Bath; 1816, Pliny Dickinson of Walpole; 1817, Daniel Merrill of West Nottingham; 1818, William Allen of Hanover; 1819, Nathan Parker of Portsmouth; 1820, James B. Howe of Claremont; 1821, Ephraim P. Bradford of New Boston; 1822, Jonathan French of North Hampton; 1823, Daniel Dana of Londonderry; 1824, Bennet Tyler of Hanover; 1825, Phineas Cooke of Acworth; 1826, Ferdinand Ellis of Exeter; 1827, Nathaniel W. Williams of Concord; 1828, Nathaniel Bouton of Concord; 1829, Humphrey Moore of Milford; 1830, Jaazanaih Crosby of Charlestown; and 1831, Nathan Lord of Hanover.

While the Legislature occupied its own home in 1819, Concord's election sermons were always at the Old North Meetinghouse, where it first met.

After Dr. Lord, later president of Dartmouth College, presented the 1831 sermon, entitled "Charity Seeketh Not Her Own," Representative Charles F. Gove, a Goffstown Quaker who rose high in public life, terminated them. When Representative Benjamin W. Farley of Hollis offered a traditional motion that the Speaker hire a clergyman for the next ceremony, Gove demanded "indefinite postponement" of the custom, and prevailed on a 107 to 81 roll call vote.

Ouster of the Chaplain

THE ONLY OUSTER of a Granite State legislative chaplain occurred on June 8, 1798, a Friday, at Hopkinton. Joshua Heywood of Amherst, thirty-seven-year-old divinity student, was discharged on his second day on the job for failure to pray for President John Adams and the Congress, and favoring France in its war with Great Britain. The House dismissed Heywood with the following resolution:

That in consequence of certain expressions used by Mr. Heywood, in his prayer in the House, and his omitting to pray for the President and the Congress of the United States, this day, that this House do not wish any further services from him as chaplain—and the assistant clerk be directed to furnish him with a copy thereof.

There is no official record of the disputed prayer, for the chaplain's remarks were not then incorporated into legislative records as they now are and long have been. But William Plumer of Epping was Speaker in that session, and Lynn Turner's 1962 biography of that noted New Hampshireman says:

It was Plumer, the deist, who took the initiative in dismissing the House chaplain in the June (1798) session of the Legislature when the rash young preacher prayed for the success of the French armies and neglected to recommend President Adams to divine favor.

Plumer wrote his wife "For the Court to live without prayers will, I believe, be less offensive to Heaven, than Jacobinical sacrifices."

Heywood filed a memorial for a hearing against his discharge but withdrew it on June 19. A Dartmouth College graduate of 1795, Heywood was ordained into the Congregational ministry a year after his legislative rebuke, at Dunstable (now Nashua).

The 1830 Legislature had three chaplains from three denominations, for a first time.

A special committee recommended the Reverend Enos George of Barnstead for the post and he was voted down. The Reverend Squire B. Haskell of Poplin (now Fremont) was next rebuffed, even though he was a member of the House.

Finally, at the suggestion of Representative Isaac O. Barnes of Barnstead, three Concord clergymen were hired to deliver the daily prayers, and each was paid $15 for the entire session. This represented economy, for they did not require mileage remuneration. The trio were Congregationalist Nathaniel Bouton, who became a state historian; Baptist Nathaniel W. Williams; and Unitarian Moses G. Thomas.

Just after the Civil War, the 1867 House of Representatives staged a historic debate on the merits of morning prayers. The argument centered on the Reverend Zedekiah S. Barstow, veteran Keene Congregational cleric, then starting his second term as a House member.

A routine committee headed by Representative Francis E. Towle of Claremont recommended the Reverend Daniel C. Babcock of that town for chaplain. This precipitated the "Battle of Prayers."

Representative Mark True of Antrim launched the debate. He offered an amendment that the dozen clergymen then serving in the House "be invited alternately by the Speaker to officiate." Representative Wolcott Hamlin of Dover, longtime chairman of the House Education Committee, said that True's proposal was "so unusual in character" that he hoped "the subject [would] be ventilated a little" before being put to a vote.

True shot back he favored a thorough discussion. He said his amendment was in the interest of economy, for he felt sure the clergy members not only would be willing to offer prayers for free, but would welcome such service. True estimated such an innovation would save the State Treasury upwards of $100.

Hamlin replied he favored economy but not of the True sort. He pointed out that a House member had served as chaplain in the previous session and was given double the $5 per diem pay collected by a member, for the added service. Hamlin disclosed two of the House clergymen had emphatically told him they wanted no part of such a gratis arrangement, and he argued "the state still is not so poor it must beg for prayers."

Representative Samuel B. Page of Warren sided with the True stance. He testified its intent apparently was being misunderstood. He argued that having members offer prayers for each other would bring the legislators "into closer communion with each other, which is highly desirable." Page declared he preferred gratuitous prayers "which distilled like the gentle dews from heaven" to prayers which were "bought and paid for."

True took the rostrum again to insist that while he agreed the House pastors "do not covet being chaplain," he continued to feel certain they would fill the position if asked to do so. True added that his proposal would give the Legislature prayers from various denominations rather than just one, and that "it seems a mark of courtesy not to hire prayers when so many potential ones are so handy."

Taking the floor for a third time, Hamlin asserted he personally felt "the most excellent way was for each man to pray for himself. That would be better than either voluntary, or paid prayers. But so long as the Legislature favors some one to implore the Divine blessing upon them in public, then decency and justice requires the chaplain be paid for his service."

Page replied to the Hamlin sally by saying he supposed it would be better for himself "and the gentleman from Dover for each in his own station to work out his own salvation." But then he added he did not believe "that when a man sent up a request for prayers, he should enclose a greenback, not that the size of the greenback made any difference in the effect of the prayer."

Representative Samuel Davis of Warner told the House the discussion "was assuming a tone of levity that was unbecoming; in view of the question under consideration." Davis declared it was "universal practice to have a regular chaplain," and he challenged anyone to point out a contrary instance anywhere.

Representative William C. Sturoc of Sunapee terminated the floor battle with a recommendation that the committee proposal be amended to reemploy the Reverend Mr. Barstow for a second term as chaplain. Speaker Simon G. Griffin of Keene put the question, and on a standing count, Barstow was retained as the official legislative contact with God, by a 106 to 90 vote. His daily remuneration of $5 as a legislator was again doubled, and he again served as vice chairman of the House Education Committee with Hamlin.

A year later, the 1868 House approved free prayers. As the session organized, Representative Page of Warren moved that the clergymen members alternate in giving gratis invocations, under supervision of the House clerk, rather than the Speaker.

Representative William H.Y. Hackett of Portsmouth asked that Page's proposal be tabled and that a customary committee of ten, one member from each county, be appointed to recommend a chaplain. But the House voted 141 to 106 against pigeonholing the free prayers, after which there was a luncheon recess. When the afternoon session opened, Page demanded action on his proposal, and it was passed, on a standing tally, 130 to 103.

Representative William Clark of Amherst offered the free prayers on the second and third days, followed by Representatives Cyrus W. Wallace of Manchester and George Beebe of Gosport. As the session progressed, Clark contributed more praying than any colleague. And when the next Legislature convened in 1869, on motion of Representative Ossian Ray of Lancaster, Reverend Clark, no longer a legislator, was hired as chaplain, with pay, without opposition!

Guest Chaplains

GUEST CHAPLAINS became legislative custom in 1949. Legislators had the privilege of sponsoring their own pastors to offer morning prayers on a voluntary basis, subject only to scheduling with the regular chaplain.

The 1951 session had its first woman guest chaplain. She was the Reverend Ethel Lee Matthews of the Bristol Baptist Church. Her April 10 invocation went:

Rev. Ethel Lee Matthews

Our Heavenly Father, as we humbly bow in Divine Presence, we welcome Thee as our unseen guest here today. May our every thought, decision and act be under the guiding control of Thy Holy Spirit.

Grant unto all, who shoulder the responsibility of our state, wisdom and strength from on high that we may please Thee in righteousness.

We thank Thee for the blessed privilege that is ours as Christians to start each new day with Thee, and as these, Thy people, start their business for today, may they have the mind of Christ in all things. We ask it in His name. Amen.

There has also been a husband-and-wife team of guest chaplains. The Reverend George T. Duke of the Colebrook Congregational Church was guest chaplain on March 7, 1957. Then Mrs. Evelyn M. Duke, his widow, was guest chaplain on January 29, 1962, as a lay minister from the Dunbarton Congregational Church.

The 1939 Legislature had the novelty of a young lay preacher as chaplain. He was Concord native H. Raymond Danforth, fresh from popularity as a member of the 1937 House and the 1938 Constitutional

Convention. He came from tiny Acworth, and was studying at the University of New Hampshire, for an education degree. Danforth took up Congregational lay preaching at nineteen, while a University of New Hampshire sophomore in 1929. He continued the practice while teaching at Keene and Claremont, during which he resided for eight years in Acworth. In 1939 he moved to Epping to become superintendent of an eight-town school district.

Danforth retired in 1969, following eleven years of service as president of the fledgling New England College at Henniker. Ever jovial and zestful, Danforth recalled in his later years that his pay as legislative chaplain was $36 per week, with a daily travel allowance of ten cents per mile for the 108-mile round-trip from Acworth to Concord, which was excellent remuneration for a teacher in the depression era of the 1930s.

A modest, quiet-spoken Goffstown Episcopal clergyman launched free prayers for the 1949 session, as austerity pangs from postwar inflation beset the General Court. They were produced by the Reverend Austin H. Reed, sixty-nine-year-old House member in his fourth term, with such success that he continued as a lawmaking chaplain up to his late 1955 death.

Reed's gratis invocations were tied to an innovation on recommendation of the committee which chose him. It suggested that in recognition of the "important contributions made by the several religious denominations to the spiritual life of the state of New Hampshire," the Speaker should "from time to time, upon application of any member," issue invitations to leaders of other denominations to share the daily devotions. Reed readily agreed to this new policy, for it was an apparent compromise to a 289 to 15 adverse vote in the 1947 House against a demand by Representative Louis I. Martel of Manchester, ardent Catholic, that the chaplaincy be divided among Protestant, Catholic, and Jewish clergymen.

The Legislature voted Representative Reed special thanks for his free prayers, and he was retained by the 1951 session on the same basis. But the second time his fellow legislators collected a purse of appreciation for Reed, and he was also given a $100 cash surplus from a testimonial given Speaker Lane Dwinell of Lebanon. Representative Reed continued his dual role in the 1953 and 1955 session. And for each of these years, he was voted a token $200 reward from the State Treasury, while increasingly using guest chaplains mustered by the membership. It was modestly estimated that Representative Reed's

Prayers and Sermons

unusual service saved the state some $5,000 of traditional prayer costs.

A legislative prayer milestone occurred on an April morning in 1953. It was a first time a member of the Christian Science Church officiated as guest chaplain. This writer reported in the *Concord Monitor:*

J. Hamilton Lewis of Concord, Christian Science reader, came up with about the most unusual demonstration the other morning that we have ever heard a guest legislative chaplain give.

He asked the lawmakers to bow with him in silent meditation for a few moments and then join in reciting the Lord's Prayer.

It turned out to be a most impressive display of humility before God, as we folks have, each in our way, come to understand Him.

The Reverend Jack Clark, Protestant chaplain at Laconia State School and Training Center, became the first black man to serve as guest legislative chaplain on June 1, 1965, and promptly became an overnight sensation. Clark called upon God to forgive Governor John W. King and the Legislature for having created the state lottery two years earlier.

Governor King remained grimly silent as the guest chaplain launched his surprise criticism, and neither he nor any legislative official ever took public issue with Clark's remarks. His prayer, as printed in the House Journal, read:

Eternal God, our Heavenly Father, we thank you for our state government and all the good it does.

Forgive our immature, irresponsible, and unprogressive legislation of a sweepstakes lottery to support the education of our children.

Give our government the vision and courage to bring out the best in the people of New Hampshire. Having been faithful to you and those whom they serve, may the leaders of our government know the joy and fulfillment of a job well done.

We ask it all in the name of Him who gave His life for the salvation, health and eternal life of all people, even our Lord, Jesus Christ. Amen.

Pay Is Slashed

WHEN MARSHALL COBLEIGH of Nashua became House Speaker in 1969, in the name of economy the chaplain's pay was slashed from $18 to $10 per working day. This rugged recompense reduction for prayers generated national attention.

When Senator John P.H. Chandler, Jr., of Warner learned of it, he took the Senate floor to disclose that Chaplain William Shafer, Rochester Methodist, was "now praying twice for half the price." He referred to the fact that the House and Senate were for a first time using different opening hours in the 1969 session, and that the chaplain was required to give separate invocations daily.

Newspapers featured stories throughout the nation telling that New Hampshire's legislative chaplain was now "praying twice for half the price." Thanks to Senator Chandler, the Senate voted to match the reduced House pay for Chaplain Shafer, and this dual arrangement was continued through the 1971 session.

Chaplain Shafer added a new dimension to the invocation in 1969 by offering prayers of the Roman Catholic, Greek Orthodox, Protestant, and Jewish faiths to commemorate the most important holy days of each.

The 1973 House of Representatives elected the first Catholic legislative chaplain in New Hampshire history as the state observed its 350th anniversary of 1623 settlement. He was the Reverend Joseph Yvon Beaulieu, forty-two-year-old pastor of St. Lawrence Church in Goffstown, who was conceived and raised in Berlin, but was born in St. Fabien, Canada, 180 miles north of Quebec City, on April 3, 1930. His parents long resided in Berlin where his father, Israel Beaulieu, worked for a half-century for the Brown Company. Father Beaulieu explained that his mother temporarily returned to her native town for his birth, for sentimental reasons.

Chaplain Beaulieu attended St. Charles College in Sherbrooke, Canada; St. Mary's Seminary in Baltimore (where he became naturalized at twenty-one); and Catholic University at Washington, D.C. He went to Goffstown in October 1972, following six years at Rochester's Holy Rosary Church and earlier service at Manchester, Nashua, Newport, and Berlin.

The 1973 General Court also set another precedent, as the Senate appointed its own chaplain for a first time since its creation in 1784. This was done primarily because the upper branch continued its new

Prayers and Sermons

policy of opening daily sessions at one o'clock in the afternoon, or two hours later than the customary House opening.

The Senate's first chaplain was the Reverend Dr. Vincent Fischer, sixty-two-year-old rector emeritus of Goffstown's St. Matthew's (Episcopal) Church, and chaplain of the McKerley Medical Center in Concord. Born in Lynn, Massachusetts, on September 29, 1910, Dr. Fischer attended University of New Hampshire, Bangor Theological School, Yale University, and Berkeley Seminary in New Haven, Connecticut. He earlier served each of Concord's three Episcopal parishes. He continued as Senate chaplain through the 1979 session.

BATTLES FOR THE CAPITOL

Early Site Feuding

THREE MAJOR CONTESTS over its site have marked the life of New Hampshire's historic granite State House. The first occurred as the 1814 Legislature authorized the structure, and Concord citizens fought over its location. The second contest developed in 1864, as the Legislature voted to enlarge the building, and Manchester offered $500,000 to erect a new State House in that largest city in the state. The third battle was staged as the 1909 Legislature voted a second Capitol enlargement, and Manchester pressed a $1 million bid to shift the government center to that city.

The 1814 Legislature resolved a threatened initial clash over the State House location, in an unusual manner. As Hopkinton and Salisbury vied with Concord for the Capitol, the legislative leaders explained the structure would have to be of granite, to be furnished free of charge by the community in which it was built. Then they named a three-man legislative committee, with one member from each of the three towns, to settle the dispute. As the only available source of granite was nearby Rattlesnake Hill in West Concord, the Hopkinton and Salisbury committee members finally agreed to let Concord have the Capitol.

The Concord site battle was between the residents of the North End, where the early settlers' families held sway, and the residents of the South End, largely comprising first-generation families. The

North Enders favored the Stickney Lot, site of the 1790 Town House which the Legislature occupied for a quarter of a century as town guests (now site of the Merrimack County Center). The South Enders proposed the swampy Green Lot, on which the Capitol finally landed.

When the location committee filed its Concord recommendation with the 1815 Legislature, it reported that New Hampshire had become the only state in the nation without its own Capitol. It also said of the Town House, which the legislators voted appreciation for in 1790:

It is justly considered derogatory to a respectable and independent state to suffer the officers of its government to sit and transact the business of the state in a building mean in its appearance and destitute of suitable quarters.

The 1815 Legislature appointed a special committee to resolve Concord's site struggle, and it recommended the Stickney Lot to the 1816 session. By then, youthful Editor Isaac Hill of the newly created *New Hampshire Patriot* had swung into action for the Green Lot. He was supported by William Lowe, former Amherst merchant who had brought Hill to Concord, and by Col. William A. Kent, onetime penniless Charlestown, Massachusetts, youth who became prosperous as a Concord business leader.

Editor Hill had an ace up his sleeve, so to speak, for Governor William Plumer of Epping, who had become a champion of the state's constitutional government, boarded at his home. Hill's pro-Green Lot editorials helped induce the 1816 Legislature to pass the buck on the site dispute. It voted to have Governor Plumer and his Council decide the location for the Capitol, and then reconvene in November to approve that decision.

No sooner had the legislators gone home than Governor Plumer swung into action. On July 2 Councilor Samuel Quarles of Ossipee had to leave town, and he exacted a promise from Governor Plumer to delay the site action until the July 4 holiday. But records show that Plumer convened the Council the following day, on July 3, the four Councilors split 2 to 2 on the opposing sites, and the Governor voted for the Green Lot, and so posted a majority defeat of the Stickney Lot.

The North Enders denounced Governor Plumer's action, even as Editor Hill editorialized praise of his boarder. The Capitol's cornerstone was laid on the Green Lot on September 24, as the feuding went on unabated, and when the legislators reconvened, Governor Plumer fell under quick attack. The Legislature appointed a committee to scan the Governor and Council records, and obtain Plumer's reasoning for his vote as part of the Council. The North Enders correctly argued that under the state Constitution the Governor can only concur with the Council, or oppose it, and cannot vote with it. This committee reported Governor Plumer at fault. It said the Governor and the Council had met on the fateful July 3 in regular format, and not as a Committee of the Whole, as claimed by Plumer.

Representative Benjamin Prescott of Jaffrey, gruff and plainspoken old soldier, precipitated an open legislative revolt against Editor Hill. He took the House floor, roundly denounced both Hill and the Green Lot, and defied Editor Hill to print his remarks.

Hill rose to the challenge. He published Prescott's remarks in full. Some of them went as follows:

I understood that thar place was nothin but a frog pond. . . . I cannot conceive how any set of men whatever should be so tarnel blind. . . . Now railly, should we want to have the House split in the middle and the frogs peeping up through the cracks. They might make so much noise as I do now.

Besides, we are likely enough to take cold as it is, and if that there State House should be built down there, we should be still more likely to catch cold.

Isaac Hill

Battles for The Capitol

Lash Back at the Editor

C OLONEL PRESCOTT and his friends quickly lashed back at this Hill gambit. They introduced the following legislative resolution:

Whereas the editor of the New Hampshire Patriot, *printed in this town, has insulted members of this House, by mutilating their observations made herein, and in other instances has basely impeached the motives of the honorable members of this House in the discharge of their official duties, and considering that this abuse is eminently different from that liberty of the press which is the glory of the American people;*

Therefore be it resolved, that the House of Representatives highly disapproves of the conduct of Isaac Hill, in mis-stating, in publications in his paper, the observations and impeaching the motives of members of this House, while in the discharge of their official duties.

Editor Hill demanded a public hearing before the House before it voted on the censure resolution, and he got it. The House then set up a special committee, with Prescott as chairman, to file a bill of particulars supporting the resolution against Hill. The upshot of this maneuver was a substitute censure resolution by the Prescott committee, which was put up for vote on December 26, as follows:

Resolved, that the House of Representatives consider the accusation preferred in the House against Isaac Hill, editor of the N.H. Patriot, *is not an offense cognizable by the Legislature, and that the House of Representatives deem it improper to express their disapprobation of said editor, individually, inasmuch as the editors of other newspapers have published equally as severe strictures and censure on the conduct and proceedings of the different branches of government.*

Following a heated floor debate, the compromise resolution was approved on an 87 to 83 roll call vote. A member of the minority in the vote then moved to strike the entire proceedings of the incident from the permanent House Journal. But he was voted down, and the details remain in legislative records to this day.

Governor Plumer also prevailed. The House repudiated the committee findings against him, by a 91 to 70 roll call vote, and gave the Governor and the Council additional funds to conclude the construction of the State House. It was in this manner that Concord's "Battle of the Boarders" went into history. More of the legislators boarded with

South Enders than with North Enders, and history has recorded that this was the determining factor in placing the State House where it has stood to this day.

The South Enders paid for their victory. They contributed $4,000 in cash toward the $86,000 cost of the State House. They also paid for splitting granite boulders on Rattlesnake Hill, having them hauled to the State Prison where the inmates cut the slabs into blocks, and then delivering them to the site.

There were tiny galleries hung on the north and south walls of the House chamber, and the Speaker's rostrum was located against the west wall. There were a dozen raised seats behind the rostrum, which were for use by members of the Senate when meeting with the House in joint session.

The only known description of the original 1819 State House was recorded by youthful Jacob Bailey Moore, Concord newspaperman and legislative printer. It is contained in his 1824 *Annals of Concord,* which was reprinted in 1970 by the Merrimack County Savings Bank for legislative use and for distribution to Concord's citizenry. Moore wrote:

The State House is situated in the center of the village, upon a gently inclined slope between Main and State streets, and has two regular fronts, east and west.

The center of the building is 50 feet in front by 57 feet in depth; the wings are each 38 feet in front by 49 feet in depth; the whole making a parallelogram of 126 feet in length by 49 feet in width, with the addition of a projection in the center of each front. It is two stories above the basement, which rises five feet above the surface of the ground; the first story is 19 feet; the second 18 feet in the wings and 31 feet in the center.

The roofs of the wings are levelled at the outer ends and rise 10 feet against the body of the center; the roof of the center rises 13 feet, presenting gable ends in front; from the middle of which, the cupola rises, 18 feet square, to the height of 15 feet above the ridge; thence in an octangular form, 13 feet in diameter, 17 feet, and is covered with a roof in the form of an inverted acorn rising to the height of nine feet, and surmounted with a gilt ball, 33 inches in height, with its wings partially expanded.

Each front on the first floor has three doors and six windows. The second floor has nine windows with a semi-elliptical window in each gable end;

Representatives Hall after the 1864 renovations showing the long desks and single-legged stools bolted to the floor which were used until 1900. The small, ceiling-level portraits and ornate chandelier were removed during the enlargement of the chamber in 1910.

there are four windows in the south and two in the north end. The outside walls of the building are of granite, hammered and built in plain style—the only ornament being a tuscan frontispiece of stone work at each central front door.

The roof and cupola are of wooden materials. The roof is ornamented with a coving appropriate to the Doric order, and a balustrade upon the wings. The square of the cupola is ornamented with 12 Ionic columns, three to each corner, placed in a triangular position, with an appropriate coping and balustrade. The octangular part has one Ionic column at each corner, surmounted with an urn.

In the second story of the centre is the Representatives' Chamber, with an arched ceiling rising 30 feet from the floor, elegantly finished with stucco work. The north wing contains the Senate Chamber, 18 feet in height, with a beautiful ceiling of plaistering, ornamented with stucco work, supported by four Ionic columns and an equal number of pilasters. This room, for its

The new fencing, walks, and lawn which were part of the 1864 renovation. Neighbors were quick to use the fence for rug beating, and the 1866 Legislature imposed a ten dollar fine for such abuse and ordered the State House "Keeper" to bar hawkers and peddlers from the yard.

neatness and elegancy of finishing, is not perhaps inferior to any in the United States.

In the south wing are contained the Council Chamber and ante-chamber, both of which are finished in handsome style. In the same wing, in the lower floor, which is divided into two parts, are the Secretary's and the Treasurer's offices, over which is a suite of committee rooms. In the north wing, under the Senate Chamber, is a spacious room intended for public hearings before committees of the Legislature.

Under the Representatives' Chamber is an open area, in which are eight Doric columns, supporting the floor above. This area, with the adjacent passages in the wings, cooled by the currents of fresh air passing through the spacious doors and windows opening into them, affords in the warm month of June, a delightful retreat to the legislators, when fatigued by long attention to their arduous duties, or heated by the ardor of debate, above stairs; and it is by no means an uncommon case to see them availing *themselves of the benefit of this pleasant retirement.*

The lot on which the State House stands contains something more than two acres, enclosed on the sides with a solid wall of hammered stone about five feet high; the front fences are of stone posts and sills and iron castings, with the gates of the same material.

Manchester's 1864 Bid

THE STATE HOUSE became overcrowded by 1863, as the House membership continued to expand owing to population increases, so the Legislature put it up for auction, so to speak. It voted that any community with adequate railroad connections could bid for the coveted Capitol. Details of what followed were voluminously reported in the newspapers.

The House action led to what everyone anticipated, a fight by Manchester to haul the government center from Concord. So when they convened in June 1864, in the depths of the Civil War, the lawmakers set themselves up as referee and bargainer for the building. The House met in Committee of the Whole on June 29 to hear spans of spokesmen for the Concord and Manchester adversaries. Speaking for Manchester were Attorney William Burns of Lancaster, and Judge Lewis Whitehouse Clark of Manchester, Jurist and legislator. On the defense for Concord were Chief Justice Ira Perley of the Superior Court and Col. John H. George, sharp-shooting Democratic party chieftain (both of Concord).

Burns led off for Manchester. He said the State House lot was too tiny for expansion. He argued that the Legislature should follow a Vermont example and erect a Capitol with spacious grounds, and that individual seats and desks should be set in such a way that each legislator could reach an aisle without climbing over another. Burns also belittled Concord. He said it was niggardly for offering "only $100,000" to retain the State House, while its people clamored that their property valuations would decrease by 50 percent if it were lost to Manchester.

Judge Perley denounced the Legislature as well as Manchester for even considering the uprooting of the State House. He rapped the solons for "fostering extravagance in the bidding, one against another, in the depths of the war drain, and need for economies at every turn." Perley insisted that Concord had a "vested interest" in the Capitol, because of its donations toward the original construction.

Judge Perley declared that Concord was at the mercy of the Legislature and emphasized that whereas the city's $100,000 offer to enlarge the Capitol was all it could afford, it was willing to go to $150,000, or any other outlay required, to keep the prized possession.

Colonel George laid down a heavy barrage against Manchester. He expressed regrets that Attorney Burns had indicated that because a mob had burned a Concord newspaper office two years earlier, because of its war stand, the city was no longer fit to have the State House. George testified that because of that "allusion," he felt it only fair play to point out that a Manchester mob had burned a Catholic church before that, and another had destroyed "two or three taverns."

Colonel George argued that the General Court would be subjected to possible evil pressures if it were moved to Manchester, because its burgeoning textile mills corporations were financed by Massachusetts capital. He contrasted Concord citizens as "steady, sober and industrious," compared with an "80 percent migratory" population in that city. George capped his presentation by stressing that Manchester millhands lived in boardinghouses, "without roots," and were given to "passions and excitements and tumults" which might be harmful to legislative deliberations.

Judge Clark, described as of modest character and much self-poise, took Colonel George sharply to task. He told the legislators that George's remarks were "contemptible" and uncalled for. Clark suggested that Concordians had a lot of nerve to bespeak corporate influences when so many of its prominent citizens (including Governor Gilmore) were on the payrolls of the railroad. He also berated George for insulting Manchester's Irish mill workers, whereupon George jumped to his feet and declared that he had not mentioned the word "Irish." Clark jabbed back that the word "migratory" meant the same thing and everyone knew it.

Judge Clark concluded his arguments by suggesting that the legislators need not fear the Manchester mill interests. He grinned as he said, "If these corporations that my friend alludes to are desiring to control your actions in regards to making laws that may affect them, they are pretty apt to come here, and they have abundant means to pay their fares and expenses after getting here."

The Legislature killed the Manchester offer by a 158 to 132 roll call vote. But Concord's State House blues did not then turn rosy. The Legislature posted official warning that Concord must produce a new street south of the Capitol within six weeks or default the Capitol to Manchester. This area included the 1819 outdoor legislative toilet facility. Mrs. Grace Amsden, Concord historian, had recorded:

The surroundings of the State House were unsightly. On the south were the ruins of Hill's brick block (also called Sanborn's), destroyed by fire a few months before, with stables, sheds, work shops and backyards as far west as State Street, all on the very edge of the State House grounds.

Concord rose to the ultimatum challenge. Mayor Benjamin F. Gale donned work clothes to help build the street. The city was short of manpower because of the war, so leading citizens also grabbed shovels and other tools to raise blisters in the community cause. But the project became snagged. The owner of a house at the western corner of the new street layout refused to budge. He threatened a court injunction, which might have eclipsed the legislative deadline and given the State House to Manchester.

Mrs. Amsden chronicled: "It was then that Mayor Gale proved himself a worthy son of the pioneers, fearless and resourceful." Newspapers were discreetly reticent in reporting what followed. This was understandable, for the Sabbath was violated. On August 14, a Sunday, Mayor Gale and a large group of citizens showed up, bright and early, with tools and rollers. By midnight the disputed house had been hauled out of the way, and the owner fumed in vain because no courts were open on the Sabbath. So on Monday morning, the deadline date, what became Capitol Street was opened to traffic, as bells pealed, factory whistles tooted, and cannon boomed another Concord achievement.

The State House was saved—but the Legislature injected a final proviso. In the bill retaining the Capitol for Concord was this last-minute amendment:

Said city of Concord shall furnish said building completed as contemplated by this act, without expense to the state of New Hampshire, upon the understanding and condition that said city shall not at any time hereafter apply to said state to refund the money expended therefor, or any part thereof.

The 1864 enlargement cost Concord $158,000, financed by a bond issue. It included a third floor on the State House, of French dormer style. The rear was extended nearly 30 feet to give more depth to the crowded House of Representatives. This gave the State Library its own quarters for a first time, in what became Room 100, on the first floor. In this enlargement, the narrow north and south wings of the Capitol were taken down and broadened, with the same granite blocks, to the same size as its center, and this adjustment remains to this day.

The House members did not fare well as Representatives Hall was renovated in the 1864 project, and the Speaker's rostrum was moved to its present north wall position. They were given individual seats, but they also got grouped desks, along which stools were anchored to the floor. The *Concord Monitor* reported:

Representatives Hall is large enough but the House is too large. There are 340 seats subject to draft and 326 members to draw. This makes the hall a little crowded, for the seats have to be pretty near together.

The chairs have the good quality of making a fair bid for a short session; otherwise they are open to criticism. The chairs to a man of moderate length, seem a little lofty and the extremities of the short-legged members will, very likely, hang dangling in the air unless they have some sort of a cricket to support them.

If the rural members, who can scarcely set out an hour's sermon on Sunday, don't conclude by the last of June (there were then June sessions) that their hoeing is more necessary than legislation, and if the hard oak chairs don't ache under them by 12 o'clock every forenoon, we shall despair of any contrivance for a short session ever succeeding.

The 1864 enlargement of the Capitol included a new dome and a two-story granite front portico, which was patterned by the Boston engineer in charge of the project, from the Hôtel des Invalides, the noted Paris shrine. The original Capitol eagle loomed 115.5 feet into the heavens. The 1864 and 1909 renovations lifted the eagle 149.5 feet into the sky. Only the Christian Science Church steeple, to the southwest, is loftier in the Concord area, with a height of 158 feet. The two stairway doors leading to the second floor were eliminated on the front and rear sides, and inside stairways were installed. D. Hamilton Hurd commented in his 1885 *History of Merrimack County* on the 1864 project as follows:

A contest of this kind between neighboring communities is much to be regretted; the placing of citizens in hostility to each other creates enmities which time alone cannot allay; and in this case the 20 years that have

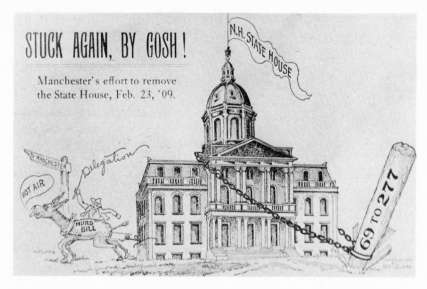

STUCK AGAIN, BY GOSH!

Manchester's effort to remove
the State House, Feb. 23, '09.

N.H. STATE HOUSE

TO MANCHESTER

Delegation

HOT AIR

HURD BILL

69 TO 277

*Postcard cartoon was sponsored by Concord to celebrate its 1909 battle to retain the
State House.*

*elapsed have failed to obliterate the scars caused by that memorable con-
test. The proposition made by the Legislature of 1864 was wrong in
principle and should never be repeated.*

Henry McFarland, prominent printer and historian, belabored the
deed, as well, in his 1899 *Concord Recollections.* He said that Concord
suffered immeasurably from the $158,000 bond issue, along with
$189,000 in interest charges before the cost was paid off.

The Granite State 1864 legislators were not unique in putting the
Capitol up for bid for its benefits. When the Maine Legislature voted a
State House, several towns vied for it, and Augusta won out with an
$11,500 donation to help build it. When Connecticut's legislators
became unhappy in the 1870s with two Capitols (one in New Haven
and one in Hartford), they sought bids on a single State House.
Hartford won out with a $500,000 ante toward its cost. Montpelier,
Vermont, had to vote funds on two occasions to keep its State House,
when renovations were required, after paying $10,000 for its original
location.

Concord Wins Again

MANCHESTER LAUNCHED its second fight for the State House in the winter of 1909. It developed as the Legislature was forced again to double its size to handle the increasing public affairs of the state's growing population. The bustling textile center this time posted a glittering $1 million bid, with a promise to erect a Capitol with spacious grounds and such elaborate accommodations as would put the Concord edifice to shame.

Representative Henry N. Hurd, Manchester lawyer, first filed a $250,000 offer. But just-retired Governor Charles H. Floyd of Manchester sponsored a $750,000 ante, which soon soared to $1 million. City Councilman Joseph H. Geisel, who later became a prominent legislator, joined in the contest. And merchant Thomas B. Varick insisted that Manchester had earned the State House by having mushroomed into the "biggest, brightest and busiest" spot in New Hampshire.

Governor Floyd sparked formation of a Committee of One Hundred, and overflow Manchester rallies generated enthusiasm for the Capitol. Manchester's city government once again played host to a delegation of legislators, to view proposed sites, even as it did in 1864. The *Manchester Union* reported some of the spots were the same as proposed forty-five years earlier.

Concord came up with an unusual defense of its possession of the State House. Its defenders enlisted Representative Clarence E. Clough, Lebanon coal and grain dealer, to publicize Concord's right to keep the Capitol. They helped Clough with a letter which outlined the Concord claim, which he sent to the *Manchester Union*. The newspaper printed Clough's statement, with banner black headlines, much to the surprise but pleasure of the Concord partisans.

The Clough statement emphasized that Concord had paid long and substantially to retain the state seat of government. He catalogued other Concord contributions besides the 1819 and 1864 payments to keep state affairs within its boundaries. He recalled the city gave cash and land for the State Prison in 1812, along with 121 acres of land and a $9,500 cash gift (nearly doubled by private donations) for the State Hospital in 1841. There was also a $25,000 contribution to help erect the State Library building of 1895.

The *Manchester Union* complained that Concord leaders were unfairly treating the $1 million offer as a joke. But, as expected, the House of Representatives gave this Manchester bid a 277 to 69 roll call burial. And Concord's ridicule continued. Penny postcards with a cartoon depicting a donkey, tagged "Rep. Hurd," trying to pull the State House southward while anchored to a stake labeled "277-69" became prized souvenirs.

This second enlargement, costing $400,000, widened Representatives Hall once again, added a three-story expansion westward to North State Street, and was financed entirely by the Legislature. Concord's equity in the state government center had apparently become so secure it no longer was required to make another payment to keep it.

Both enlargements were made with granite quarried out of Rattlesnake Hill. The difference between this stone, said by geologists to be 20 million years of age, and the rust-streaked boulders of the 1819 structure, said to have been deposited upon Rattlesnake Hill 20,000 years earlier in an ice age, remain clearly visible to this day.

Memorial Services

THE GRANITE STATE HOUSE of the Granite State has hosted all sorts of public events, since its gala 1825 tribute to General Lafayette, the French hero of the American Revolution. It has entertained many national Presidents and other distinguished New Hampshire guests of honor, and its walls have long displayed portraits of the state's warriors and political leaders.

The Capitol has even been the scene of memorial services for a handful of nearby citizens. Early in 1862, the bodies of the first three Concord area men to give their lives in the Civil War, were displayed in state in Doric Hall, as the present Hall of Flags was first named, before final rites were held in neighboring churches. They were Lt. Charles W. Walker of Concord, Capt. Leonard Drown of Penacook (then called Fisherville), and Capt. A.W. Colby of Bow.

When Franklin Pierce, New Hampshire's only President, died on October 8, 1869, President Grant ordered national mourning, and his body was placed on brief display three days later, on a Monday morning, in Doric Hall. He had been a Concord resident for some thirty years, and Mayor Lyman D. Stevens asked merchants to close their stores for an hour at noon. The schools were closed at 11:00 A.M., and hundreds of children lined their respects in hushed awe in the Capitol's main foyer. After early afternoon final services at adjacent

St. Paul's (Episcopal) Church, Pierce was buried in the Old North Cemetery, with Mayor Stevens and Governor Onslow Stearns of Concord serving as pallbearers.

Governor Wesley Powell of Hampton Falls sponsored the only funeral services ever held in the State House, for United States Senator Styles Bridges of Concord, who died on November 26, 1961. He ordered emergency repairs for the flooring of Hall of Flags and emptied the Capitol for two days for the ceremonies.

Governor Powell arranged for two days of public display of the body of the Maine farmboy who died in the full flower of political power and prestige, at sixty-three, after a quarter of a century of service at Washington, following a single term as Governor in 1935-36. An honor guard of 70 soldiers escorted the Bridges casket from his East Concord home (now the Governor's official residence), and 100 state troopers and soldiers stood rigid duty around it in the Hall of Flags for forty-eight hours.

Workmen labored in the basement throughout a night to shore up the 1819 flooring of the chamber, for the public safety, because it had developed sags after being thronged for the 1955 visit of President Eisenhower, to honor the Old Man of the Mountain, on the sesquicentennial of its discovery by white men in Franconia Notch in 1805.

The final rites on the afternoon of November 29 were limited to 250 top state and national political luminaries. The eulogy was delivered by Senator Everett Dirksen of Illinois, the sonorous-voiced Republican champion of national renown. Governor Powell exalted his long-time political associate, and brief addresses were given by Senate Chaplain Fred B. Harris and House Speaker John McCormack of Massachusetts. A special combined choir from the University of New Hampshire and the two state colleges at Plymouth and Keene sang from an adjacent corridor.

Epilogue

Struggles for Democracy

THIS COMPILATION of the story of New Hampshire's Legislature, from its 1680 birth as a royal province, and through its two centuries of self-government, offers much for contemplation.

Throughout its first century of provincial existence, the Legislature, initially called the Assembly, struggled against executive and judicial authority for self-determination. In this period, the tiny Assembly (of never more than thirty-four members) doggedly persisted in establishing the basic principles of self-strength, which blossomed out of the Revolutionary War into a free constitutional General Court, and continue to this day.

From this provincial and Revolutionary heritage, New Hampshire's House of Representatives has developed into the most democratic legislative body, on a per capita basis, in the world. Its membership size has long been criticized as an efficiency obstacle. This criticism was the subject of an address by this writer before a legislative seminar for new members, at the convening of the 1970 session, which went in part as follows:

We have come a long way in a short time to join here in this schooling on democracy—New Hampshire style.

Aerial view of the State House and surrounding downtown Concord area taken in 1979 by Robert Swenson.

It was only 186 years ago that New Hampshiremen created our present government and dedicated it to betterment of the common life.

We pioneered the world's first common government for the common welfare, and dedicated it to the proposition that common people can rule themselves.

Historians warned that this experiment, born out of the war for democratic freedoms, would fail. They said that common people were too plain, too simple, and not smart enough, to govern themselves.

Some folks continue to insist that we common folks are not fit to make our own laws and determine our public affairs. They claim there are too many of us in this great General Court of New Hampshire. They yap that our 400-member House of Representatives comprises too many common men and women, who do not know much and are not smarter than their neighbors who send them to Concord.

These critics vow we should have more select and more intellectual legislators. They say the way to achieve their goal is to slash the size of the House and boost the pay.

To This Day

All this, the critics carp, is in the name of efficiency. They hold that too many of our 400 legislators are worthless and a drag on progress.

We oppose this smear and its smack of smugness. We deny that common people are unfit to determine their own destiny. It deprecates democracy to say that special folks with special intellect, special talents and special interests can better enhance the common welfare.

Professor James P. Richardson of Dartmouth College, compiler of New Hampshire constitutional history, expressed unusual tribute to the elephantine House while serving as a member in the 1925 session. In an address before the Manchester Rotary Club he said, in part:

The big Legislature is a great institute of civics. The majority of New Hampshire people know their representative personally and a very large number of them call him by his given name. Before the coming of women's suffrage, this was quite generally the case.

Knowing their member, the voters feel free to tell what is what, as they see it, to discuss pending legislation when he is home, and we have an even better system in this informal referendum than the one conducted according to the rules.

In no state do so many people have a wide and intelligent acquaintance with public affairs. Trained first of all to investigate and study state affairs, our people inform themselves on national affairs.

The big Legislature takes the art and science of government back into the small towns and we have had men of real statesman calibre in little mountain hamlets.

The big Legislature has been a big thing for New Hampshire. Yet we have apologized for it, rather than vaunted it, derided it rather than lauded it. Rarely does anyone point out, what we have tried to point out, its immense educational influence in the state. . . .

Because we have a big Legislature, we have a large number of men who have learned parliamentary practice, how meetings should be conducted, how to guide discussion, bringing out the facts, curbing the verbose. Because of this enormous Legislature, in any moderate sized gathering of New Hampshire citizens, almost certainly there will be one or more men of

Epilogue

legislative experience. Because the Legislature is so large, no member can speak long, and so all have to learn to shoot quick and shoot straight. If they do not, their colleagues scuff them down.

Interestingly, Professor Richardson told the Manchester Rotarians that the House size, then at 421, would have to soon be curbed, because of constant population gains, and predicted it would be cut below 300. The curb came in 1943, but was pegged at its present 400.

National Accolade

THE DEMOCRACY of the House of Representatives won a surprise national accolade in 1934. When a *Collier's Weekly* reporter came to Concord to extol Governor John G. Winant and his state government reforms, he became so impressed by the size of the House that its membership, rather than Winant, was featured in his illustrated article.

The report, by Walter Davenport, was headlined:

You CAN'T FOOL NEW HAMPSHIRE. *Just try to put something over on the Legislature of New Hampshire. You can't do it. For one thing, it's too big—nobody could afford to bribe the boys even if they could all be seen. Besides, politics is a pastime, not a business, in New Hampshire.*

Davenport, who found the Legislature in special session to launch the State Liquor Monopoly System, which continues to this day, observed of the House in the July 14, 1934, issue of the magazine:

In session it is healthily suggestive of the old-fashioned town meeting, a form of government still to be found without much seeking in New England. As numerically it has the unwieldiness of the true Republican form, in action it comes as close to the old Jeffersonian idea as any legislative body you'll find anywhere.

To be sure, it has had members who have been less than zealous in pursuit of the general welfare, men who have not been above listening to reason if backed up with cash; but to talk of corrupting New Hampshire's House of Representatives is to squander anyone's time in a most shameless manner. Any aspiring agency that could afford to buy up this House wouldn't need to resort to bribery to get what it wanted. And for those who deplore the prevalence of lawyers in our legislative bodies—Congress, for example—the New Hampshire House should be a pleasant sight and a grateful sound. Of the 418 members, not more than a score are lawyers.

Prof. Thorsten V. Kalijarvie and William C. Chamberlain observed in their 1939 *Government of New Hampshire*, sponsored by the University of New Hampshire:

The Legislature of New Hampshire, like most similar bodies, in the United States, is weak in shaping its legislative program, spends a great deal of time in committee work, lacks a strong bureau of legislative reference, and is very cumbersome in operation.

On the other hand, it has thus far succeeded in representing the people as faithfully as any other similar body in this country, and does bring the average citizen and his state government close together. As long as this state has its present small population (465,000), it may well afford to continue a not too efficient Legislature, which nevertheless serves a splendid democratic purpose.

Jonathan Daniels, retired Raleigh, North Carolina, newspaper publisher and author, presented a unique report on the Granite State's giant House of Representatives, in his 1940 book, *A Southerner Discovers New England*, as follows:

It was Tuesday, and the members of the General Court of New Hampshire, which boasts of the biggest House of Representatives among American state legislatures, were coming into Concord and the Capitol to legislate and sign the mileage book which assures them every week ten cents a mile for the trip home and back in addition to the $200 a term which they get in salary.

That year there were 427 members of the House representing the half million people of the state. While I waited for the session to begin, I amused myself with some comparative mathematics. Roughly, there is one member of the House for every thousand people in New Hampshire. If New York state elected an assemblyman on the same basis there would be 12,000 members in its lower House, and if the national Congress used that ratio in representation there would be well over a hundred thousand Congressmen in America. That prospect was so appalling that I worked it backwards: If New Hampshire elected on the New York basis, there would be only half a dozen members in the House, or no more than two members if they elected on the same basis as the Congress.

Epilogue

But apparently the size of the House makes everybody happy. No young man need break his heart because of the slimness of the chance of becoming a statesman. . . .

There are only three real working days each week—Tuesday, Wednesday and Thursday. Even on those days in the past there were often more seats in the big hall than legislators in them. But in 1939 Representative George H. Duncan, Democrat of Jaffrey, introduced a resolution at the first of the session calling for installation of time clocks in both Houses and requiring the representatives of the people of New Hampshire to punch them on penalty of having compensation reduced to the terms of their attendance. The resolution raised such an uproar among the thrifty Yankees that it was withdrawn; it helped fill the hall during the rest of the session nevertheless.

The *State Government* magazine of the Council of State Governments reported on this House of Representatives' size in its March 1942 issue:

Since the House is the people's Assembly, its size will never be substantially reduced. . . . Inasmuch as a large percentage of its members are actively engaged in some business, they insist upon returning home each weekend. There is, however, an advantage in having legislators who are successful in their business or profession, for the state is thus assured leaders in its legislative assembly.

John Gunther, the late noted author, gave attest to Professor Richardson's evaluation of New Hampshire's elephantine Legislature, in his 1946 book, *Inside USA*. In surveying the characteristics of each state, he asked by whom and how its government operated. He reported, for example, that oil interests dominated Texas and that the rural populace influenced Vermont public life.

When Gunther posed the same questions to half a dozen leading Granite State citizens, he compiled the surprising answer—"The voters." He wrote that because of that unusual summation, he then asked who ran the voters, and the consensus was "All sorts of things."

This is a fitting accolade, for a democracy, by its very nature, comprises all sorts of people with all sorts of ideas. Gunther also observed:

Because the Legislature is so enormous, it is hard to control. Pressure groups can operate in the Senate—membership 24—to some extent. But the lower House is too unwieldy.

The meticulous *National Geographic* magazine said of the House size, in a January 1951 article by Albert W. Atwood:

This particular feature of the New Hampshire government is both good and bad. It brings government close to the people, but on the other hand, it brings some not too highly educated persons into the lower branch.

The *Reader's Digest* featured an article in its May 1953 issue in which Lester Velie criticized New Hampshire's House of Representatives, and extolled Nebraska's experiment with a unicameral, or single-branch legislature. Velie's views on the Granite State's House were, in part:

Legislators who don't make enough to cover room and board at the state capital live off lobbyists who expect favors in return. No state, says the National Municipal League, should pay its legislators less than $4,000 yearly. . . .

Not only does a small Legislature cost less money; there is more prestige to being in it. As a contrast to Nebraska's 43-man unicameral, let's visit a session of New Hampshire's lower House at Concord. It has 399 members, but the confusion that washes over you as you enter makes them seem twice as many. There is no room for desks; the lawmakers are jammed in theater seats, elbow to elbow. Many, unable or unwilling to crawl over the laps of colleagues, stand in the rear of the chamber, where they fidget uncomfortably, often three deep.

When the opening bell rings, the doors are locked, and no one can leave except by permission of the Speaker. Lawmakers used to absent themselves in such droves from the jammed sessions that the Speaker ruled that members couldn't collect traveling allowances unless they signed in with the Sergeant-at-Arms. When they took to signing but bolting immediately, the Speaker had them locked in.

A debate rages over a sales-tax measure, and House members fight to get the Speaker's attention—a tough job, with scores of them demanding recognition at once. The debate is futile, anyway, for the sales-tax bill is already doomed. In so big a House, there will be at least thirty storekeepers, who form a bloc to talk the sales tax to death or else to kill it by demanding roll calls on technicalities. There is no electric voting board, and the polling of 399 members can be endless.

Epilogue

Robert B. Dishman, professor of Political Science at the University of New Hampshire, called for a reduction in the House of Representatives membership in his 1956 pamphlet, *A New Constitution for New Hampshire*, in part as follows:

On the basis of comparative size and population, the New Hampshire House would appear to be disproportionately large. This would present no real problem except for the fact that experience has shown that unduly large legislatures, particularly at the state level, tend to be unwieldy, inefficient, and vulnerable to organization pressure. No one has put the case against an oversize Legislature better than the men who framed the New Hampshire Constitution. They were convinced that a House of more than fifty members would be a mistake, and in their address to the people in 1781 urging support for an earlier draft of the Constitution they (vainly) explained:

"Experience must have convinced every one who has been, in any degree, conversant with the transacting of business in public bodies, that a very large assembly is not the most convenient for that purpose. There is seldom so much order, and never so much dispatch, as is to be found in a smaller body. The reason is obvious. This has given birth to the mode of choosing committees out of the whole body; and experience hath demonstrated its utility. The convention, therefore, were of the opinion that confining the second branch (the House of Representatives) to the number of fifty, which appeared to them sufficiently large for every purpose, would be attended with the following salutary consequences—

"There would be probably a greater proportion of suitable men, than in a larger body. . . . The debates would, of course, be conducted with more wisdom and unanimity. From their numbers merely, there would be much less confusion, and infinitely more dispatch. This would of itself, produce an amazing saving in expense, independent of the difference between paying fifty, and three times that number. For these and many other reasons, the reducing and confining this branch to a small number, was surely an achievement devoutly to be wished."

More recently a committee of the American Political Science Association reached the same conclusion after a careful study of the American legislatures.

The late Raymond P. Holden of New York City, who became an

army cavalryman and then a poet and novelist of national repute, penned a unique tribute to the House of Representatives after serving in the 1953 session from Newport, his retirement home. He reported in his 1958 book, *The Merrimack*, a history of New Hampshire's famous river and its environment, in part:

Members of the General Court are, for the most part, fearful of the concentration of power, suspicious of experts and fairly certain that their individual judgment could not be improved upon. Voting is conducted more by instinctive reaction than by adherence to party lines. Lobbying is, as in other states, a factor, but in spite of the low salary of the legislators, is seldom profitable. New Hampshire lawgivers do not like to be told what to do. Some of them are not above accepting favors or entertainment, but few pay for what they get by voting as a lobbyist expects them to do. . . .

Common sense in the Capitol is, happily, as it has been for 140 years, more common than emotion. The New Hampshire General Court is, on the whole, as honest, sober and effective a body of legislators, as is to be found in any state of the Union. It often reflects, perhaps wisely, the tendency of the people to be slow to destroy existing things.

Reflections on the Membership

H ARLAN LOGAN of Meriden, sponsor of this legislative history, presented a classic reflection of the giant House membership when he, then sixty-five, served as House Republican majority floor leader in the 1969 session, which went in part:

Mr. Speaker: Within the past week my attention was called to a statement made by one of our younger freshman members—a statement in which he called the New Hampshire House of Representatives "A Den of Antiquity."

My first reaction was defensive and angry. I thought of recommending some severe rebuke, such as erasing his name from the mileage boards.

My second thought was that he might have said many more damaging things about us. The key words in his comment were "den" and "antiquity." I looked them up in the dictionary.

It is true that "den" may be defined as the lair of a wild beast—a cave or cavern—a place of resort for nefarious or prohibited purposes. But all the meanings are not derogatory; a "den" is also a private place for study, for thinking and making decisions, for escape from the noise and confusion caused by younger members of a family or of a community.

Also, "antiquity" is not by any means an entirely negative word. In addition to meaning "ancient or of great age," it also carries the connotation of respect because of age, of a lasting quality, of long experience, of stored up wisdom, and of value as when we speak of a "priceless antique."

So—I decided not to pursue my vendetta against our freshman member, but instead to ask permission of the House to say a few words in praise of age and experience as they are represented by a high percentage of the membership of this body.

I should, perhaps, begin by admitting that taken collectively, the leadership of both sides of the aisle must be considered a youthful group. With this I have no quarrel. We need energetic, vigorous, eager and ardent young bucks and tigers, just as any organization needs them.

But—It is also well to remind ourselves and them that in human affairs there is no substitute for seasoning, for aging, for long term individual experience. We need muscle, but not at the expense of patience and prudence. We need valor, but not as a substitute for discretion. We need speed, but we also need control.

. . . I am not one to place a high value on the mere passage of years, to say that the best is yet to be for us tribal elders, or to bow my head in worship of the good old ways, or of age as such. But I do believe as Sophocles said that "Age and the wear of time do teach us many things."

All this is in no way intended to belittle youth, energy, drive or alacrity. It is only my way of saying that we have other assets, and we need other assets in the House. We have a body of knowledge that was hard to come by. We have maturity. We have tradition. We have a rounding of the sharp corners that comes only from use, and a mellowing of the flavor that comes only from age.

This writer was asked to share his observations of three dozen years as a newspaperman reporting legislative activities, before the Blue Ribbon Legislative Advisory Committee in 1970, composed of private citizens, to recommend improvements in legislative operations. The address said, in part:

We are happy to see our Legislature acting in its own interest for a change. For all too long, its repute has deteriorated from lack of such attention.

Our legislative image has shrunk to such shameful degree that many members shy from self-respect, and carping criticisms are their only reward for doing their best. It's about time our Legislature flexes its purpose and improves its posture. . . .

Most of all, our Legislature lacks the vitamins of viability and visibility. It should revive itself to its original purpose of serving as the most important one-third of our state government. It should return to its own two feet and do its own thinking, rather than depend upon the Executive branch for guidance in fulfilling its constitutional obligations to the people.

It's pleasing that the Legislature has begun improving its viability. We now have staffs to help members resolve their chores, and we need more such tools.

But the visibility remains untapped. The doings of the Legislature continue too cloaked in obscurity. Much of its warp and woof is not fully communicated back to the people it speaks and acts for.

The Legislature votes improvements in state agencies and grants funds to

Harlan Logan

Epilogue

publicize and explain their affairs to the people back home. It also grants funds to local communities to promote their images and welfare.

In contrast, the Legislature doesn't even disseminate modest reports of its own accomplishments, let alone its virtues, to the people, for fear someone might snidely say it is sinful. As we suggested to the Legislature last year, this business of relying upon everyone else to cast our image is for the birds. It will be only as good and only as merited, as we ourselves reflect it.

Our General Court needs a stiff dose of public relations for restoration of public good will and understanding. . . . This will cost a bit of money. But it still would be only a fraction of what is now spent for the same purpose in the Executive and Judicial branches of our state government.

Finally, the Legislature should have its own home. The Governor got one last year and the state Supreme Court has just moved into its own quarters for a first time.

For all too long, the Legislature has crimped its affairs into odd sections of the State House. It should assume complete occupancy of the Capitol, except for modest space for the Governor and its constitutional officers.

Legislative quarters in the over-crowded State House are a disgrace. The lawmakers haven't even fitting space for their headgear, or to cool their tonsils following heated debate. Their housing situation has become so shabby that most of the members must trundle to the basement to hang their hats in less space than prison inmates enjoy. And the rank-and-file legislators now don't even have a square inch they can call their own when they come to Concord on official business when the General Court is in adjournment.

May we emphasize in conclusion that the Legislature should respect its own worth before it can expect others to appreciate it.

These 1970 suggestions have borne fruit. The Legislature now has its own $4 million office building, renovated out of the old federal Post Office adjacent to the State House, and several state agencies have been moved out of the Capitol to give the lawmakers needed elbow room. Most of these improvements have been sparked by House Speaker George B. Roberts, Jr., who headed a 1973 committee which sponsored the new legislative center. The handsome Legislative Office Building was dedicated on November 14, 1975.

Marshall W. Cobleigh, Nashua insurance executive who served as House Speaker in the 1969 and 1971 sessions, testified before a study commission of the 1974 Constitutional Convention, in part:

I came to the Legislature in 1963 convinced that we needed to cut the size of the House. I ran and was elected to the 1964 Constitutional Convention pledged to cut the size of the House and I voted that way. It was unsuccessful. Since that time, with additional service in the House, I saw the wisdom of the large legislative body and decided that I was wrong in adopting the public viewpoint that the House should be cut.

After a period of years in observing the Legislature in action and moving into the leadership rank, my position changed. . . . I think it is possible for us to reduce the size of the House, still retaining our position as the largest in the nation, while at the same time making a more efficient body, and allowing for increased compensation that will attract a better cross section of the population.

There is an old saying that if you live long enough in New Hampshire, you will land in the Legislature before the grave. That may sound odd, but it is still likelier than anywhere else in the world, because the state's 400-member House of Representatives constitutes more democratic representation than any other legislative body on earth.

This giant House of Representatives is so close to its people that each member represents a population of only 2,200. If populous California were to have such democracy, its Assembly of 80 would soar to more than 10,000. In contrast, if the Granite State were restricted to California's legislative measurement, its House would be limited to three members.

A unique feature of this New Hampshire democracy is the truism that most of its voters know their legislator personally or live within a mile with easy access to their lawmaker. Also unique, service in New Hampshire's Legislature is not legally considered as employment. The biennial salary of $200 is so meager that legislators have, on occasion, collected standard unemployment compensation when severed from their regular jobs.

Finally, as this legislative history has frequently emphasized, the

Epilogue

self-reliance and sturdiness of this 400-member body developed through three centuries of effort, and its democratic principles continue to this day. This feature so impressed Dr. J. Duane Squires, the Granite State's noted historian who served as editor of this manuscript, that he suggested "To This Day" should become the distinctly appropriate title for this history.

Appendices

TEXT OF THE ROYAL COMMISSION

The royal commission by which King Charles II created New Hampshire's state government three hundred years ago, on September 18, 1679, has long been a prized relic in the custody of the Secretary of State's office.

The complete text, with its original spellings, as provided by State Archivist Frank C Mevers, is presented on the following pages:

The Commission
constituting a
PRESIDENT AND COUNCIL
for the
PROVINCE OF NEW HAMPSHIRE,
in New-England

CHARLES ye SECOND to all to whom these Presents shall come,

GREETING:

WHEREAS, our Colony of ye Massachusetts, at Mattathusetts Bay, in New-England, in America, have taken upon themselves to organize a government and jurisdiction over ye Inhabitants and Planters in ye Towns of Portsmouth, Hampton, Dover, Exeter, and all other ye Towns and lands in ye Province of New-Hampshire, lying and extending from three miles northward of Merrimack River, or any part hereof, into ye Province of Maine, not having any legall right or authority so to so; which said jurisdiction, and all further authority thereof, we have thought fit, by the advice of our Privy Council, to inhibit and restrain for the future; And do hereby inhibit and restrain ye same. And whereas ye Government of ye part of the said Province of New-Hampshire, so limited and bounded as aforesd, hath not yet bin granted unto any person or persons whatsoever, but ye same still remains under Our immediate care and protection: To the end, therefore, yt Our loving subjects, ye planters Inhabitants within ye limits aforesaid, may be protected and defended in their respective rights, liberties and properties, and yt due and impartiall justice may be duly administered in all cases, civill and criminall and yt all possible care may be taken for ye quiet and orderly government of ye same, now Know ye, that We, by and with ye advice of our Privy Council, have thought fit to erect, and by these presents for us, or heirs and successors, do erect, constitute & appoint a President and Council to take care of ye said Tract of land called The Province of New-Hampshire, and of the Planters and Inhabitants thereof, and to order, rule and govern ye same according to such methods and regulations as are herein after provisied and declared. And for ye better execution of Our Royall pleasure in this behalf, We do hereby nominate and appoint Our trusty and well beloved subject, JOHN CUTT, of Portsmouth, Esq., to be ye first President of Ye said Councell, and to continue in ye said office for the space of one whole year next ensueing ye date of these presents, and so long after, untill We, Our heirs or successors, shall nominate and appoint some other person to succeed him in ye same. And we likewise nominate and appoint Our trusty and well beloved subject, Rich: Martin, Esqr., William Vaughan, Esqr., and Tho. Daniel, Esqr., all of Portsmouth, aforesaid; John Gilman, of Exeter, aforsd, Esqr., Christopher Hussey, of Hampton, afrsd, Esqr., and Rich: Walden, of Dover, aforesd, Esqr., to be of the Councell within ye said Province of New-Hampshire: And we do hereby authorize and appoint the said President and Councell to nominate and make choice of three other persons out of ye severall parts of the said Province whom

Appendices

they shall judj to be most fitly qualified to be of ye said Councell, and to swear them in to ye same. And yt the said Jo: Cutts, and every succeeding President of ye said Councell, shall nominate and appoint any one of the members of the said Councell for ye time being to be his deputy, and to preside in his absence.

And yt the said President, or his deputy, and any five of the said Councell, shall be a quorum. And our express will and pleasure is that no person shall be admitted to sit or have a vote in the said Councell, until he have taken ye oath of allegance and supremacy herein after mentioned, for ye one and impartiall execution of justice, and ye faithful discharge of ye trust in them reposed. Which oaths we do hereby authorize and direct ye said Ric. Martin, W: Vaughan, T: Daniel, Jo: Gilman, Christ: Hussey, R: Waldron, or any three of them first, to administer to ye said Jo: Cutt, having taken ye said oaths, we do will, authorize and require him ye said Pres., for ye time being, to administer ye same from time to time to all and every other the members of ye said Councell. And we do hereby will, require and comand ye said Jo: Cutts R: M: and every of them, to whom this our pleasure shall be made known, that, all excuses whatsoever set aside, yt they fail not to assemble and meet together at ye sd town of Portsmouth in ye Prov. of New Hampsh. aforsd within ye space of 20 days next after ye arrival of this Commission at Portsm. aforesaid, and there to cause this Our Commission, or Letters pattents, to be read before them, or as many of them as shall be there assembled, and having first duly taken the said oaths, to proceed to choose, nominate and appoint such officers and servts as they shall think fit and necessary for their service. And also to appoint such other time and place for their future meetings as they or ye major part of them (whereof ye Pres: or his deputy to be one) shall think fit and agree. And Our Will and pleasure is, that Our said Councell shall from time to time ahve and use such Seal only for ye sealing of their acts, orders and proceedings as shall be sent unto them by us, our heirs or successors, for yt purpose. And we do by

these prts, for us, our heirs and successors, constitute, establish, declare and appoint our said Pres. and Councell, and ye Pres: and Councell and their successors for ye time being, to be a constant and setled Court of record, for ye administration of justice to all our subjects inhabiting within ye limits aforesaid, in all cases, as well criminall as civill, and yt ye Pres: and any 5 of the Councell for ye time being, shall have full power and authority to hold plea in all causes from time to time, as well in pleas of ye Crown as in mattrs relating to ye conservation of ye peace, and in punishment of offenders, as in civill suits and actions between parties and parties, or between us and any of our subjects there; whether ye same do concern ye realty, and relate to a right of freehold and inheritance, or whether ye same do concern ye personality, and relate to some matter of debt, contract, damage, or other personal injury, and also in all mixt actions wch may concern both realty and person, and therein, after due and orderly proceeding and deliberate hearing on ea. sides, to give judgmt, to award execution, as well criminall as in civill cases as aforesaid: so always yt ye forms of proceeding in such cases and ye judgment thereupon to be given, be as consonant and agreeable to ye Laws and Statutes of this Our Realm of Engd, as ye prent state and condition of our subjects inhabiting within ye limits aforesaid, and ye circumstances of ye place will admit. And ye Pres: and Councell for ye time being, and every of them respectively, before they be admitted to their severall and respective offices and charges, shall also take this Oath following:

You shall swear well and truly to administer justice to all his Mates subjects inhabiting within ye Province of New Hampsh. under this Government: and also duly and faithfully to discharge and execute the Trust in you reposed, according to the best of your knowledj. You shall spare no person for favour or affection, nor any person grieve for hatred or ill will. So help you God.

Notwithstanding it is Our will and pleasure, and so we do hereby expressly declare, yt it shall and may be lawfull from time to time to and for all and every person and persons, who shall think himself or themselves aggrieved by any sentence, judgmt or decree pronounced, given or made (as aforsd) in, about or concerning ye title of any land, or other reall estate, or in any personall Action, or suit above the value of 50l and not under, to appeal from such Judgmt, Sentence and Decree unto us, Our heirs and successors, and our and their Privie Councell. But with and under this caution and limitation: That ye Appellant shall first enter into and give good security to pay full costs, in case no relief shall be obtained upon such decree. And our further will and pleasure is, and so do we hereby declare; That in all criminall cases, where ye punishmt to be inflicted on ye offenders shall extend to loss of life or limb (ye case of willfull murder excepted) ye psn. convicted shall either be sent over into this Our Kingdom of Engd with a true state of his case and conviction; or execution shall be respited untill ye case shall be here presented unto us, our heirs and successors, in Our and their Privie Councell, and orders sent and returned therin. And for ye better defence and security of all our loving subjects within ye Province of New Hampshr, and ye bounds and limits aforesaid, our further will and pleasure is, and hereby we do authorize, require and command ye said Pres: and Councell for ye time being, in our name and under the seal by us appointed to be used, to issue, seal and give commissions from time to time to such person and persons, whom they shall judg shall be best qualified for regulating and discipline of ye militia of Our said Province; and for ye arraying and mustering ye Inhabitants thereof, and instructing them how to bear and use their arms, and that care be taken that such good discipline shall be observed, as by ye said Council shall be pscribed; yt if any invasion shall at any time be made, or other destruction, detriment, or anoyance made or done by Indians, or others upon or unto our good subjects inhabiting within ye said Prov. of New Hamp. We do by these presents for us, our heirs and successors declare, ordain and grant, that it shall and may be lawfull to and for our

said subjects so comissioned by our said Council from time to time, and at all times for their special defense and safety to encounter, expell, repell and resist by force of arms, and all other fitting means whatever, all and every such person and persons as shall at anytime hereafter attempt or enterprise ye destruction, invasion, detriment, or anoyance of any of our said loving subjects, or their plantations or estates. And above all things, We do by these prsents will, require and comand our said Councell to take all possible care for ye discountenancing of vice and encouraging of virtue and good living; and that by such examples ye infidel may be invited and desire to partake of ye Christian Religion, and for ye greater ease and satisfaction of he sd loving subjects in matters of religion, We do hereby require and comand yt liberty of conscience shall be allowed unto all protestants; yt such especially as shall be conformable to ye rites of ye Church of Engd shall be particularly countenanced and encouraged. And further, We do by these prsents, for us, our heirs and successors give and grant unto ye said Councell and their successors for ye time being, full and free liberty, power and authority to hear and Determine all emergencies relating to the care and good Government of our subjects within ye sd Prov: and also to sumon and convene any person or persons before them, and punish contempts: and cause ye Oath of allegiance to be administered to all and every person who shall be admitted to any office, freedom, preferments, and likewise with what convenient speed they can, to cause and their successors for ye time being, full and free liberty, power and authority to hear and Determine all emergencies relating to the care and good Government of our subjects within ye sd Prov: and also to sumon and convene any person or persons before them, and punish contempts; and cause ye Oath of allegiance to be administered to all and every person who shall be admitted to any office, freedom, preferments, and likewise with what convient speed they can, to cause proclamation to issue out and be made in our name to ye Inhabitants of ye said Prov. of N. Hamp:

thereby signifying that we have taken them into our imediate Governmt and gracious protection, and letting them further know that We have written to ye Governour and Councell of the Massachusetts Bay, to recall all such commissions as they have granted for exercising any jurisdiction in ye parts aforesaid. And that we have inhibited and restrained them for ye future from exercising any further authority or jurisdiction over them. And further, yt ye sd Inhabitants within ye said Prov. of N. Hampr. and limits aforesaid, do and shall from henceforth repair for justice and redress unto them ye said Pres. and Councell, whom we have constituted and appointed to be a standing Court for administration of justice as aforesaid, and intrusted them with ye care of their quiet and orderly Government, and therefore requiring that they give obedience unto them: And our will and pleasure is, that these, with such other generall intimations shall be given unto ye people as by ye said Pres. and Councell shall be thought necessary. And for supporting the charges of the Government of said Prov. of N. Hamp, Our will and pleasure is, we do by these pts authorize and require the said Pres. and Councell to continue such taxes and impositions as have bin and are now laid and imposed upon the Inhabitants thereof: and yt they levy and distribute, or cause the same to be levyed and distributed to those ends, in the best and most equall manner they can, untill a generall assembly of ye sd Prov. shall be called, and other method for yt purpose agreed upon. To which our will and pleasure is, and we do by these prts authorize, require and command ye said Pres. and Councell that they within 3 months after they have bin sworn (as aforesaid) they shall issue forth sumons under ye seal bu us appointed to be used, ye return of writs for ye calling a Generall Assembly of the said Prov., using and observing there such rules and methods (as to the persons who are to chuse their Deputies and ye time and place of meeting) as they shall judge most convenient At ye meeting of which Gen. Assemblu we do hereby will, authorize and require ye Pres. of ye said Councell to

mind them in ye generell, what is to be intimated in ye proclamation aforesaid.

That he recomend them ye making of such Acts, Laws, and Ordinances, as may most tend to ye establishing them in obedience to our authority; their own prservation in peace and good Governmt, and defend against their enemies, and that they do consider of the fittest ways for raising of taxes, and in such proportion as may be fit for ye support of ye sd Governmt. And our will and pleasure is, and we do hereby declare, ordain, and grant, that all and every such Acts, Laws and ordinances, as shall from time totime be made in and by such general Assembly or Assemblies, shall be first approved and allowed by the Pres. and Councell for the time being, and, thereupon shall stand and be in force until ye pleasure of us, our heirs and successors, shall be known, whether ye same Laws and ordinances shall receive any change or confirmation or be totally disallowed and discharged.

And therefore, our will and pleasure is, that ye Pres. and Councell do, and shall from time to time transmit and send over unto us, our heirs and successors, and our and their Privie Councell for the time being, all and every such Acts, Laws and Ordinances, by the first ship yt shall depart thence for Engd, after their making. Also, our will and pleasure is, and We do hereby direct and appoint, that if ye said Pres. of ye Councell, shall happen to dye, that there from and after ye Death of ye said Pres., his Deputy shall succeed him in ye office of Pres., and shall, and may nominate and choose any one of he said Councell to be his deputy, to preside in his absence; and ye said deputy so succeeding shall continue in ye said office of Pres. untill our further will and pleasure be known therein, and We shall think fit to nominate and appoint some other to succeed therein. And if any of ye members of ye said Councell shall happen to die, our will and pleasure is, and We do hereby direct and appoint ye remainder of ye Councell to select some other person to be a member of ye said Councell for the time being, and to send over the name of such person so chosen, and the name of two more whom they shall judg fitly qualified for that sd appointment, that we our heirs and successors, may nominate and appoint which of the three shall be ye member in ye place of such member so dying. And we do hereby declare, that We, our heirs and successors, shall and will observe and continue this method of grace and favor toward our loving subjects, in convening them in their Assembly, in such manner and form as is herein before mentioned and provided, unless, by inconvenience arising from thence, We, our heirs or successors, shall see cause to alter ye same.

And whereas ye said province of new hampshire, have many of them bin long in posession of severall quantities of lands, and are said to have made considerable improvements theire upon, having noe other title for ye same than what hath bin derived from ye Government of the mattihusetts Bay, in vertue of theire Imaginary line, wch titell as it hath by ye opinion of our Judges in England, bin altogether set aside, soe ye Agents from ye saide Colony have consequently disowned any righte, either in the people or government thereof, from the three mile line aforesaid; and it appearing unto us that ye ancestors of Robert Mason, esquire, obtained grants from our greate Councill of Plimoth, for ye tract of Land aforesaid, and wheare at very greate expence upon ye same, until molested and finally driven oute, which hath occasioned a lasting complainte for Justice, by ye said Robert Mason, ever since our restoration; how ever, to prevent in this case any unreasonable demands wch might be made by the said Robert Mason, for ye right he claimeth in ye saide soyle, we have obliged ye said Robert Mason, under his hand and seal, to declare that he will demand nothing for ye time paste, untill the 12th of June last past, nor molest any in the posession for ye time to come, but will make out titles to them and theire ayres forever, provided they will pay to him upon a fair agreement, in Lieu of all

others Rents, six pence in ye pound, according to ye Juste and trew yearly value of all houses builte by them, and of all lands, whether gardens, orchards, arribell or pasture, wch have been Improved by them which he will agree shall be bounded out unto every of ye partyes concerned, and that ye residue maye remaine unto himself to be disposed of for his best advantage. But notwithstanding this overture from ye said Robert Mason, wch semeth to be faire unto us, [if] any of ye Inhabitants of ye saide province of New Hampshire shall refuse to agree with ye Agent of ye said Robert Mason, upon ye terms aforesaid, our will and pleasure is yt ye president and Councell of new hampshire aforesaide, for ye time being, shall have power and are hereby impowered to Interfere and reconsile all Differences if they can, That shall or maye arise between said Robert Mason and ye said Inhabitants; but if they cannot, then we do hereby commande and require the said president and Councill to send into England such coppies, fairly and Imparsially stated, together wth their one opinions upon such cases, that we, our ayres and successors, with ye advice of our and their Councill may determine therein according to equity; and lastly, our will and pleasure is, that the said president and Councill for ye time being, doe prepare and send to England, such rules and methods for their own proceedings, as may best suite with the constitution of the saide prov. of New Hampshire.

For ye better establishing our authority theire and the government thereof, that we and our privie Councill may examine and alter or approve the same, in witness whereof, we have caysed these our letters to be made patent.

Witness our self, at Westminster, the 18th of September, In the one and thirtieth year of our Reigne.

per Ipsum Regem, Barker.

New Hampshire's pioneer Constitution read as follows:

We, the members of the Congress of the colony of New Hampshire, chosen and appointed by the free suffrages of the people of said colony, and authorized and empowered by them to meet together and use such means and pursue such measures as we should judge best for the public good, and in particular to establish some form of government, provided that measure should be recommended by the Continental Congress, and a recommendation to that purpose having been transmitted to us from the said Congress, have taken into our serious consideration the unhappy circumstances into which this colony is involved by means of many grievious and oppressive acts of the British Parliament, depriving us of our natural and constitutional rights and privileges; to enforce obedience to which acts, a powerful fleet and army have been sent into this country by the ministry of Great Britain, who have exercised a wanton and cruel abuse of their power in destroying the lives and properties of the colonists in many places with fire and sword, taking the ships and lading from many of the honest and industrious inhabitants of this colony employed in commerce agreeable to the laws and customs a long time used here.

The sudden and abrupt departure of His Excellency John Wentworth, Esq., our late Governor, and several of the Council, leaving us destitute of legislation; and no executive courts being open to punish criminal offenders, whereby the lives and properties of the honest people of this colony are liable to the machinations and evil designs of wicked men;

Therefore, for the preservation of peace and good order, and for the security of the lives and properties of the inhabitants of this colony, we conceive ourselves reduced to the necessity of establishing a form of government, to continue during the present unhappy and unnatural contest with Great Britain; protesting and declaring that we never sought to throw off our dependence upon Great Britain, but felt ourselves happy under her protection while we could enjoy our constitutional rights and privileges, and that we shall rejoice if such a reconciliation between us and our parent state can be effected as shall be approved by the Continental Congress, in whose prudence and wisdom we confide.

Accordingly, pursuant to the trust reposed in us, we do resolve that this Congress assume the name, power and authority of a House of Representatives, or Assembly, for the colony of New Hampshire; and that said House then proceed to choose twelve persons, being reputable freeholders and inhabitants within this colony, in the following manner, viz.: Five in the county of Rockingham, two in the county of Strafford, two in the county of Hillsborough, two in the county of Cheshire, and one in the county of Grafton, to be a distinct and separate branch of the Legislature, by the name of a Council for this colony, to continue as such until the third Wednesday in December next, any seven of whom to be a quorum to do business.

That such Council appoint their president; and in his absence that the senior councilor preside.

That a secretary be appointed by both branches, who may be a councilor or otherwise as they shall choose.

That no act or resolve shall be valid and put into execution unless agreed to and passed by both branches of the Legislature.

That all public officials for the said colony and each county for the current year be appointed by the Council and Assembly, except the several clerks of the executive courts, who shall be appointed by the justices of the respective courts.

That all bills, resolves, or votes for raising, levying, and collecting money, originate in the House of Representatives.

That at any session of the Council and Assembly neither branch shall adjourn for any longer time than from Saturday till the next Monday without consent of the other.

And it is further resolved that if the present unhappy dispute with Great Britain should continue longer than this present year, and the Continental Congress give no instructions or directions to the contrary, the Council be chosen by the people of each respective county in such manner as the Council and House of Representatives shall order.

That general and field officers of the militia, on any vacancy, be appointed by the two houses, and all inferior officers be chosen by the respective companies.

That all officers of the army be appointed by the two houses, except they should direct otherwise in case of any emergency.

That all civil officers for the colony and for each county be appointed and the time of their continuance in office be determined by the two houses, except clerks of courts, and county treasurers, and recorders of deeds.

That a treasurer and a recorder of deeds for each county be annually chosen by the people of each county respectively; the votes for such officers to be returned to the respective courts of general sessions of the peace in the county, there to be ascertained as the Council and Assembly shall hereafter direct.

That precepts in the name of the Council and Assembly, signed by the president of the Council and the speaker of the House of Representatives, shall issue annually, at or before the first day of November, for the choice of a Council and House of Representatives, to be returned by the third Wednesday in December then next ensuing, in such manner as the Council and Assembly shall hereafter prescribe.

HOUSE RULES OF 1784

The 1784 House of Representatives operated with nineteen rules of conduct, as compared with the list of ten pioneered by the Provincial Assembly of 1699. They were as follows:

First - That as it is essential to the public interest, so it shall be considered and enjoined as the incumbent duty of each member of this House seasonably and punctually to attend in his place, and not to absent himself without leave.

Second - That freedom of deliberation, speech and debate in the House, be allowed to each member thereof; yet if any member by his misbehavior in speech or action, in the House, shall give just cause of offence to another, he shall for the first offence be fined at the discretion of the House, and for the second offence be admonished.

Third - That every member when he would make a motion, speak to a matter in debate, or for any other purpose whatsoever shall rise from his seat and address himself to the Speaker; but on being called to order by the Speaker, or any other member, he shall be silent; though if such silenced member shall think himself injured thereby, the Speaker shall take a vote of the House thereon, to whose decision such member shall submit on pain of displeasure.

Fourth - That no member speak more than twice to a subject in debate, 'till each member (if he pleases) shall offer his opinion.

Fifth - No motion shall be debated, until the same shall be seconded.

Sixth - When a motion is made and seconded, if desired by any member, it shall be reduced to writing before any debate shall be allowed thereon.

Seventh - While a question is before the House, no motion shall be received, unless to amend or commit the same, or to postpone the consideration of the main question, or for having the yeas and nays entered on the journal.

Eighth - If a question in debate contains several points, any member may have the same divided.

Ninth - That no vote passed in the House shall be reconsidered by a number inferior to that present, when it was passed.

Tenth - That if the House shall adjudge that any person returned as a member is not duly qualified to have a seat therein, agreeably to the Constitution, it shall at any time be in the power of such part of the House as are competent, to pass a valid vote or resolve to dismiss such person, giving notice to the town or district from which he came to choose another in his stead.

Eleventh - That every member having been present at a debate, and the vote thereon being challenged, or the yeas and nays being called for, shall be obliged when called upon by the Speaker to vote on one side or the other of the question, unless special reasons be assigned, the validity of which shall be determined by the House.

Twelfth - That no member speaking by leave shall be interrupted by another but by rising to call to order or to correct a mistake.

Thirteenth - That every bill offered to the House shall be read three times, and that there be two adjournments before it pass to be enacted.

Fourteenth - That no bill be sent to the Senate Board without notice thereof being first given to the House by the Speaker, and the title of the bill thereof being read.

Fifteenth - That no member nominate more than one person for one committee, provided the person by him nominated shall be chosen.

Sixteenth - That no member be on more than two committees at the same time, unless by his own consent; and no member chosen on any committee shall have liberty to nominate another for the same committee.

Seventeenth - That no petition be received by the House but from a member thereof, and on motion made for that purpose.

Eighteenth - Every morning the minutes of the preceeding day shall be read in the House previous to their entering upon any new business.

Nineteenth - That no person except members of the General Court be admitted above the bar of the House without permission of the Speaker, or special invitation from some member of the House.

FIRST TWELVE SENATE DISTRICTS OF 1792

368

District 1 - to contain - Portsmouth, New Castle, Rye, Greenland, Newington, Stratham, North Hampton, Hampton, Hampton Falls and Seabrook.

District 2 - to contain - Exeter, Epping, Brintwood, Newmarket, Kensington, Poplin, Kingston, East Kingston, New-Town & South Hampton.

District 3 - to contain - Atkinson, Londonderry, Chester, Plastow, Salem, Windham, Sandown, Hawke, Hampstead & Pelham.

District 4 - to contain - Nottingham, Northwood, Deerfield, Epsom, Chichester, Pittsfield, Allenstown, Pembroke, Canterbury, Loudon, Northfield, Raymond & Candia.

District 5 - to contain - Dover, Durham, Lee, Madbury, Barrington, Rochester, Somersworth & New Durham.

District 6 - to contain - Gilmanton, Barnstead, Conway, Eaton, Effingham, Meredith, Middleton, Moultonborough, New Hampton, Sanborntown, Ossipee, Sandwich, Tamworth, Tuftonborough, Wolfeborough, New Durham-Gore, Wakefield & Burton, - & Samuel Stark's, Archibald Stark's & Hugh Starling's Locations.

District 7 - to contain - Amherst, Holles, Dunstable, Nottingham-West, Litchfield, Merrimac, Bedford, New Boston, Duxbury, Raby, Dunbarton, Goffstown, Bow & Derryfield.

District 8 - to contain - Concord, Andover, Boscawen, Bradford, Campbells-Gore, Henniker, Hillsborough, Hopkinton, Keisarge, New London, Salisbury, Sutton, Warner & Weare.

District 9 - to contain - Antrim, Dearing, Francestown, Hancock, Lyndeborough, Mason, New Ipswich, Peterborough, Sharon, Temple, Wilton, Society Land, Greenfield, Rindge, Jaffrey & Dublin.

District 10 - to contain - Keene, Swanzey, Winchester, Hinsdale, Richmond, Chesterfield, Marlborough, Sullivan, Packersfield, Fitz William, Westmoreland, Gilsom & Surrey.

District 11 - to contain - Charlestown, Plainfield, Grantham, Protectworth, Cornish, Croydon, Wendell, Claremont, New Port, Unity, Langdon, Acworth, Lempster, Goshen, Walpole, Alstead, Fisherfield, Marlow, Stoddard & Washington.

District 12 - to contain - The County of Grafton excepting Burton.

THE SENATE'S 1820 RULES

1. The President shall take the chair at the hour to which the Senate shall have adjourned, and on the attendance of a quorum shall call the Senate to order, and cause the journal of the preceding day to be read. He shall have the right to name any member to perform the duties of the chair, but such substitution shall not extend beyond adjournment.

2. The President shall preserve order and decorum, and decide all questions of order, subject to an appeal to the Senate by any member.

3. Each member shall seasonably and punctually attend to his duty in the Senate.

4. No member, after having been chosen on any committee, shall have the privilege of nominating a person for the same committee, nor shall any member be allowed to nominate more than one person for the same committee.

5. Every member, when he speaks in debate, or wishes to communicate any matter to the Senate, shall rise from his seat, and respectfully address the President.

6. When any motion is made, it shall be reduced to writing, if the President or any member request it.

7. Any member may call for a division of the question, when the same is divisible.

8. When any motion is before the Senate, no other motion shall be received except for an amendment, for the previous question, for a postponement of the same question, for a commitment, or for an adjournment.

9. The yeas and nays may be required by any member, and shall be in alphabetical order, when every member present shall give his vote, unless for special reasons excused by the Senate.

10. No petition or bill shall be introduced into the Senate, those received from the House of Representatives excepted, unless by a member, on motion for that purpose, after stating the object of the petition, or title of the bill, and whenever a bill shall not be rejected on its first reading, a time shall be assigned for a second reading of the same. And no bill shall pass to be enacted until it shall have had three several readings, nor shall any bill be read a third time until an adjournment take place after its second reading, unless this rule be dispensed with by vote of the Senate.

11. No member shall absent himself from the Senate without leave.

12. There shall be a standing committee of three members, to whom shall be referred all petitions for acts of incorporation; also, a standing committee of three members, to whom shall be referred all matters in relation to the militia; also, a standing committee of three members, to whom shall be referred all military accounts; also, a standing committee of three members, to whom shall be referred printers' and all other except military accounts. All other committees shall consist of three members, unless a motion is made for a different number.

13. All committees shall be nominated by the President, unless otherwise ordered by the Senate.

14. When the Senate shall concur in the appointment of a joint committee consisting of not more than five members from the House, one member only shall be added on the part of the Senate; but when such committee shall consist of more than five members from the House, two members shall be added thereto on the part of the Senate.

15. No resolve or vote shall be reconsidered when there is a less number of members of the Senate present, than there was at passing the same.

16. The Senate shall on no occasion meet the House in Convention, until they shall

have previously passed a vote for that purpose.

17. Whenever the subject matter on which the Senate shall meet the House in Convention shall be finished, the Senate shall immediately retire to their chamber.

18. Whenever the Senate propose to concur with the House in the passage of any vote, bill or resolve, with amendments proposed by the Senate, provided the House adopt the proposed amendments, the Senate are not at liberty to withold their concurrence.

19. The standing committees shall attend at their respective committee rooms one hour before the meeting of the Senate in the morning, and at such other times as the Senate shall order.

20. The Senate shall adjourn to meet at nine o'clock in the forenoon, and at three o'clock in the afternoon of each day, unless otherwise specially ordered by the Senate.

SENATE PRESIDENTS

Twenty of the one hundred and fifteen men who have served as President of the New Hampshire Senate from 1784 into 1979, went on to become Governor, and a few others served as Acting Governor. The score who became Governor, with some serving several terms, as listed in the *General Court Manual*, with the year they first held that office, were:

William Plumer of Epping, 1812.
Samuel Bell of Londonderry, 1819.
David L. Morril of Goffstown, 1824.
Matthew Harvey of Hopkinton, 1830.
William Badger of Gilmanton, 1834.
Jared W. Williams of Lancaster, 1847.
William Haile of Hinsdale, 1857.
Joseph A. Gilmore of Concord, 1863.
Onslow Stearns of Concord, 1869.
Ezekiel A. Straw of Manchester, 1872.
Natt Head of Hooksett, 1879.
Charles H. Bell of Exeter, 1881.
Moody Currier of Manchester, 1885.
Frank W. Rollins of Concord, 1899.
Chester B. Jordan of Lancaster, 1901.
John McLane of Milford, 1905.
Charles W. Tobey of Temple, 1927.
Robert O. Blood of Concord, 1941.
Charles M. Dale of Portsmouth, 1945.
Lane Dwinell of Lebanon, 1955.

Senior Senator John Pickering of Portsmouth became Acting President of the state for three months in 1789, when President John Langdon of Portsmouth resigned following his election by the Legislature as one of New Hampshire's first United States Senators in the newly-created federal government. President Joseph M. Harper of Canterbury became Acting Governor in 1830 for four months, when Governor Harvey resigned to accept appointment as judge of the United States District Court in New Hampshire.

Sixty-seven of the Senate Presidents served in the ninety-five year period from 1784 to 1879, when the Legislature met in annual sessions. Amos Shepard of Alstead set an all-time record with seven terms, 1797-1803. Jonathan Harvey of Sutton presided for six terms, 1817-22. Other extra-term Presidents included Ebenezer Smith of Meredith, four terms beginning in 1790; Moses P. Payson of Bath, three terms, beginning in 1809, and Matthew Harvey, brother to Jonathan Harvey, also served three terms, the first in 1825.

Ten men each served two consecutive annual terms as President. They were, with the year of their first term:

John McClary of Epsom, 1785.
John Pickering of Portsmouth, 1788.
Clement Storer of Portsmouth, 1805.
Samuel Bell of Francestown, 1807.
William Plumer of Epping, 1810.
Benning M. Bean of Moultonborough, 1831.
Jared W. Williams of Lancaster, 1833.

Josiah Quincy of Rumney, 1841.
Harry Hibbard of Bath, 1847.
John S. Wells of Exeter, 1851.

Oliver Peabody of Exeter set a unique record as Senate President. He was elected to that position in 1794 and resigned to become State Treasurer. He became President again in 1813 and again promptly resigned to become a judge.

The forty-four other Senate Presidents of the 1784-1878 period, each of whom served single annual terms, were:

Woodbury Langdon of Portsmouth, 1784.
Joseph Gilman of Exeter, 1787.
Moses Dow of Haverhill, 1792.
Abiel Foster of Canterbury, 1793.
Nicholas Gilman of Exeter, 1804.
Joshua Darling of Henniker, 1812.
Josiah Bartlett, Jr., of Stratham, 1824.
Nahum Parker of Fitzwilliam, 1828.
Abner Greenleaf of Portsmouth, 1829.
Samuel Cartland of Haverhill, 1831.
Charles F. Gove of Goffstown, 1835.
James Clark of Franklin, 1836.
John Woodbury of Salem, 1837.
Samuel Jones of Bradford, 1838.
James McK. Wilkins of Bedford, 1839.
James B. Creighton of Newmarket, 1840.
Titus Brown of Francestown, 1843.
Timothy Hoskins of Westmoreland, 1844.
Asa P. Cate of Northfield, 1845.
James U. Parker of Merrimack, 1846.
William P. Weeks of Canaan, 1849.
Richard Jenness of Portsmouth, 1850.
James M. Rix of Lancaster, 1853.
Jonathan E. Sargent of Wentworth, 1854.
Thomas J. McIvin of Chester, 1856.
Moody Currier of Manchester, 1857.
Austin F. Pike of Franklin, 1858.
George S. Towle of Lebanon, 1860.
Herman Foster of Manchester, 1861.
William H. Y. Hackett of Portsmouth, 1862.
Charles H. Bell of Exeter, 1864.
Daniel Barnard of Franklin, 1866.
William T. Parker of Merrimack, 1867.
Ezra A. Stevens of Portsmouth, 1868.
John Y. Mugridge of Concord, 1869.
Nathaniel Gordon of Exeter, 1870.
George W. M. Pitman of Bartlett, 1871.
Charles H. Campbell of Nashua, 1872.
David A. Warde of Concord, 1873.
William H. Gove of Weare, 1874.
John W. Sanborn of Wakefield, 1875.
Charles Holman of Nashua, 1876.
Natt Head of Hooksett, 1877.
David H. Buffum of Somersworth, 1878.

When the Legislature shifted to a biennial basis in 1879, it became custom to limit Senate Presidents to single terms. Only once, up to 1967, was anyone reelected to that position, which constitutionally ranks next to the Governorship. John McLane of Milford served two terms in 1891 and 1893, and was then elected Governor. When Stewart Lamprey of Moultonborough became Senate President in 1965, following a record three biennial terms as House Speaker, he proceeded to win two succeeding terms in that position. Then in 1975, Alf E. Jacobson of New London became President for two terms.

A total of forty-eight men have served as biennial Senate Presidents over the past century, including seven who became Governor. The thirty-nine not already listed, all of whom were elected for single terms, have been:

Jacob H. Gallinger of Concord, 1879.
John Kimball of Concord, 1881.
Charles H. Bartlett of Manchester, 1883.
Chester Pike of Cornish, 1885.
Frank D. Currier of Canaan, 1887.
David A. Taggart of Goffstown, 1889.
Thomas N. Hastings of Walpole, 1899.
Bertram Ellis of Keene, 1901.
Charles W. Hoitt of Nashua, 1903.
George H. Adams of Plymouth, 1905.
John Scamman of Exeter, 1907.
Harry T. Lord of Manchester, 1909.
William D. Swart of Nashua, 1911.
Enos K. Sawyer of Franklin, 1913.
George I. Haselton of Manchester, 1915.
Jesse M. Barton of Newport, 1917.
Arthur P. Morrill of Concord, 1919.
Leslie P. Snow of Rochester, 1921.
Wesley Adams of Londonderry, 1923.
Frank P. Tilton of Laconia, 1927.
Harold K. Davison of Woodsville, 1929.
Arthur R. Jones of Keene, 1931.
George D. Cummings of Peterborough, 1933.
Anson C. Alexander of Boscawen, 1937.
William M. Cole of Derry, 1941.
Ansel N. Sanborn of Wakefield, 1943.
Donald G. Matson of Concord, 1945.
Charles H. Barnard of Manchester, 1947.
Perkins Bass of Peterborough, 1949.
Blaylock Atherton of Nashua, 1951.
Raymond K. Perkins of Concord, 1955.
Eralsey C. Ferguson of Pittsfield, 1957.
Norman A. Packard of Manchester, 1959.
Samuel Green of Manchester, 1961.
Philip S. Dunlap of Hopkinton, 1963.
Arthur Tufts of Exeter, 1969.
John R. Bradshaw of Nelson, 1971.
David L. Nixon of New Boston, 1973.
Robert B. Monier of Goffstown, 1979.

Appendices

Provincial Assembly

Twenty-three men served as Speaker of New Hampshire's tiny provincial Assembly through its ninety-five years of existence from 1680 into 1775. They presided over fifty-five assemblies, some of which held many sessions, and nine of the Speakers served two or more terms.

Richard Waldron, Jr., of Portsmouth became the first Speaker, when the Assembly was created early in 1680, as New Hampshire was given its own government for a first time. He presided over six additional assemblies in a four-year period up to 1685, when a royal Governor abolished the Assembly. By royal decrees, New Hampshire then had no Assembly until 1692, when it was reestablished, with Richard Martyn of Portsmouth as Speaker for a single term.

Andrew Wiggin of Stratham set a provincial record by serving twelve terms as Speaker of the Assembly from 1728 into 1742. John Pickering of Portsmouth served six terms as Speaker, 1697-1704, and Henry Sherburne, Jr., of Portsmouth presided for four terms, 1755-1762.

Richard Gerrish of Portsmouth had the unusual experience of becoming Speaker in 1709, for an Assembly which rolled up sixty-one sessions in five years, and then served for two more terms. Also serving as Speaker for three terms each were George Jaffrey of Portsmouth, 1693-1695, and John Wentworth of Somersworth, the final Speaker of the provincial Assembly, from 1771 into 1775. Two-term Speakers were John Plaisted of Portsmouth, 1696 and in 1717, and Peter Gilman of Exeter, 1766-1768.

Richard Waldron, III, of Hampton, son of the first provincial Speaker, served a history-making three-year term as Assembly Speaker, starting in 1749. Governor Benning Wentworth refused to approve his election, the legislators insisted they had the sole right to name their own presiding officer, so this Forty-Fifth Assembly held twenty sessions without doing any official business, except to announce that it would appreciate having anyone publish its Journal, because funds could not be legally voted for that purpose.

The dozen other provincial Assembly Speakers, all with single terms, were:

John Gilman of Exeter, 1693.
Henry Dow of Hampton, 1698.
Samuel Penhallow of Portsmouth, 1699.
Daniel Tilton of Hampton, 1703.
Mark Hunking of Portsmouth, 1709.
Thomas Packer of Portsmouth, 1717.
Joshua Peirce of Portsmouth, 1719.
Peter Weare of Hampton Falls, 1722.
Nathaniel Weare of Hampton Falls, 1727.
Nathaniel Rogers of Portsmouth, 1744.
Ebenezer Stevens of Kingston, 1745.
Mesheck Weare of Hampton Falls, 1752.

The Revolutionary Period

Three men served as Speakers of New Hampshire's new House of Representatives through its nine annual terms of the Revolutionary War period, from January 5, 1776, to

June 2, 1784.

Phillips White of South Hampton became the first House Speaker under the state's first-in-the-nation Constitution, and served one term. John Langdon of Portsmouth next served six consecutive terms as Speaker. Then John Dudley of Raymond was Speaker for two terms. Langdon later served seven terms as Governor.

Speakers Under The 1784 Constitution

New Hampshire's House of Representatives has had 101 Speakers, in the 195-year period since the state's permanent constitutional government became effective in 1784. Thirteen of them went on to become Governor. They were, with their Speaker terms, as follows:

> John Sullivan of Durham, 1785.
> William Plumer of Epping, 1791-2 and 1797.
> Samuel Bell of Chester, 1805-6.
> David L. Morril of Goffstown, 1816.
> Matthew Harvey of Hopkinton, 1818-21.
> Levi Woodbury of Portsmouth, 1825.
> Nathaniel B. Baker of Concord, 1850-51.
> Charles H. Bell of Exeter, 1860.
> Chester B. Jordan of Lancaster, 1881.
> Charles W. Tobey of Temple, 1919.
> Sherman Adams of Lincoln, 1943.
> Lane Dwinell of Lebanon, 1951.
> Walter R. Peterson of Peterborough, 1965-67.

Fifty-four of these one hundred and one Speakers served annually up to 1879, when the Legislature shifted to the present biennial system. John Prentice of Londonderry set an all-time record, according to the *Laws of New Hampshire*, with eight consecutive terms as Speaker, beginning in 1794. Serving four consecutive annual terms were Thomas Bartlett of Nottingham, as of 1787, and Charles G. Atherton of Nashua, 1833. Three-term annual Speakers included Charles Cutts of Portsmouth, 1807-8 and 1810; Henry Hubbard of Charlestown, 1825-8, and Moses Norris, Jr., of Pittsfield, 1839-40 and 1847. Eighteen other Speakers who each served two annual terms were:

> George B. Upham of Claremont, 1809 and 1815.
> Clement Storer of Portsmouth, 1811-2.
> Thomas W. Thompson of Concord, 1813-4.
> Edmund Parker of Nashua, 1823-4.
> Franklin Pierce of Hillsborough, 1831-2.
> Ira A. Eastman of Gilmanton, 1837-8.
> Samuel Swazey of Haverhill, 1842-3.
> Harry Hibbard of Bath, 1844-5.
> Samuel H. Ayer of Hillsborough, 1848-9.
> Edward H. Rollins of Concord, 1856-7.
> Napoleon B. Bryant of Plymouth, 1858-9.
> Edward A. Rollins of Great Falls
>   (Somersworth), 1861-2.
> William E. Chandler of Concord, 1863-4.
> Austin F. Pike of Franklin, 1865-6.
> Simon G. Griffin of Keene, 1867-8.

Samuel M. Wheeler of Dover, 1869-70.
Charles P. Sanborn of Concord, 1875-6.
Augustine A. Woolson of Lisbon, 1877-8.
Twenty-two Speakers given single annual terms were:

George Atkinson of Portsmouth, 1784.
John Langdon of Portsmouth, 1786.
John Sparhawk of Portsmouth, 1787.
Nathaniel Peabody of Atkinson, 1793.
Russell Freeman of Hanover, 1796.
Henry B. Chase of Warner, 1817.
Ichabod Bartlett of Portsmouth, 1821.
Charles Woodman of Bridgewater, 1822.
Andrew Pierce of Dover, 1823.
James Wilson, Jr., of Keene, 1828.
James B. Thornton of Merrimack, 1829.
Samuel Webster of Kingston, 1830.
John S. Wells of Lancaster, 1841.
John P. Hale of Dover, 1846.
George W. Kittridge of Newmarket, 1852.
Jonathan E. Sargent of Wentworth, 1853.
Francis R. Chase of Northfield, 1854.
John J. Prentiss of Claremont, 1855.
William H. Gove of Weare, 1871.
Asa Fowler of Concord, 1872.
James Emery of Hudson, 1873.
Albert R. Hatch of Portsmouth, 1874.

Speakers Since 1879

Forty-seven men have served as Speaker of the House of Representatives since the state government went onto a biennial basis of operations in 1879. As was true of the State Senate, it became custom to give the House Speakers only single two-year terms. It was not until 1961 that a Speaker won reelection. He was Stewart Lamprey of Moultonborough, who went on to win that post for a total of three terms. He was followed by Walter R. Peterson of Peterborough with two terms, 1965-67; Marshall Cobleigh of Nashua with two terms, 1969-71, and George B. Roberts, Jr., of Gilmanton, who became Speaker in 1975, and won a third term in the 1979 session.

The forty-two other biennial House Speakers have been:

Henry H. Huse of Manchester, 1879.
Chester B. Jordan of Lancaster, 1881.
Samuel C. Eastman of Concord, 1883.
Edgar Aldrich of Colebrook, 1885.
Alvin Burleigh of Plymouth, 1887.
Hiram B. Upton of Jaffrey, 1889.
Frank G. Clarke of Peterborough, 1891.
Robert N. Chamberlain of Berlin, 1893.
Stephen S. Jewett of Laconia, 1895.
James F. Briggs of Manchester, 1897.
Frank D. Currier of Canaan, 1899.
Cyrus H. Little of Manchester, 1901.

Harry M. Cheney of Lebanon, 1903.
Rufus N. Elwell of Exeter, 1905.
Bertram Ellis of Keene, 1907.
Walter W. Scott of Dover, 1909.
Frank A. Musgrove of Hanover, 1911.
William J. Britton of Wolfeboro, 1913.
Edwin C. Bean of Belmont, 1915.
Olin H. Chase of Newport, 1917.
Charles W. Tobey of Temple, 1919.
Fred A. Jones of Lebanon, 1921.
William J. Ahern of Concord, 1923.
George A. Wood of Portsmouth, 1925.
Harold K. Davison of Haverhill, 1927.
George A. Foster of Concord, 1929.
Harold M. Smith of Portsmouth, 1931.
Louis P. Elkins of Concord, 1933.
Amos N. Blandin of Bath, 1935.
Oren V. Henderson of Durham, 1937.
Ansel N. Sanborn of Wakefield, 1939.
Charles H. Barnard of Manchester, 1941.
Sherman Adams of Lincoln, 1943.
Norris Cotton of Lebanon, 1945.
J. Walker Wiggin of Manchester, 1947.
Richard F. Upton of Concord, 1949.
Lane Dwinell of Lebanon, 1951.
Raymond K. Perkins of Concord, 1953.
Norman A. McMeekin of Haverhill, 1954.
Charles Griffin of Lincoln, 1955.
W. Douglas Scamman of Stratham, 1957.
James E. O'Neil of Chesterfield, 1973.

Basic sources for this history of New Hampshire's colorful General Court have been the *State Papers* of forty volumes, and the *Laws of New Hampshire,* in ten volumes, which include legislative data for the 156-year period from the 1679 birth of this legislative body up to 1836. Both of these sets of documented history were sponsored by the Legislature, and published in such limited quantities that they have become prized collectors' items in recent years.

The *State Papers* were compiled by state-employed historians from records in the Secretary of State's files, through a span of seventy-seven years, or from 1866 to 1943. Production of the *Laws of New Hampshire* began in 1902 and was completed in 1922.

The first ten volumes of the *State Papers* were produced by the Reverend Nathaniel Bouton, Concord historian, over a ten-year period, following his 1866 retirement from forty-two years of pastoral work. In 1882 Deputy Secretary of State Isaac W. Hammond of Concord was appointed state historian. He labored nine years during which he became librarian for the New Hampshire Historical Society, to produce eight segments of the *State Papers.* They included a monumental compilation of the rolls of New Hampshiremen in the Revolutionary War, which continue of inestimable worth to this day.

Attorney Albert Stillman Batchellor of Littleton became state historian in 1890, following three terms in the House of Representatives and service on the Governor's Council. He compiled thirteen volumes of the *State Papers,* and launched the *Laws of New Hampshire,* through twenty years during which he became blind, and then died in 1913. Batchellor's output included reproduction of the legislative *Journals* from 1784, under the permanent Constitution, up to 1792 when that document was remodelled.

Henry Harrison Metcalf of Concord, veteran publisher and historian, authored volumes 32 and 33 of the *State Papers* in 1913-16. Finally, Director Otis G. Hammond of the New Hampshire Historical Society and son of Isaac Hammond, who had been Batchellor's assistant, produced the concluding seven books of the *State Papers* in the 1933-43 period. Each of the forty volumes was published by the Legislature and limited to eight hundred copies.

The *Laws of New Hampshire* were compiled by Batchellor, with a concluding assist by Metcalf. Their declared purpose was for a first time to make available, in published form, not only all the laws enacted in the 1679-1835 period, but the membership of each Legislature, and related historical data. It was not until 1836 that the Legislature published its annual statutes for general distribution, a custom which continues to this day. Actual publication of the final five volumes of the *Laws of New Hampshire* was delayed to 1917, through 1922.

Interestingly, the five concluding *Laws of New Hampshire* volumes were labelled *Second Constitutional Period,* even though New Hampshire actually has never had a second permanent Constitution. Batchellor used that title, however, because it was officially used by the Legislature, and the courts, for more than half a century following the wholesale remodelling of the 1784 Constitution in 1792. It was not until 1889 that the State Supreme Court ruled in a minor liquor nuisance dispute, that the title "Second Constitution" was a "misnomer." The court explained that while the 1792 voters approved several dozen amendments to the Constitution, much of its details continued in force from 1784 and were not laid before the 1792 electorate. This opinion is contained in Volume 66, page 72, of the *New Hampshire Reports.*

These state historians bore the title of "Editor and Compiler of State Papers," and were paid salaries, with modest spending allowances. Batchellor, for example, had a salary of $2,500 in his final year (compared with $3,000 for the Governor), along with $1,300 for clerical hire and $400 for incidentals.

Concord and Manchester newspapers were of major assistance in compiling legislative lore not recorded in the House and Senate Journals, starting in the 1850s, when shorthand developed. These primary sources were the 1809 *New Hampshire Patriot* and the 1864 *Concord Daily Monitor*, which merged in 1923, and the 1863 *Manchester Union*, which became the *Manchester Union Leader* in 1946.

The *New Hampshire Registers* provided substantial legislative details for ninety years up to 1889, when the *General Court Manual* took over the function of listing election statistics and general state government information. The annual *Registers* of the 1822-1866 period were of special value because they presented carefully researched legislative data never otherwise compiled. These editions of the pocket-sized *Register* were compiled by John Farmer, Concord apothecary and historian, who was appointed by the 1837 Legislature as first state historian and died soon thereafter from tuberculosis, and G. Parker Lyon, Concord book dealer and historian.

Rare information was obtained from unique manuals of the Constitutional Conventions as compiled by Professor James F. Colby of Dartmouth College for the 1902 convention, and by Deputy Secretary of State Hobart Pillsbury for the 1918 convention. Equally rare as a research source was the reproduction of details of the 1791 Constitutional Convention by Dr. Bouton for the 1876 convention's delegates. Other research sources have included:

The Journals of the House and Senate and their session laws.

Reverend Jeremy Belknap's 1784 and 1791 *History of New Hampshire.*

William Plumer, Jr.'s 1857 *Life of William Plumer.*

Governor Charles H. Bell's 1888 *History of Exeter,* featuring legislative sessions in that town through the Revolutionary War period.

James O. Lyford's 1906 *Life of Edward H. Rollins,* an 1857 founder of New Hampshire's Republican Party, which presents the first half century history of that political organization and its legislative leadership.

Lyford's 1903 *History of Concord.*

The 1908 *New Hampshire Tax Commission Report,* presenting the history of the development of legislative taxes, by an interim study commission comprised of William B. Fellows of Tilton, John B. Morrill of Gilford and Harry G. Sargent of Concord.

Richard F. Upton's 1936 *Revolutionary New Hampshire,* an interpretive analysis of that eight-year conflict, which became so valued that it was reprinted in 1971.

J. Duane Squires's 1956 *Granite State of the United States,* presenting well illustrated and perceptive details of the state government, and the affairs of its people, from the 1623 settlement, into the mid-1950s.

Charles F. Whittemore's 1961 *Life of John Sullivan of New Hampshire.*

John K. Gemmill's unpublished 1966 Columbia University thesis (on file in the State Library) *From Colony To State - The Emergence Of Home Rule In New Hampshire 1775-1783,* featuring legislative life and multiple officials.

Mrs. Grace Amsden's unpublished manuscript history of Concord's first century, and its legislative affiliations, on deposit with the New Hampshire Historical Society.

Jere R. Daniell's 1970 *Experiment In Republicanism,* a detailed resumé of New Hampshire politics in the formative half century of 1741 through to 1794.

Historical New Hampshire, published by the New Hampshire Historical Society.

Early editions of the biennial *General Court Manual,* dating from its first 1889 issue, containing rare legislative and state government data never otherwise compiled.

The biennial legislative biographical *Brown Book,* dating from its 1881 origin.

Special thanks go to Director Thomas K. Reynolds of the Legislative Reference Service, and his predecessor, Richard M. Serena, and the staffs of the State Library, the Concord City Library, and the New Hampshire Historical Society, for their ever-friendly and helpful cooperation. Also appreciated have been the assistance of former United States Senator Thomas J. McIntyre, and retired United States Senator Norris Cotton, in processing research material from the Library of Congress.

Appendices

LIST OF ILLUSTRATIONS

The illustrations listed below in the order in which they appear in this volume were gathered from many sources over the extended period during which the manuscript was in preparation. The author is deeply grateful to all those who so willingly provided guidance and assistance.

INDEX

A

Abbott, George W., 189
Academies chartered, 119
Adams, Benjamin C., 223, 248-250
Adams, James O., 148, 150
Adams, John, 318
Adams, John Quincy, 124
Adams, Sherman, 216, 217, 247, 265, 278, 294, 295
Ahern, William G., 189
Ahern, William J., 202, 292
Ainley, Greta M., 220
Alcoholic beverages, state control, 215, 263
Aldrich, Edgar, 262
Alexander, Anson L., 239
Alexander, Norman, 219
Allen, Pardon W., 202
Allen, Samuel, 24, 35
Allen, William, 318
Alphabet, all letters in one sentence, 206
American Legion, 9
American party, 137
Amherst, legislative session, 109
Amidon, Charles J., 233
Amoskeag Falls, canal, 285-287
Amoskeag Mills, 10
Amsden, Charles H., 262
Amsden, Grace, 120, 123, 336
Anderson, Leon, 10, 313, 343, 352
Anderson, Samuel, 134
Andros, Sir Edmund, 23-24
Anne, Queen, 35, 36
Apportionment
    House, 158, 186-187
    Senate, on basis of
        population, 251
        wealth, 227-228
Armistice Day, 212
Ashley, Samuel, 53
Assembly. See also: House of Representatives
    authority to impose taxes, 17, 23, 26
    clerks, 28, 29, 36, 51, 52
        members serving as, 33, 51
    created by council under royal commission, 15
    meetings in taverns, 33

members, 16, 53
    election, 16
    privileges, 31-32
    qualifications, 31
    salaries, 32
    rules, 27-28, 32, 33
    seating, 33
    sessions, 35-36
        annual, 31
    speakers, 16, 28, 29, 36, 43, 45, 51, 52, 374
        choice vetoed by Gov. Wentworth, 37, 43
    statutes, 17-18
Association of Women Legislators, 273
Atherton, Blaylock, 247, 280
Atherton, Henry B., 171, 177
Atkinson, George, 79, 84, 105
Atkinson, Theodore, 28, 29, 32, 36-37, 52
Atwood, Albert W., 349
Auditor of accounts, 257, 260
Austin, Daniel B., 153
Australian ballot, 187
Ayer, Samuel, 134

B

Babcock, Daniel C., 319
Bachelder, Nahum J., 184-185, 189-190, 200
Badger, Joseph, 85
Bailey, Joshua, 85
Baker, Mary, 21
Baker, Moses, 85
Baker, Otis, 53, 68, 84
Banks chartered, 119
Barefoote, Walter, 23
Barker, Benjamin, 68
Barnard, Daniel, 245
Barnes, Isaac O., 319
Barnum, P. T., 306
Barrett, Alonzo D., 198
Barrett, Edwin S., 260
Barstow, Zedekiah S., 319, 321
Bartlett, Emma L., 274
Bartlett, Ichobod, 117
Bartlett, John C., 160
Bartlett, John H., 209, 211

E

F

apportionment, 158
expelled, 201-204
first Black and first Indian, 223
number limited, 216
related, 198, 223-224, 229, 275-276
salaries limited by constitutional
    amendment, 170
salaries paid by state, 106
salaries paid by towns, 68
youngest, 224
mileage, 68, 216, 217-218, 229-230
official formation, 66
officially designated by Gov. Coote, 26
privileges, 221
rules of 1784, 366-367
seat 13 eliminated, 219-220
seating lotteries, 143, 150, 287-293
speakers, 71, 85, 105, 125, 183, 190, 193,
    197, 201, 210, 216, 218, 251, 258,
    292, 309, 321, 323, 325, 354, 355,
    374-377
Howard, Charles W., 311
Howard, Donalda K., 282
Howard, Timothy J., 241
Howe, James B., 318
Hulme, John T., 304, 308
Humphrey, Howard, Sr., 223
Humphrey, James A., 223
Humphrey, Stillman, 186
Humphreys, Cecil C., 248-249
Humphreys, Moses, 207
Hunking, Mark, 29, 36, 52
Huntington, Newton S., 177, 189
Hurd, D. Hamilton, 337
Hurd, Henry N., 339, 340
Hussey, Christopher, 15

I

Ide, Daniel, 160
Immigration bureau, 184-185
Impeachment of Woodbury Langdon,
    98-100
Incompatible offices, college faculty and
    representative or senator, 83-84
Independent Democrat, 139, 302
Indian, legislature, 223
Indian raids, 5
Indian Stream Republic, 115

Inflation, 76-77
Ingalls, Robert, 127
Inheritance tax, 190
Insurrection fears, 186
Interest and dividends tax, 212
Isles of Shoals, 15, 52

391

J

Jackson, Andrew, 124, 126, 174
Jackson, James R., 149, 150
Jackson, Katherine, 281
Jacobson, Alf E., 252-253
Jaffreys, George, 29, 52
James, Alexander, 236
Jameson, Nathan C., 179
Jeffrey, James, 51
Jenkins, Augustus, 127
Jenness, Advid, 163
Jenness, Mary, 163
Jenness, Samuel, 53
Jewett, Louis M., 183
Jewett, Stephen S., 187, 261-262
Johnson, Richard M., 189
Johnson, Thomas F., 148
Joint legislative committee on elderly af-
    fairs, 272
Jones, Frank, 171-172
Jones, Samuel, 134
Jordan, Richard, 77
Jose, Richard, 29, 52
Judiciary system reorganized, 26

393

Index

N

395

399

401

Index